11-1-73

Minority
Group
Relations

MERRILL SOCIOLOGY SERIES

Under the editorship of

Richard L. Simpson

University of North Carolina, Chapel Hill

and

Paul E. Mott

Minority Group Relations

James G. Martin
University of Northern Iowa

Clyde W. Franklin
The Ohio State University

CHARLES E. MERRILL PUBLISHING COMPANY
A Bell & Howell Company
Columbus, Ohio

The authors are grateful for material reprinted from *The Tolerant Personality* by James G. Martin by permission of the Wayne State University Press.

Published by
Charles E. Merrill Publishing Company
A Bell & Howell Company
Columbus, Ohio 43216

ISBN: 0-675-08953-0

Library of Congress Catalog Card Number: 72-97539

1 2 3 4 5 6 7 — 78 77 76 75 74 73

Printed in the United States of America

1777193

To Doris
JGM

To Alice and the late Bernice
CWF

.

Foreword

The number of books dealing with race and ethnic problems is staggering, and it continues to increase at an amazing rate. Sociologists have made notable contributions to this body of knowledge, and so have historians, anthropologists, psychologists, journalists, and others. Those who teach courses in race relations nowadays suffer no dearth of excellent source material.

This wealth of information which we have at our disposal is not, however, an unmixed blessing for the teacher, and it is often baffling to the student who seeks to organize, integrate, and comprehend it. In recent years several earnest attempts have been made to develop a systematic, conceptual framework for this mass of data, and the present volume by Drs. Franklin and Martin represents a commendable effort to do just that.

Their presentation is organized around the core concepts of prejudice and discrimination. Some would doubtless prefer other key concepts, such as power, status, values, or self-concept, but these authors have chosen to remain in the older sociological tradition, without, however, neglecting other concepts which contribute to an understanding of the phenomena. In this volume they subject prejudice and discrimination to a penetrating analysis, and then they proceed to ascertain the social and personality consequences and to evaluate the various strategies employed for their alleviation.

The book has numerous other merits. It avoids the provincialism so characteristic of much of the writing on racial problems, drawing much of its data from societies other than our own. It also eschews the sentimentality, moralization, and dogmatism which are all too prevalent in the literature in this area. It is, accordingly, a sociological presentation, which is what it purports to be.

Brewton Berry

Professor Emeritus

The Ohio State University

Preface

A plethora of books and articles have been used, in recent years, as literature for "race relations" or "minority groups" courses. Much of this material has been polemical in nature. Although it has enhanced awareness and provided acute observations, it has been of little value theoretically and methodologically. Our intent is to attempt to correct this deficiency.

While this textbook is meant primarily for the conventional course in minority groups, the scope is somewhat broader. It aspires to treat intergroup relations in a theoretical and methodological vein without sacrificing the rich imagery which characterizes much of the substantive material on minority groups. In fact, an effort has been made to integrate this kind of knowledge with a theoretical framework which will enable the student to analyze intergroup relations situations which currently exist as well as those which may emerge in the future regardless of what groups are "minority" or "majority."

A major premise of this volume is that the study of intergroup relations should have a higher priority than the study of particular minority groups as such. Consequently, much of the material pertaining to minority groups is cited primarily for illustrative purposes. Most of the discussion dwells upon racial, ethnic, and religious groups, especially Black-white relations in contemporary American society, but there are occasional references to other forms of intergroup relations including occupational groupings, sex substructures, and a few other social categories. These references are essentially for comparative purposes and are marginal rather than central to the basic thrust of the book.

The study of intergroup relations, although primarily a sociological enterprise, also is dependent upon knowledge from such areas as psychology, genetics, anthropology, history, and social psychology. The approach in this monograph is best characterized as postivistic and social psychological. Underlying theses of "symbolic interactionism" and "social exchange" also may be detected since both of us subscribe to much of these theories in social psychology. The emphasis is upon the dynamics of intergroup relations rather than the static structural aspects. The reader will find, however, numerous references to literature concentrating more heavily upon the social structural factors. The traditional sociological perspective, to be sure, has stressed the role of social structures in intergroup relations. The treatment had dealt largely with the relative positions of majority and minority groups in society. There are indications, however, that sociology in general has moved toward a more social psychological orientation, and this seems to be especially so in the area which is now generally referred to as intergroup relations.

Our interest in the field of intergroup relations and our presumption to write a textbook on the subject are the product of a combination of circumstances, influences, and collaborative interests. The most prominent of these are: (1) long standing personal and professional interest in the field; (2) experiencing the responses of students in classes in intergroup relations, race relations, and social psychology; (3) various kinds of research activities in the area; (4) consultation experiences in the field; (5) association and service with organizations concerned with improvement of intergroup relations; and (6) a mutual feeling that the field has moved away from an emphasis of the scientific study of intergroup dynamics, and a perception that this is inimical to the true aims of any behavioral science. The kind of textbook which has emerged doubtless reflects these experiences and activities.

We cannot acknowledge all of our intellectual debts to our teachers, colleagues, and students; we only hope that we have adequately cited sources of formal data and ideas by footnotes and other references. We should like to express our appreciation, however, to George Greider for the tremendous assistance given us in this endeavor. The tolerance and inspiration of our wives is affectionately appreciated.

Contents

Introduction to Theory and Methods in Intergroup Relations

Theory in the behavioral sciences facilitates research, however, research can only be guided if theories are logically and operationally adequate. Unfortunately, theories in intergroup relations have not always been distinguished by logical and operational adequacy. On the contrary, much theorizing in this area has been characterized by emotionalism and controversy. While the models which result from such theoretical attempts often appeal to the beginning student, they should not be confused with scientifically constructed theories. Gunnar Myrdal's classic contribution to the field of intergroup relations, *An American Dilemma,* had a tremendous impact on the social order, but it lacked operational and empirical adequacy. These inadequacies existed for twenty years until Frank R. Westie designed a study and tested some of the implications of Myrdal's primary theory.[1] While the study generally supported the theory, there were some additional findings which refined certain aspects of the model. We suggest that only through such means can theories advance reliable and valid knowledge about intergroup relations.

This chapter is devoted to an explication of elementary theorizing and research strategies which may be used in scientific inquiries into the phenomenon of intergroup relations.

THE THEORETICAL AREA OF CONTENT IN INTERGROUP RELATIONS

Sophisticated research techniques and theory in intergroup relations are often de-emphasized. Reasons for this de-emphasis are varied, however, one apparent reason stems from the emotional and political nature of the substantive content. This area of sociology, perhaps more than any other, has been characterized by popular writings in the field being accepted as conclusive evidence. More recently, however, researchers have devoted their energies to this area. In view of this development it becomes necessary to specify the assumptions under which these investigators operate.

Research involving intergroup relations takes as its basic unit of analysis the group. An assumption is made that the group represents an entity that is more than the sum of its parts. In other words, when individuals come together in groups, unique attributes emerge which are different from the individual elements acting alone. This has important implications for theory and research methodology. For instance, the naive researcher may be inclined to use isolated individuals from several ethnic, racial, or substructural groups as imagery sources for theorizing and testing of intergroup theories. Such a strategy, however, is fraught with difficulties due to the fact that there is a high risk of obtaining invalid results when individual cases are studied in instances where group data should be used. In other words, if one is interested in studying the dynamics of group interaction between Black Panthers and Ku Klux Klansmen, he should use, as his basic units of cognition, groups of Black Panthers and groups of Ku Klux Klansmen. However, if the investigator *specifies* that he is interested in individual interaction between members of the two groups then he would be justified in selecting *individuals* as cases in his study.

While the above discussion may appear to be a petty methodological issue, it should be stressed that there are numerous theoretical and research advantages to be gained from correct selection of cases for theory testing—the most important being empirically adequate results.

THEORY IN INTERGROUP RELATIONS

A theory of intergroup relations refers to *a set of interrelated propositions, nominal definitions, operational definitions, and imagery which purports to explain, predict and control intergroup relations phenomena.* Obviously, such a definition of theory in intergroup relations does not distinguish it from theory in other areas of sociology nor other fields in the behavioral sciences. What *does* distinguish intergroup relations theory is the content of the area in which the theory is to be constructed. In other words, the above definition of theory should be altered to include the social phenomena which are the units of cognition. In this case the social phenomena include coordinated lines of thought, affectivity, and behavior as well as social norms, roles, and exchange relations emerging within and between social groups.

Theorizing in intergroup relations is not a novel procedure. What is novel is the formal style of theorizing which is currently being done in the area. For instance, John Dollard's *Caste and Class in a Southern Town* and W. E. B. DuBois' *The Souls of Black Folk* are both classical theoretical statements about intergroup relations. They epitomize as well many other works of the same time period, a *literary style* of theorizing. This style of theorizing is characterized by an unfolding plot—a behavior sequence which has certain significance and is occupied by individuals, particular persons or sets of events.[2] It tends toward description, though speculation is also a characteristic of the style, and serves as a tool of explanation. Such a style of theorizing is still in use especially among popular writers such as John H. Griffin (*Black Like Me*) and Grace Halsell (*Soul Sister*). Richard Wright's *Black Boy* is another example of the literary style of theorizing. Consider the following excerpt from Wright's work:

> Yet, deep down, I knew that I could never really leave the South, for my feelings had already been formed by the South, for there had been slowly instilled into my personality and consciousness, black though I was, the culture of the South. So, in leaving, I was taking a part of the South to transplant in alien soil, to see if it could grow differently, if it could drink of new and cool rains, bend in strange winds, respond to the warmth of other suns, and, perhaps, to bloom. . . . And if that miracle ever happened, then I would know that there was yet hope in that southern swamp of despair and violence, that light could emerge even out of the blackest of the southern night. I would know that the South too could overcome its fear, its hate, its cowardice, its heritage of guilt and blood, its burden of anxiety and compulsive cruelty.
>
> With ever watchful eyes and bearing scars, visible and invisible, I headed North, full of a hazy notion that life could be lived with dignity, that the personalities of others should not be violated, that men should be able to confront other men without fear or shame, and that if men were lucky in their living on earth they might win some redeeming meaning for their having struggled and suffered here beneath the stars.[3]

Inherent in the above paragraphs are causal explanations related to black migration from the southern to the northern regions of the United States during the 1920s and 1930s. While these paragraphs pertain directly to the life of a southern Black man, it is important to realize the significance of the events in this man's life as it relates to numerous Black migrants of that period. In other words, while it may be almost impossible to discern postulates, theorems, definitions, and imagery in literary theorizing, the style may produce, nevertheless, insightful and imageric impressions of social phenomena. There are several difficulties with literary theorizing within the purview of this chapter, which include a lack of explanatory and predictive power. Descriptively, this style of theory is quite adequate, however, due to the fact that laws and conditions are not conspicuous aspects of the structure of such theories, inferences beyond the scope of the content presented cannot be made and, consequently, explanation and prediction are not enhanced.

Another type of theorizing which has been popular in literature is the *academic style*.[4] This style is much more precise, abstract, and general than the literary style. Furthermore, the materials dealt with tend towards ideationalism rather than observation and tend to be highly postulational and technical though not necessarily formally constructed. Examples of such theorizing can be found in Eldridge Cleaver's *Soul On Ice*, William H. Grier and Price M. Cobbs' *Black Rage*, and E. Franklin Frazier's *Black Bourgeoisie*. An example of this type of theorizing is presented in the following passages from *Soul On Ice*:

> Since each society projects its own sexual image, the Unitary Society will project a Unitary Sexual Image. We can thus postulate, following the model of Marx, that in ancient communal society, which was not cleft into antagonistic classes, there existed a Unitary Society in which a Unitary Sexual Image was in natural coincidence with the way of life of the people. This is the lost innocence of the Garden of Eden.

> The Class Society projects a fragmented sexual image. Each class projects a sexual image coinciding with its class-function in society. And since its class-function will differ from that of other classes, its sexual image will differ also and in the same proportion. The source of the fragmentation of the Self in Class Society lies in the alienation between the function of man's Mind and function of his Body. Man as thinker performs an Administrative Function. These two basic functions I symbolize, when they are embodied in living men functioning in society, as the Omnipotent Administrator and the Supermasculine Menial.

> Since all men are created equal, when the Self is fragmented by
> the operation of the laws and forces of Class Society, men in the
> elite classes usurp the controlling and Administrative Function of
> the society as a whole—i.e., they usurp the administrative com-
> ponent in the nature and biology of the men in the classes below
> them. Administrative power is concentrated at the Apex of society,
> in the Godhead of the society (paraoh, king, president, chairman).
> Administrative power beneath the apex is delegated. Those in
> classes to which no administrative power has been delegated have
> the administrative component in their personalities suppressed,
> alienated, denied expression. Those who have usurped the Adminis-
> trative Function we shall call the Omnipotent Administrators.
> Struggling among themselves for higher positions in the administra-
> tive hierarchy, they repudiate the component of Brute Power in
> themselves, claim no kinship with it, and project it onto the men
> in the classes below them.[5]

While the above excerpt certainly does not constitute a formal theory,
it is a portion of a theory and the entire contribution conforms to an
academic style of theorizing. If portions of the excerpt were formalized,
we would be able to identify propositions such as the following: Each
society projects its own sexual image; Each class projects a sexual
image coinciding with its class function in society; and, Differences in
sexual images in a society will be a function of the society's class
function differences.

In addition to propositions, formalization of academic theories also
results in nominal definitions such as the *Omnipotent Administrator*
defined as "those who have usurped the administrative function." It is
important, however, to realize that differentiation between postulates,
theorems, definitions, and imagery in academic theories often is rather
difficult to accomplish, and this is perhaps the chief criticism of this
style of theorizing. This criticism is valid since prediction, control, and
explanation are affected by vagueness or lack of precision in a theory.
If, in fact, the elements of a theory cannot be discerned, then precision
is lacking.

The final type of theorizing offered in this chapter is a synthesis of
Kaplan's symbolic, formal, and postulational styles of theorizing,
which we have labeled *formalistic theorizing*. Examples of formalistic
theorizing can be seen in Richard A. Schermerhorn's *Comparative
Ethnic Relations*, Pierre Van Den Berghe's *Race and Racism*, and
Hubert M. Blalock's *Toward a Theory of Minority Group Relations*.
Included in this style of theorizing are symbols subjected to mathe-

matically standardized transformation, as well as systems bound together by chains of logical derivations which may or may not be dependent upon any content. In the formal style of theorizing, logical derivations are dependent only upon the pattern of relationships holding among the symbols themselves.[6] The following propositions taken from Blalock's work epitomize the formal style of theorizing.

(1) In general, the larger the number of feasible alternative means for achieving a given goal, the less likely it is that this goal will be incompatible with a second goal, in the sense that the achievement of the former will reduce the probability of attaining the latter, or vice versa.

Note: To the extent that the possession of resources increases the range of alternative means to a given goal, then the greater the resources the less the likelihood that this goal will be incompatible with others in the above sense.

(2) Those goals which permit the least flexibility with respect to choice among alternative means can be expected to have the greatest influence in determining the direction of one's behavior (choice behavior), though not necessarily its intensity or persistence.

Note: This proposition is based on the assumption that individuals will act more or less rationally so as to maximize their chances of attaining all important goals. They are expected to select the more efficient means toward goals that do not permit flexibility, and then to choose means toward other goals (that do permit flexibility) according to their compatibility with the most efficient means toward the first goals.

(3) Economic and status factors are most likely to be major determinants of minority discrimination if *both* of the following hold:

(a) there is a relatively small number of means to status and economic goals that are perceived to be efficient; and

(b) discriminatory behavior is perceived to be instrumental, either for large numbers of persons or for influential elites, in achieving status objectives by these most efficient means.[7]

The above type of theorizing has the advantages of potentially providing more precise explanations, predictions, and controls. Furthermore, because the structure of such theories is of such a nature that postulates, definitions, and theorems are explicitly stated, there is a greater likelihood that logical adequacy can be achieved with the above theoretical style. There is one major disadvantage which has characterized much theorizing of this type in intergroup relations but which does not *have* to be a disadvantage—imagery inadequacy. Imagery inadequacy refers to the lack of a rationale which would explain why a particular independent variable is linked to a particular dependent variable. Herbert Blumer has recently renewed his criticism of theoretical formulations lacking imagery, indicating that such an inadequacy often results in pseudo-explanations of social phenomena.[8]

The nature of Blumer's criticism centers around the belief that social interaction is dynamic and cannot be adequately described or explained through the use of definitive concepts. Rather, because interpretation is a crucial aspect of social interaction, researchers and theorists should place much more emphasis on the development of sensitizing concepts. Blumer states that "human beings interpret or define each other's actions instead of merely reacting to the actions of one another."[9] Furthermore, "their response is not made directly to the actions of one another but instead is based on the meaning which they attach to such actions."[10] If the latter comments are taken into account, it should be easy to understand why Blumer feels that simple linkages of independent variables are fallacious. They do not take into account "the process of definition intervening between the events of experience pre-supposed by the independent variable and the formed behavior represented by the dependent variable."[11] A proper procedure seemingly should involve first of all a careful selection of variables which reveals thoughtful reflection on problems in an effort to identify their genuine parts. There must be an intensive and extensive investigation into the problem area. Following such a procedure, presumably, one can concentrate on attempting to establish cause-effect relationships, though Blumer does not emphasize this point.

Structure of Theories

We have suggested that the formalistic style of theorizing is a superior style in intergroup relations due to its explicitness, precision, and potential research fertility. Let us now turn to the structure of this type of theorizing. Formalistic theories contain postulates, theorems, nominal definitions, operational definitions, and imagery. *Postulates* refer to the basic assumptions of a theory—the givens. *Theorems* are the testable, logical propositions derived from the basic assumptions. *Nominal definitions* refer to assignment of meaning by substitute expressions while *operational definitions* indicate the procedures to be used in obtaining the variable. *Imagery,* as previously stated, refers to the rationale of a theory.

Because the above features of a theory and their definitions may still be difficult to comprehend, we will illustrate a type of theory construction technique which can be used in intergroup relations. Before moving directly to the illustration, it may be more clarifying first to delineate several general strategies: *induction, deduction,* and *retroduction.* Induction is a theory construction strategy which begins with empirical content and moves to a more general level of abstraction through the development of general postulates, nominal definitions, and imagery. Deduction involves a strategy whereby the investigator constructs a set of general principles, definitions, and imagery from which logical derivations are made and operational definitions constructed. Retroduction as a theory construction strategy is perhaps most in vogue. This strategy entails both induction and deduction. The researcher begins to induce a theory from empirical data; however, in the process of inducing, with the aid of explanatory and intervening variables, general principles are developed which not only explain the empirical content observed but go beyond it and have implications for other matters of fact (deduction). This strategy is especially useful when theories are constructed in under-researched areas or when syntheses of opposing lines of thought are being attempted.[12] Let us now turn to an illustration of an initial state of theory construction.

Much research in sociology would tend to support the following assumptions:

Postulate 1: The formal socialization process functions to legitimate societal norms for superordinate substructures and subordinate substructures.

Postulate 2: The informal socialization process functions to legitimate societal norms for superordinate societal substructures and attenuates perceived legitimacy for subordinate societal substructures.[13]

These assumptions may be used as postulates in this illustration. Before deriving the theorems, however, it would be necessary to discuss the rationale behind the assumptions. In other words, some effort should be devoted to an explanation of the reasons why the variables have been linked together in the stated fashion.

For instance, one set of substructures within the United States may have its genesis in race, ethnicity, or some combination of the two. The resultant categories may be labeled *majority group* and *minority group*. Through an intensive and extensive examination of the formal socialization institutions and techniques in the United States, and by assessing majority and minority groups' acceptance or rejection of societal norms, it should be possible to observe some relationship between formal socialization and perceived legitimacy of societal norms. A similar procedure should be followed for postulate 2 in order to derive imagery prior to formal theorizing. In other words, if the investigator hopes to avoid charges of being mechanistic and/or naive in his theory construction, he should be reasonably certain that his postulate variable linkages are based on as much prior evidence as possible.

Following such an explication, one may derive new propositions which could be subjected to empirical tests such as the following:

Theorem 1: Increasing consistency in formal and informal socialization leads to increasing perception of the legitimacy of societal norms.

Theorem 2: Increasing inconsistency in formal and informal socialization leads to increasing perception of illegitimacy of societal norms.[14]

Before the actual test it is necessary to produce operational definitions for the variables used in the study. In other words, consistency in formal and informal socialization and perception of the legitimacy of societal norms must be measured. For example, certain questions on an interview schedule could be designed to reveal information about the interviewee's formal and informal socialization experiences as well as perceived "correctness" of societal norms. An index of consistency would be constructed from the formal-informal socialization items and a perceived legitimacy index would be developed from the correctness question.

Theoretical Adequacy of Formulation

Whether or not a theory constructed by induction, deduction, or retroduction is adequate can rarely be discerned from a cursory examination of the formulation. Instead, it is necessary to subject the theory to close logical, operational, empirical, and pragmatic scrutiny. One may want to determine whether or not the theory is contradictory or if the theorems have been logically derived from the basic assumptions. Another concern may be with the key variables (independent, intervening, and dependent). Can these variables be operationalized? If they cannot, then the theory cannot be tested, and thus should probably be labeled as an impractical exercise. Concerning pragmatic adequacy, one should be interested in the utility of the formulation. Can it be feasibly applied to the "real world"? Finally, following a test of the theory, the theorist should be interested in the degree to which the theory was supported by the findings. In other words, is there reason to suspect that the theory is empirically adequate? One can never be certain about this aspect of the scrutiny; however, support for the theory does tend to indicate some degree of empirical adequacy, and the test enables the theorist to revise and reformulate the theory if necessary.

While there are many facets of theory construction which may remain vague to the reader, this introduction to theory building should not only illuminate the importance of theory construction in intergroup relations but also should demonstrate the need for more theorizing if we are ever to have reliable and valid explanations of social phenomena pertaining to intergroup relations.[15]

METHODS IN INTERGROUP RELATIONS

When methodology is mentioned in the social sciences, the beginning student often envisions long formulas, abstract postulates and theorems, and statistics. Just as often, he may feel that there is little need for this type of thinking in a field where the substantive material is variable and subject to seemingly unexplained variations.

While it is true that the subject matter in an area like intergroup relations is not as sharp and as focused as some in the natural sciences, this does not negate the very crucial functions performed by methods in intergroup relations and other areas within the social sciences. Some of these functions include providing procedures for concept formation, hypothesis building, making observations, deriving measurements, experimenting, theory building, providing explanation, and predicting relationships between social phenomena.

Other functions of methodology in intergroup relations are to deline-ate and examine various methods used, in short, to facilitate compre-hension of the scientific inquiry process. For instance, it is important to know whether experimentation or survey research will yield the most valid intergroup relations findings. If, for example, one is interested in studying the nature of the relationship between prejudice and discrimination, or more specifically how well one can predict a per-son's discriminating behavior from his prejudiced attitudes, experi-mentation may prove to be the most suitable technique. It should be possible to conclude from a comparative examination of this tech-nique and others that experimentation is superior with respect to the establishment of *causal relations* between variables, the controlling of extraneous influences, the manipulation of independent and interven-ing variables, and the measurement of change in the dependent vari-able. Provided that such a conclusion of superiority of technique can be reached, the study of methodology should be mandatory for students and researchers in intergroup relations. The crucial importance of the study of methodology in intergroup relations becomes apparent when one realizes that the substantive content of intergroup relations and the utility of the content will only be as good as the techniques used to *acquire* and *evaluate* the content.

The Development of Disciplined Thinking

In order for any area to advance substantively *and* methodologically, it is necessary for that area to cultivate and maintain disciplined thinking. For an area such as intergroup relations, which is relatively new and still in the exploratory stage, the aforementioned necessity becomes an indispensable requirement which must be met by contributors to the field.

Disciplined thinking in intergroup relations involves affectivity-free cognitions. The process does not refer to a specific type of thinking, *à la* the scientific method. It does, however, involve making use of objective and logical rules in an effort to explain, predict and control social phenomena. For example, the propositions that "*All* whites are racists" and "*All* Blacks are lazy" are constructed in such a way that the logical derivations are inadequate. In other words, because racism and laziness are, in actuality, variables which are not usually defined independently of race designation, theorems derived from the postulates may be logical but not objectively valid. Thus one would find it difficult to categorize such thinking as disciplined, unless there were some ulterior motive.

Any discipline characterized by either illogical derivations or by extreme subjectivism runs the risk of falling by the academic wayside. Intergroup relations is an area which can be exceedingly fruitful from a sociological point of view; however, it is currently important, and will become even more important in the future, to extricate the intergroup relations area from polemics and emotionalism if scientific advances are to be made.

Coping with Novel Developments in the Field

Because intergroup relations remains relatively underdeveloped, there is much room for "discoveries," serendipity, and so on. However, while the field is new, it is also an area which has been bound by the shackles of traditionalism. In fact, one could venture to say that some current polemical and emotional literature is a reaction to traditional and somewhat antiquated thought in intergroup relations.

One of the most potentially fruitful techniques in intergroup relations is small group research. This approach can be used to study intergroup tension, conflict, harmony, intersex interaction, and other processes. A classic experiment which illustrates the utility of small group research in intergroup relations was conducted by Muzafer Sherif in 1949 and replicated in 1953 and 1954. The experiment was designed to produce group formation and particular relations between groups. Twenty-five boys of approximately twelve years of age were invited to a summer campsite and were divided into two experimental groups. During their stay at the camp, the experimenter manipulated a number of variables which enabled him to confirm the following hypotheses:

  1. When individuals having no established relationships are brought together to interact in activities with common goals, they produce a group structure with hierarchical positions and roles within it.

     The interaction process tends to produce common norms for the group, which constitute the basis of attitudes of individual members, at least in matters of consequence to the group.

2. When two in-groups are brought into functional relationship under conditions of competition and frustration, negative out-group attitudes toward the outgroup and stereotypes will arise and be standardized.[16]

In many instances, however, funding agency restrictions, legislative restrictions, educational administrative restrictions, and traditional thought render small group techniques almost sterile. These restrictions also extend to theoretical discussions which may be somewhat different or socially unacceptable. Obviously, then, for some, one way of coping with novel developments in intergroup relations has been to restrict dissemination of information. This is directly antithetical to the scientific process. In fact, unless researchers and theoreticians are "free" to explore such phenomena in novel ways, there is a distinct possibility that the advancement of knowledge in intergroup relations will be stifled. For example, if a researcher designed a laboratory experiment which would involve intense interaction between Black males and white females or white males and Black females, one could speculate that the researcher might be subjected to a great deal of pressure inimical to the research process—even outside of the much maligned deep South. It is obvious that knowledge suffers since this is information which cannot be gleaned without intergroup interaction. Yet, positive and negative interracial social interaction occurs. Furthermore, if we are to learn anything about such interaction, it is necessary for us to study the phenomenon regardless of individual predilections to the contrary.

As intergroup relations matures as an area, it will be necessary to replace traditional thought concerning *proper* methodological strategies with more progressive strategies devoid of restrictions, such as societal norms, governing relationships between ethnic, racial, and other aggregates.

The "Soft" Methodological Approach

When one speaks of a "soft" methodological approach, it is important to emphasize that the adjective is not meant to convey any meaning antithetical to the scientific process. On the contrary, it can be argued that occasionally such an approach actually has enhanced the scientific process to a much greater extent than so-called more rigorous approaches. The scientific process benefits by empirical data, not a particular type of methodology.[17] Regardless of the methodology, if the data do not imply verification of the theory, the science of human behavior will not be appreciably advanced.

The soft approach may be thought of as *the application of empirical techniques of investigation designed to discern directions in which concepts or issues might be explored rather than the development of definitive findings.* The soft approach in intergroup relations, then, while less rigorous in terms of technique, may contribute immensely to imagery. Such approaches are commonly employed during the exploratory stages of the study of social phenomena. However, some social scientists have contended that the subject matter of social behavior is of such a nature that disciplines using social variables would be better off using soft approaches. Indeed, the contention is that much of human behavior remains uncontrollable, unexplained, and unpredictable precisely because of the fact that definitive concepts often have been established with little imagery and sophisticated techniques of analysis have been used resulting in little-explained variations in the phenomena investigated.

Regardless of one's methodological predilection, the soft approach can be viewed from several perspectives. We will look briefly at the techniques of exploration, case study, deviant case analysis, analytic induction, and empathetic explanation.

Exploration

Exploration has been characterized by both narrative speculation based on cursory, deliberate, and incidental investigation, and statistical pilot-type studies. Both types of exploration can be exceedingly informative if they are viewed as the beginning steps of investigation rather than as an end in themselves. Narrative investigation in exploration can be very fruitful and rich in content. The technique, however, is *not* usually objective in the strict sense of the term. Rather, it often involves subjective judgment from a few cases. Yet, as Blumer has pointed out, a few competent observers may be much more important than carefully selected samples of individuals who can shed little light on the social phenomenon under investigation. In fact, a common criticism directed at empirical studies is that they often lack imagery and richness of content. A contrasting view is that such a weakness is probably inherent in the methodology since human behavior should be approached from an introspective point of view.

More positivistic researchers have tended to use pilot studies which may be replicas of empirical studies. For these students of the behavioral sciences, this type of exploration is superior to the more humanistic technique explicated above. It is suggested that the canons of *scientific* lines of exploration are followed more closely by this method; that is, by the specification of independent, intervening, and dependent variables, provision of a rationale for such specification, operationalization of such variables, and finally testing relationships between the variables. To be sure, not all pilot studies will follow this procedure—some have proceeded without any such specification. Nevertheless the ultimate aim of the study has been to test relationships between variables regardless of whether or not the relationships were specified a priori.

Case Study

Case study refers to a method of exploratory investigation where few assumptions are made concerning the nature of the relationships among variables. It should be noted, however, that descriptive findings from a case study may enhance the investigator's knowledge about other cases which are similar to the case researched.

For instance, the case study by Inge Powell Bell essentially is a description of a southern Congress of Racial Equality group in 1962.[18] The study includes a descriptive explication of the following: the backgrounds of CORE members; the structure of CORE; the action tactics of CORE; and, CORE's relationships to the Black and white communities. While this study is not inferential it does provide the rudiments of a conceptual framework which should prove fruitful for future investigations. If, for example, any of us decides in the future to study inferentially a civil rights group, it may be possible to use, as propositional bases, empirical regularities observed by Bell and others who have used the case study approach.

Deviant Case Analysis

Another approach to the case study method which yields very informative results is deviant case analysis. In deviant case analysis, the selection of a case is predicated on the assumption that it deviates from the normal order of such cases. For instance, if a superordinate and a subordinate group defy predictions regarding emergent tensions as a consequence of power imbalance, then deviant case analysis of this atypical situation may prove informative.

Stanley Lieberson has observed that there is less early conflict between majority and minority groups when a minority population migrates to a society in an economically, politically and socially inferior position.[19] In order to empirically validate this assertion, Lieberson pointed to the movements of many European and Oriental populations to the United States and the lack of warfare, nationalism, and other forms of conflict. Suppose, however, a migrant population inferior socially, economically, and politically enters a society and conflict immediately occurs. In order to determine possible causes of the deviation, a researcher may decide to intensively examine the migrant group for possible clues. If, for example, the migrant members are found to have unusually high levels of aspiration then prior assumptions regarding the behavior of migrant groups with certain social, economic and political characteristics must be altered.

Analytic Induction

This approach represents a type of soft methodology whereby there is a persistent search for cases which are not supportive of some theory being tested. If such cases are discovered, the theory is then altered in such a way that it includes an explanation of the deviant cases. For instance, one might originally hypothesize that Protestants are prejudiced toward Catholics in Northern Ireland simply because of religious differences. However, in the process of confirming this hypothesis, a Protestant might reveal that his prejudice is solely related to economic factors. To be sure, such factors may be inextricably interwoven with religion. However, the hypothesis might be altered to include the integrated nature of economics and religion. Following such a theoretical alteration. the investigator searches for additional cases which may result in further theory modification. The process is then continued over and over until the theory has reached an acceptably refined status.[20]

Empathetic Explanation

As a strategy, this involves investigation which is empirically cursory. Speculation possibly characterizes much of the technique. This type of research involves integrating emotion, ideas, and purpose in an effort to explain some social phenomenon. *Black Rage* by Grier and Cobbs and *Talley's Corner* by Elliot Liebow are examples of empathetic explanation, which some researchers have suggested is unusually adapted to the study of human behavior since it stresses an "in-depth" understanding of the case and the situation. Such an approach is closely related to Blumer's suggested technique for empirical study of social interaction where emphasis is placed on understanding the phenomenon from the actor's point of view. Such an approach would be exceedingly difficult to use in intergroup relations due to the enormous number of variables, many of which may not be directly relevant to the phenomenon being researched. Nevertheless, the approach has become increasingly popular among persons calling for an increase in applied research.

The "Hard" Methodological Approach

"Hard" methodology is the pseudonym generally applied to survey, laboratory, and field experimental procedures. It has been known as "positivistic," "empirical," "naturalistic," and even the "scientific" approach. What hard methodology generally implies is that a set of hypotheses, or a formal set of theorems derived from a set of postulates or basic assumptions, are systematically tested and disproved or *not* disproved. Also, the method involves the construction of sampling designs and the use of statistical inference techniques.

Hard methodology in intergroup relations has been chiefly of two varieties—experimental and survey. We will devote our attention first to the experimental approach.

The Experimental Approach

Experimental approaches may be of two types: laboratory and field. The aims of both approaches are the same, that is, the investigator manipulates a situation so that different groups of persons will represent, in varying degrees, the dependent variable conditions to be assessed. The simplest form an experiment can take is where the researcher has one experimental group and one control group. He measures the groups one at a time with respect to some dependent variable. Then he manipulates some independent variable in the experimental group and compares the experimental and control groups on the dependent variable which should have been influenced by the manipulation process.

It may be pointed out, however, that very complex designs can be developed which control, in varying degrees, threats to the generalizability of experimental findings.[21] These threats to "external validity," as it is called, tend to be much more prevalent in laboratory experiments. This is due to the fact that such experiments generally permit the control of many extraneous influences which may contaminate the study but which, nevertheless, do not allow for generalizability to other situations in the real world. In the real world, such influences may be operating in such a way that the dependent variable is affected in some manner. For example, suppose that an investigator is interested in studying the dynamics of prejudice in face-to-face interaction between Arabs and Jews. He might design an experiment which would bring together for an extended time a number of two-person groups representing the two nationalities. In an effort to control extraneous influences, the researchers may decide to restrict external interaction and other influences. Interestingly though, such extraneous factors may actually contribute enormously to the dynamics of prejudice in face-to-face interaction between Jews and Arabs. In other words, friends, parents, mass media, and so on may all interact with the experimental variables. Thus, a manipulated variable in an experiment may explain little of the variation in the "real world" dependent variable due to the fact that situational variables are absent.

The field experiment has been used as a possible solution to the problem of generalizing from experimental findings. Because the experiment takes place in a natural setting, researchers have felt that internal and external validity would be accomplished. Internal validity refers to *the extent to which the independent variable actually explains changes in the dependent variable when extraneous influences have been controlled.* Obviously, however, in a field experiment, the likelihood that extraneous influences will be contributing to changes in some variable under scrutiny is considerably greater. Also, while the field method increases the possibility of achieving some measure of external validity, it decreases the likelihood of achieving internal validity. For instance, if, using the above example, the Arab and Jewish subjects are allowed to remain the "field" and an experiment is conducted whereby the researcher manipulates the "degree of authoritarianism perceived by other" as a causal variable in the dynamics of prejudice, it is anticipated that he will have a very difficult time assessing the effect of the manipulated variable on the dependent variable.

Survey Designs

The survey design has been the most frequently used methodological strategy in intergroup relations. The approach is characterized by the production of data through such techniques as questionnaires, interviews, and surveys. Criticism of this mode of investigation has ranged from charges of internal invalidity to external validity inadequacy. This technique remains, however, the chief methodological approach to the study of intergroup relations.

One of the most distinguishing features of survey designs is the manner in which the independent, intervening, and dependent variables are conceived. In contrast to experimental designs, where the variables are induced, literally manipulated and observed sequentially in terms of time-order, the survey design produces data without regard to time-order. In fact, it is not uncommon for a survey to assess dependent variables prior to the assessment of independent or intervening variables. Because time-order cannot be controlled in survey designs investigators generally refer to *inferring* causality rather than *establishing* causality.

Survey designs in intergroup relations have usually taken conventional steps in the investigation process. Generally speaking, these steps are different from experimental analyses only on specific points. We will list these steps and discuss possible divergencies from the experimental approach where it is deemed necessary. Steps in a survey design generally include problem formulation, data organization, case definition and selection, data production, data analysis, and reporting of data.

Problem Formulation. For intergroup relations, problem formulation can be especially acute. This is due mainly to the fact that intergroup relations as an area can deal with two-person groups or nations depending on how one defines the concept "group." Moreover, since man is an interacting being, most of his behavior in some way involves groups of people. Thus, one problem which confronts the survey analyst and the experimenter is topic formulation and delimitation. While human behavior is complex, multifaceted, and problematic, investigators *have* been able to study intergroup relations, however, the generalizability of their findings often has been dubious. The main reason for the skepticism has been due to the fact that many purported studies of intergroup relations have, in actuality, been a concentration on one minority group or another (e.g. Blacks, women, Jews) devoid of any intergroup phenomena. A problem in intergroup relations should be concerned with a delineation of two or more groups of individuals and an explication of the process whereby they act in awareness of each other and adjust their responses to each other's responses.

Data Organization. Following problem delimitation, it is necessary to specify the research procedures to be employed in the survey. Ordinarily investigators begin by conceptualizing the variables to be used. For survey designs, this basically means that measuring devices must be constructed in such a way as to yield the best possible indicators of phenomena under investigation. Since observation and literal variable manipulation are not defining characteristics of surveys, the analyst must rely on constructed indices placed in interviews, questionnaires, or surveys to accomplish what the experimenter might actually induce or literally observe. In addition, the investigator in intergroup relations should be keenly aware of the fact that variable measurement must be amenable to intergroup phenomena.

Case Selection. This is where the most common errors are made in intergroup relations investigations. Theoretical formulations in this area should imply that groups will be the obvious units of analysis, yet, due to a variety of reasons, such as, time, money, effort, and even naiveté, groups have not always been used as units of analysis in intergroup relations investigations. A failure to use appropriate cases in research has implications for types of conclusions which can be drawn from the results.[22] Illustratively, if one is interested in the relationship between conflict and group variables such as social cohesion, group morale, and intragroup interaction, then the proper units of analysis will be groups. Should the researcher design a study which involves interviewing individuals about their relationship to a particular group and their attitudes and participation in conflict with other groups, little information will be revealed about the original problem. This is due to the fact that an assessment of attitudes, cognitions, and behavior will not divulge information about group variables. In order to gain information about group variable influence, it would be necessary to construct group indices.[23]

Data Production. Data production may be difficult due to the lack of measures designed to assess intergroup relations phenomena. However, if such measures are constructed and used as survey procedures then data gathering should be rather axiomatic. This is not to say that data production is a simple process, as it is often fraught with many difficulties; however, if stringent rules regulating intergroup investigations are adhered to with respect to data production, then the process should be similar to those found in other types of investigation.

Data Analysis. What should one do with survey data once they have been produced? An answer to this question depends upon such things as levels of measurement employed in the study, intent of the investigator, case selection procedures used, and other less important considerations. Any analysis of survey data is sure to include statistical inference procedures in order to facilitate summarizing the results of the study.

First it is necessary to transform raw data into the variables desired for the analysis. Second, it is important to categorize differentially variables. Third, procedures for controlling certain influences and variables must be made specific and, fourth, there must be some designation of "successful" and "unsuccessful" outcomes and what they mean. The experimental analyst also would be concerned with the above consideration, however, as previously pointed out, his procedures would be different, especially with respect to step three. Control procedures, due to the diverse nature of surveys and experiments, would be statistical rather than literal in surveys, although selection control procedures might be similar for the two approaches.

Thus, survey designs and experimental designs are similar in terms of intent, however, procedures are somewhat different. In intergroup relations, it is suggested that both of these procedures must be refined, and there must be improved usage if they are to be useful and valid techniques for investigating phenomena in this field.

Notes

1. Frank R. Westie, "The American Dilemma: An Empirical Test," *American Sociological Review* 30 (August 1965): 527-38.
2. Abraham Kaplan refers to this theoretical type as a cognitive style of presentation in *The Conduct of Inquiry* (San Francisco: Chandler, 1964), p. 259.
3. Richard Wright, *Black Boy*, 5th prtg. (New York: Harper and Row, 1966), pp. 284-85.
4. Kaplan, *The Conduct of Inquiry*.
5. Eldridge Cleaver, *Soul on Ice* (New York: Dell, 1968), pp. 178-79.
6. Kaplan, *The Conduct of Inquiry*, pp. 260-62.
7. Hubert M. Blalock, *Toward a Theory of Minority Group Relations* (New York: Wiley, 1967), p. 204.
8. Herbert Blumer, *Symbolic Interactionism: Perspective and Method* (Englewood Cliffs, N.J.: Prentice-Hall, 1969).
9. Ibid.
10. Ibid.

11. For a concise discussion of this problem, see Herbert Blumer, "Sociological Analysis and the Variable," *American Sociological Review* 21 (December 1956): 683-90.
12. For a concise introduction to social theory, see Clarence Schrag, "Elements of Theoretical Analysis in Sociology," in *Sociological Theory: Inquiries and Paradigms,* ed. Llewellyn Gross (New York: Harper and Row, 1967).
13. These postulates are abstracted from "Toward A Paradigm of Substructural Relations: An Application to Sex and Race in America," by Clyde W. Franklin, Jr. and Laurel R. Walum, *Phylon* (Fall 1972): 242-53.
14. Ibid.
15. This view is advanced for all of the social and behavioral sciences by Robert K. Merton, *Social Theory and Social Structure* (New York: The Free Press, 1957).
16. For the entire study see Muzafer Sherif et al., *Intergroup Conflict and Cooperation: The Robbers Cave Experiment* (Norman: University of Oklahoma Book Exchange, 1960).
17. For a collection of papers on this position, see Blumer, *Symbolic Interactionism.*
18. See Inge Powell Bell, *CORE and the Strategy of Nonviolence* (New York: Random House, 1968). For another case study in the area, see Michael Lipsky, "Rent Strikes: Poor Man's Weapon," in *Racial Conflict,* ed. Gary T. Marx (Boston: Little, Brown, 1971), pp. 326-35.
19. When the population migrating is superior socially, economically, and politically, Lieberson contends that warfare often occurs early in the contacts between the indigenous and migrant groups. See Stanley Lieberson, "A Societal Theory of Race and Ethnic Relations," *American Sociological Review,* vol. 26, no. 6 (December 1961): 902-10.
20. See Donald Cressey, *Other People's Money. A Study of the Social Psychology of Embezzlement* (Glencoe, Ill.: The Free Press, 1953).
21. For an excellent and concise statement on types of experimental designs, see Bernard Phillips, *Social Research: Strategy and Tactics* (New York: Macmillan, 1968), pp. 87-104.
22. The classic statement on external and internal validity in experimental design can be found in Donald T. Campbell, "Factors Relevant to the Validity of Experiments in Social Settings," *Psychological Bulletin* (1957), 54: 297-312, and Donald T. Campbell and Julian C. Stanley, *Experimental and Quasi-Experimental Designs for Research* (Chicago: Rand McNally, 1963).
23. See Paul Lazarsfeld and Herbert Menzel, "On the Relation between Individual and Collective Properties," in *A Sociological Reader on Complex Organizations,* ed. Amitai Etzioni (New York: Holt, Rinehart, and Winston, 1969). Also see W. S. Robinson, "Ecological Correlations and the Behavior of Individuals" in *Studies in Human Ecology,* ed. George Theodorson (Evanston: Row Peterson, 1961), pp. 115-20.

Group Classification   2

INTERPERSONAL AND INTERGROUP RELATIONS

The phrase "human relations" implies the study of human interaction in a rather broad sense. Its customary usage does not always indicate precisely what area of behavior is intended. It may refer to relations between two persons, to interaction within a family, or to relations between religious groups. Part of the ambiguity may be excused on the grounds that it is not always feasible to classify human behavior into neat semantic compartments. The scientific study of behavior requires, however, that objective and rigorous definitions of units of analysis be formulated and consistently applied. This is especially important in the complex area of intergroup relations and is also a major challenge. Of fundamental significance for the student of intergroup relations is the task of specifying the scope and boundaries of this field. A first step is to attempt to differentiate between interpersonal and intergroup relations.

Let us subsume both interpersonal and intergroup relations under the general rubric of human relations. Nominally, we may regard interpersonal relations as interaction between (and among) individuals, that is, individuals responding to each other *as individuals*. The last phrase is crucial in the distinction, because we do not always react to others as individuals in the strict sense. One may be treated as a group member with little reference to one's individuality. Consequently two people may be engaging essentially in intergroup interaction if they are responding to each other primarily in terms of group classification. The distinguishing characteristic of interpersonal relations, therefore, is that the interaction involved is on a personal plane. We may ordinarily surmise that two persons interacting are indeed engaging in interpersonal relations, but allowances must be made for the possibility that they represent different groups to each other and are interacting accordingly. "Friends" would presumably interact on a personal basis, whereas the interaction between the leaders of two national states could be, in effect, on the intergroup level.

In the case of two groups confronting each other directly, such as two armies or two athletic teams, the interaction is obviously intergroup. *Intergroup relations are between collectivities.* Responses tend to be on a categorical basis, and individuals are perceived and treated categorically. It is probably not without significance that the individual is rather obscured in these situations, such as in the military. The group is considered to be of paramount importance and loyalty to it is demanded. There are, of course, interpersonal relations within groups. All instances of intergroup relations are not as simple and manifest as a war or an athletic contest, and the interaction may not be as dramatic as conflict. The process may be much more latent, subtle, and subdued. Relations between two religious groups within a community, for example, may be virtually "invisible" to one who is unfamiliar with the social organization of the community. In fact, the relations may actually occur in the privacy of a voting booth with, of course, only one person present.

Interpersonal relations are not the concern of this book. Prejudice and discrimination against individuals *as individuals* can be ignored from our standpoint. Similarly, conflict between persons does not interest us unless there are group overtones. Whenever the group membership of the individuals involved is a factor in modifying the behavior, the matter comes within our jurisdiction. To be sure, it may not always be an easy job to determine whether the interaction is strictly interindividual or whether or not the group consideration has some effect.[1] We can make the distinction simply enough at the logical level, but in the absence of experimental controls we may have to resort to inference and speculation in real situations.

The most familiar forms of intergroup relations to the layman seem to be "race" conflict, ethnic discrimination, religious prejudice, and the like. These are indeed commonplace and important, but there are many other kinds of groups and interaction. There are innumerable possible combinations of interactive situations involving a wide assortment of groups, including complex multiple group interrelations. Although we shall confine ourselves to the more familiar situations, it is essential that in our theoretical formulations, at least, we take into account these other possibilities, such as social class relations, ideological groupings, age groupings, and rural-urban relations.

GROUPS AND GROUPINGS

It is necessary for us to depart somewhat from the orthodox sociological usage of the term group. In its conventional meaning in sociology a group consists not merely of an aggregation of people but also entails established relationships and common social norms.[2] The definition requires that there be some degree of social organization and social control. Our usage will be somewhat broader and will encompass not only groups in this strict sense but also collectivities; for example, it will be expedient to regard "races" as groups, and the only requirement for this classification will be that there is some common identification *either* by those inside the group or by others whose arbitrary classification has practical sociological consequences. These kinds of groups may have little cohesion and membership may be very subjective and vague. Furthermore, a person may be classified as a member of a group even though he would not prefer such classification. The critical consideration in this sense of group membership is usually how one is classified by others. Thus the kinds of groups considered in intergroup relations are not necessarily synonymous with the types associated with "small group" analysis in sociology.[3] In many instances, in fact, we are dealing with large, loosely organized collectivities which may seldom, if ever, act in any concerted fashion as a unit. These groups may not have norms peculiar to them and they may not have any policies as groups, although there may be norms and policies which are attributed to them by other groups. Racial groups would be a typical case in point.

The kinds of groups which we shall consider are in some cases hardly more than statistical categories of people who are responded to as a category. In other instances, of course, the groups involved will approximate a strict sociological definition. It may be a very cohesive social unit with a distinctive cultural pattern and a strong sense of common identity. The relevant point is the kind of relations that occur between groups rather than the organization of the groups themselves, though in some cases the latter factor has an important bearing upon the character of those relations. Finally, we must recognize that we may consider a category of people as a group for our purposes either because of some "consciousness of kind" emanating from within the group or because there is an externally imposed classification. The latter circumstance, as will be discussed later in this book, may contribute to the former.

GROUP MEMBERSHIP AND GROUP CLASSIFICATION

The ordering and identification of people can be a mysterious business. Psychologists, for example, employ a device which probes a person's self by requiring him to ask himself "Who am I?" In the area of intergroup relations we might well ask two similar questions, namely: "Who are you?" "Who is he (or she)?" The first question would be asked *of* a person and the second *about* the same person. The answers to these questions will not always reveal group identification, but in many cases this is the principal means of identifying the person. The answers do not always coincide in terms of group classification. The way in which we classify ourselves does not always square with that of others; social class offers an interesting case in point. It is not necessary or inevitable to perceive oneself or another person as a group member but it is certainly quite common and almost unavoidable in some respects in giving a full description of an individual. Identification by national citizenship, sex, and occupation can be informative about an individual even though such groupings are quite heterogeneous.

Subjective and Objective Classification

All classification of people is arbitrary and subjective to some extent. A given person might be classified in a variety of ways (age, sex, nationality, ethnicity, race, religion, occupation, political affiliation, residence, social class, wealth, legal status, personality, family, community, or education, to mention some of the more popular forms) and to cite any particular one as paramount for identification would be difficult to justify.[4] Social taxonomy is not an exact science; we are confronted with such problems as whether or not to recognize the person's own classification as valid or to consider his classification by others as authoritative. It also must be acknowledged that group boundaries are often quite indefinite and this confounds the problem. On the other hand, one cannot deny the reality of classification as it is practiced in everyday life. People are almost constantly grouping each other and the consequences are by no means academic; whether one is classified as ally or enemy can be a matter of life and death.

In the Republic of South Africa one's racial classification is of cardinal importance because of the strict segregation laws pertaining to non-Europeans, especially the Bantu. These laws sometimes create awkward and even amusing situations as the following newspaper story reveals.[5]

JOHANNESBURG, SOUTH AFRICA (AP)—"The legal position of Japanese in this country," remarked the Johannesburg *Star* recently, "remains as tangled as a Chinese puzzle, despite the efforts of the minister of interior to clarify the position."

The Johannesburg *Rand Daily Mail* editorially suggested, only half in jest: "Visiting Japanese would be wise to travel about South Africa accompanied by lawyers who would advise them when they were white and could swim in a municipal pool or sit on a 'Europeans only' park bench. Unless, of course, they were here on pig iron buying business—then the customer is always white."

A Stern Warning

These wry comments deal with the latest twist in South Africa's apartheid (racial separation) policy. And they are accompanied by a stern warning from Interior Minister Jan de Klerk that henceforth no exceptions would be made on declaring people white who are not ethnically white—or don't look white.

He added that no amount of agitation by political opposition or press is going to persuade the government to bend its apartheid laws, because these efforts represent "a plot to undermine the South African traditional way of life and a move to get the public to accept integration."

The Japanese got the front page headlines in this situation although there are only a handful of them here—diplomats or businessmen—compared to 500,000 long-resident Indians and at least 6,000 Chinese.

The Japanese recently obtained concessions which the government refuses to give the Indians and Chinese. For instance, a Japanese swimming team toured this country and (after a local row in Pretoria) was allowed the use of "whites only" pools. A Japanese gymnastic team competed against South African whites and was widely applauded.

But the main thing in the Japanese puzzle, which de Klerk tried to explain to heckling opposition in Parliament, is that the Japanese have been exempted under South Africa's group areas act, which restricts all nonwhites to segregated housing districts.

This means Japanese diplomats may live in white areas, send their children to white schools; and visiting Japanese businessmen stay at "whites only" hotels and use such restaurants.

Official Listing Unchanged

But de Klerk made plain that while the Japanese thus might enjoy some privileges as "honorary whites," the government has never declared them officially white and continues to list them as nonwhite Asians (along with Indians, Chinese, Malays) under the population registration act.

As things stand, now, a Japanese might stay at one of Johannesburg's white hotels and use its dining room. But if he wanted to eat out at another restaurant he'd risk being taken for a Chinese and refused service. The same might happen if he tried to sit on a park bench marked "Europeans only."

In fact, a Pretoria bus driver got into a scrape with the authorities when he refused to let a member of the Japanese Consulate board his bus. The bus driver said he thought the man was a Chinese "and anyway, nobody ever told me about special privileges for Japanese."

De Klerk denied allegations that special privileges were given the Japanese because their country is an increasing market for South African pig iron, iron ore and wool. He said attempts to gain similar concessions for Malays, Chinese and Indians would fail— nor would multiracial sports be allowed.

Cultural Definition of Groups

Culture provides certain general guidelines for the grouping of people; it indicates categories and their relative significance. It also furnishes linguistic symbols to facilitate identification of groups. The culture serves as a kind of "score card" which informs us how to classify people and what the distinguishing characteristics of various groups are. There also are built-in judgments in culture about the relative importance of different groups. In short, our culture informs us how to classify, identify, judge (and prejudge) and treat people in terms of groups.

Priority of Groupings

Since any person can be classified in various ways, the question of the priority of his group arises. What is his most important group? We again are faced with the possibility of disagreement between the person and others who judge him by group membership. To some the person may be a Black first and foremost regardless of occupation, sex, political affiliation, religion, or any other phylon. If one is strongly prejudiced against Blacks, then the perception of an individual as a member of this group seems to obscure all other of his categories.

To the racist, the single most important social classification will be race with other categories being relegated to secondary importance. To the person who is extremely politically conscious, race will be less significant than political affiliation or ideology in judging an individual. If one attaches great significance to religious group membership, this classification tends to transcend both racial and political membership.

Take Mr. J. M. Stonetree, for example. What is his most important group membership for purposes of social identification and evaluation? Which social category is most important to him in his social image of himself? Let us hypothesize that he is, in alphabetical order: an architect, a Christian, a citizen of the U.S.A., an ex-convict, a man, a member of the Whig political party, and a Stonetree. Who is he to you and who is he to himself? Which grouping is most important and which is least significant? Of course we must acknowledge that our perception of him and his perception of himself will depend in large measure upon the social context. If he is traveling abroad he is more obviously an American, and at work his occupational category may loom larger than any other social category. Nevertheless, at any given time it is plausible to postulate some rank order of group memberships, either as he is perceived by others or as he regards himself. There is hardly any time at which we are simply an individual, either to ourselves or to other people. It is very difficult for Mr. Stonetree to ignore his social classifications entirely or to escape the consequences of social grouping by the people with whom he interacts. This is not to say that this does not occur; we merely emphasize that most of the time we function in some kind of group context, either explicitly or implicitly, as defined by our own judgments or as imposed upon us by the judgments of those with whom we associate.

Effects of Grouping

The principal effects of group classification are prejudice and discrimination. Either the prejudice or the discrimination can be positive *or* negative. One's principal group classification can determine where one may live, eat, work, attend school, play, and be buried.

An interesting case of "confused" group classification is that of people known as "Turks" in South Carolina. These people, who could be classified sociologically as an ethnic group with some justification, are believed by some to be descended from early Caucasians of Arab origins but are more probably a combination of North American Indian and Black ancestry. Despite their generally dark complexions, they have been classified as white by the U.S. Census Bureau for over a century. In the city of Sumter, S.C., they have mingled freely with whites, attending the same schools and movie houses and being served at the same barber shops. In the rural areas of Sumter County, however, the Turks were required to attend a separate school because local officials did not regard them as white. This segregation was protested in the courts, even before the 1954 Supreme Court decision on segregation in the public schools, but the case was lost on technical grounds. Eventually, an appeal was successful and the local school board closed the Turks school and admitted them to the public schools which the white children had been attending.[6]

Changing Group Membership

Although some kinds of group membership, such as race, may be impossible to change in the strict biological sense, in other cases a change may be effected. Even in the case of race, although one cannot alter his genetic heritage, people do switch race categories. In the United States there are many people who could claim either Black or Caucasian classification with social success. The evidence indicates that when there is a choice possible, it is in the direction of the group which is in the most favorable situation with respect to discrimination.

Thus "passing" in the U.S. means that racially marginal persons tend to prefer classification as whites in order to avoid negative discrimination against Blacks or other non-whites.

The amount of passing by persons of some Black ancestry in the U.S. is obviously difficult to determine under the circumstances of discrimination against people who are classified as Black and the tendency to regard any person as Black with any degree of such ancestry. A seemingly reliable estimate has been made by one sociologist, Caroline Day, by inquiring about the number of passes in 346 mulatto families. She concluded that about 10 percent of these families had members who had passed, presumably on a permanent basis. In an extrapolation based upon these data another sociologist, John H. Burma, has estimated that there were over 110,000 passers around 1940 and that the number passing each year would be about 2,750.[7]

Changing one's group membership may entail migration, religious conversion, social mobility, or the same result sometimes can be accomplished by modifying one's visibility in some way, such as acquiring a new name. One often can escape the effects of group membership, such as negative discrimination, by influencing how one is classified by others.

Perception and Visibility

In order to respond to a person as a group member it is first necessary to recognize him as such; this requires a certain visibility plus a discerning eye. Perception is selective and is influenced by predispositions. One must be aware of the category involved and be able to identify members, in order to express prejudice and to discriminate.[8] Visibility is a necessary condition for prejudice and discrimination but not a sufficient one in itself. Physical differences, names, language, dress, and the like may facilitate group identification, but they do not guarantee prejudice or discrimination. Prejudice itself affects perception and is likely to make the prejudiced person selectively perceptive to the members of the object group.

In identifying individuals as members of groups we are evidently influenced more by the total visual field than by actual characteristics of the individual himself. This was borne out in a study by Alice B. Riddleberger and Annabelle B. Motz on the relationship between perception and prejudice.[9] Their findings indicated that subjects define an individual in terms of the total situation to a greater extent than in terms of any clues gained from the individual's facial or physical features. Individual characteristics which would serve to identify a person as a member of a particular group are not inherently conspicuous. They "stand out" only if the scene is psychologically structured by us to render them highly visible.[10]

Visibility is relative and subjective. A man's necktie is "conspicuous" if the color indicates his school affiliation, if this is considered to be an important social classification and if the perceiver is aware of this kind of social distinction. The same notion is applicable to coloration of skin, the principal difference being the objective amount of surface exposed to one's vision. Everything else being equal, the objective, physical dimensions determine what is perceived, of course, but this is seldom the case. It is more likely that the viewer singles out some particular characteristic, such as skin color or name, for selective attention in accordance with his preconceptions and predispositions. As we shall learn subsequently, stereotypes exercise a profound effect upon perception and the relative visibility of "distinguishing" characteristics of group members.[11]

The role of visibility in the objective sense can be more fully appreciated when one considers that sightless persons also hold various kinds of group prejudices and manage to identify group membership by means other than visual perception. A religious amulet or the chain from which it is suspended is also "obvious" only in a subjective sense. Some people do not notice it, to others it is quite manifest. It is indeed quite difficult to talk meaningfully about objective visibility in the area of intergroup relations. Such a statement is probably quite disconcerting and puzzling to many laymen who are likely to insist that they can "tell black from white." The answer of course is that such a distinction is indeed a relatively easy one to make if one is predisposed to single out skin pigmentation for special attention and if the shades of coloration are as distinct as implied in the words "black" and "white." More realistically, we discriminate in our perception between persons of light and dark complexion because these distinctions have social-psychological significance for us and because we have been conditioned by our culture to notice these kinds of differences in appearance.

GROUP BEHAVIOR

To what extent do groups behave collectively? The answer depends upon the homogeneity of the composition of the group and how cohesive it is. Some groups are deliberately organized for collective action and attempt to foster a common pattern of behavior. Other groups, such as racial groups, may have very little sense of common allegiance and may display very little collective action. One can hardly attribute policies to racial groups as a whole. Ethnic groups can hardly speak with one voice either. Religious groups often have the ideal of unified beliefs and actions but seldom achieve them in practice. Even political parties do not always present a profile of accord.

Reputations of Groups

A significant fact in intergroup relations is that groups of the sort we have been discussing come to have reputations. Whether they are "earned" or imputed amounts to the question of asking if they are "deserved" or are due to prejudice. This is a fundamental and critical question, and much of the energy expended in the field of intergroup relations is for the purpose of answering it. Objectivity would require that a distinction be made between deliberately organized groups which formulate and execute policies as such, and such collectivities and racial groups which ordinarily do not act as a unit.[12] For a group to acquire any kind of reputation at all requires, of course, that the persons constituting the group be perceived and conceived as a category in the first place. Thus one would not be likely to ascribe group characteristics to left-handed people since they are seldom regarded or perceived as a social unit. It seems almost inevitable that we would associate some kind of reputation with a group merely as a result of categorizing the people involved.

In an era of mass media communication and widespread concern with public opinion, propaganda, and public relations, such units as ethnic groups are almost obliged to concern themselves with their public "image." It is frequently necessary for a group to undertake some kind of publicity activity to counteract defaming communication circulated by those prejudiced against the group. The problem of group reputation is magnified by the rise of mass media communication. The mass media are ideal for the perpetuation of stereotypes, and groups feel it necessary to protect themselves from the adverse effects of being stereotyped on television, radio, and other media. Protests have been lodged with radio and TV stations and networks by various racial and ethnic groups against unfavorable portrayal. Blacks complained about the "Amos 'n' Andy" program and persons of Italian ancestry expressed resentment about the extensive use of Italian names for gangsters on the "Untouchables" program. Ethnic minorities often have been cast in the role of villain and criminal in the mass media, but apparently this practice has been curtailed somewhat and is doubtless due in no small measure to the increased sensitivity on the part of both minority and majority groups.[13]

TYPES OF GROUPS

In-Groups and Out-Groups

A general kind of sociological classification of groups is that of in-groups and out-groups. This distinction is not merely academic or the product of sociological imagination. In numerous instances in real life one encounters a classification of people into "we" and "they." Indeed, these distinctions are firmly rooted in our language, so much so, in fact, that it is exceedingly difficult to speak of people except in terms of in-group and out-group classifications. We must either talk about ourselves or about them! One owes allegiance to his in-group and tends to be condescending or hostile towards the out-group. In extreme cases of intergroup conflict, such as war, one is obliged to sacrifice his life for the in-group and to kill out-group members on sight. One has a positive prejudice towards the in-group and a negative prejudice toward the out-group. We praise the in-group and disparage the out-group.

There are various levels of classification. The in-group may be as small as a couple or theoretically as large as the entire population of the earth, and the out-group can be the rest of the world or the family next door battering at your fallout shelter entrance. A given person could be classified as part of your in-group or as an out-group member depending on one's sociological perspective. John Smith could view Enrico Antonelli as a fellow Christian, a fellow American, a fellow New Yorker, or as a Catholic, an Italian, or as a New Yorker of the city variety as distinct from upstate residents. The boundaries of the in-group vary and are subjective in that they are contingent upon one's social-psychological perspective of the moment. This is not to deny that there are some rather permanent and enduring group boundaries. The French and Germans offer a case in point, but even its validity as an example depends upon restricting the generalization to a particular historical period. The younger generation in these countries are increasingly inclined to view themselves as "European."

The out-group sometimes assumed the form of a kind of residual category; that is, the people "left over" after the social circumference of the in-group had been specified. The out-group in this case would consist simply of everybody who was not included in the in-group. There are semantic labels available for designating these groups: foreigner, alien, barbarian, gentile, heathen, enemy, to mention only a few. There is a certain deceptiveness involved in these distinctions, however. In-groups and out-groups do not exist independently of each other, and one's own classification is not an absolute matter. To be sure, "we" are always the in-group, but we are they to them and they are we to themselves. In war it is indispensable to have two enemies and also two in-groups. We are also the enemy although we are not inclined to admit it. Psychologically we seem to prefer to emphasize our in-group memberships rather than to acknowledge our out-group status. The latter may be forcefully and dramatically called to our attention at times. When one peers out of a foxhole and is greeted by enemy fire he will realize that he is very much in an out-group situation, or when one is asked to sit in the rear of the bus it is difficult to avoid the same conclusion.[14]

The process by which in-group and out-group distinctions develop has been demonstrated by Muzafer Sherif in a series of brilliant and imaginative social-psychological experiments. The studies were conducted at summer camps, employing as subjects boys who had been carefully selected so that matched groups could be established, and the subjects were not aware that they were participating in any kind of scientific experiment. Without making it apparent to the boys the experimenters (serving in such roles as camp director and counselors) created conditions which gave rise to two groups, out-groups to each other. This was accomplished by such techniques and devices as transporting the two groups in separate buses, arranging athletic competition between them, and assignment of housing by group membership. Consequently, characteristic attitudes and behavior began to emerge in the relations between the in-group and the out-group. There was mutual animosity between the two groups and on one occasion overt conflict occurred. This was in line with the main hypothesis of one of the studies: "When two in-groups are brought into functional relationship under conditions of competition and frustration, negative out-group attitudes toward the out-group and stereotypes will arise and become standardized."[15] (As we shall see in chapter 6 the barriers between the two groups were subsequently broken down by arranging cooperative activity aimed at achieving common goals important to both groups.)

From the standpoint of discrimination, there is positive (favorable) for the in-group and negative (unfavorable) for the out-group. The degree of discrimination depends upon the sharpness of the distinction and the intensity of the prejudice.

Reference Groups

Although it is difficult to imagine intergroup relations occurring between reference groups in the strict sense, the concept nevertheless has considerable relevance. These kinds of groups are close conceptual kin of in-groups and out-groups. The basic idea of reference groups is that individuals *identify with and relate themselves to* groups or collectivities. These may be "real" social entities such as a family, community, or political party, but they may also assume the form of "abstract collectivities" such as "farmers," "liberals," "conservatives," "veterans," or "Southerners." Membership in a reference group is primarily psychological in character, that is, the identification with the group emanates from the individual. The person may be a member of a group in the strict sociological sense and also identify strongly with it, of course, but one's behavior also can be influenced by an allegiance which is aspirational in nature. As Shibutani has eloquently expressed it: "Each man acts, then, for some kind of audience, and it is important to know what this audience is and what kinds of expectations are imputed to it."[16]

The impact of reference group identification can be illustrated by political behavior. Voting decisions are apparently influenced by a variety of reference group loyalties. The critical identification may be in terms of political party affiliation, sex, religion, occupation, social class, regional identification, family membership, community, neighborhood, age, race, ethnicity, or some kind of social collectivity. The crucial question is which of these identifications will be of paramount importance in determining how the person will vote. If he conceives of himself as a farmer rather than a veteran, the voter will probably reach a different political decision. Religion may claim a stronger allegiance than social class identification or the appeal of a common sex may be stronger than nominal political party affiliation.

The types of groups which occupy the attention of the student of intergroup relations—ethnic, religious, and so on—obviously serve as reference groups on occasion. Behavior is affected by the norms and values we associate with and attribute to these groups. In addition to political behavior, our actions and attitudes in many other areas are evidently conditioned by reference group identification: jury decisions, ity itself.[17] It seems likely that our self image reflects the kind of consumer preferences, esthetic judgments, style of dress, and personal-reference group to which we relate ourselves.

By postulating positive and negative reference groups we can relate them to in-groups and out-groups. It is logical to associate positive reference groups with in-groups and to view out-groups as the counter-part of negative reference groups. Hence it is to be expected that a person would take behavioral cues from a positive reference group in much the same sense that one's behavior would be shaped by the expectations and demands of an in-group. Conversely, one would respond to the standards and values associated with a negative refer-ence group in somewhat the same manner as reacting to the norms of an out-group.

Reference groups are of especial significance in the context of mass society, in which an individual has multiple group memberships and identifications. The mass media of communication make it possible for an individual to identify himself sympathetically with a variety of groups. He can identify with labor or the company in an industrial strike; he can relate himself to the communist bloc or to the West; he can psychologically take the side of Israel or the United Arab Republic; and he can align himself in similar fashion with diverse groups in the disputes, conflicts, and issues that are so vividly called to our attention by the mass media. It would seem in fact that we are almost forced to form reference group attachments as a result of the way in which we are dramatically confronted with these struggles and issues by the channels of mass communication. It is difficult to remain neutral and not to evaluate events from the standpoint of one's reference groups. Indeed, knowing another person's reference groups is often an impor-tant key to understanding his behavior. Actions which otherwise perplex us sometimes become meaningful when we learn the individ-ual's reference groups and their priority to him. It is not a simple matter to determine the reference group allegiances of another person.

It is possible to conceal one's true sentiments; a management official may actually identify with labor, and a capitalist could secretly sympathize with the communist movement!

Ethnic Groups

Although chapter 4 is devoted entirely to the subject of ethnic groups, a preliminary introduction should serve a useful purpose here. Ethnic groups are distinguished by cultural homogeneity. Sociologists tend to view them as subcultural entities; that is, subgroups of society with cultural patterns which differentiate them significantly from the main cultural stream. This designation of a group implies that it has not been fully assimilated culturally. The term is frequently employed to describe immigrants and their descendants who have retained cultural traits from the "old country."

Racial Groups

Race is a term which almost defies rigorous definition. It is also the subject of a subsequent chapter in this volume, but it deserves a brief introduction here. *Scientifically* speaking, race refers to subdivisions of the species differentiated by distinguishing physical characteristics which are genetically transmitted. Sociologically, race tends to be whatever people define it to be; that is, one's racial group membership is largely a matter of how society classifies him, regardless of the biological validity of the classification.

National Groups

Nationality in the strict legal sense is rather easy to define; it merely refers to citizenship in a national state. Thus virtually everybody is a citizen of some national state or other today because the political organization of the world today almost precludes one's legal existence otherwise. The shift of social organization from tribe to nation during the past several centuries has decreed that the individual must "belong" to a state and have some kind of national identity. This has become a basic form of identification and classification of people in the modern world; we have become Frenchmen, Italians, Japanese, Nigerians, Hungarians, Lebanese, Brazilians, Norwegians. Changing nationality has become a difficult and complex process, subject to many restrictions and conditions.

The term nationality is sometimes used synonymously with ethnicity by the general public. This is understandable and excusable when one considers that state and culture are somewhat coterminus in modern times. Information forms which inquire about one's nationality presumably seek to learn the national origin of his forbears and this is almost tantamount to asking his ethnic group membership. It should be understood, of course, that immigration makes it possible for a person to become a citizen of a different national state while retaining the cultural earmarks of his former country.

National states undergo changes in territorial sovereignty and population. Wars, treaties, revolutions, invasions, plebiscites, and the like have resulted in the creation and reformation of states and consequently defined and re-defined the citizenship of the people affected. The geographical area commonly referred to as the Balkans is the most famous example in modern times. Individuals have been classified as citizens of two or three national states during the course of a lifetime without changing residence.

Minority Groups

The term minority is obviously suggestive of groups which are of less than majority size, and its sociological usage does indeed have this connotation. The crucial component of its meaning in intergroup relations, however, is the relative position of the group in the social structure.[18] *A minority group is regarded as having an inferior, subordinate position in the society.* Its social status is low relative to other groups; one might say that it is sociologically "underprivileged." Although it is not required by orthodox definition to be statistically minor, this is nonetheless typically the case. A small group, everything else equal, is likely to have less social power. There are power elites, but we do not view these, social-psychologically, as minorities. To reiterate, the distinguishing feature of a minority is its subordinated social status and lack of effective social power to combat unfavorable treatment by dominant majority groups.

Minority groups are, by definition, especially susceptible to prejudice and discrimination. As Louis Wirth expressed it, "Minority status carries with it the exclusion from full participation in the life of the society."[19] This idea also can be expressed as lack of social assimilation of the group. In some cases this is due to a desire to remain separate and distinct; the group may resist social osmosis, but frequently it is a matter of facing barriers and obstacles to assimilation. Similarly, the original classification of people into a minority group may be the product of their own desires or the group consciousness may be imposed from without, but it is more likely to be the latter.

Traditionally, the concept of minority group has been restricted to racial, ethnic, and religious types. These categories are sufficiently broad to allow inclusion of almost any sort of collectivity that is treated as a minority. There are political minorities and groups such as migrant workers who are oppressed by dominant groups and their behaviors and relationships to the rest of the society can be profitably analyzed as minority situations.

Some form of visibility is essential for minority groups, otherwise differential treatment is thwarted. The means of identification is sometimes physical and in other instances behavioral (cultural), but unless it is present in some form it is not possible to distinguish the majority from the minority. When "natural" symbols are unavailable the dominant group may require that distinctive ensignia be worn by the minority, as in the case of Nazi Germany compelling Jews to wear the Star of David.

Majority (dominant) groups are frequently numerically superior but there are many historical instances in which a relatively small group has subjugated a much larger one. The whole history of colonialism is replete with examples in fact. The British in India, the Dutch in South Africa, the French in Algeria, and the Portugese in Angola have all been familiar examples of this phenomenon. The technique for establishing and preserving a superordinate position varies, but the most effective device is to institutionalize the basis of control. An instructive analogy would be the idea of the divine right of kings. When this kind of doctrine is embedded in the mores, it is implicitly accepted by those affected. Consequently it is the most effective kind of social control available to a power elite. The controlling group needs only to suppress countervailing ideologies in order to preserve its favored status. The most fearful eventuality, and the one that causes the most anxiety and dread, is the inversion of the power situation. In fact this becomes a basis for rationalizing the status quo, and one often hears the remark from these circles that, "They would do the same thing if the situation were reversed," or words to that effect.

Implicit in the concept of minorities is the notion that they are unable to defend themselves from exploitation and discrimination by dominant majority groups. They are forced to work for lower wages and to pay higher rents; they are excluded from private associations and subjected to personal indignities, in contrast to the favorable treatment of majority group members. The particular pattern of prejudice and discrimination depends upon the minority and majority groups involved, of course. Christians were cast into the arena with lions by the Romans; Indians were herded into reservations by "Americans"; and gypsies were incarcerated into concentration camps in Nazi Germany.

Other Groups

Most of the kinds of groups which are of concern to the student of intergroup relations can be subsumed under the categories which have been described thus far. However, there are a few other groups that warrant our brief attention because the same principle of interaction applies, even though they will not be systematically discussed later in the book. *Families* are social units which are important in intergroup relations. Family membership in ancient Chinese society was a primary means of social identification. Interfamily conflict in the form of feuding is a matter of legend and fact in the United States; the Hatfields and the McCoys, for example. The *clan*, although of relatively little social significance in the Western world today, still looms large as a social category in some societies.

The *tribe* remains a grouping of vital importance in parts of the world, especially in Africa. A major source of political conflict in many African societies today is between the proponents of a strong central government on the one hand and tribal autonomy on the other. In addition, some intertribal conflict remains in many African states, the Congo and Nigeria being the most publicized recent examples. Tribes can, of course, be classified as ethnic groups within the context of a larger society.

Castes are also rather unfamiliar to the contemporary Western world although caste conditions are still approximated in Black-white relations in certain parts of the American South.[20] India offers the classic example of castes, although official government policy there now discourages caste distinctions. Despite the efforts of Ghandi and Nehru the caste system in India evidently has not entirely disappeared. The chief characteristic of a caste system is its prevention of mobility; one's caste membership is fixed at birth and it is theoretically impossible to alter it. Castes function as communal groups in job allocations; caste and type of work are closely related in India. Relations between castes are defined by the culture and, to the extent that these definitions are socially accepted, result in accommodation. Friction occurs when the legitimacy of the system is challenged, especially by the lower castes.

Communities, by definition, tend to be self-contained social entities, and there is always the possibility of conflict of interest between different communities. In ancient Greece city-states were often rivals and engaged in warfare, and the Italian city-states were similar entities in many respects; even today Venice and Rome manifest ancient animosities. In modern times intercommunity relations are more likely to assume the form of economic and political competition, and the division is frequently on a rural-urban or urban-suburban basis. In the United States communities compete for industry and trade and for federal and state aid, and not least important, in athletics.

Communities have reputations and members may be prejudged accordingly. That a community is an in-group can be appreciated by observing the differential treatment a visitor sometimes receives from the police for traffic violations. It also can be inferred from the practice of law enforcement officials in foregoing prosecution if the offender promises to leave town.

Gangs of male youths in urban communities in the U.S. are of interest to us not only because they interact on an intergroup level but also because they provide something of a model of intergroup relations on a larger scale. It is indeed unfortunate that we have not exploited this "natural laboratory" more fully to discover basic principles of the dynamics of intergroup interaction, especially the conflict aspects. These gangs have been studied primarily from the standpoint of their deviant norms and the delinquent behavior of their members. They manifest strong in-group characteristics such as prejudice and discrimination against out-groups, and violent conflict between gangs is not uncommon.[21]

Age represents still another basis for grouping and intergroup relations. Adolescents and the elderly are frequently singled out in American society. The former group is said to possess a subculture and to exhibit prejudice towards adults, and the elderly also apparently feel set apart and claim to suffer discrimination. Young people seem to resent the designation of "teens" and protest newspaper stories identifying juvenile offenders as "teens." The elderly prefer to define themselves as "senior citizens" and are the recipients of an admixture of favorable and negative discrimination. Both groups are subjected to stereotyping. Age grouping is subjective and arbitrary, to be sure, but it is quite real to the person who is referred to as a "kid" or an "old man." The generational conflicts which occur are sociologically genuine also.

The decade of the sixties in American society gave rise to a new and more dramatic version of generational conflict. The advent of this conflict seemed to have been signalled by a slogan of students at Berkeley during the early stages of the student movement, namely, "don't trust anybody over thirty." This edition of the generation conflict featured four principal areas of conflicting attitudes: (1) attitudes in the area of sexual morality, (2) drugs, (3) religion, (4) the Vietnam War and the draft. Some observers even postulated a youth counter-culture with a radically different life style covering such areas as dress, music, sex, religion, drugs, politics—in short a generalized rejection of traditional values. Whether a myth or reality, the generation gap gave rise to a large amount of literature purporting to analyze and explain the phenomenon; for example, Edgar Friedenberg and Charles Reich offered a sympathetic analysis, whereas Lewis Feuer had an explanation which did not flatter youth. In any event, there seemed to be little doubt of some hostility and prejudice between the generations; one of the most dramatic manifestations of this was an attack on youthful peace protesters in New York City by construction workers (hard hats) in 1970.

Sex

The battle of the sexes may not reach the stage described so amusingly by James Thurber in "The War Between Men and Women," but it would be naive to overlook sex groups in the study of intergroup relations.[22] We should not be deceived by the existence of marriage into believing that men and women do not identify with their own sex on many issues. The loyalty to one's sex may be moderated by attachment to one's spouse but it does not entirely nullify it. Furthermore, there is undeniably prejudice based upon sex, and discrimination (both positive and negative) can be easily demonstrated.[23] Perhaps we should be more grateful than we are that there is a strong interpersonal attraction between men and women; otherwise Thurber's story might not be fantastic.

In American society during the last few years we have witnessed the rise of the Women's Liberation Movement evidently sparked in no small measure by the publication of *The Feminine Mystique* by Betty Friedan in 1963. American women had protested inferior status in an earlier period of American history but the feminist movement in the 1920s had focused primarily on voting. Between that period and the advent of the Women's Liberation Movement there was no large-scale, vigorous protest against subjugation of women. Inspired perhaps by the efforts of Black people to achieve social justice, Women's Liberation has become more militant in tone; sexism was denounced with the same kind of fervor as the denunciation of racism. The following passage from *Sexual Politics* by Kate Millett, one of the most dedicated and forceful advocates of liberation of women, conveys the spirit of the movement and the grievances of its supporters.

> The study of racism has convinced us that a truly political state of affairs operated between the races to perpetuate a series of oppressive circumstances. The subordinated group has inadequate redress through existing political institutions, and is deterred thereby from organizing into conventional political struggle and opposition.
>
> Quite in the same manner, a disinterested examination of our system of sexual relationship must point out that the situation between the sexes now and throughout history, is a case of that phenomena Max Weber defined as *herrschaft*, a relationship of dominance and subordinance. What goes largely unexamined, often even unacknowledged (yet is institutionalized nonetheless) in our social order, is the birthright priority whereby males rule females. Through this system a most ingenious form of "interior colonization" has been achieved. It is one which tends moreover to be sturdier than any form of segregation, and more vigorous than class stratification, more uniform, certainly more enduring. However muted its present appearance may be, sexual dominion obtains nevertheless as perhaps the most pervasive ideology of our culture and provides its most fundamental concept of power.[24]

Political groups strive to promote a common identity and to discredit their political opposition. The solidarity of the political in-group is dependent in large measure upon a shared contempt for common foes. If one defines politics as a struggle for power, it obviously follows that the power struggle will be waged at the intergroup level to a considerable extent, because political success seems to be very much dependent upon organization. Political group consciousness is at its apex during election contests, but for the professional and the person with highly salient political attitudes, the political identification of people is never out of season.

Political group membership may be a prime determinant of one's general social status in a society, as in the case of the Communist party in either the U.S.S.R. or the U.S.A. Political parties themselves are composed of persons who are also members of various other kinds of groups. This is especially so in the United States where parties have been formed more on the basis of ethnic, religious, regional, or racial interest groups rather than upon ideological considerations. To the extent that political groups reflect socioeconomic class views and interests, political conflict has overtones of interclass conflict.

In American society in particular *voluntary associations* play an important role in social, political, and even economic life. Since many Americans are members of a variety of such groups, the membership in any one is frequently nominal. In the case of groups such as Masons, social fraternities, and the like, the membership may be of some advantage or disadvantage in employment, promotion, or admission to other associations. These groups possess a varying quantity of power and influence as well as prestige. They interact with each other as well as with the "general public." The AFL-CIO and the Farm Bureau share some common views but are in opposition on other issues. The National Association for the Advancement of Colored People and the National Association of Manufacturers seldom come into contact but it is conceivable that they could confront each other on some issue of mutual concern. Occasionally two important and influential organizations who usually have friendly relations and similar attitudes on many matters will find themselves on opposite sides, as in the case of the American Medical Association and various veterans organizations over government paid medical care for veterans.

The functional significance of these associations is enhanced by the social conditions of mass society in which individual identification with society is filtered through various kinds of reference groups such as voluntary associations. The politics of mass society similarly require collective action to influence social policy. In fact the characteristic social-psychological posture of Americans in modern mass society according to David Riesman is "other-directed."[25] In view of the penchant of Americans for organizations it is rather ironic that we regard ourselves as highly individualistic.

There are numerous other social categories which are of some relevance in intergroup relations beyond the major ones we have already considered.[26] There are, for example, occupations and professions which are reference groups of high priority for many people. For many persons it is their most important social identification; being a medical doctor or a clergyman or a railroader means much more than performing a particular kind of work. There are very real intergroup relations between occupational groups; physicians and nurses, plumbers and carpenters, and teachers and janitors interact on a group basis in many instances. Indeed, the whole field of occupational sociology devotes itself to a considerable extent to the study of relations between and among occupational groups.

Other groupings which merit mention in passing are those based upon such criteria as attitudes, personality, handicaps, physical characteristics, regional residence, neighborhood, education, and abilities and talents. There are also combinations of groupings such as the temporary alliances that might be formed during a bond issue campaign or a fluoridation of water referendum. There are issues which sometimes divide communities into two camps, cutting across other group boundaries. Long industrial strikes have produced schisms in families, churches, and PTA's; controversies over school problems and officials have split communities along uneven sociological lines.

One of the most intriguing questions in the sociology of intergroup relations is what the evolution of groups will be; for example, what existing groups will fade or merge and what new groups will emerge and become more prominent? Will race identification become less important and social class more significant? Will new groups develop which we cannot conceive at the present time; for example, will new kinds of categories based on age, education, occupation, or other criteria come into existence and produce dramatic forms of intergroup conflict? Such questions challenge our sociological imagination, insight, and foresight.

MARGINALITY

Group boundaries are not always clear and distinct, and an individual's membership status may be ambiguous and indefinite. Admission to a group or expulsion from it is often gradual rather than sudden and the psychological transition does not always equal the sociological in pace. The immigrant changes his national residence and perhaps eventually his citizenship, but this does not automatically cancel his sentimental attachment to his native land. In fact, there are hardly any group memberships which are absolutely fixed. One's "race" cannot be altered in the sense of revising one's genetic constitution, but his social classification can be changed by a legislative act, a new theory in anthropology, or a shift in popular beliefs concerning the idea of race. A person's religion, culture, nationality, and social class are subject to change.

Sociology is indebted to Everett V. Stonequist for the most intensive treatment of the concept of the marginal man.[27] Since its formulation by Robert Park, the concept has been employed primarily in analyzing the behavior and attitudes of immigrants in American society. The interest of American sociologists in this phenomenon is obviously related to the large amount of immigration to the United States during the past century. Examples of cultural marginality have been ubiquitous, and some of the most famous sociological studies have dealt with this subject, including the classic *The Polish Peasant in Europe and America* by William I. Thomas and Florian Znaniecki.

The marginal man is subjected to cross pressures resulting from dual cultural participation. He finds it difficult to abide by the demands and expectations of two different cultures. The Navajo Indians are a striking example of this situation. The Navajo way of life and American culture are divergent in many beliefs, values, and customs. The individual Navajo is torn between two alternative courses of action and two systems of values which are essentially irreconcilable. He cannot obey both sets of behavioral expectations which makes it difficult to develop a high degree of personal organization. This condition contributes to a confused self-image; he is not unambiguously Navajo or American. He cannot identify exclusively with either group.

The concept of marginality also can be applied profitably to the analysis of the social-psychological status of various minority groups and their members. If the dominant religion is Christianity, a member of the Jewish faith in such a society is faced with peculiar problems of adjustment in connection with the celebration of religious holidays. Christmas in American society poses this kind of problem for non-Christian faiths as it is not a simple matter to celebrate the holiday as some kind of secular occasion when it is fraught with such obvious religious significance. Majority group members are so accustomed to associating manger scenes with the holiday observance that they are prone to overlook their religious symbolism and to express bewilderment when objection is raised by non-Christians to placing these scenes on public property.

One of the personal problems created by marginality is that one never can be certain how he will be classified and thus treated by other people. There is always some degree of uncertainty as to how one will be perceived by others and how they will respond to you. If there is some divergence between the person's self-image and his perception by others, it creates psychological conflict and tension. The immigrant who conceives of himself as an American but who is referred to as a "wop" will experience emotional strain. Indeed, as Stonequist has noted, this kind of situation can lead to various personality difficulties such as ambivalence of attitude and "dual personality." On the other hand, of course, marginality may provide a perspective which enables one to gain keen insight into society and human behavior and can contribute to urbanity and sophistication. The challenge of marginality for the individual is to exploit the opportunity rather than to become a victim of it.

Notes

1. See James M. Fendrich, "Perceived Reference Group Support: Racial Attitudes and Overt Behavior," *American Sociological Review* 32 (December 1967).
2. The concept of group in sociology is expertly treated in George C. Homans, *The Human Group* (New York: Harcourt, Brace, 1950).
3. See Michael S. Olmsted, *The Small Group* (New York: Random House, 1959).
4. Classification changes with time as new categories are developed and old ones fade. Cf. William Petersen, "The Classification of Subnations in Hawaii," *American Sociological Review* 34 (December 1969).
5. Chicago *Sun-Times*, 10 May 1962. Similarly, see Leslie Melamed, "Race Awareness in South African Children," *Journal of Social Psychology* 76 (1968): 3-8.
6. *Feature Press Service*, American Civil Liberties Union, Weekly Bulletin, 1962. Cf. Brewton Berry, *Almost White* (New York: Macmillan, 1963).
7. John H. Burma, "The Measurement of Negro 'Passing'," *American Journal of Sociology* 52 (July 1946): 18-20.
8. For an example of this process see William M. Kephart, "Negro Visibility," *American Sociological Review* 19 (August 1954): 462-67.
9. Alice B. Riddleberger and Annabelle B. Motz, "Prejudice and Perception," *American Journal of Sociology* (March 1959): 498-503.
10. On situational visibility see Barry Williams, "Social Identities in Black and White," *Sociological Inquiry* 41 (Winter 1971): 57-66.
11. See Dilavin Porier, "Police Encounters with Juveniles," *American Journal of Sociology* 70 (September 1964), and Gerald Engel and Harriet E. O'Shea, "Group Characteristics as Perceived by Members of Religious and Racial Groups," *The Journal of Social Psychology* 68 (1966): 347-75.
12. For example, a labor union or business organization in contrast to Blacks.
13. See Norman A. Scotch, "The Vanishing Villains of Television," *Phylon* 21 (Spring 1960): 58-62, and Melvin DeFleur, "Occupational Roles as Portrayed on Television," *Public Opinion Quarterly* 28 (Spring 1964): 57-74.
14. "We" often tend to deny the humanity of out-groups, e.g. Huckleberry Finn, on being asked if anyone was injured in a particular accident replied that nobody was killed, "only a nigger." Cf. Thucydides on the thickness of the Persian skull and the difficulty of doing damage to such infra-human heads.

15. Muzafer Sherif and Carolyn W. Sherif, *An Outline of Social Psychology* (New York: Harper and Bros., 1956), p. 293.
16. Tamotsu Shibutani, *Society and Personality* (Englewood Cliffs, N.J.: Prentice-Hall, 1961), p. 257.
17. On the relationship between ethnicity, religion, and other reference groups and voting behavior see Samuel Lubell, "The Politics of Revenge," *Harper's* 212 (April 1956): 29-35.
18. See Donald Young, *American Minority Peoples* (New York: Harper and Bros., 1932).
19. Louis Wirth, "The Problem of Minority Groups," in *The Science of Man in the World Crisis,* ed. Ralph Linton (New York: Columbia University Press, 1945), p. 347.
20. On the subject see Anthony de Rerick and Julie Knight, eds., *Caste and Race: Comparative Approaches* (London: J. & A. Churchill, Ltd., 1967), esp. the George DeVos paper.
21. For a sociological analysis of gang behavior see Albert K. Cohen, *Delinquent Boys: The Culture of the Gang* (Glencoe, Ill.: The Free Press, 1955), and Frederick M. Thrasher, *The Gang* (Chicago: University of Chicago Press, 1936).
22. James Thurber, *The Thurber Carnival* (New York: Dell, 1964).
23. Helen M. Hacker, "Women as a Minority Group," *Social Forces,* October 1951, pp. 60-69.
24. Kate Millett, *Sexual Politics* (New York: Doubleday, 1970).
25. David Riesman, Nathan Glazer, and Reuel Denney, *The Lonely Crowd* (Garden City, N.Y.: Doubleday, 1954).
26. See Edward Sagaran, ed., *The Other Minorities* (New York: Ginn & Co., 1970). Women, adolescents, homosexuals, cripples, dwarfs, ex-convicts, and the aged are among the nonethnic minorities treated in this reader. Similarities and differences between their statuses and those of the traditional minorities are discussed.
27. Everett V. Stonequist, *The Marginal Man: A Study in Personality and Culture Conflicts* (New York: Scribner's, 1937). For the original formulation of the concept of the marginal man see Robert E. Park, "Migration and the Marginal Man," in *Personality and the Social Group,* ed. Ernest W. Burgess (Chicago: University of Chicago Press, 1929). The idea is critically evaluated in Arnold Green, "A Re-Examination of the Marginal Man Concept," *Social Forces* 26 (December 1947): 167-71.

Biogenetic Classification: Race

3

"Race" has come to be an important category for classifying people. For some persons it is almost obsessive, in the sense that racial classification transcends in importance all other social categories. It is also a critical mode of classification for other people who may not regard it as significant themselves, because of the real consequences it has for them as *objects* of classification. In a society where racism is rampant, an individual member of a racial minority cannot escape the consequences of classification, and therefore he has a racial consciousness imposed upon him which may be repugnant to him.

As a result of this it behooves us as students of intergroup relations to pay serious attention to this category and try to make some sense of it. Objectively and soberly, however, we must recognize that the task of defining race and describing the concept and its consequences is a formidable one; we should caution fellow students against the illusion that by the end of this chapter they will be sophisticated about the subject. However, there are certain dimensions of the topic which warrant careful analysis, and we have arranged these in what we think is an appropriate analytical and pedagogical sequence. First and foremost, we need to come to grips with the *concept* of race. Having laid as solid a constructed conceptual foundation as possible, we then examine the process of *race formation* (to the extent that it has occurred) by evolutionary processes. These insights should contribute to an understanding of the next area of analysis of *racial classification*, because race formation has not resulted in distinct, discrete species subdivisions. There are some curious beliefs about racial classification, however, which have profound effects, so in the next section we examine race mythology. The final section of this chapter attempts to peer into the sociological and biological future to catch a glimpse of what race may mean to other generations of human beings.

THE CONCEPT OF RACE

Scarcely a word in the English language is fraught with more ambiguity, emotionality, and mastery than race. Its meaning is varied and depends in large measure upon the person who is using it at the moment and the context. Its intended meanings include nationality, culture, mankind, religion, ethnicity, language groups, and even sex.[1] For instance, there are references to the Hindu race, the human race, the Aryan race, the Polish race, the Jewish race, and the female race, to mention only a few of the common usages of the concept. Of crucial importance here is the fact that efforts to develop a systematic and rigorous definition of race are thwarted somewhat by the ambiguous meaning and inconsistent usage of race as a concept. The term is not only employed loosely but also irresponsibly, as the geneticist, William Boyd, suggests:

> The concept of race has probably been of some use in the past, employed as anthropologists formerly used it, although there are some today who would doubt that; but the word has latterly fallen into disfavor, partly because it has been much misused by fanatics and unscrupulous persons to further their purposes of gaining political power. Such persons apparently knew little, and cared less, about possible true scientific meanings of the term.[2]

First and foremost, race is an idea. It can be considered as the most powerful ideational force in the world or it can be ignored. Although it is difficult for the contemporary world to grasp, the idea of race is of recent historical origin.[3]

Socially speaking, race is defined in the same way as any other symbol—by social consensus. In this sense a person's racial group membership is largely dependent upon the collective judgment of other members of his society and not on biological characteristics.[4] Even a person's own opinion as to what race he "belongs" carries less weight than public opinion. (The same statement is also applicable to social class of course.) This insight helps to explain why persons who are deemed to have any Black ancestry are classified as Black in the United

States even though the proportion of Black ancestors is only a small fraction. While this type of classification is not logical it *is* sociological. Thus, an individual's racial classification, from a sociological point of view, depends primarily upon how he is perceived by other members of his society.

The same principle is obviously involved in legalistic definitions of race. Legislative decisions on racial classification presumably reflect public opinion on the subject. An individual's racial classification is dependent upon ideas about race held by members of the legislature, and as one might expect, such definitions vary considerably. Historically, as we have already noted, the concept of race did not become prominent until the last few centuries. Commensurately the practice of legalistic racial classification is also of rather recent origin and is plagued by similar inconsistencies and discrepancies in usage. For instance, persons classified for one purpose, such as burial, may be defined differently for other purposes, such as marriage or school attendance.[5]

Frequently legalistic definitions make reference to the amount of "blood" of some "race" an individual has to establish his racial category. Fractional distinctions are frequently made; in some states in the U.S. a person is considered to be Black if he has as much as "one-eighth Black blood." Blood may be taken to mean ancestry of course, but some of the laws actually refer to "a drop of Black blood," and one encounters such phrases as "Black blood flowing in the person's veins!" The courts have not presumed to take blood samples of individuals whose racial group membership has become the object of litigation, rather they have followed the practice of determining race in terms of the presumed race of his ancestors. Interestingly, the race of the ancestors is similarly reckoned. Legally then, therefore, race is defined in an arbitrary, subjective, common sense manner. Indeed, it is not unreasonable to suggest that legislation defining race is produced by legislators acting, directly or indirectly, under the influence of racists' ideas. Otherwise it is difficult to explain why there should be any laws containing definitions of race in the first place.

When one reflects upon the concept of race in historical perspective, it is difficult to disavow entirely the contention of *some* racists that race is essentially a matter of intuitive definition. In other words one must grant some credence to the racist view that race is something of the "heart" rather than the "mind," in the sense that it is a rather mystical and subjective idea that is a function of arbitrary judgment. To be sure, racists are not always consistent in their definitions, and many do emphasize the purely biological aspects, but when hard pressed for scientific evidence on race, subjective definitions often emerge. To some extent the sociologist can agree with this view, for it is a case of what sociologists refer to as the principle of "the self-fulfilling prophecy."[6] It can also be expressed as an instance of the sociological principle: "that which is regarded as true tends to be true in its consequences."[7]

Despite the elusive and subjective meaning of race, it is possible to formulate a satisfactory biological definition. The challenge inheres in the application of the definition to racial classification because the latter tends to be social. *Essentially, race refers to a subdivision of the species which is differentiated by distinctive physical characteristics which are genetically transmitted.*[8]

Genetic Kinship

Each individual is biologically unique, excluding identical twins, but all of us in the human species share a substantial number of genes in common. The closer the consanguineous (that is, "blood") relationship the greater probability of similarity in genes. If it were possible to assign a number to each gene and to identify a person's genetic composition, each individual would have a kind of genetic serial number. Since the number of genes in man has been estimated as high as 50,000, the number would be an extremely long one. We could compare the number of common digits between two persons and determine the degree of genetic kinship. The closer the degree of genetic kinship the more similar the genetic serial number. Two offspring from the same parents could be expected to have more genes in common than two persons selected at random. Cousins would probably have more different genes than siblings, and identical twins would have the same number.

We can understand the nature of genetic relationships also by thinking in terms of social kinship. One might say that all members of the human species are related to each other genetically to some degree, that is, sharing some common ancestry. We are all "related" in the sense of kinship. This can be expressed in terms of "cousinhood"; that is, two persons can be first cousins, second cousins, and so on. The highest degree of cousinhood would theoretically be the two most dissimilar persons genetically.

EVOLUTIONARY DIFFERENTIATION
OF THE SPECIES: RACE FORMATION

Since the origin of man is still shrouded in mystery, it is probably unreasonable to expect to discover a sudden point of transition in biological evolution from nonhuman animal to human being. Evolution, by definition, is a gradual process. Our task, however, is to consider the formation of biologically distinctive subgroups within the human species. That the present subdivisions of man are descended from common ancestors seems virtually beyond dispute.

Man, as a species, is "polytypical," which means that there are different types or modalities within the species. These may be called races for want of a better term, although some prefer to designate these subdivisions as strains, or even racial stocks. How did these subdivisions or races develop? What kinds of physical and social conditions gave rise to this variation?

At the theoretical level it is reasonably easy to answer these questions. Our knowledge of patterns of variation in other species is helpful in providing answers. In general, we may attribute race formation to the following factors, each of which will be considered in turn in some detail: (1) natural selection; (2) isolation and migration; (3) mutation; (4) genetic drift; and (5) mixture.[9]

Natural Selection

All organisms are potentially adaptive. The principal means of biological adaptation is selection. This occurs as a result of the differential survival and reproductive value of hereditary traits. Certain physical characteristics have a positive value for survival and reproduction under given environmental conditions whereas others are disadvantageous in adaptation. Some traits, such as those often produced by mutations, are lethally disadvantageous. Inasmuch as these hereditary characteristics are transmitted through reproduction and since offspring closely resemble parents in genetic constitution, the genetic composition of each succeeding generation will reflect selective survey and reproduction. Those persons who have characteristics which enable them to survive and reproduce offspring will be disproportionately represented in the next generation. Consequently, a population will undergo a certain amount of biological transformation over a period of many generations. The direction of the evolution will depend upon the kind of environmental pressures and demands that a population faces. If a disease such as malaria is present, those who have the strongest physical defenses against it will be favored because they are "the fittest" to survive. In the long run the population will develop a natural immunity to the disease.

The human species has undergone evolution by means of natural selection which has produced our polytypicality. It is not always possible to know exactly how distinctive heredity traits were developed through selection. For example, we do not know definitely how the distinctive eye fold of Mongoloids developed or if it was originally a universal human characteristic. It seems plausible that it represents an adaptation to geographical conditions, since it does afford considerable protection for the eyes from cold, wind, and dust. One can imagine the Mongoloid face developing as a result of intense natural selection in a physical environment which was cold and windy and conducive to sinus infections. By the same token the physique of inhabitants of areas where the temperatures are frigid reflects natural selection. The Eskimo in the Arctic has a bulky physique which tends to conserve body heat. Conversely, the tall, slender body of the Nilotic Black of the Sudan suggests an adaptation to the climate of that region since a greater body surface facilitates heat dissipation.

There also has been some natural selection in man with respect to skin pigmentation. There is an observable relationship between dark skin and a sunny climate. The function of the darker skin presumably is to protect against ultraviolet rays from the sun. That heavier pigmentation has a positive value in climates with bright sunlight is a reasonable hypothesis but it is difficult to verify conclusively. However, there are exceptions to this rule, as in the case of the Bushmen who are yellowish-brown in coloration, yet they live in a sunny environment. Dark skin also would serve as protective coloration, and could have other advantages of which we presently are unaware. In any event it seems quite likely that a darker hue has some kind of adaptive advantage in geographical areas where there is considerable sunlight and that a fair complexion is of some slight value in areas farther removed from the Equator. At least this kind of relationship does prevail; the skin color of native inhabitants darkens as one approaches the Equator.

Thus we can understand that natural selection operates to produce relatively distinctive traits that are hereditary in a population and thus differentiate it from other subdivisions of the species. Selection is a slow and complex process, however. Even if a particular trait has as much as a 1 percent advantage it may require a few thousand generations to produce a distinctive characteristic in a population. It also must be recognized that selection operates in conjunction with other processes by counteracting or reinforcing them. In combination with mutation, isolation and migration, genetic drift, and mixture, selection has produced the variations which exist within *Homo sapiens* today.

Migration and Isolation

The human animal is quite mobile; he has lived in a variety of climates and has been able to subsist on almost any kind of food. Wandering over almost the entire earth, larger groups split into smaller units, with one faction migrating. These migrations often resulted in geographical isolation with physical barriers, such as mountains and rivers, to the exchange of genes. In addition, migration resulted in the development of cultural variation which, in turn, prevented cross-mating.

The impact of isolation upon differentiation of the species can be more fully appreciated by imagining a hypothetical case in which a population migrates to an area surrounded by mountains.[10] Assuming that the mountains serve as an effective barrier against immigration and sexual contact with persons outside of this population, we can illustrate the genetic effects of this situation, at least at a theoretical level. A major consequence of these conditions will be a high degree of inbreeding, since mates can be selected only from within the isolated population. In concert with natural selection this can result in a population with certain hereditary physical traits which would be peculiar to that particular group. Thus if the altitude and atmosphere are such that there emerge particular structural characteristics of the respiratory system, we may expect that eventually the population will adapt accordingly. The inbreeding will have the general effect of homogenization of the gene pool. The band of people will come to have various physical uniformities which will differentiate them from other groups.

In addition, various kinds of social barriers such as religion, nationality, and culture can prevent mating and reinforce other barriers to genetic contact. Gypsies are a classic example of social isolation since they almost never select a marriage partner from outside their own ranks. It is a highly inbred group; one might even say a rather "pure" strain. (This is quite ironic when one considers that this group was viciously persecuted by that vigorous proponent of racial "purity," Adolf Hitler!)

Mutation

A mutation refers to a change in the chemical composition of a gene. Mutations are, of course, the basic source of hereditary variety. Many mutations are lethal, especially if they have the effect of altering major organs significantly; however, mutations are statistically rare occurrences. It is assumed that an organism at any given time is in a rather optimum adjustment to its environment, so that any kind of genetic change will be disadvantageous.

Occasionally a mutation occurs which has some positive adaptive utility for the organism and it may ultimately become prevalent in the population. However, in a large population even a gene with a 1 percent advantage in selection—a relatively large advantage—has in the long run only a 0.0197 probability (less than 2 percent) of establishing itself. This is offset to some extent by the fact that some genes mutate repeatedly. In fact, if a mutation occurs often enough it can counteract a selective disadvantage.

Mutations provide a kind of "raw material" which, when acted upon by natural selection, isolation, and genetic drift, result in the formation of groups with different gene frequencies. One can plausibly imagine, for example, a situation in which a mutation occurs in a population confronted with some kind of unusual environment condition, such as the presence of some new disease, for which the mutation would afford some measure of protection. Under these circumstances the mutated gene would become established in the population over a period of many generations.

Genetic Drift

Random genetic drift is essentially a function of the small size of a population. Small size makes it more probable that chance fluctuations in the gene frequencies will occur. Genetic drift, as we have mentioned previously, operates in conjunction with isolation. It seems very likely that during the early history of man these two conditions must have prevailed frequently in combination. The smaller the size of the group, the more likely that genetic drift will operate to change the original gene frequencies. This is simply due to the operation of change in mating and reproduction; a particular gene which was initially present in an individual may be lost to the population if it is not transmitted to offspring (unless it should reappear as a mutation). The gene composition of succeeding generations is thus permanently affected unless mixture or mutation can replace it.

The process of genetic drift has been vividly described by William W. Howells in the following passage:

> Genetic drift is a force without direction, an accidental change in the gene proportions of a population. Other things being equal, some parents just have more offspring than others. If such variation can build up, an originally homogeneous population may split into two different ones by chance. It is somewhat as though there were a sack containing 50 red and 50 white billiard balls, each periodically reproducing itself, say by doubling. Suppose you start a new population, drawing out 50 balls without looking. The most likely single result would be 25 of each color, but it is more likely that you would end up with some other combination, perhaps as extreme as 20 reds and 30 whites. After this population divides you make a new drawing, and so on. Of course at each subsequent step the departure from the then-prevailing proportion is as likely to favor red as white. Nevertheless, once the first drawing has been made with the above result, red has the better chance of vanishing. So it is with genes of hereditary traits.[11]

Both genetic drift and selection would have a more pronounced effect in populations which are small and isolated from other gene pools.

Mixture

Still another influence which modifies the gene frequencies of a population is interbreeding. New genes are introduced into the pool by intermarriage. A mate chosen from a different gene pool could have the effect of introducing new genes into the population. The extent of genetic change will depend upon the rate of "gene flow"; that is, the amount of interbreeding. The mere introduction of a gene does not guarantee its survival or growth in frequency in a population; this will depend upon whether or not it has any selective value or is favored by genetic drift.

Mixture is probably the principal agent of gene frequency modification at the present time. Immigration is fairly common and marriage across community, national, and continental boundaries is not unusual. Changes in social norms and rapid means of transportation facilitate intermarriage and interbreeding today.

These evolutionary forces—mutation, natural selection, isolation, mixture, and genetic drift—have interacted during the course of man's existence to produce the patterns of genetic variation (races, stocks, subraces) that are to be found today within *Homo sapiens*. It is exceedingly difficult to unravel the evolutionary processes that have contributed to these developments, partly because of man's genetic complexity and partly because of our incomplete knowledge of his evolutionary history and the mechanics of heredity. It is doubtful if we shall ever be able to discern more than a general outline of what has transpired genetically in view of the interbreeding and recombination of genes that has occurred.

RACIAL CLASSIFICATION

Man's penchant for ordering his world is nowhere more manifest than in his efforts to establish systematic categories within his species. Whether or not he has been successful in this endeavor depends largely upon one's standards in taxonomy. Although the quest for racial classification seems to have subsided somewhat in *scientific circles* in recent years, one detects a persistence and in some instances an enhancement of the notion among laymen that there are definite and discernible races. Indeed, many laymen seem to expect that there should be experts who can glance at an individual and pronounce his racial pedigree forthwith. As we shall presently discover, the matter is not quite that simple.

When one considers the question of racial classification it is imperative to recognize at the outset that each individual within the species, excepting identical twins, is genetically unique. Any effort at classification must take this kind and amount of variation into account. Furthermore, the human species, as compared to other species, is remarkably homogeneous. In contrast to many other species of animals, there has been no tendency in man towards further speciation; the existing races of man are certainly not emergent species. This has been virtually guaranteed by the continuous crossbreeding that obviously has characterized man throughout his existence.

It also is pertinent to point out that man, as a species, has undergone scarcely any biological evolution during the last 50,000 years. If a specimen of Cro-Magnon man were alive today and dressed in conventional attire he would probably not be identifiable to most of us. Indeed, it can be convincingly argued that there has not really been any fundamental biological change in man since he first appeared as a bipedal primate. The most impressive changes during this period, as far as man is concerned, have been social and cultural.

Thus we are confronted with two salient facts in any efforts to establish categories within the human species: individuals are genetically unique, and the whole species is rather uniform. The task of racial classification would be greatly simplified if we had "duplicates" in quantity who differed markedly from other genetic "carbon copies." It would enhance our insight into the nature of race and the problems of racial classification to imagine that there were several genetic "models" or "patterns" with millions of individuals with identical genetic constitutions as "duplicates." If these pattern types were significantly different, in terms of the number of hands or fingers or some other critical biological trait, then we would have definite and conspicuous races and there could be no equivocation about classification, and the ordering of individuals into categories would be quite unambiguous and systematic. Unfortunately, there are no clearcut categorical physical differences between the so-called races of man.

Anthropometric Classification

Anthropologists have labored diligently and conscientiously for many decades to classify man accurately into different races. In more recent years there appears to be a diminution of interest on the part of anthropologists in this area, at least in the traditional approach to racial classification. With the advent of human genetics and particularly race genetics, the task has been taken up to some extent by geneticists, and we shall review their efforts and conclusions subsequently in this chapter. The advancement of knowledge in genetics has exerted an influence upon anthropologists and their conceptual approach to race; this will become more evident after we have described and compared the anthropometric and the genetic methods of race classification.

Essentially the anthropometric approach to race classification is a matter of measuring physical traits which are determined by heredity and deriving race categories from these assessments. This is what geneticists would call a phenotypical approach, that is, observing the actual traits as they exist in a group of people, as distinct from tracing the genetic transmission of traits from one generation to the next. Geneticists concentrate upon *genotypes* in their analysis; they are interested primarily in the genes which ultimately are expressed as phenotypical traits in living persons.

The anthropometric classification approach is necessarily limited to characteristics which are visible or observable in some manner. This imposes a limitation on the method in that those characteristics that are observable are not always the most significant ones from a biological standpoint; rather they may be superficial and unimportant as far as their relevance to adaptation is concerned. Furthermore, a person may carry genes for some trait which he does not manifest himself. A person with brown eyes may possess genes for blue eyes.

> Serviceable though the racial classification method of physical anthropology is when used by experts, it has one prime shortcoming for the student of evolution: it can tell us almost nothing about the frequencies within the different populations of the genes associated with physical characteristics, simply because we cannot deduce the genotypes from the phenotypes of the metrical characters which have been traditionally used. These, like head form, for example, depend on the interactions of many genes with each other and are influenced by the physical environment and customs of different peoples.[12]

One should also realize that this kind of classification is based upon statistical inference; that is, anthropometrically speaking a race is a kind of statistical profile of a category of people derived from sample observations. These statistical descriptions are ordinarily expressed in terms of averages, as in the case of height. This is a legitimate and valuable method of scientific analysis, but one should bear in mind that a statistical model of a race almost certainly will not fit any particular member of that category. The relationship between the statistically constructed model and the characteristics of any given member of the race is a probability relationship. As the anthropologist Weston La Barre has expressed it: "What we construe as 'races' are statistical inferences based upon genetic facts. That is, all true racial traits are inherited through the germ plasm but can be seen only in the actual living individual."[13]

A problem that has plagued anthropologists in their attempts to classify man racially has been how much emphasis to place on adaptive traits. If one concedes that there are really no human hereditary traits that are not adaptive to some extent the question becomes academic, and apparently modern anthropologists increasingly take this view of the matter. The advantage of using characteristics which are of little adaptive significance is that, since they are not appreciably modified by selection, they provide a more enduring and conservative basis for classification and for tracing the ancestry of contemporary races.

Anthropometric classification begins with a selection of the inherited traits upon which the process will be based. Among those which have been employed are: head form, hair texture, skin pigmentation, nose form, lip shape, and various other morphological and skeletal characteristics such as the ratio of the length of different bones. These criteria have been applied singly and in combination to achieve race classification.

The form of the head frequently has served as a basis for developing race categories. *Craniometry,* in fact, was once a very important area of physical anthropology, although it receives less attention in the field today. One major reason for the emphasis upon head measurement has been the availability of skulls and the feasibility of comparing the size and form of the head of contemporary man with prehistoric specimens. Head form has been studied primarily in terms of the *cephalic index,* the ratio of the width of the head (x 100) to the length. Variations have been discovered between different racial groups; natives of the Nordic area have been found to have a longer head, on the average, than residents of southern (Alpine) Europe whose heads tend to be rounder. The continent of Africa is actually somewhat heterogeneous in head form, with considerable uniformity within certain tribal groups. Longheadedness is the most prevalent form, especially among Blacks. In general, the whole species of man is evidently becoming more round headed (*brachycephalic*). Any given racial group is likely to display more variation within it than between itself and another "race." Nevertheless, these average indices give some general indication of the genetic proximity of different races, at least when interpreted by qualified persons.

Although the cephalic index is of some utility in ordering people by race, it is subject to one serious limitation which materially reduces its values; namely that geographical mobility has been shown to affect the shape of the head of the offspring of immigrants.[14] As a consequence of this discovery, the use of head form as a basis for race classification has been somewhat discredited. Anthropologists specializing in this area may develop considerable skill in identifying skulls by race, but the role of guesswork is still evidently large. The prominent anthropologist William W. Howells has suggested that while it is generally possible to distinguish between the skull of an Australian aboriginal from that of an Eskimo or of a European, the skulls of Blacks and Mongoloids are more difficult to differentiate.[15] Even if the various difficulties which we have mentioned could be overcome, a classification of races based upon head measurements would still not yield mutually exclusive categories. This is obviously so because differences in head shape are relative in nature.

Much of what has been said about the problem of ordering races by head form would also apply to other physical characteristics, such as skin coloration and nasal index. These are characteristics which vary in degree and will yield only approximate results. There are rather obvious differences in skin pigmentation among individuals and broad differences between groups, but it is really a matter of a continuum from the darkest shade to the lightest. Any division of mankind into racial groups on the basis of color will inevitably be arbitrary. The boundary between one group and another may be the difference between two imperceptible gradations of color. One can envision mankind arrayed in one long line from the darkest complexion to the lightest, and this will suggest the kind of problem involved in classifying by color.

To be sure, most Africans are much darker in complexion than most people from Northern Europe and this is essentially the result of genetic factors. Some slight difference might be attributable to exposure to sunlight, of course. There is also the albino who has no pigmentation, due to a mutation, but he may be either "Black" or "white." (In this connection it is interesting to ask what we really mean when we say "colored." A person of black complexion could certainly be considered as "uncolored" in a very strict sense. People generally referred to as "white" are most certainly colored in the strictest sense. Only the albino can legitimately be referred to as white.) References to yellow men or red men are patent misnomers. The fact of the matter is that we are almost all brown in some shade or another. Some African Blacks are dark chocolate brown and some can be properly described as black, but there are others such as Bushmen and some Nigritos who have yellowish and reddish tinges.

At the most general level, there is considerable agreement that mankind can be divided into three main divisions with some overlap and some exceptions. These three basic stocks are generally identified as Caucasoid, Mongoloid, and Negroid. Geographically speaking, these groups generally inhabit Europe and North America, Asia, and Africa respectively. These racial stocks are loosely referred to as "white," "yellow," and "black," although these are obviously rather inaccurate descriptions in any technical sense.

This scheme does not make allowances for such marginal racial groups as the Australian aborigines, the Ainu of Japan, even Indians (of either variety), or American Blacks. It merely identifies the three major gene pools of the world in a general way. It is an intermediate step in classification between the species and the individual. Of course, one can choose the level of classification he wishes between the limits of the rather uniform species and the biologically unique individual.

Other schemes of classification go beyond this very general level, identifying as separate races the natives of Australia, the Ainu, the Veddoid, and the Polynesians. E. A. Hooton has even postulated "composite races" with various subgroups.[16] He refers to racial groups which are "predominantly Caucasian," "predominantly Black," "predominantly Mongoloid," and so on.

The more intensive the classification the more subdivisions there are; thus the Caucasian group has been subdivided into the Nordic, Alpine, and Mediterranean types. These in turn can be differentiated into ethnic groups or even nationalities as some have done. It would be possible to identify even more specific gene pools such as communities. Ultimately, of course, the categories would reach the level of small mating groups until the logical and biological limit of the individual was reached. The Negroid stock has been similarly subdivided; one finds references in anthropological literature to Bushmen (who seem to have some Mongoloid characteristics), the Negrito (who could very well be classified as a rather distinct race separate from Negroes with considerable justification), the "Forest Negro," the Bantu (who are really a collection of tribes who share a kind of common linguistic base), the Nilotic (of the upper Nile region), and the Oceanic Negroes (principally in Melanesia and New Guinea). The American Black is considered by some students of race classification to constitute still another subvariety of Negro while others view it as a composite type or even a new race.

The Mongoloid stock is also alleged to have its subvarieties, and these include a number of tribal and ethnic groups on the continent of Asia which have been "mating groups" with consequent inbreeding. There are the Japanese, the Koreans, and the Tibetans, for example, who might be said to be genetic subdivisions of the Mongoloid stock in the sense that historically, and to some extent currently, they have constituted gene pools, with relatively distinctive frequencies of genotypes. The Chinese are certainly Mongoloid, but this is a rather diverse population; in the broad geographical area designated as China there are many different "local races," and along the boundaries (Tibet, U.S.S.R., Korea)[17] there are genetic similarities with adjacent populations. The Eskimo is also considered to be of Mongoloid extraction, that is, descended from that basic stock. American Indians are generally regarded as representing an offshoot of the main Mongoloid stock. It is theorized that they originally migrated via a land bridge across what is now the Bering Strait. In the case of North American Indians one might postulate a number of local races, inasmuch as each of the numerous tribes evidently constituted rather endogamous mating groups. Then too, the people who inhabit the areas of Malaya, Indonesia, the East Indies, and the various islands of the South Pacific seem to have shared some common ancestry with the Mongoloid racial groups previously mentioned.

The people of Hawaii present an even more vexing problem to the racial taxonomist. Although there are some individuals who are rather obviously of Chinese or Japanese descent there are many whose genetic background is a blend of many different combinations, including some unknown degree of European and Oceanic and African Negroid stocks. The original population apparently consisted of Polynesian migrants who later mixed with Spanish sailors and other Europeans. The most populous group today is "Japanese Hawaiians" who are, of course, also Americans. There can be little doubt that the population of Hawaii is the most polyracial in the world today.

In what physical respects do these various racial groups differ? This is a question which is better left to physical anthropologists, at least in the specific aspects. The physical differences which separate "subraces" or "substocks" are of a rather particularistic nature and involve some rather fine discriminations of a technical character. These distinctions are based upon those physical characteristics which are observable and measurable in some manner. What these discernible differences "prove" is in the final analysis a matter of subjective judgment.

The Genetic Approach

The science of genetics is not the most ancient of the sciences, and human genetics is of even more recent vintage. The field of race genetics, nevertheless, has made impressive strides in a remarkably short span of time in the face of frustrating methodological obstacles; although it does not necessarily follow that we are on the threshold of any monumental discoveries in this area, the genetic approach has provided some enlightening insights into the nature of race.

The development of race genetics has had the dual effects of supplanting and supplementing the anthropometric approach to the study of race. With the advent of race genetics there apparently has been a decline in the interest of physical anthropologists in the problem of race classification. (This may also be due to a general trend away from the whole idea of race classification in anthropology and the other social sciences.)

The genetic approach to the study of race is largely a matter of the application of known principles of heredity to the special problem of patterned variation within the human species. It is implicitly assumed that a particular individual will resemble the composite genetic pattern for the whole group only in a probability sense. A gene pool is a discrete collective biological unit (a "race") to the extent that it has maintained genetic isolation. This simply means that the "race" must be a population in which mate selection is endogamous. The barrier to outbreeding can be geographical, cultural, social, or psychological.

In short, "races are populations which differ in their relative commonness of some of their genes." This variation is relative; one village will differ from the next, and yet the total number of genes involved in the differences may be only a very small percentage of the total number of genes in man.

Essential to the genetic study of race is the analysis of family lines. It is by the tracing of lines of descent that geneticists can discern the pattern of the inheritance of traits. In the case of racial classification in man the crucial problem is the determination of the degree of genetic homogeneity in a population. In a highly inbred group, the lines of family descent are simplified in that a member of the current generation will have fewer ancestors than in the case of a group that has experienced considerable mixture with other groups. When mating occurs between two persons who are closely related, such as third cousins, there will be more ancestors in common than in the case of tenth cousins. As Melville J. Herskovits has put it: "From the genetic point of view, a race is thus to be considered not as an aggregate of individuals whose physical characteristics are similar, but as a series of *family* lines. These produce offspring, who, when they are adults, resemble each other because they are the product of similar genetic strains."[18]

One of the difficult problems faced by geneticists in the study of race is the "unravelling" of the patterns of physical characteristics in living people in terms of the inheritance of these traits from various ancestors. The problem is so complex in fact that it is practically impossible to identify ancestral types with any real assurance of accuracy. For much the same reasons, the idea of "pure races" existing at some point in the distant past can be dismissed as ridiculous. There has been so much mixture that even if there were relatively pure strains that existed in the past, the probability of any "pure type" emerging today would be virtually nil.

Differences in races, according to the genetic viewpoint, are simply a matter of the number and kinds of genes involved. One distinguished geneticist, Bentley Glass, has estimated that the total number of genes which differentiate Blacks and whites ("typical" representatives) are on the order of a half dozen pairs.[19] This is hardly an impressive number when one considers that apparently individuals within the same "race" may differ in at least twice that many genes. Also, it is pertinent here to emphasize that these genes in which races differ are evidently independent of each other on the whole. A narrow nose and straight black hair are presumably unconnected genetically!

In recent years the genetic approach to race has explored the use of blood types for classification. There is a note of irony in this, in that many popular superstitions about race dwell on the notion of blood. The interest of geneticists, however, is quite objective and analytic. The initial interest in blood types stemmed from a very practical consideration—their utilitarian value in blood transfusions. It was discovered that blood with certain *antigens* (rather obscure chemical components) would not coalesce smoothly with blood containing different antigens. The principal antigens are identified by the symbols A, B, AB, and O. These types have become well known in recent times, particularly because of the use of blood typing during World War II by the armed forces and the development of "blood banks" for transfusion purposes by the Red Cross and other agencies after the war.

Blood type, as defined in terms of these antigens, is a hereditary trait transmitted in a known pattern which facilitates its use for the genetic study of race. It is generally supposed that these traits have no particular adaptive significance, although it is possible that future research will reveal at least some indirect connections between these chemical components in the blood and other physical characteristics. One of the major advantages of blood groups in race classification is that they are very easy to determine. Moreover, the categories are discrete and exact; it is a matter of being in one group or another without any continuous variation, in contrast to a characteristic such as skin color.

What is important in this system of classification are the relative frequencies of blood types in different populations. On this count, the person who expects gross differences is likely to be disappointed. As table 1 indicates, there are "races" which are similar in terms of blood type frequencies but rather diverse with respect to other physical characteristics. Concentrations of one type are most likely to occur in rather small and isolated groups, such as American Indian tribes.

TABLE 1

FREQUENCIES (IN PERCENT) OF INDIVIDUALS OF THE
FOUR BLOOD GROUPS AMONG THE INHABITANTS
OF DIFFERENT COUNTRIES

	O	A	B	AB		O	A	B	AB
EUROPE					ASIA				
English	48	42	8	1	Chinese	34	31	28	7
Spanish	41	47	9	2	Buriats	32	20	39	8
French	40	42	12	6	Japanese	30	38	22	10
Germans	36	43	15	6	Siamese	37	18	35	10
Poles	32	38	21	9	Javanese	30	25	37	8
Russians	32	34	25	9	Indians				
Swedes	38	46	10	6	(Bengal)	33	20	39	8
Finns	34	42	17	7					
Hungarians	36	42	16	6	AUSTRALIA				
Italians	46	34	17	3	Aborigines	48	52	0	0
Greeks	42	40	14	4					
					AFRICA				
AMERICAN (INDIANS)					Egyptians	27	39	25	9
Blackfeet	24	76	0	0	Ethiopians	43	27	25	5
Navajo	78	22	0	0	Madagascans	46	28	22	4
Utes	97	3	0	0	Pygmies	31	30	29	10
Maya	98	1			Negroes	43	23	29	5

Perhaps the most striking difference in these frequencies is the larger amounts of type B among Asian peoples. The Indian populations have little, if any, B. Africans and Europeans do not differ significantly in percentages of the various types. The incidence of B declines as the distance from Asia increases. Type A is obviously the most widely dispersed. (There are still other blood types, such as M and N, but these antigens have little practical significance as far as blood transfusions are concerned.)

What is the value of blood grouping for race classification? Opinion is divided, for races based upon serological criteria do not necessarily correspond to the conventional idea of races being visibly distinguishable in terms of morphological characteristics. Races arrived at by this technique could very well be heterogeneous in skin coloration, for example. Thus far no relationship has been discovered between blood type and external physical characteristics. The question of how important blood groups are as a basis for classification depends, in the final analysis, upon what one thinks race "ought to be." If one insists that race be based only upon nonadaptive characteristics, then blood groups would qualify on that score.

More specifically, what groupings have actually been developed using blood types? One effort has been made by Boyd.[20] Using the Rh factors as well as O, A, AB, and M and N antigens, he has postulated the following six categories: (1) Early European group (hypothetical —represented today only by their modern descendants, the Basques); (2) European (Caucasoid) group; (3) African (Negroid) group; (4) Asiatic (Mongoloid) group (the inhabitants of India might prove to be an Asiatic subrace, or even a separate race if more serological evidence were available); (5) American Indian group; and (6) Australoid group. Dr. Boyd concedes that this classification does not involve sharp distinctions or boundaries between these groups. He also acknowledges that it is only a general classification and that some populations, such as Pacific peoples, do not have sufficiently distinctive gene frequencies to permit them to be regarded as separate races or as part of the major groupings.

To be sure, knowledge of gene frequencies for blood types may enable us to infer more accurately the lines of descent of present populations; it may illuminate, for example, the genetic relationship between the Eskimos and American Indians, but it is too much to expect that genetic analysis will produce finite "races." One of the most useful applications of the approach is in making predictions about the effects of different gene combinations in parents on their offspring, that is, hybridization and amalgamation. In the final analysis we are left with the fact of the statistical relativity of races. Beyond this, race becomes a social question.

RACE MYTHOLOGY

An elaborate mythology concerning the idea of race has developed within the last two centuries. Prior to the eighteenth century the notion of race was apparently rather obscure and insignificant. Race did not seem to be considered an important type of social classification; its advent seems to be due in large measure to the need for a rationalization of the exploitation of certain groups. Race has been closely associated with the institution of slavery, especially after slave holding came under moral attack.[21] It was spuriously argued that since Blacks were *racially* inferior they were not entitled to equal rights; the implication was they were subhuman and thus not deserving of humane treatment. This proposition was also advanced to justify the imperialism and colonialism that flourished during substantially the same period. Racism became a convenient ideological defense for social practices which patently and flagrantly violated basic social and institutional principles.

The idea of race was given great impetus by an intellectual movement generally known as "Social Darwinism." This school of thought, exemplified in the writings of Herbert Spencer, emphasized such ideas as "struggle for survival," "survival of the fittest," biological determinism, competition, and race. It was a social doctrine or philosophy based upon the principle of evolution. Critics of the doctrine have regarded it as a perversion of Darwin's ideas. (It also should be mentioned that others who were more inclined towards liberalism and social reform applied Darwin's concept of evolution to social issues and the general question of social change and progress. Their positions were that man is able to choose and shape the kind of social order he prefers. This viewpoint is epitomized in Lester Ward's concept of *social telesis*.[22]) Social telesis refers to adaptation which is the result of a correspondence between the organism and the changed environment. Basically this means that man's action is purposive and based on his cognition and anticipation. Social Darwinism was also propagated by social theorists and philosophers of the "conflict school."[23] A leading exponent of this doctrine was a sociologist, Ludwig Gumplowicz, who emphasized *Rassenkampf* (race struggle) as the key social process.

The intellectual foundations of modern racism received even more emphatic and ardent reinforcement by such propagandists as Arthur De Gobineau, Madison Grant, Houston Chamberlain, Lothrop Stoddard, Henry Osborn, and Josiah Strong.[24] De Gobineau was a vigorous opponent of equality, brotherhood, democracy, the French Revolution, and so on, and an apologist for aristocratic domination of society. Grant was a stern foe of race mixture and lavishly praised "Nordic" stock while expressing disdain and contempt for other racial groups. Chamberlain, the son-in-law of another celebrated racist, Richard Wagner, glorified the Germanic "race" and was a precursor of Adolph Hitler. Stoddard and Osborn dwelled on the same racist themes with only slight variations; Stoddard viewed with alarm a "rising tide of color" which he alleged threatened the noble white race, while Osborn was a racial determinist who preached the superiority of Anglo-Saxons. It was Strong's dogmatic opinion that God had a "mission" for Anglo-Saxon Protestants. The most notorious advocate of racism in the twentieth century has been Hitler, whose ideas were expressed in *Mein Kampf*. His thesis was that the "Aryan race" was superior, pure, and to be found primarily in Germany. That the term "Aryan" referred to a linguistic category rather than biological classification did not deter Hitler. By extremely irresponsible demagoguery, perverse logic, corrupted science, appeal to base emotions, and outright falsification Hitler managed to disseminate his racist doctrines in Germany. Their appeal was irresistible to many Germans because they were so flattering to them. The German people were told that they constituted a "master race" who were destined to dominate inferior races. Coupled with this assertion was a campaign of vile denunciation and persecution directed against Jews in Germany. Jews were made the scapegoat for virtually every social problem in the country.

Although racism has evidently waned in the wake of World War II, many of its constituent myths persist. In spite of the fact that both the West and the Communist Bloc officially reject racism, the appeal of racial ethnocentrism is still strong in many areas. The United States, ironically, offers a certain amount of "leadership" in this respect. Its closest rival would be the Union of South Africa. The most outspoken racists are frequently persons of relatively low social status, especially when education is weighted heavily in the reckoning of status, although in the deep South it has been traditionally necessary to be something of a racist in order to become a political leader. In intellectual circles in the U.S. racism in blatant form is rare.

According to the new political left in the United States, racism is a hallmark of the radical right. Militant Blacks have described American society as being racist to the core, and other antiracists have applied the term "institutionalized racism" to refer to the pervasive and deeply imbedded nature of racism in American society and to suggest that many people are unconsciously racist in their actions. Consequently racism has become a kind of political slogan and epithet. In this kind of atmosphere it has become difficult to discuss a subject such as intelligence and race in a calm atmosphere. This is, we submit, ironically one of the insidious consequences of racism itself; it encourages an intellectual atmosphere in which rational discourse is quite difficult.

Some of the more prevalent and enduring of racial myths deserve our special attention; no discussion of race is complete without a consideration of them. The term myth, as used here sociologically, refers to unverified beliefs that are uncritically accepted and perpetuated in a society because of their emotional appeal.

The Myth of Racial Superiority

One of the most persistent of all racial myths is the belief that some races (races as defined by the subscriber to the myth) are innately superior to others. The emotional appeal of this belief is quite obvious. It is invariably "our" race which is claimed to be superior. History does not record any case of a race which even acknowledges, much less claims, its own inherent inferiority. It is one of mankind's favorite delusions, and we must admit that it is one which is exceedingly difficult to resist, even for people who have been exposed to scientific reasoning. It is a convenient rationalization for exploitation and domination of other groups. This myth can justify the institution of slavery, colonialism, and various forms of discrimination and segregation.

The doctrine of racial superiority is essentially mystical in character, but it usually assumes the form of a claim of greater mental ability. This is often expressed as some kind of quality which is and can only be conveyed by the term "spiritual." This seems to imply that not only is there a difference in intellectual ability, but also in such other respects as morality, temperament, and even sexual drive. It is interesting to note that there is seldom if any claim of *physical* superiority per se. Perhaps this is because it is relatively easy to validate or refute this kind of contention. Propositions which are scientifically testable *don't make good myths*. It would be quite legitimate for Germans to claim to be physically superior—at least in the sense of average size and strength—to Japanese, but this is obvious and consequently would not have the "mystique" appeal that seems to be so essential in racial mythology.

When one considers the subjectivity of the concept of race and the fallibilities of our instruments for measuring intelligence, it is apparent that it is virtually impossible to verify any thesis of racial mental superiority. When this question is posed to anthropologists, who might be considered the most competent to give an authoritative answer, the response is that "there are apparently no discernible differences in innate mental abilities among the various racial groups of the world. Hence on biological grounds and as a consequence of the common ancestry of all peoples—however much they may differ from one another in their physical characters—there is every reason to believe that innate mental capacity is more or less equally distributed in all its phases in all human groups."[25] This seems to be the most authoritative and objective opinion that is available on the question of racial differences in mental ability. To those who derive ego gratification from the belief that their race is the most gifted intellectually, such evidence is not likely to carry much weight. Myths have an emotional basis and cannot be destroyed merely by scientific evidence and rational arguments. Hence we should not expect that the notion of racial superiority will disappear in the near future.

"Mongrelization"

Racial mythology is replete with beliefs derived from what might well be called "barnyard genetics." Much of this folklore seems to date from prescientific agriculture. This is somewhat ironic in that agriculture has benefited enormously from the science of genetics. Unfortunately there are many who benefit from the results of science without understanding it. In addition to the more grossly superstitious beliefs about the effects of hybridization in human beings, there are some quaint notions about "improvement of the stock" inspired by selective breeding in subhuman animals.

"Blood" and Race

The word blood is similar to the word race in many respects; it has all sorts of mystical, romantic, and superstitious overtones, and there is a vast body of folklore associated with it. It has been traditionally regarded as *the* vital substance of life and there is considerable justification for this idea. One can very well imagine prehistoric man concluding that this red liquid had magical properties which animated the human body and which halted life when drained.

According to the mythology which has developed concerning the relationship between blood and race, blood is supposed to be the agent of heredity. References are made to "Black blood," "Spanish blood," "white blood." It is implied that physical traits are somehow transmitted by means of blood. The fact of the matter is that it is the genes which are the agents of heredity. Nevertheless, this superstition persists, and one even encounters this usage among people who would be otherwise considered well educated.

The tenacity of this mythology is manifested in the U.S. in objections to blood transfusions from persons of other "races." During the early part of World War II the American Red Cross, under pressure from racists (American, not German), "segregated" blood by "race." It eventually discontinued the practice as a matter of national policy, but the state of Arkansas later passed a law requiring that blood taken from Blacks and whites be separately identified. In spite of considerable publicity of the scientific facts about the irrelevancy of race in blood transfusions, many people apparently still are opposed to receiving blood from individuals of a different "race." It is ironic that such attitudes should exist in view of the fact that a transfusion from a sibling could be fatal if it is not of a compatible type, whereas blood from a person from another continent might save one's life if it were of the correct type.

An underlying assumption of this mythology seems to be that the blood of the mother actually circulates in the fetus. This is a mistaken notion. The child may be of a different blood type from the mother. Blood type is inherited, to be sure, and parents with certain type combinations cannot produce offspring with other types (parents with types A and AB cannot produce offspring with type O, for example), but this is a matter of gene determination. The blood supply of the fetus is independent of that of the mother. The blood of the parents does not flow in the veins of their children in any literal sense. Offspring are not really the "flesh and blood" of their parents but rather are the product of the *genes* transmitted to them.

The central idea implied in the term "mongrelization" is that race mixture has certain adverse effects. This in turn is predicated on the supposition that there are differences in "quality" between different races. It is argued that a superior race will be contaminated by mixing its blood with an inferior race. Belief in this myth is accordingly coupled with a vigorous opposition to interracial marriage. Defenders of this myth cite other myths such as race purity to sustain their position. All of the emotionality associated with love, marriage, sex, and children is aroused to promote inbreeding.

The very language employed to propagate the myth reveals a fundamental ignorance of biology, genetics, and anthropology. The term "mongrelization" is favored because of its inflammatory value. The correct technical terms used by geneticists to describe the mixture of diverse stocks—hybridization, amalgamation—are eschewed by racists.

This doctrine alleges also that if two persons of dissimilar racial background mate, the resultant offspring will suffer certain bad biological effects. It is contended that there will be "disharmonious" individuals; that is, persons will have physical disproportions, such as short arms and long legs. The evidence from crosses does not bear out this contention, however. In fact, if one were to draw any conclusion from the scientific data on inbreeding and outbreeding it would be that, everything else equal, outbreeding is generally preferable. There is some positive evidence to suggest that hybrid offspring are more vigorous and viable than those of parents of the "same" race. This phenomenon is known as *hybrid vigor* by geneticists. Also, it produces new genetic combinations which are valuable for species survival.[26]

Crossbreeding is as old as mankind. Racists prefer to say "miscegenation," probably because of the unsavory psychological sound the word seems to have for most people. If there had been any deleterious effects the human species would have become extinct long ago. *No matter how divergent they may be racially, people engage in reproductive behavior regardless of whether or not it is socially sanctioned.*

By all odds it would seem that the rate of mixture is on the increase today. Contacts resulting from rapid and less expensive means of transportation undoubtedly contribute to this trend. Many of the other barriers of the past also seem to be declining: geographic, cultural, legal, social, and even psychological. Prejudice itself remains as the principal barrier to intergroup mating. In this connection it is ironic to observe the militant opposition of bigots to interracial marriages. As long as one is strongly prejudiced against a particular group this should surely insure against marrying a member of that group. One wonders, on clinical grounds, if there is an unconscious fear on the part of the bigot that he will lose his prejudice and thus his protection against what he dreads most, affection for one member of a group he presently detests.

Evolutionary Stages of Races

This myth still has widespread acceptance, but it does seem to be on the wane. The quintessence of it is that the various "races" of man represent different stages of evolutionary development. The myth assumes that there has been a differential rate of biological evolution among the subgroups of the human species, and that it is possible to classify racial groups today according to how "advanced" they are. As one would expect, there is a pronounced tendency to regard one's own racial group as the least primitive. It is customary to compare contemporary races with simian anthropoids in an effort to determine which is more "apelike."

According to the version of this myth which prevails among Western racists, Blacks are most similar to nonhuman anthropoids and hence the most primitive. Caucasians of course are alleged to be the most advanced or the most highly evolved. It is obvious that this belief is inextricably connected with the larger myth of racial superiority-inferiority. It is one of the arguments cited to sustain the general thesis that there are qualitative racial differences.

The scientific evidence on this matter emphatically refutes the claims of racists. It simply cannot be demonstrated that any of the living races of man (ignoring for the sake of argument the problem of defining separate races of mankind) is any more advanced or retarded on some kind of evolutionary scale. Different racial groups (again overlooking the ambiguity of the term race) may be compared with respect to how "humanoid" particular traits are, but there is no distinct pattern or cluster of advanced or primitive traits in any particular group. If one defines as primitive a trait which is shared with our remote human ancestors, it is legitimate to refer to advanced and primitive characteristics, with proper qualifications. Hence it is possible to prepare a comparison, such as in table 2 by Edward Hoebel.

It is obvious from the chart in table 2 that none of these basic racial stocks is "ahead" or "behind" on any kind of evolutionary scale. Given a particular selection of traits, one could "prove" that any of these groups was the most advanced, that is, the furthest removed from our primate ancestors. We can only agree with La Barre that: "The generalization remains that the living races of man can*not* be placed in any linear or evolutionary 'ladder' from 'high' to 'low' in objective physical terms."[27] In fact, the whole comparison is somewhat ridiculous when one considers it in the light of the probability that racial differences in man do not have any great evolutionary (adaptive) significance!

TABLE 2

	MOST SIMIAN-LIKE	LESS SIMIAN-LIKE	LEAST SIMIAN-LIKE
Cephalic index	Mongoloid	Caucasoid	Negroid
Cranial capacity	Negroid	. . . .	Mongoloid, Caucasoid
Eye color	Negroid, Mongoloid	. . . .	Caucasoid
Nasal index	Negroid	Mongoloid	Caucasoid
Hair form	Mongoloid	Caucasoid	Negroid
Hair length	Caucasoid, Mongoloid	. . . .	Negroid
Body hair	Caucasoid	. . . .	Negroid, Mongoloid
Lip form	Mongoloid	Caucasoid	Negroid
Lip color	Mongoloid	Caucasoid	Negroid
Facial prognathism	Negroid	Caucasoid	Mongoloid
Eye form	Caucasoid, Negroid	. . . .	Mongoloid

SOURCE: E. Adamson Hoebel, *Man in the Primitive World.* Copyright 1958 McGraw-Hill Book Company. Used with permission of McGraw-Hill Book Company.

"Pure" Races

One of the most fantastic racial myths is the idea of "pure" races. It is closely correlated with the doctrines of mongrelization and racial superiority. Belief in the notion of pure races is evidently on the decline, due in part, no doubt, to the general advance in scientific thinking in the modern world. The idea of racial purity seems to be regarded as utterly absurd to anybody of any genetic sophistication.

The term pure race is in itself rather ambiguous. What constitutes a pure strain in biology is a matter of relative definition. It is essentially a question of the intensity and duration of inbreeding. The longer and more intense the inbreeding the purer the strain becomes. In the human species it is rather obvious that there has been incessant crossbreeding throughout the history of mankind. There may have been isolated populations which were characterized by a fairly high rate of inbreeding for a number of generations, but the mobility of man and his sexual appetite have surely operated to prevent this kind of situation from enduring.

The views of anthropologists and geneticists on the question of pure races is epitomized in the following paragraph from the "Statement on the Nature of Race and Race Differences" prepared for UNESCO:

> There is no evidence for the existence of so-called "pure" races. Skeletal remains provide the basis for our limited knowledge about earlier races. In regard to race mixture, the evidence points to the fact that human hybridization has been going on for an indefinite but considerable time. Indeed, one of the processes of race forma-tion and race extinction or absorption is by means of hybridization between races. As there is no reliable evidence that disadvanta-geous effects are produced thereby, no biological justification exists for prohibiting intermarriage between persons of different races.[28]

An even more emphatic rejection of the idea of pure races is ex-pressed by some who imply that the idea of a pure race is not a legitimate abstraction. If man is essentially a polyploid form, one can hardly talk of pure races in the formal sense and probably not even of a pure species. In the final analysis the future of this myth depends upon the weight of scientific evidence and expert opinion versus the romantic appeal of "purity."

The foregoing racial myths do not exhaust the folklore of racism by any means. There are various other unscientific notions alleging con-nections between race and culture, race and temperament, race and morality, race and sexuality, and race and politics. They are corollaries of the general concept of race and the dogma of racism. These myths would be a source of amusement if they were not so tragically dangerous.

THE FUTURE OF RACE

What is the social future of the concept of race? What are the evolu-tionary prospects for variation within our species?

As a social concept and as a political rallying device, race seems to be on the demise. The Nazi era in Germany may have represented the apex of a historical trend with respect to the social and political significance of race. As a reference group it is being replaced by such identifications as ideology, political and economic alliances, and nationalism. The decline of colonialism and the rise of new national states in Africa should contribute to this trend. To be sure, one hears reference to "Negritude"[29] which is supposed to represent some kind of "Black nationalism" in Africa, and there is the reactionary racial situation in the Union of South Africa and the U.S.A., but it seems likely that racial identification as such will be supplanted by other allegiances.

Racist doctrines seem to be losing their appeal, and this is supported by public opinion polls in the U.S. which show decreasing opposition to racial interaction. This is doubtless due to the decline in emphasis upon Social Darwinism. Many of the fallacies and myths of racial superiority have been effectively dispelled, and there are fewer and fewer adherents to theories of racial determinism. Race prejudice, at least in the abstract, is going out of vogue. People seem to be viewing race in a less absolute fashion and from a more relativistic perspective. This appears to be the trend, but the social concept of race is not likely to become extinct in the immediate future.

The future course of human evolution, as it pertains to patterned variation within the species, depends upon the kind of variables we have previously analyzed in connection with race formation. In the modern world, however, we seldom find a replication of the conditions which presumably gave rise to the present differentiation of the species. Selection today is not "natural" in the sense that it was for primitive man with very little culture to assist him in adjusting to his natural environment. There is still selection, to be sure, but it is more on the basis of social and economic factors. Infant mortality is closely related to the income of the parents. Reproduction rates are correlated with occupation, education, religion, social attitudes, income, and many other variables. Mating is still largely a matter of geographic proximity but the mobility of man today has resulted in many persons from different continents mating. In any metropolitan community in the world one can expect to find all of the major racial stocks to be represented to some extent. Admixture of genes is commonplace. Genetic isolation is also much rarer, so that there is less chance for genetic drift to have a decisive effect on gene frequencies.

It can be convincingly argued that cultural evolution has come to replace biological evolution in importance in man. Man adapts himself to his natural environment today by means of his cultural devices to a considerable extent. Furthermore his scientific knowledge, which is a part of his culture, now enables him to influence his own genetic future. As his familiarity with genetic processes increases, he will be able to determine his biological destiny to an even greater extent, perhaps to the point that he can choose rather exactly the genetic traits he wishes in his offspring and how many "copies" of each genetic edition. The problem is not so much a matter of the technical knowledge required, because this almost surely will be acquired, but rather a question of the values and social ethics involved in such an enterprise. The same basic issue is present today in the issue of population control, which incidentally seems likely to be a more important "biological" development than species variation.

There probably will be a higher degree of biological uniformity in the species in the future, at least as far as race differences are concerned. The amount of *individual* variation could even increase, partly due to the new combinations of genes resulting from outbreeding. The amount of inbreeding should decline and the amount of hybridization should increase, especially as the process of urbanization continues throughout the world. Any social development which extends the area of mate selection will reduce the amount of inbreeding.

Boyd, after surveying the evidence from mixtures of different racial groups and after projecting other current genetic trends in man, concludes that:

> . . . the man of the future will be brachycephalic, perhaps about as tall as present-day inhabitants of Southern Europe, with dark brown eyes, a brown skin, and straight (or perhaps slightly wavy) hair. The population of the world, after the miscegenation which is here predicted, will be fairly uniform in appearance. We thus have reason to suppose that, whether or not we began with a heterogeneous species of *Homo sapiens*, we shall probably finish with a fairly homogeneous species at the end.[30]

Notes

1. William C. Boyd, *Genetics and the Races of Man* (Boston: Little, Brown, 1956), p. 184.
2. Ibid.
3. Michael Banton, *Race Relations* (New York: Basic Books, 1967), p. 12. Banton does state, however, that racial differences appear to have been discerned from the earliest periods of human history. For further discussion of this point and the general idea of race see: Earl W. Count, ed., *This Is Race* (New York: Henry Schuman, 1950); Edgar T. Thompson and Everett C. Hughes,

eds., *Race: Individual and Collective Behavior* (Glencoe, Ill.: The Free Press, 1958); and Philip Mason, *Race Relations* (London: Oxford University Press, 1970).

4. See C. Eric Lincoln, "Color and Group Identity in the United States," in *Color and Race*, ed. John Hope Franklin (Boston: Houghton Mifflin, 1968), pp. 249-63.
5. Mason, *Race Relations*, refers to this conception of race as "notational race" which is to be distinguished from biological race, p. 10. Also see Robert K. Merton, *Social Theory and Social Structure* (Glencoe, Ill.: The Free Press, 1949), chapter VII.
6. Howard W. Odum, *Race and Rumors of Race* (Chapel Hill: University of North Carolina Press, 1943).
7. For other definitions of race see Boyd, *Genetics and Races of Man*; Carleton S. Coon, Stanley M. Garn, and Joseph B. Birdsell, *Races: A Study of the Problems of Race Formation in Man* (Springfield, Ill.: Charles C. Thomas, 1950); William W. Howells, "The Meaning of Race" in Richard H. Osborne, *The Biological and Social Meaning of Race* (San Francisco: W. H. Freeman, 1971); and almost any introductory anthropology textbook.
8. E. A. Hooton, *Up from the Ape* (New York: Macmillan, 1946). Also see James C. King, *The Biology of Race* (New York: Harcourt Brace Jovanovich, 1971), pp. 8-12.
9. For a more detailed treatment of these processes see Leslie C. Dunn, *Heredity and Evolution in Human Populations* (Cambridge: Harvard University Press, 1959); Coon, Garn, and Birdsell, *Races: A Study*; and Cyril D. Darlington, "The Genetic Understanding of Race in Man," *International Social Science Bulletin* II (Winter 1950): 479-88. See also Robert E. Kuttner, ed., *Race and Modern Science* (New York: Social Science Press, 1967).
10. For an excellent discussion of the opposite of isolation, genetic mixture, see Mason, *Race Relations*, pp. 29-34.
11. William W. Howells, "The Distribution of Man," *Scientific American*, September 1960.
12. Dunn, *Heredity and Evolution*, p. 93.
13. Weston La Barre, *The Human Animal* (Chicago: University of Chicago Press, 1955), p. 133.
14. See Franz Boas, *Changes in the Bodily Form of Descendents of Immigrants* (New York: Columbia University Press, 1912), and Harry L. Shapiro, "Migration and Environment," in Count, *This Is Race*, for evidence on this phenomenon.
15. William W. Howells, *Mankind So Far* (New York: Doubleday, Doran, 1944), pp. 296-99.
16. Hooton, *Up from the Ape*, pp. 607-52.
17. Garn, Coon, and Birdsell, *Races: A Study* have postulated the idea of "local races" and "geographical races."
18. Melville J. Herskovits, *Cultural Anthropology* (New York: Alfred A. Knopf, 1955), p. 71.
19. Bentley Glass, *Genes and the Man* (New York: Columbia University Press, 1943).
20. Boyd, *Genetics and Races of Man*, p. 268.
21. For a fuller treatment of this subject see E. Franklin Frazier, *Race and Culture Contacts in the Modern World* (New York: Alfred A. Knopf, 1957), especially chapter XIII, and Edgar T. Thompson, "The Plantation as a Race-Making Situation," in Leonard Broom and Philip Selznick, *Sociology* (Evanston, Ill.: Row, Peterson, 1958), pp. 506-7.
22. Lester F. Ward, *Dynamic Sociology I* (New York: D. Appleton, 1910), p. 72.
23. See Banton, *Race Relations*, pp. 36-54.

24. Arthur De Gobineau, *The Inequality of Human Races* (New York: G. P. Putman's Sons, 1915); Madison Grant, *The Passing of the Great Race* (New York: Scribner's, 1918); Houston S. Chamberlain, *The Foundations of the Nineteenth Century* (New York: John Lane, 1913); Lothrop Stoddard, *The Rising Tide of Color Against White Supremacy* (New York: Charles Scribner's Sons, 1920); (Henry Osborn's views are contained in his Preface to Grant's book); and Josiah Strong, *Our Country* (New York: Baker & Taylor, 1885).
25. This statement is made in spite of Arthur Jensen's findings in "Social Class, Race and Genetics: Implications for Education," *American Education Research Journal* 5 (1968): 1-42. See also Howard F. Taylor, "Quantitative Racism: A Partial Documentation," *The Journal of Afro-American Issues* 1, no. 1 (1972): 1-20.
26. David Rife, however, contends that there is a lack of positive evidence for hybrid vigor in contemporary ethnic groups of mixed origin. Nevertheless, he does state that there is no reason to believe that intermixture results in deterioration in mankind. It does result in greater individual variability and simultaneously reduces group differences. There appears to be no biological advantages or disadvantages from interbreeding. In Kuttner, *Race and Modern Science*, p. 167.
27. La Barre, *Human Animal*, p. 113.
28. For the full statement, see Harry L. Shapiro, "Revised Version of UNESCO Statement on Race," *American Journal of Physical Anthropology* 10 (1952): 363-68.
29. The concept of "Negritude" is discussed in Georges Balandier, "Race Relations in West and Central Africa," in *Race Relations in World Perspective*, ed. Andrew W. Lind (Honolulu: University of Hawaii Press, 1955). A typical reference to the idea is found in George A. Shepperson, "External Factors in the Development of African Nationalism," *Phylon*, Fall 1961, p. 208.
30. Boyd, *Genetics and Races of Man*.

Ethnic Groups

4

THE CONCEPT OF ETHNIC GROUP

Ethnic groups are identified by their cultural distinctiveness. Although the term varies in usage among sociologists, there is general agreement that the principal identifying characteristic of ethnic groups is culture.[1] This means that an ethnic group within a larger society constitutes, in effect, a subcultural unit. We also might refer to this group as a cultural minority, since, ordinarily, such units are minority groups too. In addition to common cultural bonds, ethnic groups are characterized by some sense of mutual allegiance and identification. Ethnic groups tend to be in-groups, and this is reflected in such areas of behavior as dating, socializing, and voting.

The term ethnic group is frequently used synonymously with nationality, referring to national origin. Thus, Americans (meaning citizens of the U.S.A.) who were born in Italy and were formerly Italian citizens are regarded as an ethnic group or a nationality group. (It should be borne in mind, however, that nationality also may be used in the strict sense of current national citizenship. One is often at a loss to know exactly which type of information is sought on questionnaires and forms in the U.S. which inquire about "nationality.") It is legitimate of course to refer to the "French people" (that is, citizens of France) as an ethnic group, but the term is more frequently reserved to designate cultural minorities, such as Canadians of French cultural background, or American citizens of German cultural heritage.

Ethnic group boundaries should not be considered precise, even in the sense of individual classification. A person may be divided in his ethnic loyalties and, as a result, it can be difficult to decide whether one is, for instance, German or English if he lives in Canada and has both kinds of ancestors. Furthermore, cultural boundaries are not likely to be exact as exemplified by the fact that one can find some common elements in German and English cultures.

One may even encounter the term ethnic employed as a substitute for the word race. This practice is apparently the result of ignorance of the technical distinction, especially in popular literature. There are some social scientists, however, who favor this usage. Ashley Montagu, for instance, proposed that we dispense with the term race and employ ethnic group instead. (He argued that aside from the "major groups" of mankind—Negroid, Australoid, Caucasoid, and Mongoloid—it is preferable to designate any further subdivisions as ethnic groups.[2]) In spite of arguments to the contrary, we are inclined to feel that a valid distinction exists between the concepts race and ethnic and as a consequence, this chapter is devoted to ethnic relations.

The cultural bonds which unite members of ethnic groups include language, religion, mores and folkways, style of dress, occupational specialization, esthetic standards, social values, and personality models; in short, the various components of culture. This can be illustrated from any number of ethnic groups within American society (identified here in terms of the "native" culture): Italian, Greek, Hungarian, Swedish, Mexican, Japanese, Polish, Czechoslovakian, the various Amerindian tribes, and many others.[3] These groups share some sense of mutual identity based upon common cultural background. The sentimental attachment to this cultural heritage varies from one individual to another and decreases as the whole group becomes more fully assimilated into a larger culture. The first generation immigrant clings more tenaciously to the culture of the "old country" than does the second generation, and by the third generation, for example, there is virtually no knowledge of the native language of the grandparents.

We have previously suggested that ethnic groups, especially when they are found within the context of a larger society, are usually minority groups. This is not invariably the case, but ethnic groups are frequently subordinated to some extent in the social structure and would hence qualify for the designation of minorities. They are also frequently the targets of prejudice and discrimination, which would also make them eligible for this label. In fact, it is our contention that an ethnic group may be aptly defined as a cultural minority. Consequently, we shall refer on many occasions to ethnic minorities.

Charles Wagley and Marvin Harris, writing from an anthropological viewpoint, have suggested five characteristics which distinguish minority groups: (1) minorities are subordinate segments of complex state societies; (2) minorities have special physical or cultural traits which are held in low esteem by the dominant segments of the society; (3) minorities are self-conscious units bound together by the special traits which their members share and by the special disabilities which these bring; (4) membership in a minority is transmitted by a rule of descent which is capable of affiliating succeeding generations even in the absence of readily apparent cultural or physical traits; (5) minority peoples, by choice or necessity, tend to marry within the group.[4] One must concede that most groups generally regarded as minorities would probably not satisfy all of the conditions stipulated, but as an abstract model these characteristics certainly have theoretical utility in the study of minority groups.

Although our analysis of ethnic minorities will be confined primarily to American society, there are some important distinctions to be made vis-à-vis the European situation. American ethnic minorities generally expect to be "Americanized" (assimilated) eventually. This is regarded as desirable and normal. In fact, often the second generation immigrant is impatient to be considered a full-fledged "American" and may resent the sentimental attachment of his parents to their native culture. In contrast to this we have the European tradition, epitomized in the Balkans, wherein ethnic minorities are more often "national" groups who aspire to be politically independent if not politically dominant and do not aspire to be assimilated into the dominant cultural group. Each group desires to preserve its cultural identity, and there is rather strong political identification in terms of ethnicity. Moreover, in the U.S.A. the ethnic minority, excluding American Indians, is of "foreign" origin, whereas in the Balkans an ethnic group, such as the Magyars or Croatians, would not be immigrants.[5] The concept of assimilation is a very important topic in race relation interaction and is treated at length in chapter 5.

The distinction between race and ethnicity is based on the difference between physical and cultural factors in the classification of people. While it is true that ethnic groups are somewhat endogamous in mate selection which would mean that the gene frequency in one group might differ slightly from another, it seems doubtful today that any ethnic groups in America have sufficient inbreeding to produce a pattern of distinctive physical traits. Suffice it to say that ethnicity is frequently a *barrier* to mating but hardly an insurmountable obstacle. Persons of Italian descent marry persons of German descent, people of Swedish and Mexican backgrounds marry, and in the U.S. this kind of exogamy tends to prevent genetic homogeneity in ethnic groups.

In order to maintain its cultural distinctiveness, an ethnic group must successfully insulate itself from the cultural influences of the larger society. This can be accomplished by some form of physical or sociological isolation. The Amish in the United States attempt to achieve it by maintaining their own community, church, schools, and other institutions and by restricting the interaction of their young people to Amish social circles. There is a ban on attending motion picture theatres, listening to radios, watching television, and reading for pleasure, and this prevents infiltration of the outside culture. "Members of the community are removed from contacts which would serve as stimuli or models for the learning of outside customs and outside cultural drives."[6]

Most ethnic minorities in American society do not strive to preserve their cultural system, at least not as diligently as the Amish. After the first generation, as we have suggested, it is exceedingly difficult to maintain a minority culture unless strong measures, like those the Amish use, are employed. This is especially so in contemporary American society which is replete with various heterogenizing influences. Ethnic minorities found preservation of their cultural system easier during the period in American history when the rate of immigration was much higher than it is presently, thus providing a source of continuing reinforcement of the native culture. There is some attempt, however, to identify ethnic affiliation in the U.S.

America has been referred to as a country of ethnics in view of the fact that its composition consists of people of nearly every different cultural background. Table 3 represents the characteristics of the total population of the U.S. by selected ethnic origins. An important point offered by Andrew Greeley is that not only is America a nation of ethnics but it is also a nation of ethnic groups, which implies cultural pluralism.[7] While some authorities for years have felt that ethnic emphasis would become a thing of the past, the term "ethnic group" has remained, implying the existence of cultural heritages among large numbers of Americans. The reasons for the persistence of ethnicity in this country are varied. However, the chief reasons appear to be *the immigrant group's socialization experiences, group consciousness, and isolation.*

TABLE 3
ETHNIC COMPOSITION OF THE UNITED STATES

	Approximate Number	Percent
English	19,060	9.6
German	19,961	10.1
Irish	13,282	6.7
Italian	7,239	3.7
Polish	4,021	2.0
Russian	2,152	1.1
Spanish	9,236	4.3
Other*	105,633	53.3
Not Reported	17,635	8.9

SOURCE: U.S., Department of Commerce, "Characteristics of the Population by Ethnic Origin," *Current Population Reports*, Series P-20, no. 221, p. 4.
* Blacks and Jews constitute approximately 14 percent of the total population in America numbering approximately twenty-two million and six million respectively.

Greeley uses Germans as an ethnic group that had experienced nationhood to such an extent prior to their entrance into America that it was almost inevitable that they would attempt to form a German nation in this country. On the other hand, Scandinavians did not immigrate from nations and thus did not embrace the nationhood concept. It was only when these people settled in America that they began to think of themselves as culturally different. This is important because it implies the development of group consciousness. Group consciousness refers to a state of group existence characterized by identity awareness with respect to some peculiar life and characteristic spirit. The development of group consciousness can be a function either of internal or external factors or some combination of the two. For instance, Blacks in the United States are in the process of developing group consciousness as a consequence of many years of prejudice and discrimination (external factors), and Jews had a sense of nationhood prior to their arrival in the United States as a consequence of external prejudice and discrimination. While we admit that a group can be in existence without group consciousness if another group perceives it as having group consciousness, group consciousness would facilitate the emergence of group identity when identifying characteristics are less external than others.

Isolation is a major cause of ethnicity persistence. While we could consider the case of Blacks' isolation in America, because of the numerous discriminating variables inextricably interwoven with this position we will look instead at the Scandinavians who migrated to this country. These migrants formed communities in rural America, and as a consequence of their rural living, many did not learn English nor did they become "acculturated." Nationality enclaves were created directly as a function of language and cultural barriers. As a result of isolation, ethnicity persisted for large numbers of this group.[8]

Andrew Greeley has stated that if one wishes to accomplish change in America, he should be cognizant of the ethnic pluralism in the large American centers.[9] Emphasizing ethnic pluralism, however, has become a subject of debate in recent years. For example, one argument is that ethnic identification is unnecessary since in America the primary emphasis is upon unity instead of diversity. Another argument alleges that ethnic emphasis generates racism. While there may be some debates over ethnic emphasis, ethnic identification is still very much a part of the American way of life, as evidenced, for example, in the many ethnic holidays such as St. Patrick's Day and the various Jewish holidays.

It is necessary to consider the voluntary as opposed to the involuntary nature of ethnic group identification. There are numerous Blacks in America who have attempted to disengage themselves from their Black brothers (though this tendency presently is declining in many areas), yet they have been largely unable to do so because of their high visibility (in fact, this may be one reason why growing numbers of upwardly mobile Blacks are finding their way back home). The visibility factor makes some group ethnicity voluntary and other group ethnicity involuntary. Too, while there can be little disagreement with the contention that Irish, Polish, and German ethnic groups may experience some prejudice and discrimination in the United States if they make themselves visible, the question "Why can't they be like us?" is not raised to as great an extent for these groups. Unfortunately, Blacks, Indians, Chicanos, Puerto Ricans, and Orientals do not always have such a choice. As a result, one may want to differentiate between factors contributing to voluntary ethnic group identification and those contributing to involuntary group identification. Perhaps in both cases the ethnic groups' socialization experiences, degree of group consciousness, and extent of isolation will be crucial factors. We submit, too, that certain groups' visibility, i.e. their physical characteristics, may influence all of these factors in such a way as to render the above variables relatively sterile for involuntary ethnic group analysis.

Are Jews an Ethnic Group?

This question poses an intriguing problem of identity for both Jew and Gentile.[10] In a sense Jews may be regarded as a religious group, though religion is not a universal denominator of Jews. However, for many who define themselves as Jews, religion remains an essential common bond. It should be obvious that Jews are racially heterogeneous and that there are many diverse cultural strains represented in the aggregate. This is especially apparent in the state of Israel where Jews of a wide variety of cultural backgrounds have settled. For instance, one can find Jews who have immigrated from Spain, Germany, the U.S.S.R., and the U.S.A., as well as many other cultural parts of the world.[11] Jews obviously have not been fully united by a shared language as evidenced by the fact that many immigrants to Israel have had to learn Hebrew. The only sense in which Jews might be justifiably referred to as an ethnic group, at least in the sense of the term as we have used it, would be one which assumed that Judaism pervaded virtually every aspect of life for its followers. Such an assumption seems difficult to sustain without considerable qualification. It is probably no more or less tenable than an assumption that Christians constitute an ethnic group because their religious beliefs affect every facet of their behavior. To assume otherwise inclines one to pursue some kind of magic ingredient which is supposed to characterize all Jews and to render their behavior distinctive. If there is such a factor it is indeed elusive and has escaped the attention of social scientists. If there are any special Jewish qualities, and scientific caution requires us to suspend any categorical judgment about the question, the most plausible would seem to be the historical minority position of the group, particularly in the social context of a dominant Christianity. In any event, we must remain skeptical of any allegation of universal Jewish traits, especially when one considers the cultural and genetic diversity of this group.

 Although it is difficult to resolve the question of whether or not Jews constitute an ethnic group, there can be little dispute that they are and have been a *minority* group. In fact, Jews might be cited as the classic example. Historically Jews have almost always been in a minority situation, and this seems partly due to the relatively small size of the group. This is also, doubtless, one of the reasons why Jews have been a favorite scapegoat group. Small groups are preferable to large ones for scapegoating purposes, unless they are very powerful and have great prestige. Since the advent of the Christian era Jews have been a religious minority within the framework of Christian-dominated societies, and as such have been subjected to a kind of "stepchild" treatment. On logical grounds one would not suspect this; on the contrary, one would expect that since Christ was a Jew and inasmuch as Christianity is an offshoot of the Hebrew religion, Jews would be the object of a certain amount of respect and esteem on the part of Christians. This has hardly been the case, whatever the complex psychological reasons may be.

What is so remarkable about the Jewish group is its survival despite its minority status and the vicious persecution to which it has been subjected. It is extraordinary indeed when one examines the historical record of harassment, discrimination, exploitation, and attempted extermination. This has led some to conclude that there *is* some special Jewish quality which transcends the religious factor and to argue that this group is more on the order of an ethnic group. Perhaps the answer to this puzzling question lies in the character of Judaism. Perhaps it can be partly answered by posing another question: what are the chances of a religious tradition, such as that embodied in the Old Testament, disappearing because of social persecution? One answer might be that a tradition which can produce a Moses is not likely to be destroyed by a Hitler! It must be acknowledged, however, that the "Jewish religion" may have somewhat broader ramifications for its adherents (including those whose affiliation is only quite nominal) than other religions. This is especially so for those who are scrupulous in obeying the numerous religious rules pertaining to diet, ritual, observance of holidays, belief, and morality. Pertaining to this, the point of view of an American historian, Oscar Handlin, merits our consideration. In discussing the question of the identity of "the American Jew," he writes of the group that:

> Its complexity, diversity, and variety defy a neat categorization in terms of origin, status, or even religious affiliation. The most that can be said is that the Jews of America today constitute a group loosely held together by a consciousness of common elements of tradition, experience, and antecedents. In part, their cohesion springs from the recollection of a long religious tradition that some of them have abandoned but that nevertheless has left its mark upon their ideas and their way of life; in part it springs from the history of their settlement in the United States. In any event, these people significantly act as an ethnic group and may intelligibly be discussed as such.[12]

It is noteworthy that Handlin judges (American) Jews to be an ethnic group. His usage may reflect a more liberal interpretation of the term rather than a strict sociological meaning. In any event, one can easily agree with the proposition that the principal source of social cohesion among Jews is religion. It serves as a unifying force in the absence of any other common allegiance.

Another consideration which relates to the question of Jewish ethnicity is the decline of Zionism and the establishment of Israel as a national state. To be sure, Israel is not a "Jewish state" in any official sense, and religious freedom is constitutionally guaranteed. Nevertheless, the nation was settled primarily by persons who regarded themselves as Jews, and the founding of Israel was promoted as a "Jewish homeland." The ideal of Zionism (a movement devoted to the establishment of a Jewish state, preferably in the Palestine area) was substantially, but not completely, realized when the state of Israel came into existence. Accordingly, the *raison d'être* for Zionism disappeared. This has meant that "Jewish nationalism" has been psychologically transferred to the state of Israel. It also has meant that many Jews have had to decide what their nationality would be, a choice which was merely hypothetical previously. As far as American Jews are concerned, the emergence of Israel apparently has not affected the deep social, psychological, and cultural roots they have in the United States, if we are to judge from the small number who have emigrated. In many respects the question of national allegiance has been simplified by the establishment of this new state. There is no longer the question of dual loyalty which may confront the American immigrant from some European nation.

The net effect of this development is that the psychological aspects of assimilation and enculturation have been facilitated for Jews. That is to say, it is psychologically more feasible to identify with a particular national state, say France or the U.S.A., and its national culture and still maintain one's religious integrity and loyalty, now that the agonizing question posed by Zionism has been settled. This might be inferred from the tone of contemporary anti-Semitic propaganda. One rarely encounters nowadays the theme that Jews are not capable of loyalty to the national state because of a strong secret allegiance for Israel. (This theme is to be found, however, in anti-Jewish propaganda from Egypt.) Hence one could argue that Jews are becoming more of a religious group and less of an ethnic group. This process should be accelerated by a reduction of anti-Semitism, which would remove some of the present barriers to assimilation.

Jews are an ethnically diverse group in a very real sense. This is reflected not only in modern Israel but among American Jewry, though to a lesser extent. Jewish immigrants (employing this identification for the sake of analysis) to the United States came primarily from

Germany, Russia, and Poland, but there were many other ethnic back-grounds represented. The German Jews proved to be the most inclined towards rapid assimilation, especially in conjunction with their support of Reform Judaism. The later influx of Jews from Russia and Poland produced something of a check on this trend. The present situation seems to be one in which a general cultural homogenization is occur-ring, expedited by a diminution of religious differences (beliefs, prac-tices, moral doctrine), a decline in Zionism (as a result of the establishment of the state of Israel), a reduction of the number of Jewish immigrants in recent years, an increasing percentage of Ameri-can Jews who have been born in the U.S.A., a weakening of patterns of involuntary segregation, and a general secularization in American society. (It should be noted in passing that a similar process may very well be underway in the U.S.S.R. as well, but for rather different reasons. It has become increasingly difficult for Jews in the Soviet Union to preserve their religious traditions as a result of the generally unfriendly attitude towards religion on the part of the government and the Communist party. It is not so much that Jews are persecuted as an *ethnic* group, but that it is difficult for them to practice their religious traditions in an atmosphere that is rather hostile toward religion in general.)

In the final analysis, apart from the question of whether or not Jews can be legitimately regarded as an ethnic group, we must resort to the same sociological device employed in defining a racial group. The question of definition of the Jewish group reduces itself to the same subjective proposition; Jews are people who consider themselves to be Jews and who are regarded by others as Jews. In this case, in con-trast to racial classification, the judgment of the people being classified probably looms larger. This is partly due to the fact that it is more feasible to change religious group membership than racial classification. It would be easier for a Jew to define himself "successfully" as a Christian than for a Black to have his claim to being white validated socially.

Ethnic Marginality

Reference has been made previously to the sociological concept of marginality, but it remains for us to apply it to the area of ethnic groups.[13] The marginal man has one foot in one culture and the other in a different one. This is exemplified in the case of the immigrant. It presents a dilemma for the individual who must adjust his old culture to a new one. This adjustment is seldom without pathos, and American literature is replete with examples of the psychological struggles of individuals to reconcile different and often conflicting cultural patterns. Indeed, this has been a favorite theme in American novels, especially during the era when immigration was at its peak—the first two decades of the twentieth century. One of the most eloquent expressions of the theme is found in *My Antonia* by Willa Cather.[14] Oscar Handlin has written a moving chronicle of the trials and tribulations of immigrants in *The Uprooted*.

Ethnic marginality is also portrayed dramatically in a sociological classic, *The Polish Peasant in Europe and America,* as the following excerpt reveals:

> Since the immigrant is no longer a member of the society from which he came, since he lives in the midst of American society, is connected with it by economic bonds and dependent on its institutions, the only line of evolution left to him seems to be the one leading to a gradual substitution in his consciousness of American cultural values for Polish cultural values and of attitudes adapted to his American environment for the attitudes brought over from the old country.[15]

Other examples of ethnic marginality are to be found among American Indian tribes. The individual is caught between the cultural crosscurrents of, for example, the "Apache" way of life and the "American" way of life. It is virtually impossible psychologically to accept one culture completely and exclude the other. Some kind of compromise is inevitable, and the resultant mixture may not be a congruous one for personal adjustment. The Navajo Indians provide a case in point:

> The Navaho are torn between their own standards and those which are urged upon them by teachers, missionaries and other whites. An appreciable number of Navahos are so confused by the conflicting precepts of their elders and their white models that they tend, in effect, to reject the whole program of morality (in the widest sense) as meaningless or insoluble. For longer or shorter periods in their lives their only guide is the expediency of the immediate situation.[16]

For the member of a minority ethnic group marginality is an ever present fact of life. It affects his personality and his social status. The condition need not always be detrimental to the individual however, since it may offer a vantage point for rare insights into human behavior and the social order.

ETHNIC PLURALISM VS. ETHNIC ASSIMILATION

There are two general avenues of social policy open to a society which contains various ethnic minorities. On the one hand it can pursue a course which encourages assimilation and acculturation, or it can place a premium on cultural diversity. In the first case social pressures are exerted to effect cultural conformity throughout the society. In the second instance there can be a permissive attitude toward cultural heterogeneity or even internal and external rewards for preserving ethnic identity.[17] One seldom finds a situation, however, where social policy on the matter is clear cut, except in totalitarian systems. In American society, for example, there has not been any explicit official policy on the question of ethnic assimilation. In the one area where one might expect a formal and consistent policy, American Indians, there has been considerable uncertainty and ambiguity.

The whole question of assimilation is, of course, a controversial one. There are strong convictions and compelling arguments on both sides of the issue. Basically it is a question of what the optimum level of social organization should be: should the national state be a homogeneous cultural unit, or should the ethnic group within the national state be "culturally autonomous"? The avocates of a pluralistic system argue that the whole system is enriched by cultural diversity. Ideally, different ethnic groups maintain their own cultural patterns and tolerate and respect those of other groups. Each group is able to preserve its own traditions and values and harmonious intergroup relations prevail. Any assimilation which occurs is supposed to be on a voluntary basis. There should be no coercive homogenization of culture. The freedom to be culturally different is regarded as a value of cardinal importance. It also is contended that cultural pluralism and political democracy are inextricably connected, as Oscar Janowsky eloquently argues:

> Cultural pluralism affords the means of achieving mutual respect and cooperation. I urge it not only because it provides the only alternative to continued oppression and strife—a necessary evil, as it were. I maintain that it is desirable in its own right, because I regard it as a fulfillment of democracy in regions of mixed national-

ity. Democracy rests on the assumption that human progress depends on variety of cultural patterns, on the impact of clashing ideas; that uniformity, certainly enforced uniformity, stifles thought and experimentation and results in stagnation.[18]

Those who favor an emphasis on assimilation maintain that it is necessary in order to promote cordial intergroup relations and to prevent conflict.[19] Cultural unity contributes to national strength and social cohesion. It operates to eliminate prejudice and discrimination by removing ethnic group distinctions. The proponents of this view also maintain that assimilation tends to result in a general social-cultural consensus that mitigates against the occurrence of social disorganization and social problems. This viewpoint, as one might infer, is often associated with an emphasis upon nationalism. Minority groups are expected to adopt the national culture and exhibit loyalty to the national state and its traditions. Unassimilated minorities are sometimes viewed as "social problems."

The crux of the dispute about pluralism and assimilation is whether or not acculturation is to be voluntary. There are some who would employ intimidation and coercive measures to effect "Americanization" (or some other substantive form of assimilation). An example of this approach in the U.S. would be legislation which required fluency in English for voting eligibility. On the other hand there is a body of opinion which favors a laissez faire policy which would leave the question to the cultural minorities themselves. In effect, this would mean that an ethnic group could decide for itself (collectively or individually) whether to adopt the culture pattern of the larger society, and if so, how rapidly. The "choice," however, is always somewhat illusive, because what it actually amounts to is a determination of the issue by the relative weights of cultural forces (majority and minority) and public opinion. Thus there will be rewards and costs accompanying acculturation, namely social and psychological pains, regardless of what the choice happens to be. In contemporary mass society it is virtually impossible to resist cultural homogenizing influences such as the mass media of communication, and unless an ethnic group is willing to isolate itself by extraordinary means, it can hardly avoid being swept into the cultural mainstream.

As we shall have occasion to point out subsequently, the issue of pluralism vs. assimilation continues to be contested in such societies as Malaya, the U.S.S.R., and Canada. In the U.S. the matter is still essentially unresolved as far as American Indians are concerned and recently the issue has become relevant also for Blacks.

Cosmopolitanism

A social policy permitting cultural diversity but emphasizing cultural sophistication might be called "cosmopolitanism." In its ideal form there would be diverse cultural strains represented in a society, and tolerance of cultural variation. Additionally, members of the society would be conversant with various cultural patterns, and a certain common core of culture would provide some measure of stability and unity for the social order. Essential for the success of this kind of social system is subscription by almost all members to a set of values which would sustain such a policy. It is probably closer to the idea of "pluralism" than that of "assimilationism," but it does not seem to combine elements of both. It certainly smacks of utopianism, but it also has its practical appeals. The closest approximation of it today probably would be Switzerland, although the United States would qualify also in many respects.

In Switzerland one finds a cosmopolitan atmosphere, especially in the cities, although there is less of the "hippie" or "street" culture. The democratic political ethic appears to be deeply imbedded in Swiss culture, and this is undoubtedly a sustaining force in its tolerance. German ethnicity is the most widespread but one notes the lack of any militant ethnocentrism that has characterized Germany at times in its history. The Swiss version of Germanic culture is more akin to the Austrian variety, as though it had been imported from Vienna rather than Prussia. Swiss culture is rather more subdued, and the Italian and French cultural strains in Switzerland also lack any aggressive overtones. Thus the Swiss have achieved a remarkable degree of success in maintaining a national cohesion of diverse ethnic factions without fostering a belligerent nationalism as a corollary.

We have considered previously the polyethnicity of American society, but as an illustration of cosmopolitanism, albiet an imperfect one, the city of New York deserves mention. It is the most heterogeneous large city in the world as far as ethnicity is concerned. Virtually every ethnic group in the world is represented in its population, and if one includes United Nations delegates the representation is even more catholic. The bulk of the population is of European cultural descent, but one also finds immigrants from China, Japan, India, Korea, all parts of Africa, Latin America, and almost every other part of the world. The cultural atmosphere is cosmopolitan; one is likely to hear several different languages spoken in the course of a twenty-minute subway ride. There exists voluntary segregation on the basis of ethnicity and involuntary segregation. Ethnicity is a political factor of some consequence; the notion of a "balanced ticket" (meaning a "proper proportion" of candidates of the various ethnic and religious groups) is considered to be a fundamental political principle in New York City politics. On the whole, however, intergroup relations are relatively harmonious, especially when one takes into account the amount of ethnic variance, though in recent years the people of Harlem have become much more intolerant of their position in the New York City social structure.

A cosmopolitan social system is one which is culturally rich. The "cultural capital" can pay high dividends for its members, however, it requires some unifying factors to insure the necessary cooperation for the social system to function. Tolerant intergroup attitudes are indispensable. It offers a large measure of personal freedom in that there are a number of different cultural patterns from which an individual could conceivably choose. This "freedom of choice" may exact a certain psychological toll however, if the individual is faced with conflicting norms. Instead of becoming culturally sophisticated he may become culturally alienated, and in more extreme cases, culturally disorganized to the point of personal disorganization. In any event, the prospects for the extension of cosmopolitanism seem bright, particularly with a decline in nationalism. It also should be expedited with continued improvements in communication and transportation technology. For example, the advent of international television transmission should have a tremendous impact.

Religion and Ethnicity

Religion is often a core ingredient in a culture. Its influence is likely to be reflected in many facets of the culture. Religion and ethnicity are also frequently associated in a statistical sense. One finds high correlations between ethnic group membership and religious affiliation. Hence an American of Italian extraction is very likely to be Roman Catholic in religion. An immigrant from Sweden will probably be Lutheran. The overwhelming majority of American Blacks belong to Protestant denominations, principally Baptist and Methodist, although some are Catholic and a small percentage are of the Jewish faith.

Most people acquire their religion as they adopt other cultural factors; that is, by social inheritance. The individual who changes his religious group affiliation, excluding denominational changes within Protestant Christianity, is rare indeed. Contemporary religions seem to profess "universality" rather than a "tribalistic" scope and consequently make some efforts to avoid narrow identification with a particular ethnic group. Nevertheless, there remain identifications which are quasi-religious and quasi-ethnic, such as Hindus in India. Buddhist and Muslims are less closely associated with national or ethnic groups. Muslims are to be found in Asia, Africa, the Middle East, India, and a variety exists in the U.S. in the form of the Black Muslims. Buddhists are more populous in Laos, South Vietnam, North Vietnam, and Cambodia. Europe is almost exclusively Christian, and missionary efforts in the Orient and in Africa have enjoyed only modest success (either in spite of or because of colonialism).

In analyzing intergroup prejudice, it is often difficult to determine whether prejudice towards a group is primarily due to ethnicity per se or religion. In order to ascertain the "reason" for the prejudice it is necessary to hold one of the factors constant, as in comparing attitudes towards Catholic and Protestant Italians, or Moslem and Hindu Indians.

There are ethnic group relations within religious groups and religious group relations within ethnic groups. Among Roman Catholics in the United States there have been minor tensions between Poles and Irish and between Germans and Italians. These rivalries have often occurred in the context of political activities. Similarly, Americans of German extraction are sometimes divided along Catholic and Lutheran lines. Religion offers a basis for social unity across ethnic lines, but ethnicity may at times alternate such unity if it is attempted or achieved.

ETHNIC GROUPS IN OTHER SOCIETIES

We can hardly undertake an exhaustive analysis of ethnicity even in a particular society, but at least we can attempt to gain some insights into the nature of ethnic groups by considering a few examples in different societies. We feel that the U.S.S.R., Malaya, and various parts of Africa should provide sufficient and diverse illustrations which will be instructive.

The Soviet Union

The U.S.S.R. is rivaled only by the U.S.A., ironically, in its ethnic diversity. There are so many ethnic groups in the Soviet Union, in fact, that it is rather inaccurate to refer to that nation as "Russia," since the "Russians" are only one ethnic group within a larger society, about *70 million out of 200 million people.*[20] The Soviet government makes much of its "liberal" policies with respect to the freedom and "integrity" of its ethnic groups. The U.S.S.R. has always insisted that it follows a policy of cultural autonomy for its minorities, and it is true that concessions were made in the early days of the regime when J. Stalin was "People's Commissar for Nationalities." The proclamation quoted below suggests why promises of cultural autonomy were made.

> Mohammedans of Russia, Tartars of the Volga and Crimea; Kirghiz and Sartes of Siberia and Turkestan; Turks and Tartars of Transcaucasia, your beliefs and customs, your national institutions and culture, are hereafter free and inviolable. You have the right to them. Know that your rights, as well as those of all the peoples of Russia, are under the powerful protection of the Revolution, and of the organs of your soviets for workers, soldiers, and peasants. Lend your support to this revolution, and to its government.[21]

One surmises that the Soviet government actually brings strong, if subtle, pressures to bear to encourage cultural conformity. This is accomplished by means of the definitions of various ethnic group customs as conflicting with the goals of a (Marxist) socialist society. It is somewhat analogous to the situation in art and literature in the U.S.S.R. in which there is official intolerance of any theme or emphasis which does not coincide with the idea of "socialist realism." Whatever the effects of formal government policy with respect to cultural minorities, ethnic variation in the Soviet Union remains an indisputable sociological fact.

The most populous ethnic group in the U.S.S.R. are the Russians, who comprise about 35 percent of the total population of the country according to the available evidence.[22] The next most numerous group are the Ukranians, who might be regarded as somewhat more "European" in cultural tradition than the Russians.[23] When the Germans invaded the Soviet Union during World War II they were welcomed in some instances as liberators by many Ukranians who were smarting under the authoritarian rule of Stalin. (German atrocities soon reversed the situation, however.) Following in order of size are the Kazaks, "White" Russians, Uzbeks, Tartars, and Georgians (Stalin was a Georgian), to mention only some of the larger ethnic groups. In addition, there are many people in the Soviet Union whose ethnic background is Polish, Lithuanian, Latvian, German, Estonian, Arme-

nian, Turkish, Mordovian, Moldavian, and Azerbaijan. In the eastern
part of the country there are many people who are ethnically and
racially more Mongolian than European.[24] One can only speculate of
course about the number of Hungarians, Czechoslovakians, or Poles
now residing in the U.S.S.R. as a result of the peculiar political relationship between the U.S.S.R. and these and other similarly situated
countries.

Despite vicious persecution condoned and even initiated under
czardom and the shabby treatment (especially under Stalin) accorded
them by the communist regime, the Soviet Union still may have as
many as two and one-half million Jews.[25] The figure is necessarily speculative of course, since the U.S.S.R. has been somewhat coy and eva-
sive in releasing statistical data of this sort. Some Russian Jews have
migrated to Israel, but leaving the Soviet Union has not always been a
simple matter.

The total number of different ethnic groups in the Soviet Union is
reputed to be as high as 200,[26] but most researchers agree that there
are at least 100 distinct groups.[27]

Rather typical of the kind of official pronouncements on the question
of cultural minorities is the following objective formulated by Stalin
for the Sixteenth Conference of the Communist Party of the U.S.S.R.:

> The flourishing of national cultures and languages during the
> period of the dictatorship of the proletariat in a single country but
> with the purpose of preparing conditions for the dying out and
> amalgamation of these cultures and languages into a single social-
> istic culture and common language in the period of victory of
> socialism in the whole world.[28]

This policy statement seems to indicate that although the ultimate
goal is single culture for all citizens of the Soviet Union, there is
recognition that some toleration of ethnic differences is necessary in
the meantime. When cultural unification is ultimately achieved, it
probably will have a strong Russian flavor. Russian literature, history,
and the language appear to have been given a favored status.[29] (This
is ironic in view of the Czarist emphasis upon "Russification" which
was resented among the various minorities and which was one factor
that stimulated the revolution.) At the present time the Soviet Union
must be regarded as a multi-ethnic state. It is presumably becoming
more uniform in culture, but there are still many vestiges in the form
of folk patterns and language. It remains to be seen whether a "Soviet

people" or culture will emerge under the impact of Communist doctrine.[30]

Federation of Malaya

Another interesting society from the standpoint of ethnic composition is the Southeast Asian country of Malaya,[31] as shown in table 4. In addition to the native Malays, who constitute approximately 45 percent of the population of the Federation of Malaya, about 36 percent of the population is of Chinese background, and about 10 percent are from India or Pakistan. The Indian community in Malaya dates from the period of British rule, though the Indian immigration into Malaya took place primarily during the first three decades of this century.[32] There are a few Europeans and persons of partial European ancestry, including a few of Portugese and Dutch descent. The Portugese and Dutch held portions of Malaya prior to British possession. The Japanese occupied Malaya during World War II but there are very few there today. There are some residing in Malaya representing Japanese business firms. There are also some immigrants in Malaya from Thailand and Indonesia.

TABLE 4
ETHNIC COMPOSITION OF MALAYA

	NUMBER	PERCENT
Malays	4,381,000	44.90
Chinese	3,472,000	35.60
Indians & Pakistanis	932,000	9.50
All Others	972,000	10.00

SOURCE: *Europa Year Book 1969* (London: Europa Publication, 1968), p. 895.

Malaya is also quite varied in religion. The Malays are predominately Muslims. (The Malays originally migrated from southern China and came under Islamic influence in the fifteenth century.) The Chinese population in Malaya consists primarily of Confucians and Buddhists, though there are Taoists and Christians. The Indians (including the Pakistani, who are almost entirely Moslem) in Malaya are almost all Hindus, and a few are Muslim, Christians, or Sikhs. An almost minute number are Jews and Parsees.

The Malays are largely engaged in agriculture and fishing and dwell mainly in rural areas. Since 1957, approximately 20 percent of the Malays have lived in cities of more than 1000 population in comparison to 50 percent of the Indians and 75 percent of the Chinese. (The Chinese comprise about 80 percent of the population of Singapore.) The Chinese dominate in business activities in the country, and this has caused some resentment among the Malays. The Indians are mainly laborers on rubber plantations, but some are shopkeepers, bankers, and money lenders.

In spite of the fact that Malaya has been bothered by problems of intergroup tensions, but considering its ethnic and religious diversity and the economic and political problems it has had to face, including communist guerilla activity, there has been some modicum of tolerance and cooperation. The Malays tend to claim certain rights as a result of their indigenous status and to regard the Chinese, and to a lesser extent the Indians, as foreigners. The Chinese, in turn, have contended that they have been discriminated against in civil service employment, land ownership, citizenship, voting, religion (Islam has been given a favored official status in the constitution), language (Malayan was made the official language of the Federation), and in provisions for schools. The Chinese maintained their own educational system largely at their own expense, which emphasized Chinese culture and language rather than Malayan nationalism. The new policy of the Federation has stressed "Malayanization." A major instrument for producing this result is to be the public school, as evidenced in the following excerpt:

> Long range education policy in the Federation looks toward the establishment of free and compulsory national primary schools open to children in the 6-12 age group of all races, with the language of instruction Malay or English, according to the majority decision within the district. In Malay schools pupils will be taught English from the first year; in English schools the study of Malay will begin in the third year. The plan provides for inclusion of courses in Mandarin or Tamil at the request of 15 or more parents within any district.[33]

There has been some Chinese resistance to this plan. They have reservations about foregoing their own cultural heritage, and the Malays view the opposition as a kind of national disloyalty.

Another source of tension has been the suspicion on the part of the Malays that the Chinese schools were instilling communist ideas, especially because some of the teachers were trained in China and some of the textbooks were printed there. The Malays have feared that there is some latent loyalty to China and even sympathy for the communist regime despite the fact that the majority of the Chinese in Malaya were born there. This fear was stimulated by the fact that the communist guerrillas were almost all Chinese. Malayans of Chinese descent have proclaimed their loyalty to the Federation and their opposition to communism. They have argued that, as businessmen, they would have the most to lose if communism should come to power in the Federation.

The friction between the native Malays and the Chinese is also manifested in the opposition of the Malays to the inclusion of Singapore in the Federation. To do so might tip the political scales in favor of the Chinese since they comprise about 80 percent of the population there. Actually, most of the Chinese have been rather apathetic about political affairs, being more interested in commercial activities. It is likely that they will take a more active part in politics in the future in order to gain and protect their civil rights. Under the British the Chinese paid little attention to politics, depending upon the British to insure their rights and freedoms in relation to the Malays. Since the Malays are politically dominant under the Federation, it has become necessary for the Chinese to take a more active role in political affairs. In recent years the naturalization laws have been relaxed to allow a greater number of persons of Chinese descent to become Malayan citizens and this has served to allay some of the apprehensions of the Chinese about their status and to symbolize the "Malayanization" of these residents.

The Indian community in Malaya, with the exception of those with considerable education, has displayed relatively little concern about political matters.[34] This has been partly due to the fact that most of the Tamils have returned to South India after working a few years, mostly on rubber plantations. Their main concern has been wages and working conditions and possible land ownership. More recently the Indians have become permanent residents and citizens. As this trend continues one may expect that the Indian-Malayans will exhibit an increasing interest in political issues, particularly those affecting minority rights and privileges. Malay-Indian intermarriage is not unusual when both parties are Moslem.

The political parties in this young nation mirror the racial and religious differences within it as well as the spirit of tolerance and unity which exists. The major political organization, the United Malays National Organization (UMNO), was originally formed to oppose a union of Malay states (and inclusion of Singapore) proposed by the British because that arrangement would have given equal citizenship rights to non-Malays, principally the Chinese, of course. Subsequently it promoted the cause of independence and after success in that venture gained political control in the Federation which was established. UMNO managed to reserve a number of rights and privileges for the Malays on the grounds that they were the indigenous racial/ethnic group. Its position on such questions of immigration, naturalization, civil service employment of non-Malays, religious freedom, Chinese "squatters" (Chinese who had settled in rural areas to escape the Japanese occupation in Malaya during World War II), land tenure, and so on, has evidently mellowed somewhat in recent years, especially as its fears about the loyalty of the Chinese-Malayans to the new government have subsided. Consequently its social base of appeal has been broadened.

The Malayan Chinese Association (MCA) was organized to protect the interests of the Chinese community and to demonstrate support for the government's efforts to combat (communist) terrorist activity. It has favored inclusion of Singapore in the Federation, citizenship by right of birth in Malaya, and a policy which would condone a certain amount of cultural pluralism. It has modified its opposition to "Malayanization" after its alliance with UMNO and the Malayan Indian Congress (MIC), although not without some loss of some of its Chinese support. The Indian party represents the interests of the Indian community in an enlightened way, but it is not very powerful. In the 1955 general elections these three political parties allied into the Malay-Chinese-Indian Alliance party (MCI) and won fifty-one out of fifty-two legislative seats in a remarkable display of national unity and cooperation. The remaining seat went to the Pan-Malayan Islamic Party. A cabinet was chosen representing the three major political groups. The Communists are not recognized as a legal political party.

The ethnic profile of Malaya presents many familiar intergroup situations. The apprehensions of minority and majority about the distribution of power and rights, with the corresponding political controversy, are not unusual in intergroup relations. All in all, there has been considerable harmony and tolerance in the general intergroup situation in Malaya. There has been hardly any of the bitter, hostile prejudice that gives rise to violent conflict. Nor has there been much of the vicious kind of racism that one can encounter in the West. Presently, however, the nationalistic Malays have begun to question their economic and social position in the social structure vis-à-vis the Chinese and Indians. They contend that not only have these groups entered the country but that the Chinese and Indians have also taken control of the country's wealth. The native Malays have blamed the British for initiating a system which would permit Chinese and Indians to gain economic control of Malaya and have castigated Chinese and Indians and people who do not know how to enjoy life. The Chinese and Indians of Malaya have suggested that native Malays are ignorant, lazy, and infirm.

There appears, then, to be some real problem associated with national integration in Malaya. Due to cultural and social differences, assimilation of Chinese and Indians appears to be out of the question at the present time. Cheng Char Gan has suggested recently that a combined political party consisting of the Democratic Action Party, the PMIP (an extreme Malay ethnic organization), and the Malaysia People's Movement, which in 1969 was able to challenge traditional political parties due to relative ineffectiveness in protecting the rights of the non-Malay communists, may play a major role in achieving national unity in Malaya in the future. Gan makes the following assertion:

> The writer believes, on the basis of its principles of freedom, justice, equality, and solidarity in the multiethnic society of Malaysia, that the DAP-Gerakan-PPP political structure is capable of bridging the communal gulf and promoting the formation of a collective identity by facilitating and intensifying social communication among dissimilar cultural groups. Should it control the federal political machinery, not only the communal division be gradually ended, but also the ultimate goals of national integration be eventually achieved.[35]

The prospects for friendly and cooperative intergroup relations in Malaya are fairly bright. As the Malay group makes concessions in the direction of equal rights for others who consider Malaya their permanent home and as the Chinese and Indians and other minorities demonstrate an intention of making Malaya the focus of their national and political loyalty, conditions should continue to improve. The rate and degree of cultural assimilation will doubtless remain a disputed issue, but as the younger generation of Malayans enters the political scene, from a background of native birth and common education in the public schools, it is probable that ethnic competition and conflict will subside.

Africa

The continent of Africa, where human culture is often said to have originated, contains a large number of ethnic groups.[36] The variation ranges from the Berber tribesmen north of the Sahara, to the Swazi and Bushmen in South Africa, to the Ethiopians and the Nandi in East Africa, to the Ashanti and Yoruba in West Africa. Indeed, one can justifiably regard all of the many tribal units as essentially ethnic groups. To be sure, tribalism is apparently on the decline in contemporary Africa, but one of the major challenges facing the new national states there is to establish sufficient cultural unity beyond the tribal level to permit establishment of a durable national society.

Village and tribe have been the traditional units of social organization in Africa. Ethnicity has developed accordingly from this sociological base. This probably has been due in part to the problems in transportation and communication presented by geographical conditions on the continent, such as the Sahara and the jungle areas. In any event, it has resulted in a multiplicity of tribal-ethnic groups with relatively little cross-cultural contact and exchange, especially south of the Sahara. In the past few decades intercultural contact has increased considerably. Prior to this the principal sources of "outside" cultural change had been traders, missionaries, and colonialists. It is ironic that today many of the new African states find that much of what they have in common culturally speaking is of European origin. A conference of African states might be conducted in French or English, for example, since these would likely be the only languages spoken in common.

African ethnicity is often obscured, in the eyes of those unacquainted with its cultural variation, by a tendency to regard Africa in a racial perspective. This preoccupation with race, which persists in spite of the fact that Africa is a racially heterogeneous continent, serves to becloud our perception of ethnic differences. We have been educated in recent times in this respect by such dramatic political events as the strife in the Congo. Reports in the daily newspaper have made us aware of not so subtle ethnic distinctions even within a particular "nation."

We are gradually becoming aware that Africa is by no means culturally homogeneous, even within the emergent national states. This is one reason, incidentally, why federalism will likely precede nationalism in many of these new states. This is illustrated not only in the Congo, but also in Nigeria which has achieved a remarkable degree of political stability in a short span of time, considering the amount of religious and tribal pluralism. The northern part of the country is predominantly Moslem and rural, and it has tribal groups whose culture contains traits suggestive of Arab influence, while the southern part is more urban and European in cultural tone, with Christians, Animists, and various other religions. One finds different tribal groups represented in a modern city such as Lagos, although tribal identification and culture appear to be on the wane in the urban setting.[37]

The ethnic diversity of Africa is revealingly reflected in the multiplicity of languages and religions found there.[38] The number of different languages and dialects runs in the hundreds, the exact number depending upon the mode of classification (Ottenberg claims that are more than 800),[39] and the number of distinct religions may be almost as high, depending upon how rigorously one defines religion. One finds all of the major religions of the world practiced in Africa and most of the principal languages spoken. The *Regional Economic Atlas* lists seven basic language "stocks," with some thirty-two subgroups, and there are a considerable number of "branches" of these subgroups.[40] (This does not include Indo-European languages.) The Hamito-Semitic stock, for example, includes Berber, Iraqu, Chado, Cushitic (which has four branches based on regions), Arabic, and Semitic.[41] Some of these branches can be subdivided still further.[42]

Africa is populated by hundreds of different tribal-ethnic groups, although in some cases the cultural distinctions are relatively minor ones.[43] An inkling of the magnitude of this variation can be garnered from the following passage from a volume by George P. Murdock on African peoples and cultures. The Voltaic peoples are subsumed under "Sudanic Agricultural Civilization" in the author's classification and they reside in Western Sudan.

> The Voltaic peoples attain today a total population of approximately six million, or appreciably more than the Nucleor Mande. Unlike the latter, however, they do not consist of a few great and relatively homogeneous nations but rather, probably because of their relative isolation, form a large number of culturally distinct tribes. In the classification that follows, even extensive combination has been unable to reduce the number of separate ethnic groups below forty-eight. These are divided into clusters on the basis of linguistic affiliations. Unless otherwise noted, each tribe is to be understood as pagan in religion and as belonging to the appropriate branch of the Voltaic subfamily of the Nigritic stock.[44]

The author proceeds to enumerate the forty-eight ethnic groups which are divided into nine different clusters. The Lobi cluster, for example, contains the Dian, the Dorosie, the Kulango, the Lobi, and the Tusyan.

In addition to native African ethnic groups there also are various European cultures represented in Africa, even in postcolonial situations. There are the Portugese in Angola, the British in Southern Rhodesia, the French in Algeria, the Belgians in the Congo, and the Dutch descendants in South Africa. There are Indians in South Africa; many other European nationalities present in other parts of Africa on a small scale in commercial and technical roles; and there are even Americans present as Peace Corpsmen in many of the new African states such as Nigeria and Ghana.

Ethnic relations in Africa seem to have been relatively peaceful when compared to Europe. Interethnic warfare has existed but usually on an intermittent basis. Until recently it had not involved a high number of casualties and was seldom conducted for gaining territory or political domination. This form of conflict became less frequent after the influx of Europeans and the establishment of African colonies by the European states. The only significant organized warfare in Africa in recent historical times was in World War II in North Africa between the Allies and the Germans and Italians. More recently there have been instances of violent conflict involving Africans and colonialists, and the civil war between Nigeria and Biafra. The most notable instance of warfare between Africans and colonialists was in Algeria, but this was not actually "organized" warfare in the European tradition. The same thing could be said of the Congo, Kenya, and the Union of South Africa. In Algeria the native rebel forces fighting for the independence of the country from the French resorted to guerrilla type military tactics, and they constituted only a small fraction of the total native population. In Kenya the Mau Mau terrorists conducted periodic raids and attacks rather than waging open and full revolution, and most of the native population treated the Europeans with considerable respect and tolerance.[45] There was some violence in the Congo against Europeans and some sporadic conflict among various political and tribal groups during the period immediately after independence. There has been amazingly little resistance to the oppression of the Bantu by the Afrikaners (the Dutch descendants who settled in South Africa in the seventeenth century), and the only major violence has been the shooting of natives by government troops and police.

As the new national states emerge in Africa it will be interesting to observe whether chauvinistic nationalism, of the type that has characterized Europe in recent decades, will develop and produce international conflict. There is some evidence that such a trend may develop. For instance, one of the longest and most devastating civil wars in modern history came to an abrupt end January 12, 1970. The conflict involved the Nigerian Federal army and the Biafran army. Biafra, with a population of a little over three million, engaged the Nigerian Federal Government (population of over 36,000,000) in a civil war in the hope of becoming an independent and new nation in 1967. On January 1, 1969, the general philosophy of Biafra was revealed in what has become known as the Ahiara Declaration.[46] Essentially the philosophy revolved around the principle of egalitarianism and communalism, self-criticism, examination of new and traditional leadership, society's vices, and so forth. The declaration further asserted that the Biafran revolution would stamp out all traces of "Nigerianism." It is somewhat unlikely that this conflict was extraordinary in terms of occurrence and may well be an indication of what can be expected as new national states emerge in Africa.

Another sore spot on the continent which seems most likely to erupt into hostilities is in the Union of South Africa. The policy of suppression and discrimination against the Africans can hardly lead to any other result in the long run, despite the perseverance and patience of the Bantu. If the African population does not spontaneously revolt there is the possibility of some kind of intervention on the part of other African states. It is difficult to conceive of a continuation of the present state of affairs for any considerable period of time. The Afrikaners' rigid policies of apartheid are out of tune with the values of the contemporary world and the doctrine of Pan-Africanism which is being prepared by many Blacks throughout the world. Thus, although it may be possible to maintain the privileges of the European descendants for the short run, disaster seems inevitable unless there is some movement toward equality. The specter of racial violence must surely haunt the dreams of many South Africans.

Unlike the French in Algeria or the Belgians in the Congo, the Afrikaners have no real European "home" to return to in case of an end to their hegemony. In the Congo, for example, many Belgians have returned to assume positions of responsibility in professional and technical capacities under conditions of social equality. The principal difference between the Congo and South Africa is that the final political authority is vested in the hands of Africans. The European may still occupy an administrative position and have supervisory authority over African workers, but there is veto power which rests with an African government. The attitude of the South African government seems to reflect the fact that there is nowhere for the Europeans to go. They cannot imagine themselves working for the Bantu. Hence their "escape" is a rigid system of subordination and segregation of the Africans. It is a rather academic question whether the subjugation of the Africans is motivated by "racial" or "ethnic" prejudice. That the "whites" are in dominant social and political position in the Union is incontestable at the present time; the vital question is how long they will be able to maintain their "supremacy."

Cultural Homogeneity and Heterogeneity

There seem to be two general trends operating today which affect the composition of culture—the movement towards the standardization of culture around the world, and the increasing diversity within cultures. The standardization trend has been given impetus by such factors as increased cultural contact, which has been stimulated in turn by more rapid and less expensive means of transportation and communication. The process also has been greatly encouraged by the expansion of science, which aspires to transcend cultural biases in its search for reliable knowledge. Science has established, as a matter of fact, something of a universal culture pattern which is shared by scientists in many different cultures. Modern war also has probably made a perverse kind of contribution to the same process. It has probably accelerated the rate of cultural diffusion, as in the case of the exposure of the inhabitants of South Vietnam to many aspects of American culture since the Vietnam War. All in all, we observe an increased rate of cultural contact and cultural diffusion. This means that people around the world are increasingly familiar with cultural practices of other societies. Cultural isolation is becoming increasingly rare. Abetting this trend has been the "technical assistance" programs undertaken by various nations (principally the U.S.A. and the U.S.S.R., although the U.N. also has sponsored projects) to aid "underdeveloped nations." Inevitably, there is some diffusion of nontechnological culture, some of it not altogether unintentional in the context of the ideological cold war. Whatever the motives, the net result has been to reduce cultural differences, and not merely on a unilateral basis.

This reduction of cultural differences also has served to diversify particular cultures in the sense that new elements from other cultures are to be found together with existing traits. Hence, there is an interaction of the two trends, one making for diversity within particular cultures and the other representing a movement towards more similarity among the various cultures of the world. To the extent that these are powerful forces and ones which will continue to operate in the future, they should result in a diminution of ethnic group differences. One would expect that ethnic distinctions will tend to fade as the cultural basis for these distinctions disappear. To be sure, this is not likely to occur in the immediate future—one can hardly imagine the adoption of an international language during the next generation, for example—but it will almost certainly modify the course of ethnic group relations in the future. As we have mentioned previously, the nature of group distinctions is subject to change, and ethnic group classification may well give way to some other mode of social organization, for example political or ideological.

Notes

1. Cf. E. K. Francis, "The Nature of the Ethnic Group," *American Journal of Sociology*, March 1947, p. 395. See also Brewton Berry, *Race and Ethnic Relations*, 3d ed. (Boston: Houghton Mifflin, 1965), and Pierre L. Van Den Berghe, *Race and Ethnicity: Essays in Comparative Sociology* (New York: Basic Books, 1970).
2. M. F. Ashley Montagu, *Man's Most Dangerous Myth* (New York: Harper & Bros., 1953), p. 5.
3. For a sociological analysis and description of various ethnic groups within American society see Francis J. Brown and Joseph S. Roucek, *One America* (New York: Prentice-Hall, 1945); Everett C. Hughes and Helen Hughes, *Where People Meet* (Glencoe, Ill.: The Free Press, 1952); Charles F. Marden, *Minorities in American Society* (New York: American Book Co., 1952); Richard A. Schermerhorn, *These Our People* (Boston: D. C. Heath, 1949); Arnold Rose and Caroline Rose, *America Divided* (New York: Alfred A. Knopf, 1948); George E. Simpson and J. Milton Yinger, *Racial and Cultural Minorities* (New York: Harper & Bros., 1958); Stuart Hills, "Negroes and Immigrants in America," *Sociological Focus* 3, no. 4 (1970): 85-96; and Melvin Steinfield, *Cracks in the Melting Pot: Racism and Discrimination in America History* (Beverly Hills: Glencoe Press, 1970).
4. Charles Wagley and Marvin Harris, *Minorities in the New World* (New York: Columbia University Press, 1958), p. 10.
5. Cf. Francis Deak, "Eastern European Nationality and Ethnic Groups," in *Group Relations and Group Antagonisms*, ed. R. M. MacIver (New York: Harper & Bros., 1944), pp. 11-30.
6. Joe Wittmer, "Homogeneity of Personality Characteristics: A Comparison between Old Order Amish and Non-Amish," *American Anthropology* 72, no. 5 (October 1970): 1063-67.
7. Andrew Greeley, *Why Can't They Be Like Us?* (New York: Dutton, 1946), pp. 20-35.
8. Ibid.
9. Ibid.
10. For literature on this question see Louis Finkelstein, ed., *The Jews, Their History, Culture, and Religion* (New York: Harper & Bros., 1949); Karl

Kautsky, *Are the Jews a Race?* (New York: International Publishers, 1926); Isacque Graeber and S. H. Britt, eds., *Jews in a Gentile World* (New York: Macmillan, 1942); and Henrik F. Infield, "The Concept of Jewish Culture and the State of Israel," *American Sociological Review*, August 1951, pp. 506-13.

11. W. D. Borrie, *The Cultural Integration of Immigrants* (Paris: UNESCO, 1959), p. 243. The problem could become acute for a small country such as Israel unless other countries are willing to aid her. There are already appeals being made for such aid (*The Columbus* (Ohio) *Dispatch*, 26 March 1972).

12. Oscar Handlin, "The American Jew," in *Understanding Minority Groups*, ed. Joseph B. Gittler (New York: John Wiley, 1956), p. 58.

13. For an excellent example of ethnic marginality see Irvin L. Child, *Italian or American?* (New Haven, Conn.: Yale University Press, 1943).

14. Also, Edna Ferber, *A Peculiar Treasure* (New York: Doubleday, Doran & Co., 1939).

15. W. I. Thomas and Florian Znaniecki, *The Polish Peasant in Europe and America* (New York: Alfred A. Knopf, 1927), p. 1468.

16. Evon Z. Vogt and Clyde Kluckhohn, *Navaho means People* (Cambridge, Mass.: Harvard University Press, 1951), p. 157.

17. On the issue of pluralism and assimilationism see Brewton Berry, *Race and Ethnic Relations*, 3d ed. (Boston: Houghton Mifflin, 1965), chapters 8 and 12; H. G. Duncan, *Immigration and Assimilation* (Boston: D. C. Heath, 1933); and Clyde V. Kiser, "Cultural Pluralism," *Annals of the American Academy of Political and Social Science*, March 1949, pp. 117-30. Also see J. I. Berhek, "Ethnic Group Cohesion," *American Journal of Sociology* 76, 1 (July 1970): 33-46.

18. Oscar I. Janowsky, "Ethnic and Cultural Minorities," in MacIver, *Group Relations and Group Antagonisms*, p. 169.

19. This argument is presented in H. P. Fairchild, *Race and Nationality in American Life* (New York: Ronald Press, 1947); however, such assimilation has often taken on a type of pseudo-tolerance for the minority group with expressions of love as long as the relationship was essentially paternalistic. Cf. Pierre Van Den Berghe, *Race and Racism: A Comparative Perspective* (New York: Wiley, 1967).

20. Joseph S. Roucek, "The Soviet Treatment of Minorities," *Phylon*, Spring 1961, p. 15.

21. Sidney Webb and Beatrice Webb, "National Minorities in the Soviet Union," in Alain Locke and Bernard J. Stern, *When Peoples Meet* (New York: Hinds, Hayden & Eldredge, 1946), p. 673.

22. See Erich Goldhagen, *Ethnic Minorities in the Soviet Union* (New York: Praeger, 1968).

23. For a discussion of various Soviet ethnic minorities see William H. Chamberlain, *Soviet Russia* (Boston: Little, Brown, 1930).

24. See Walter Kolarz, *Russia and Her Colonies* (London: G. Phillip, 1952).

25. For an account of the situation of Jews in the U.S.S.R. see Solomon M. Schwarz, *The Jews in the Soviet Union* (Syracuse, N.Y.: Syracuse University Press, 1951).

26. Jacob Robinson, "The Soviet Solution of the Minorities Problem," in MacIver, *Group Relations and Group Antagonisms*, p. 185.

27. Roucek, "Soviet Treatment of Minorities," p. 15.

28. Robinson, "Soviet Solution of Minorities Problem," p. 187.

29. Roucek, "Soviet Treatment of Minorities," pp. 20-23. Also, see Bernard J. Stern, "Soviet Policy on National Minorities," *American Sociological Review*, June 1944, pp. 229-35; Erich Hula, "The Nationalities Policy of the Soviet Union," *Social Research*, May 1944, pp. 168-201; and Walter Kolarz, "Race Relations

in the Soviet Union," in Andrew W. Lind, *Race Relations in World Perspective* (Honolulu: University of Hawaii Press, 1955), pp. 187-216.

30. Dinko Tomasic, *The Impact of Russian Culture on Soviet Communism* (Glencoe, Ill.: The Free Press, 1953).

31. The following sources seem to be the most comprehensive and authoritative on Malaysia: Richard H. Allen, *Malaysia—Prospect and Retrospect: The Impact and Aftermath of Colonial Rule* (London: Oxford University Press, 1968); Rupert Emerson, *Malaysia: A Study in Direct and Indirect Rule* (New York: Macmillan, 1967); Victor Purcell, *Modern Malaya* (Singapore: Eastern University Press, 1960); Lucian W. Pye, *Southeast Asia's Political System* (Englewood Cliffs, N.J.: Prentice-Hall, 1967); and Richard Winstedt, *Malaya and Its History* (New York: Holt, Rinehart, 1956).

32. See Usha Mahajani, *The Role of Indian Minorities in Burma and Malaya* (Bombay, India: Vora & Co., 1960), p. 108.

33. U.S., Department of State, Malaya Publication 6714, p. 6.

34. See Mahajani, *The Role of Indian Minorities,* for elaboration of the point.

35. See Cheng Char Gan, "Ethnic Differences and National Integration in Malaysia" (M.A. thesis, The Ohio State University, 1970).

36. For general works on Africa see Walter T. Wallbank, *Contemporary Africa* (Princeton, N.J.: D. Van Nostrand, 1956); Charles G. Haines, ed., *Africa Today* (Baltimore, Md.: Johns Hopkins University Press, 1955); and William R. Bascom and Melville J. Herskovits, eds., *Continuity and Change in African Cultures* (Chicago: University of Chicago Press, 1962).

37. Simon Ottenberg and Phoebe Ottenberg, eds., *Cultures and Societies of Africa* (New York: Random House, 1960), p. 77.

38. For example, see the *Regional Economic Atlas* (London: Oxford University Press, E. C. 4, 1965), p. 11.

39. Ottenberg and Ottenberg, *Cultures and Societies of Africa,* p. 66.

40. *Regional Economic Atlas.*

41. See Joseph H. Greenberg, *The Languages of Africa* (Bloomington: Indiana University Press, 1970).

42. *Regional Economic Atlas.*

43. This point was alluded to in an early work by Bruce Hunter, *The Tribal Map of Negro Africa* (New York: American Museum of Natural History, 1956).

44. George P. Murdock, *Africa* (New York: McGraw-Hill, 1959), p. 78.

45. Ottenberg and Ottenberg, *Cultures and Societies of Africa,* p. 75.

46. Colin Legum and John Drysdale, *Africa Contemporary Record Annual Survey and Documents. 1969-70* (Exeter, England: William Chudley and Son Ltd., 1970).

Intergroup Interaction 5

A cardinal assumption underlying the study of social behavior is that persons engage in social interaction, and, indeed, interaction may be seen as the crucial factor in all social life.[1] Without social interaction, it would be impossible to speak of instances of social or group activities. Herbert Blumer refers to two forms of social interaction originally identified by George H. Mead: "the conversation of gestures" and "the use of significant symbols."[2] Blumer identifies them respectively as "non-symbolic interaction" and "symbolic interaction." Non-symbolic interaction occurs when a person responds directly to another's action without attempting to impute meaning to that action. Symbolic interaction, on the other hand, indicates a presentation of gestures by a person and a response to the meaning of those gestures by another.[3] (A gesture is defined as any part or aspect of an ongoing action that signifies the larger act of which it is a part.[4]) Thus, when a person passes another on a busy street and unwittingly emits the familiar greeting "how are you" and the other responds "hi," it is most likely that a conversation of gestures has taken place. Indeed, the act may be so much a part of the two persons' habit orientation that if one were to call attention to the fact that they had engaged in the behavior they would not immediately remember it.[5] On the other hand, if a Black athlete, participating in the Olympic games, raises a clenched black-gloved fist while accepting a gold medal, and his act brings forth responses of applause and outrage from spectators, then symbolic interaction has occurred. Symbolic interaction places a greater emphasis on the process of gesturing than non-symbolic interaction. In line with the emphasis on gestures, then, raising a clenched black-gloved fist indicates to some spectators loyalty to a Black movement, freedom, struggle, joy; and to others, rebellion, revolution, and subjugation. Responses to the gesture will depend upon the predilections of the responders (spectators), that is, the meanings that the act has for them. Thus, in the aforementioned example of symbolic interaction, some members of the audience and the athlete will "understand" each other while for other members of the audience, this understanding will not take place. It is important to realize that understanding another does not mean agreement with another. If there is a segment of the athlete's audience that becomes outraged over his actions, understanding probably has occurred to the same extent that it has among persons reacting favorably to his gesture. Succinctly, symbolic interaction involves the forging together of joint lines of action. Blumer has delineated three features of social interaction, as follows:

> The first premise is that human beings act toward things on the basis of the meanings that the things have for them. . . . The second premise is that the meaning of such things is derived from, or arises out of, the social interaction that one has with one's fellows. The third premise is that these meanings are handled in, and modified through, an interpretative process used by the person in dealing with the things he encounters.[6]

Explanations of intergroup behavior must take into account the unique properties of the intergroup interaction in question.[7] Social interaction, as previously stated, is symbolic in character. It entails persons interpreting and defining each other's actions instead of merely reacting to each other's actions.[8] In other words, a person does not react directly to another's actions, but rather, he reacts to the *meaning* which the action has for him. Social interaction, then, is mediated by the use of symbols. This is true not only for interindividual interaction but also individual-group interaction and intergroup interaction. Regarding individual-group interaction, persons act in and toward social situations rather than toward social groups. The group enters into action only to the extent that it shapes situations in which people act, and to the extent that it supplies fixed sets of symbols which people use in interpreting their situations.[9]

Social groups may be conceived as acting social units and intergroup relations involve social groups responding to the actions of other groups in social situations. A study of relations between social groups requires at least a three-dimensional analysis. These dimensions relate to the individual as he interacts with himself; the individual as he interacts with the group; and, the group as it interacts with other groups.

The first dimension is related to the concept of self. The "self," as William James, G. H. Mead, C. H. Cooley, and others have contended, is a basic unit of analysis in social interaction. In social psychological terms, the self has at least two connotations. One meaning implies that persons have attitudes and feelings about themselves and the other meaning emphasizes the set of psychological processes which influences behavior and adjustment.[10] Paul F. Secord and Carl W. Backman have made the following observations about the self:

> One consequence of being human is that a person becomes an object to himself. Because of his possession of language and a superior intelligence, man has a unique capacity for thinking about his body, his behavior, and his appearance to other persons. Each of us has a *set of cognitions and feelings toward ourselves*. The terms most commonly applied to this set of elements are self-concept.[11]

On the other hand, Blumer illustrates a second view of the self in the following statement:

> I wish to stress that Mead saw the self as a process and not as a structure. In asserting that the human being is an object to himself, the human being may perceive himself, and act toward himself. As these types of behavior imply, the human being may become the object of his own action. This gives him the means of interacting with himself—addressing himself anew.[12]

While the former view of the self involving the notion that persons have conceptions of themselves is a crucial point, the discussion of the self in this chapter is devoted more to the latter position as stated by Blumer. This becomes apparent in the following paragraphs of this section.

The self arises through a slow and tedious process whereby the individual first becomes aware of a distinction between himself and others. As he grows and has experiences outside of himself, the individual makes even greater distinctions between himself and others. An important part of the early learning period of an individual is the identification process. The person begins to identify with his parents, peer groups, race, and nation. He develops loyalties and antagonisms toward various groups. In essence, the individual becomes equipped with the mechanisms for confronting the world.

We now turn to the second dimension, the individual as he interacts with the group. As an acting unit, persons first begin to interact with primary group members. Indeed, these groups are responsible for socialization. Such groups also aid the individual in developing his ability to interpret the actions of others, that is, to point out to him the meanings of others' actions. With the development of interpretation skills which are infused with group characteristics, the individual is ready to confront persons of similar developments from other groups.

In many instances, actual physical intergroup interaction will involve little more than individual interaction—thus the third dimension, group-group interaction. Such interaction between members of groups will be influenced to some extent by the organization and structure of the groups to which they belong. However, part of the interaction must be attributed to the social situation from the individual's point of view and the interpretative skills of these individuals. Of importance here is the fact that individuals in social situations have made and continue to make decisions which affect the outcome of groups of people. Such decisions are made by persons responding to situations, interpreting and acting. Thus, the specific form of interaction taken between two groups will vary with individual participants and social situations. A longitudinal examination of interaction between two social groups would undoubtedly attest to the dynamic nature of intergroup interaction. Yet, as has been stated, interaction between groups will be affected by the organization and structure of the groups—the values, roles, norms, and the coordination of these elements. The next section is devoted to some of the constraining forces which shape situations and contribute to the rise of certain interaction forms.

SOCIAL NORMS AND VALUES IN INTERGROUP INTERACTION

It is impossible to discuss social interaction between groups without recognizing the importance of societal norms. The nature and form of social norms are crucial influences in the structuring of interaction patterns within social groups, and therefore may have ramifications for intergroup social interaction.

Social norms are learned expectations regarding behavior *shared by group members.*[13] In other words, social norms specify appropriate and inappropriate ways of behaving for group members. They are relative in the sense that what one group defines as appropriate behavior for group members may be defined as inappropriate behavior for members of another group by their group norms. For instance, if one visited a Black Baptist church on a given Sunday morning and was asked and agreed to give an extemporaneous speech, and then stood behind the pulpit and delivered the speech, he would be in violation of a social norm. The social norm violated would be related to standing behind the pulpit. In the Black Baptist church, this is a most sacred position which is reserved for ordained ministers. On the other hand, if one delivered an extemporaneous speech in a white Presbyterian church and stood behind the pulpit, it is entirely possible that no one in the audience would experience uncomfortable feelings since the act would not be defined by church members as inappropriate behavior.

Social norms can be classified into two categories: folkways and mores.[14] Folkways are relatively unimportant social norms. These norms may be violated without the violator receiving *severe* negative sanctions. On the other hand, mores are norms which are not open to question. A failure to abide by these norms will usually result in severe sanctions in the form of ridicule, confinement, physical punishment, or some other rather severe negative sanction.

The influence of social norms (both folkways and mores) on intergroup interaction can be seen in the following manner. Some of the more influential group memberships held by persons are those that individuals have been socialized to value. As a result, racial, ethnic, religious, and sex groups, to mention a few, are felt to be important by most individuals; they represent an anchor, a referent, a point of identification. Implicit here is the idea that such groups are norm-setters; that is, they hold expectations about member behavior, and if members value their affiliation, wanton violation of important group expectations are rare. For example, if an American-Indian congressman publicly expresses his feeling that an Indian occupation of Alcatraz is unwarranted and should be ended by any means, he should be prepared for ostracism, castigation, and the label "Uncle Tomahawk." The congressman in question would have committed an "unpardonable sin," which can be summarized as a violation of group norms regarding "airing one's dirty linens before members of the 'out-group'." Groups may have unique means of punishing norm violators and only a few persons are able to assume the deviant role and remain psychologically consonant; others usually succumb to group pressures.[15] Thus, if a group decides on a given course of action, the pressure of group opinions, along with latent negative sanctions which can be made manifest, will usually bring all but the most courageous (or "irresponsible" depending upon the perspective) in line with group thinking.

In line with this contention, if a pattern of group superordination has been established vis-à-vis another group, emergent social norms will function to maintain the relationship until other variables enter in and alter the relationship. There is, of course, a good deal of speculation about what these variables can and should be. Some suggest that revolution is the only variable which can change the interaction pattern; others feel that voluntary integration is the answer; and still others have postulated enforced legislation as a solution variable to inequality between groups. Another alternative suggested and often practiced by disenchanted subordinate group members has been a rejection of the social system accompanied by social withdrawal. To be sure, these are but a few of the change variables advanced to effect social equality. In a given situation, all of these variables and more may be present; however, the effectiveness of any one or some combination has not been conclusively determined and awaits further data and scientific investigation.

VALUE ORIENTATIONS

Value orientations are sets of assumptions, partly unconscious, concerning correct and incorrect lines of action, thought, and affectivity. While every society will be characterized by a core value system, it is important to realize that subgroups also have sets of values commensurate with or different from the society's value system. In fact, when one group is socially superordinate over another group in a social system, it is not unusual for the system value orientation to reflect only the interests of the superordinate group.[16] Based on this line of thought, Blacks in the United States may find that few, if any, of the values they were able to maintain through slavery are represented in that society's core value system. Women as a group may find that system specification of correct and incorrect lines of action for them are inimical to their self-enhancement. A communist visiting a western culture of significantly different ideological perspectives can consider himself fortunate if he does not encounter many persons who categorically believe that the communist line of thought, affectivity, and actions are wrong. Whether such value sets *are* wrong is, of course, a relative question. As we have implied, what is wrong in one culture may be right in another culture, and this may be extended to include subgroups. That is, if such a subgroup leads a socially isolated existence in a social system and develops its own sets of values, norms, and ideals, it is largely a matter of conjecture whether deviant behavior attributed to members of this group by the society is, in actuality, a violation of social norms to which they subscribe.[17]

Another unique feature of value orientation is that changes in them may render social norms ineffective as constraining mechanisms for members of a group regardless of the social status of the group. As previously implied, social system values reflect the norms of the social system. Individuals within the social system, especially those who are members of the dominant group, will ordinarily internalize and perpetuate these values as a result of socialization. However, changes in value orientation may attenuate any relationship between social norms and social values. Change can come from a variety of formal and informal socialization sources—peer groups, schools, religious institutions, chance interactions.

In the United States, changes in values, reflected in young adults, have been swift and have come from all of the sources mentioned. The result has been to effect some change in normative standards. For instance, prior to the 1960s, reproduction was normatively a family function for the dominant group as well as the sexual activities which lead to reproduction. If sexual activity or reproduction were discovered outside of the family, the persons involved (more generally the female) were subjected to ridicule and scorn, especially by members of the larger social order. Interestingly, though there were members of the Black middle class who vehemently opposed extramarital sexual relations and reproduction, a majority of Blacks never reflected the strict and unyielding attitude toward premarital sex, extramarital sex, or illegitimacy as the majority of whites allegedly assumed. Of current interest, however, are the ubiquitous instances of *acknowledged* common-law marriages, abortions, and illegitimacy among prominent and prestigious members of the superordinate group. The instances of such activities are not nearly as salient as the acknowledgements. A common statement among Blacks may be "sure, it's all right *now* to (copulate) before or outside of marriage because their children do it." This is a very astute observation which should not be surprising, since, in any society, the superordinate group plays a major role in shaping the value orientations and norms of the system.[18]

Social norms and social values are best conceived as mediating mechanisms which structure social relations among groups of peoples.

While normative standards restrict the range of permissible conduct for group members, values are media of social transaction that expand the compass of social interaction and the structure of social relations through social space and time.[19] Social groups tend to be affected by the same principles of social exchange as individuals. This becomes obvious if one examines the structure of intergroup relations. Relations between social groups can be defined as balanced, unbalanced, or nonexistent. Balanced relations exist between social groups when the structural position assumed by one group vis-à-vis another is similar, that is, the duties and obligations (roles) and the rights and privileges (statuses) are synonymous for both groups. When one group enjoys a relative advantage in values and statuses over another in social interaction, intergroup relations are unbalanced. If social interaction does not occur between social groups, then nonexistent social relations characterize the intergroup relationship.

If one traces the character of intergroup relations between Blacks and whites in the United States, it is possible to note that the period of slavery was essentially an era where very little social interaction between the two groups occurred. While we recognize the subjugated position of Blacks during this period, relations could not be referred to as unbalanced due to the failure of numerous whites to recognize Blacks as human.[20] One rarely thinks of relations between humans and infrahumans in a *social* sense.

Following the emancipation proclamation, whites began to *think* of Blacks as human but as inferiors. For many, this line of thinking has persisted to the present time. Nevertheless, the period 1860–1960 can be referred to generally as a time of unbalanced, though often lawful, relations. It is important to realize that this period has not ended; however, there is reason to believe that the period is beginning to merge with a period of balanced relations. Admittedly, the dynamics of intergroup relations are such that period specification is nearly impossible. For instance, many persons will undoubtedly quarrel with the notion that substantial progress has been made on the intergroup relations front in the United States. Furthermore, one can agree that the United States may be moving back to a period of nonexistent social relations between Blacks and whites. We will address ourselves to this question in chapter 12; presently, however, an attempt has been made to illustrate some types of relations between groups.

Intergroup roles in a society are governed by the prevailing norms and values of societal members. Thus, if a group has a social advantage over another, the subordinate group may be relegated to inferior roles, i.e., economic, political, and social. Such a phenomenon has a compounding effect. If the unequal interaction process is begun, it tends to be self-perpetuating to the extent that even "serious" onslaughts designed to alter the interaction pattern may be unsuccessful. A case in point is the plight of the American Indian. While only tokenism has been in evidence on numerous occasions, some intense efforts have been made to eradicate the conditions to which American Indians have been subjected. However, the nature of American Indian subordinance, without considering the existing societal attitudes of prejudice and discrimination, was so intrinsic that it pervaded all aspects of their social life. The result was that Indians received a secured stamp of manifest and latent inferiority. This has resulted in inadequate socialization for entrance into a society which places great emphasis on technological skill, formal socialization, and, in general, the capitalistic enterprise system. Latently, feelings of alienation and resignation characterized many American Indians prior to the 1960s resulting in passive acceptance of the status quo. Since the advent of the sixties, however, American Indians have been more vehement in their opposition to inferior treatment by society. In spite of increased Indian awareness *and* external aid extended to alter existing conditions, the American Indian's position vis-à-vis the majority group has remained essentially unchanged.

If societies were homogeneous, void of developed specialities within or between them, there would be little need for a study of intergroup relations. But societies do show variations in roles, statuses, and behavior. These variations are characteristic of societies that differ on race, religion, sex, occupation, and so on. The process by which singular groups vary along these lines is called *differentiation*. Differentiation leads to processes such as competition, cooperation, accommodation, assimilation, stratification, and conflict between the demarcated parts. We will examine each of these processes as they relate to intergroup interaction.

PROCESSES OF INTERACTION

Cooperation

On the simplest level, cooperation as a process of intergroup interaction imposes restrictions on human activities. The process involves groups extending mutual aid in an effort to ascertain some goal. Thus, patterns of social interaction between groups cannot give one group a decided advantage if cooperation is to be maintained. To be sure, in cooperative social interaction, one group *can* enjoy an advantage for a period of time, however, as will be seen later, unbalanced relationships are tenuous and inevitably lead to conflict, opposition, or interrupted interaction. Consequently, cooperation is more effective if both parties are equally powerful and dependent in social interaction. In other words, it is not merely a coincidence that Russia and the United States are suddenly finding that they have more in common than previously realized, nor are the emerging forms of cooperation between the United States and The People's Republic of China pure happenstance. There may be a realization by strategic officials in all countries involved that cooperation with others can be an effective tool in enhancing one's own country—not to mention the possibilities for peaceful coexistence of antagonists.

Ordinarily, groups do not engage in cooperative exchange for long periods of time without some kind of conflict. The rationale for this assertion is obvious when one realizes that groups engage in cooperation for the attainment of specific goals that are only a part of the total goal set for which they are striving. *This means, basically, that groups do not contract to cooperate indefinitely; the process is simply one of the means groups use for a specific time to obtain their own goals.* For instance, the United States and Russia engaged in a cooperative effort during World War II. They gave each other mutual military and psychological support only to become bitter enemies following the commencement of the conflict. In short, when two groups can be distinguished in terms of social values, norms, or ideology, cooperation may characterize some interaction between them; however, the process refers to perhaps one dimension of the groups' activities—thus conflict may still ensue over some other activity or at a later point in time. For example, it may not be farfetched to visualize that at some point in the future, conflict may develop further between Russia and China, England and France, Canada and the United States.

Competition

When groups in close proximity have diverse interests and there are scarce resources available to secure these interests, some form of social conflict is likely to develop. A mild form of conflict which often develops is competition. An important prerequisite for the emergence of competition is equality. In the strict sense of the concept, competition occurs only between groups which are approximately equal in power. As a matter of fact, it is somewhat improbable to speak of Blacks as economic competitors of whites in the United States. In order to compete, Blacks would be obliged to have independent resources from which to draw as they engaged whites in an economic "game."

Perhaps what illustrates the above point more than anything else is the occasional political-economic game often played by whites and Blacks. A commonplace phenomenon presently is for Blacks to be placed in strategic positions of prestige and importance. As long as the positionholder maintains some modicum of decorum with respect to political issues regarding intergroup relations (e.g., police brutality among minority group members, Black power, brown power, riots), he may be extended respect, financial security, and even admiration. On the other hand, should the Black become a spokesman for what is frequently call the "Black revolution," it is not unusual for him to find himself without any of the previously described benefits. Oftentimes this means that visibility *and* effectiveness are greatly attenuated, and these are salient factors in competition.

While Blacks and whites in the United States cannot participate in an "economic game" in any real sense, they have begun recently to participate in "psychological games." Such participation is possible due, in part, to the intangible nature of psychological variables as compared with economic variables, and the tremendous increase in race pride among Blacks accompanied by a growing trend toward rejection of white middle-class life styles. Thus, while self-conceptions among Blacks may be a function of significant other conceptions, within the past few years there has been an alteration in many Blacks' perceptions and identification of significant others. The overall effect of this change has been to create an atmosphere of psychological equality which is necessary for the emergence of psychological "game playing" between groups.

Whenever psychological games are played by two groups, three possible outcomes for each group are possible: win, lose, or draw. If a minority group loses or draws such a game, its status remains unchanged. On the other hand, should the minority group win the psychological game, it is likely that an alteration in its status will occur. This change is due to the fact that psychological gains can be translated into gains in other areas, thus giving rise to competition and some possibility of success in these other areas.

Assimilation

"Assimilation is an elusive concept and is applied to a wide range of ethnic changes and generally with implied direction towards greater homogenity." This view was expressed by Stanley Lieberson in his book *Ethnic Patterns in American Life*. He went on to define operationally an assimilated ethnic population as a group of persons with similar foreign origins, knowledge of which in no way gives a better prediction or estimate of their relevant social characteristic than does knowledge of the total population of the community or nation involved.[21]

Assimilation refers to a blending process whereby two distinct groups form a homogeneous entity. This process implicitly means that distinctions between groups disintegrate and group members become socially and physically similar. The crucial problem here is that previously distinct groups find it difficult to give up their social and physical uniqueness. One difficult barrier which often works against assimilation is fear of amalgamation. Amalgamation occurs when there is biological intermixture or blending of two previously distinct racial or ethnic groups and tends to be viewed in undesirable terms by minority groups as well as majority groups. Because of the possibility of interracial or interethnic reproduction when assimilation occurs, many individuals do not favor assimilation. Obviously, the perceived abhorrence of amalgamation is in itself a product of some form of prejudice. Nevertheless, assimilation in its pure form involves amalgamation as well as normative, valuative, and ideological intermixture.

If a group is dominant, assimilation is normally regarded as an undesirable form of interaction because it entails a loss of power. Resistance to this form of interaction is manifested in terms of prejudice, discrimination, and so forth. From the minority group's point of view, assimilation also may be undesirable in the sense that it may be perceived as further subjugation through absorption rather than blending and as a loss of identity. In theory, some elements of the minority group would be apparent in the truly "assimilated group" and thus there should be little basis for such a fear (this view is expanded further in chapter 11). In practice, however, there may be some reason to believe that assimilation means absorption rather than intermixture.

Milton Gordon, in his *Assimilation in American Life*, has listed seven stages of assimilation.[22] He states that an alteration of minority cultural patterns to conform to those of the dominant society is *cultural or behavioral assimilation. Structural assimilation* refers to minority entrance into majority group cliques, clubs, other organizations, and institutions. *Marital assimilation* involves large-scale intermarriage between members of majority and minority groups. *Identificational assimilation* is the development of a sense of peoplehood based exclusively on the dominant group. According to Gordon, a different type of assimilation has occurred when relationships between majority and minority groups have reached a point whereby prejudice is basically nonexistent. He refers to this type of assimilation as *attitude reception assimilation.* In contrast, *behavioral assimilation* does not necessarily involve cognitive or affective assimilation, but it entails the process whereby discriminating behavior is absent. Lastly, *civic assimilation,* between majority and minority groups, is an absence of values and power conflict. In a real sense, this type of assimilation represents the ultimate form in a society which is dependent to a great extent upon the success of the aforementioned types.

To a very great extent these stages of assimilation are based on what Gordon calls the Anglo-Saxon conformity goal system. However, the melting pot and cultural pluralism goal systems emphasize the necessity for structural assimilation. It may be somewhat unfortunate that a goal system distinction was made since these types of assimilation are relevant only for one of the goal systems. In addition, it is rather difficult to accept conceptions of assimilation which do not connote a blending process between two groups where the final product is cultural fusion or a hybrid type. In other words, when Gordon discusses Anglo-Saxon conformity as a goal system, he may be referring to types of conformity rather than assimilation types, since the essential ingredients of assimilation would include a blending process involving all of the variables mentioned above.

While such a view of assimilation may be perceived by some readers as rather rigid, it takes on added significance when viewed in conjunction with life chance differences which may be noted between groups in America. Several years ago Lieberson found occupational differences between ethnic groups and stated four factors which contributed to these differences: (1) needs of the ethnic group; (2) skills of the ethnic group; (3) differences in arrival of ethnic groups to the country and the state of the economy; and (4) occupation of parents.[23] These differences obviously relate to varying degrees of cultural isolation. In other words, we would expect the least adaptable ethnic group to have pressing economic needs, few skills, and so on. On the other hand, most differences between the ethnic group and the majority group on the above points may mitigate against cultural fusion. If the assimilation process does not include cultural fusion, then, for many ethnic groups, entrance into the cultural mainstream will be impossible. With an absence of cultural fusion it is also likely that the ethnic group will be a highly visible entity, and as stated in chapter 4, visibility is a factor which cuts across numerous types of assimilation. Therefore, unless we are willing to accept a value-free definition of assimilation, we might as well dispense with its use in race relation literature.

Accommodation

When groups have experienced intergroup processes such as cooperation, assimilation, competition, or conflict, it is entirely possible that still another form of interaction will emerge. This form is called accommodation, which means that groups develop working arrangements while maintaining their distinct identities. Accommodation is a very difficult process for social groups, especially if there has been some conflict between them. Conflict between social groups ordinarily entails gains and losses for the groups involved. Accommodation between these groups is difficult since a prerequisite for such accommodation might be a return to some state prior to the conflict *or* maintenance of the present state. Either prerequisite usually will be untenable from one group's point of view. The tenuous cease-fire agreement of 1970 between the Arabs and the Jews illustrates how prerequisites for accommodation cannot please both groups. From the Arabs' vantage point, any cease-fire arrangements should have included some restoration of resources which were gained from the conflict. Jews, on the other hand, countered with a position that the cease-fire agreement, having occurred after the conflict, should impose limitations only on postconflict territorial infringements. It is not difficult to imagine the complexities which are involved in getting two groups of similar experiences, such as those illustrated above, to reach the accommodation form of social interaction. In fact, unless one party is considerably weakened by conflict, accommodation can very seldom occur except through some form of intense mediation.

In order for total accommodation to occur between any minority group and the majority group, it would be necessary for minority groups to be relatively self-sufficient. Blacks, although they do not fall into this self-sufficient category, and whites in America may be on the way toward cultural accommodation to some extent, however unwittingly. In spite of the fact that Blacks basically experienced a loss of culture during slavery, it appears that enough remnants remained which enabled them to build a unique culture. In addition, the long years of involuntary and voluntary servitude have contributed to this cultural base.

Whether Blacks and whites in America can achieve cultural accommodation obviously remains to be seen. However, the dynamic sixties seemingly set the stage for some form of cultural accommodation. Thus, we see that now it is not uncommon for Aretha Franklin, The Jackson Five, Sonny and Cher, The Rolling Stones, and Dionne Warwicke to be enjoyed by both Black and white youngsters alike. Black writers can portray the beauty of Africa and white artists can paint moving scenes of Europe and both will produce adulation from members of both Black and white groups. To be certain, the United States is far from total accommodation. In fact, we submit that until respect and tolerance are developed in areas other than these few cultural ones, accommodation will remain an unrealized facet of the American dream.

Social Stratification

If human beings were classified or distinguished from each other in terms of race, sex, age, and natural ability, and no significance was attached to the resultant categories, mobility in societies would be always horizontal instead of vertical. To the contrary, there are few societies, if any, where categories of humans are not hierarchically arranged with some groups ranked inferior to others. Social stratification is the process whereby *categories* of persons are differentially ranked with respect to some social criteria. The result of this ranking process is variation—Jewish, Mexican, or Oriental ancestry. Individual physical appearance, behavior, and beliefs assume very little importance as such in the ranking process, while social recognition is of major significance. As Malcolm X has stated in *Malcolm X Speaks*:

> What you and I need to do is learn to forget our differences. When we come together, we don't come together as Baptists or Methodists. You don't catch hell because you're a Methodist. You don't catch hell because you're a Democrat or a Republican, you don't catch hell because you're a Mason or an Elk, and you sure don't catch hell because you're an American; because if you were

an American, you wouldn't catch hell. You catch hell because
you're a black man. You catch hell, all of us catch hell for the
same reason. So we're all black people, so-called Negroes, second-
class citizens, ex-slaves. . . .[24]

The astuteness of Malcolm X's observation is substantiated by the
following excerpt from Shibutani and Kwan:

> In any system of social stratification, the people in the highest
> stratum, by interacting primarily among themselves, develop a
> characteristic style of life. They generally inhabit the most desirable
> areas in the community—either by tradition or, if the economy is a
> competitive one, by being the only people who can afford to pay so
> much for land. In these exclusive areas they have intimate and
> exclusive social access to one another. They are often immune
> from prosecution for deeds that might result in others being in-
> carcerated for years; their word of honor is respected in situations
> in which the testimony of others is not; they are exempted from
> many burdensome tasks.[25]

Social stratification appears, then, to be functional for the superior
strata, while it is less functional for the subordinate strata. In fact,
social stratification contributes to unbalanced relationships between
groups in a society which may in turn result in minority groups' usage
of power balancing techniques. Such techniques frequently have a
traumatic effect on intergroup relations and the society itself.

In a classic contribution by Davis and Moore, it was suggested that
stratification was functional for a society since positions necessary for
its maintenance are secured by social stratification. While these authors
concentrated on the functional aspects of stratification, appraisals of
the work emphasized some of the dysfunctional aspects of stratification,
including limitation of opportunities and nondiscovery of talent. Regardless of the efficacy of social stratification, one thing is certain, it
does engender a consciousness which is necessary for intergroup
conflict.

Conflict

Perceived subjugation leads to social conflict between groups. Such
conflict is inevitable when groups engage in activities which affect the
outcomes of other groups and thus, some groups can be labeled as
powerful while others are referred to as dependent. The problem
would be less complex if perception were related to immediate consequences. Unfortunately this is not the case. Past, immediate, and

future subjugation by a group may be perceived by another group. For instance, conflicts between South Vietnam and North Vietnam may be conceptualized as civil conflicts stemming, in part, from perceived subjugation. It makes little difference whether the subjugation is imagined or real; past, immediate, or future. Thus, conflict in intergroup relations involves the process whereby groups become emotionally and violently opposed to each other—the crucial objective for each being to subjugate the other as a means of ascertaining some desired end.

Conflict appears to be rather disruptive for a social system because the process ranges from subjugation to annihilation as a means of achieving superiority over another group. Unlike competition, conflict in its pure form occurs among equals and nonequals. Of course, if a group is quite subordinate to another, it takes a great risk in entering into conflict with the superordinate group. Nevertheless, from the subordinate group's vantage point, conflict may be the only available alternative which will ultimately yield balanced relations between the groups. While conflict is not a necessary factor in accommodation, it can enhance the likelihood of groups reaching working arrangements.

INTERGROUP DYNAMICS

In the foregoing section, we explained some of the forms of interaction between social groups. This section will deal more specifically with intergroup dynamics. As suggested earlier in this chapter, groups can interact on an equal or unequal basis or they can elect *not* to interact. If they interact, there are basic social-psychological factors which should be examined if a fuller understanding of intergroup relations is desired. We will consider unequal intergroup interaction and then equal intergroup relations.

If, when groups interact, one group is superordinate, then a type of power-dependence relationship exists between the groups. Since superordinate-subordinate group relations from a subordinate vantage point are salient, if groups are highly interrelated, interaction is likely to go on indefinitely.

If groups are somewhat distinct and not engaged in conflict, they may be perceived as coming together to exchange services. As a result, when groups are unequal in resources and one group exerts a good deal of power, it is entirely possible that a dependent group will withdraw from the interaction due to perceived subjugation as a consequence of extreme dependence. This also is true at the international level when subsystems within a nation-state become blocked in expansion or are threatened with dependence and retreatism or revivalist expansion occurs. The latter alternative is discussed below under a third alternative of balancing power for superordinate groups (increasing alternatives). Often however, the former alternative of retreatism is the technique used by groups within a system when extreme dependence is impending, though this may be accompanied by in-group revivalism. For instance, some have contended that the radical right in the United States may reflect a group which retreats and narrows the concept of national to include only those like themselves. We submit that withdrawal is inimical to the social system in the long run even though it may enhance intragroup relations. Coalition formation is a technique which has been successful in balancing power between groups and contributing to nonconflict intergroup interaction. The result of this mode of interaction is to decrease the powerful group's alternatives for getting its goals mediated. Such a technique is exceedingly difficult to use when the group to be affected is powerful to the extent that it controls the outcomes of several other groups whose goals might be different. Additionally, such a group usually enjoys positive interactive relations with other groups to the extent that coalition-formation against the group is difficult. Furthermore, intergroup relations between subordinate groups may not be conducive to the development of coalitions. The Israeli-Arab situation illuminates both of these difficulties. Israel is a small country bounded on all sides by Arab neighbors; yet Egypt has found it extremely difficult to subordinate this country. Of course, reasons for Egypt's lack of success have been attributed to numerous factors including a lack of technological and military development, insufficient cognitions about warfare, and even, family background factors.[26] A crucial point, though, is that the Arab world has never *successfully* coaligned, though there is a trend in that direction. Complicating the picture even more is the fact that Israel enjoys a positive relationship with other countries who can extend resources in times of crisis. Thus, any group interested in subjugating Israel would have to dilute the relationship between Israel and other countries, the United States being one of them. At the present time, this does not appear to be a possibility.

A third alternative for balancing power available to subordinate groups engaging in social interaction with superordinate groups is for the subordinate group to enhance its own alternatives. Few persons would argue with the thesis that prior to the Cuban revolution Cuba interacted with the United States from a dependent position. However, with the rise to power of Castro, and Cuba's extension of her alternative sources of aid to include the Soviet Union, "independence" was achieved and the United States' power with respect to Cuba attenuated sharply. It is important to note that this strategy may not actually mean a net increase in power for a group. With respect to Cuba, it simply meant a transference of dependency from one nation to another (from the United States to the Soviet Union). Net power gains *can* be made with respect to the former superordinate group, but unless the subordinate group has adequate resources of its own or can develop such resources, the overall gain in power will be negligible.

In order for a group to increase its alternatives, it is necessary for that group to build and maintain good will. This act, in and of itself, implies dependence on some group. Yet, if original superordinate-subordinate group relations constitute the basic unit of cognition, then the subordinate group achieves independence through the successful development and maintenance of positive relationships with other groups that can provide needed resources.[27]

A final alternative for social groups involved in unbalanced relationships with another group is for the subordinate group to increase the powerful group's dependence. With respect to nation-states, Dean G. Pruitt has made the following observation:

> By helping another nation in concrete ways, we demonstrate to the people of that nation how helpful we can be in the future. This may cause them to feel more dependent on us and thereby increase our ability to command favors from them in the future. In adopting a policy of increased responsiveness, which will produce a larger number of concrete acts of helpfulness to another nation, a nation's leaders may be trying to increase their influence over the other nation.[28]

In order to increase another group's dependence, a subordinate group must have adequate resources or be able to provide crucial services to other groups. In fact, if a group successfully transfers its allegiances from one group to another, then the subordinate group has been able to convince the other group that it has salient services to provide. In the case of Cuban-Soviet relations, for example, one important consideration for the Soviet Union was the strategic location of Cuba in the Western hemisphere. Thus, what Cuba lacked in resources was more than surpassed by her physical location, which shows that the subordinate group provides a crucial service to the superordinate group.

Intergroup relations, as some sociologists have noted, should not be regarded necessarily as a distinct theoretical area of content. Rather, it should be viewed as a subfield which is a special case of the larger discipline of human interaction. Thus, interaction between social groups is based on principles similar to those characterizing individual social interaction. These principles, as mentioned earlier, are related to the symbolic interaction social-psychological perspective.

All social groups are made up of individuals who have selves. This means that individuals, as members of social groups, make indications to themselves, toward the groups to which they belong, and toward other groups of which they are not members. For example, a group of white middle-class Brazilian students may overwhelmingly indicate feelings of antagonism toward Brazilian blacks, and on some occasions, members from these two groups may engage in forms of intergroup conflict. The symbolic process occurring for these two groups may be envisioned in the following manner. Each student from the white middle-class group and black group brings with him the ability to interpret situations, actions, and so forth from a particular learned perspective. Thus, each member of both groups interacts with himself from his individual perspective. Second, each member of the two groups is affected, to some extent, by the emergent group values, norms, perspective, ideology, and so on. The extent of the group's effect varies from one individual to another. As a result, a given member engages in self-interaction which includes his individual perspective and the group's (of which he is a member) perspective; he also, if not isolated, engages in direct interaction with his other group members and places himself in their individual and group roles; finally, he interprets the actions of the "out-group" by imagining himself in the role, notes the situation and makes indications to himself. Specific group action occurs when group members align their actions through interpretation and role taking, and intergroup interaction occurs through the symbolic processes involving two or more social groups or members from these groups. The specific form which interaction between social groups takes is dependent upon member reaction to the prevailing role of social exchange and characterizing social processes such as assimilation, stratification, accommodation, and conflict. The important point for the reader of this book to remember, however, is that relationships between social groups are analyzable in terms of the same principles developed to explain other forms of social interaction—in fact, such principles enhance our understanding of these complex social phenomena.

Notes

1. This point is made in George Lundberg, Clarence Schrag, Otto Larsen, and William Catton, *Sociology*, 4th ed. (New York: Harper and Row, 1968), p. 8. Interaction is defined as the mutual and reciprocal influence exerted by two or more persons, or groups, upon each other's expectations and behavior.
2. Herbert Blumer, *Symbolic Interactionism: Perspectives and Methods* (Englewood Cliffs, N.J.: Prentice-Hall, 1969).
3. See Jerome G. Manis and Bernard N. Meltzer, *Symbolic Interaction: A Reader in Social Psychology* (Boston: Allyn and Bacon, 1967), pp. 6-9.
4. This point is stressed in George H. Mead, *Mind, Self and Society* (Chicago: University of Chicago Press, 1934), pp. 42-51, 145-46.
5. This is important for behavior can be viewed as "social" not simply when it is a response to others, but rather when it has incorporated in it the behavior of others (Manis and Meltzer, *Symbolic Interaction*, p. 9).
6. Blumer, *Symbolic Interactionism*, p. 2.
7. Recent work by Wilson emphasizes the unique aspects of interaction which may be stressed by theorists and researchers. See P. Wilson, "Conceptions of Interaction and Forms of Sociological Explanation," *American Sociological Review* 35 (August 1970): 697-707.
8. Blumer, *Symbolic Interactionism*.
9. Ibid.
10. This distinction is made in Bernard Meltzer and John Petras' paper on "The Chicago and Iowa's School of Symbolic Interactionism," in *Symbolic Interaction*, ed. Jerome G. Manis and Bernard N. Meltzer, 2d ed. (Boston: Allyn and Bacon, 1972), pp. 43-51.
11. Paul F. Secord and Carl W. Backman, *Social Psychology* (New York: McGraw-Hill, 1964), p. 579.
12. Blumer, *Symbolic Interactionism*.
13. Lundburg et al., *Sociology*, p. 12.
14. This distinction was initially made in William G. Sumner, *Folkways* (Boston: Ginn, 1906).
15. See S. E. Asch, "Studies of Independence and Conformity: A Minority of One Against a Unanimous Majority," *Psychological Monographs* 70, no. 9, 1956. Also, because cohesion is related to the significance of group negative functions for an individual, see Leon Festinger, Stanley Schacter, and Kurt Back, *Social Pressures in Informal Groups: A Study of Human Factors in Housing* (New York: Harper and Row, 1950).
16. In order to insure a static system value orientation, superordinate groups have constructed restrictive legislation in some instances. In the United States this has taken the form of immigration laws suspending Chinese and Japanese immigration at certain times. See George E. Simpson and L. Milton Yinger, *Racial and Cultural Minorities: An Analysis of Prejudice and Discrimination*, 3d ed. (New York: Harper and Row, 1965), pp. 87-93.
17. This view is very much in line with societal reaction theory as explicated by Edwin M. Lemert in *Human Deviance, Social Problems and Social Control*, 2d ed. (Englewood Cliffs, N.J.: Prentice-Hall, 1971).
18. We do not submit that this is "right"; nevertheless, it tends to be somewhat universal. Lieberson's point concerning the relative ease of a migrant population's entrance into a society when it is socially, economically, and politically inferior has some relation to this point in the sense that the superordinate group's deterministic role in societal directions is not seriously challenged. See Stanley Lieberson, "A Societal Theory of Race and Ethnic Relations," *American Sociological Review* 26, no. 6 (December 1961): 102-910.
19. Peter M. Blau, *Exchange and Power in Social Life* (New York: Wiley, 1964).

20. See Sidney M. Willhelm and Edwin H. Powell, "Who Needs the Negro?" *Transaction* 1 (September-October 1964): 3-6. Also Norval Glenn, "White Gain from Negro Subordination," *Social Problems* 14, no. 2 (Fall 1966): 159-78, and chapter 12 of this book.
21. Stanley Lieberson, *Ethnic Patterns in American Life* (New York: The Free Press, 1963), pp. 7-8.
22. See Milton Gordon, *Assimilation in American Life* (New York: Oxford University Press, 1964), chapter 3.
23. Lieberson, *Ethnic Patterns in American Life,* p. 159.
24. Malcom X, *Malcom X Speaks* (New York: Merit Publishers, 1965), pp. 12-31.
25. Tamotsu Shibutani and Kian M. Kwan, *Ethnic Stratification* (New York: Macmillan, 1965), pp. 33-34.
26. These factors relate to the socialization process, which may be devoid of certain aspirational influences.
27. Power-dependence relationships are discussed in this chapter in the same manner that Emerson discusses them. See Richard M. Emerson, "Power-Dependence Relations," *American Sociological Review* 27 (1962): 31-41.
28. Dean G. Pruitt, "Stability and Sudden Change in Interpersonal and International Affairs," *Journal of Conflict Resolution* 13 (1969): 18.

The Concept of Tolerance-Prejudice

6

It is amazing how seldom we perceive and evaluate other people strictly as individuals. This is largely because group membership is a cardinal sociological fact—our lives are closely bound up with such groups as families, communities, associations, nations, and so on. We should not expect to be judged completely independently of our group memberships because many of our personal characteristics are a result of participation in groups. Yet even the most refined scientific-mathematical techniques will not permit us to predict individual characteristics from group memberships without considerable error. This is because (1) each individual is a unique combination of characteristics, and (2) no group is perfectly homogeneous in composition.

At a psychological level, as we suggested in chapter 2, human beings seem to have a penchant for classification. Indeed, to offer a global generalization, human cognition seems to be a process of interplay between specificity and generality. Human perception might be characterized as a process of comparing unique objects and events with similar ones. Our capacity for abstraction and our ability to manipulate abstract categories is presumably peculiarly human, and without this capacity, the human animal surely would not have developed culture. What concerns us here, of course, is the human tendency to classify other people and the consequences of that. Prejudice is a fascinating manifestation of this human proclivity to establish tidy categories.

THE UNIVERSALITY OF ETHNOCENTRISM

Ethnocentrism, as we have previously noted, refers to the allegiance and loyalty which one displays toward the in-group. This attachment is partly emotional in character, and it tends to influence one's judgment about other groups. Because, characteristically, the out-group is judged by the standards of the in-group the bias for the norms and values of the in-group is likely to result in an unfavorable comparison for other groups. This usually means, in short, that "we" are better than "they."

Ethnocentrism, in its various forms, seems to be universal among human groups.[1] Its social base assumes many forms: nation, region, community, religion, social class, ideology, ethnicity, occupation, and so forth. Its common denominator is the favoritism shown one's "own" group, whatever it happens to be. Moreover, tribalistic loyalty has almost always been considered a basic virtue in human society. It is generally encouraged and rewarded, and failure to exhibit it is customarily penalized to some extent. Much of social control, indeed, is concerned with stimulating and reinforcing group pride and devotion to group rules and goals. It is not peculiar to any particular group or to any particular period of history, and it is altogether unlikely that it will disappear as a factor in human affairs, though one should not discount the prospect that it will lessen in intensity as humankind becomes more cosmopolitan.

Everyday life is replete with examples of ethnocentrism, so much so, in fact, that only the absence of it ordinarily makes us aware of it. The occasional group member who compares his own group unfavorably with another serves to remind us of it. The spectator who doesn't "root" for the home team is looked at askance, and the citizen of the nation-state whose loyalty is suspect is in dire circumstances. Ethnocentrism is so pervasive that many laymen evidently regard it as "natural," and it is indeed normal in the statistical sense.

There are two major consequences of ethnocentrism: it tends to promote cohesion and morale in the in-group; it also contributes to intergroup tensions and conflict.[2] These two results are obviously interrelated, as is illustrated in the case of nationalism. Everything else being equal, national cohesiveness favors war, and a declaration of war usually stimulates national unity. Thus ethnocentrism can be said to be functional in the sense that almost any kind of human behavior or cultural practice performs some kind of function for the individual or society. Whether it is dysfunctional depends, in the final analysis, upon one's value judgment. It is clear that ethnocentrism tends to encourage intergroup conflict, and if one regards this as undesirable, then ethnocentrism is objectionable.

Ethnocentrism and a provincial, parochial viewpoint are closely associated; in fact, they are virtually synonymous. This is in contra-distinction to a catholic, cosmopolitan perspective. Although contact with other groups and other cultures by means of travel, education, or some other form of communication seems to moderate ethnocentrism it does not insure that ethnocentrism will be eliminated. If ethnocentrism already has deep emotional roots in one's personality it is unlikely that one's mind will be appreciably "broadened" by contact with other groups and other cultures. Such contact may only serve to reinforce it, because ethnocentrism conditions perception in such a way that the foreign is perceived automatically as inferior and unnatural. Can a person become completely cosmopolitan and devoid of ethnocentrism? We doubt it.

One of the most significant forms of ethnocentrism in recent history has been nationalism.[3] The nation-state, within the last few centuries, has come to be regarded as a basic reference group, and national identification is frequently so strong that it even transcends religious loyalties. More recently we have witnessed the advent of ideological ethnocentrism which threatens to supplant, at least to some extent, national identification. To be sure, it is not always a simple matter to differentiate, for example, between Chinese communism and Chinese nationalism, or, for that matter, to ascertain to what extent Chinese nationalism and Russian nationalism divide China and the U.S.S.R. and to what extent they share a common ideological viewpoint.

As we observed earlier, cultural ethnocentrism seems to be on the decline. This is evidently due in large measure to the increased rate of cultural diffusion and borrowing in concert with the impact of scientific technology. There are few people in the world today who are completely isolated from the mass media of communication and their dissemination of culture. News of a space flight can be known almost instantaneously throughout the world and the growth and expansion of science can be expected to accelerate this trend. Thus, the differences which divide the world today are not so much cultural as they are political. As the people of the world become more sophisticated culturally, cultural ethnocentrism will probably continue to diminish; it is much more difficult to predict what will occur when they become more sophisticated politically.

As a general concept in intergroup relations ethnocentrism is very valuable, but a concept more amenable to rigorous definition and quantification is required to deal with intergroup attitudes. Hence it seems more fruitful to pursue a definition of prejudice and its logical complement, tolerance.

DEFINITION OF TOLERANCE-PREJUDICE

The field of intergroup relations has been plagued with many semantic problems: race, prejudice, and discrimination, for example. Part of the overall problem has been the emotional overtones generated by these terms which have rendered them difficult to define. The magnitude of the task of defining prejudice objectively can be appreciated by realizing that one meaningful measure of success would be agreement of persons of all shades of prejudice that the definition was valid.[4] If prejudiced people, including those who are favorably prejudiced as well as those negatively prejudiced toward some group, can agree on a definition, then this could be taken as an indication of the objectivity of the definition. In dealing with prejudice, then, we are confronted with the task of having to satisfy a host of critics, including the prejudiced themselves.

Although the term prejudice has its limitations, it is possible to develop an operational definition for quantification and measurement. It should be made clear at the outset of this endeavor that we are concerned exclusively with *group prejudice* and not interpersonal biases. Interpersonal attitudes are irrelevant unless they are influenced by the group membership of the object. If one's attitude toward another person is conditioned by the group membership of that person, then group prejudice is involved. In other words, we are dealing with a categorical attitude. If we judged each other strictly as individuals the phenomenon of group prejudice could not exist.

Prejudice is an attitude and therefore, covert, and in that sense, it can be distinguished from *discrimination*, which is an overt process. To be sure, the two processes are frequently closely intertwined in actual behavior, but conceptually we can make a rather clear distinction between the two processes. This differentiation becomes important in regard to the question of legal measures to combat discrimination, since laws can prohibit discrimination but cannot always be expected to control prejudice. Prejudice is usually the force behind discrimination. Some discrimination is not motivated by prejudice, but the experienced student of intergroup relations is wary of claims of unprejudiced discrimination.

Group prejudice can be either positive or negative, that is, favorable or unfavorable. We customarily think of it as negative, and in the absence of any qualification, the conventional meaning is intended here. It is the negative variety which seems to produce the most social friction. Positive prejudice can seldom be divorced entirely from the negative form, however, because a favorable attitude toward one group is frequently associated with a hostile attitude toward some other group; hence, a positive prejudice toward the in-group and negative prejudice toward the out-group is the familiar pattern.

By derivation and connotation the term prejudice implies an advance judgment; in fact, many of the definitions that have been formulated emphasize the idea of *pre*judgment. In this sense prejudice would refer to judgment of a person before acquaintance with him. This is obviously often the case in group prejudice because an individual is judged in *absentia*, that is, an opinion is formed of him on the basis of his group membership, frequently before he is ever confronted as a (unique) person. Thus prejudice is to make up one's mind about a person prior to knowing his personality and observing his behavior. This conceptual approach to prejudice also implies that the prejudgment is not modified to correspond to the uniqueness of the individual after there has been an opportunity to know him. The prejudgment persists even though it is inaccurate. The advance categorical evaluation is presumably too rigid to allow modification to fit the individual case. The prejudgment has assumed that the group is homogeneous and that a blanket judgment will cover any particular case so that it will not be necessary to alter it. Such a preconception is obviously likely to condition one's perception, so that accurate perception of the individual is prevented.

As we have previously indicated in our discussion of grouping, no group is perfectly homogeneous, so that any prejudgment of an individual on the basis of group membership is fraught with error. There are certain statistical correlations between group membership and individual characteristics, to be sure, and this kind of analysis is a useful tool in social science. What distinguishes prejudice from this kind of statistical analysis is that in the case of prejudice the judgment is an emotionally rigid one. Group prejudice renders a judgment concerning the whole group, a judgment which tends to persist even when an individual member does not correspond to the preconceived categorical image.

The various definitions of prejudice which have been propounded suggest the following ingredients or characteristics: (1) Prejudice entails judgment before confrontation and acquaintance. It is a judgment based upon preconception. (2) It is an emotionally rigid attitude. Because of this, advance judgments are not altered when the individual does not correspond to the preconceived image of the group. (3) It is an irrational attitude. This is due to its emotional character. The emotional factor is associated with its rigidity, which contributes to its irrationality. (4) Prejudice tends to be a misjudgment, that is, an inaccurate judgment. This may be due to a lack of accurate information or to distorted perception. (5) Prejudice is usually an unfriendly, negative attitude, but it can also be favorable and positive. (6) Prejudice seems to have the connotation of an *unfair* attitude, in the sense of a judgment which runs counter to the basis ethical principles of a society. The following definition, offered by Allport, seems to combine most of these elements. "Ethnic prejudice is an antipathy based upon a faulty and inflexible generalization. It may be felt or expressed. It may be directed toward a group as a whole, or toward an individual because he is a member of that group."[5]

The definition of prejudice advanced below also combines most of these factors. It will serve as our "official" definition for the ensuing discussion of the subject in this book. We shall postulate prejudice to be: *a rigid, emotional attitude towards a group which may be either negative (unfavorable, hostile) or positive (favorable, friendly) and which results in prejudgment of members of the group.*[6] This definition regards group prejudice as a categorical attitude which subordinates individual distinctiveness in favor of a composite image of the group. The result is that individual identity is obscured. "They are all alike," a statement frequently heard in interviews with strongly prejudiced persons, expresses the idea well. Similarly, the remark that "I wouldn't want my daughter to marry one of them," conveys the same notion. The underlying assumption is that the group is homogeneous and objectionable. All members of the group, all prospective sons-in-law, are prejudged. (One could almost certainly "match" the eventual son-in-law of this prejudiced person with a member from any sizeable ethnic, racial, or religious group in every characteristic except the one employed to define the group—such as religious affiliation, for example.)

This definition emphasizes that prejudice tends to be a rigid attitude and implies that it is the emotional component which makes it inflexible. Were it not for this emotional rigidity, the prejudgment would be corrected to comply with the facts of individual uniqueness. Prejudice, one might say, refuses to listen to reason; it is a "My mind is made up—don't bother me with the facts" attitude. It is a predisposition with an emotional anchorage which renders it resistant to change. It is a preconception which affects perception; that is, it induces a certain "blindness." Prejudiced people "know" what the group in question "is like" and that "they are all alike," so that it is not necessary for such people to perceive and judge each member of a group as a unique case. The stronger the prejudice, the more rigid the judgment will be. Prejudice is an irrational attitude in that the emotional factor prevents an objective judgment.

We are accustomed to regard prejudice as negative, but as noted earlier in this chapter, it can also be positive. By this same logic, a "zero point" of prejudice would differentiate between the two kinds. In the case of attitudes toward Blacks we would have diagrammatically:

Zero

Positive | Negative

Pro-Black | 0 Point | Anti-Black

It is more instructive, however, to make a comparative analysis of attitudes toward Blacks in relation to attitudes toward, say, "whites." Thus our diagram would show positive and negative prejudice for both groups.

Pro-Black | Anti-Black

Anti-White | 0 | Pro-White

What is the maximum prejudice? The polar extremes might be said to be (logically, psychologically, and sociologically) the predisposition to kill any group member on sight, for negative prejudice, and deliberately sacrificing one's life for a group, in the case of positive prejudice. Warfare would seem to offer the classic example. One is expected to kill the enemy on sight in almost all situations, and to risk losing one's own life in the process. Both "we" and "they" are the "enemy" in wartime, of course. Negative prejudice, under these circumstances, is socially regarded as quite laudable (provided it is directed towards the out-group, of course.) Some cases of treason presumably are due to a positive prejudice toward the out-group. On the whole, we shall be concerned with negative prejudice in our analysis of intergroup relations, with the tacit understanding that negative prejudice toward a group is usually found in conjunction with a positive prejudice toward an "opposite" group.

For group prejudice to exist, some kind of social classification is required, as we learned in chapter 1. In the absence of culturally provided social categories such as race and nationality it is difficult to avoid judging a person as an individual. Prejudice is also facilitated by linguistic symbols which provide handy labels for these social categories. Derogatory terms for groups reinforce negative prejudice.

Tolerance

Like the term prejudice, tolerance is most useful when it is operationally defined. In its popular usage tolerance seems to imply something of a condescending attitude. Some people evidently even regard it as expressing a dislike covered only by a grudging willingness not to attempt to do anything harmful against the group. It also is used to convey the idea of "restrained opposition," that is, an inhibition of one's antipathies. Hence, the term has an obnoxious quality for many people who wish to promote "acceptance" rather than "mere toleration." There are surely many minority and majority group members who are quite willing to settle for tolerance in such a sense. They do not insist upon being loved or esteemed as long as they are not "bothered" in other respects. According to this view it is not necessary for your neighbor to love you; it is sufficient if he does not harm your family or your house. Tolerance is obviously an ambiguous word.

Whatever its popular meaning may be, we can employ tolerance here in an operational sense in conjunction with the definition of prejudice which we have developed. We shall define tolerance simply as *the relative absence of prejudice*. This makes tolerance the logical complement of prejudice; the greater the prejudice, the less the tolerance will be. We also can regard prejudice and intolerance as synonymous. In terms of our diagrammatic representation of prejudice, the zero point would be "absolute tolerance" in the sense that there would be neither positive nor negative prejudice. Movement towards the zero point on the scale means more tolerance and less prejudice.

	Zero	
Tolerance—		—Tolerance
	0	
—Prejudice		Prejudice—
(Negative)	Point	(Positive)

At the zero point on this scale the subject would have neither a positive nor a negative preference for the group in question, so he could be said to be unprejudiced, or tolerant.

Another student of intergroup relations, Oliver C. Cox, has advocated a distinction in meaning between prejudice and intolerance. He would have prejudice refer to attitudes which facilitate economic exploitation, as in the case of the economic subordination of the Blacks in the South by the dominant group. In other words, Cox views race prejudice as a device for rationalizing and sustaining economic subjugation. "Social intolerance," on the other hand, is illustrated by anti-Semitism, according to Cox. It is a refusal to respect the beliefs and practices of a subordinate group, presumably because they are regarded as obnoxious and offensive to the dominant group's own ideas and behaviors.[7] This distinction, it should be noted, is associated with a particular theoretical approach to the explanation of prejudice, namely an emphasis upon economic factors.

Van Den Berghe, in his study of prejudice, has distinguished between two types of prejudice.[8] The one, *competitive*, exists in a situation where the majority is in control and of higher status, as represented by many industrial societies, and the other, *paternalistic*, which exists under conditions where a minority is dominant, such as in a plantation economy. The U.S.A. would be an example of the competitive form and the Republic of South Africa illustrates the paternalistic model.

The concept of tolerance-prejudice which we have developed purports to be independent of any theory of prejudice (or the lack of it, tolerance) and should be applicable to any form of prejudice toward race, ethnic, religion, politics, or class. It is designed to facilitate the construction of instruments to measure tolerance-prejudice, since a rigorous definition of what is to be measured should precede scaling. Also, our definition of tolerance-prejudice has been fashioned so as to dovetail with the definition of discrimination which will be presented in chapter 9.

Ethical and Empirical Forms of Prejudice

Prejudice is a complex and elusive concept. Insight into its nature requires painstaking and thorough analysis. In our opinion, there are two significant forms or dimensions of prejudice which it behooves us to anatomize. We can conceive of prejudice in two senses, one a matter of the empirical validity of a group judgment, and the other the purely ethical quality of a group judgment.[9] In other words, we can postulate a form of prejudice which is an erroneous judgment about a group, as well as an ordinary expression of affection or dislike for a group. In the one case prejudice exists if the person has some misconception about the group, if his information about it is incorrect, and he prejudges accordingly. Ethical prejudice is simply any rigid value judgment, negative or positive, about a group. If one says, "I don't like Mexicans," he has expressed prejudice in the ethical sense. If he claims he dislikes Mexicans because they are all lazy he is manifestly guilty of prejudice in the empirical sense, because he is surely in error in his allegation. Statements of ethical prejudice usually include some "reason" for the preference. (One might refer to cases where no reason is given for liking or disliking a group as "pure prejudice;" that is, instances in which a person says, "I just don't like them; I don't know why.") It may be necessary to press a person for his reasons for disliking (or liking) a group, but it is rare to encounter anyone who cites no reason at all for his attitude. The explanation given may not always lend itself to simple empirical determination. If it is alleged, for example, that Germans are materialistic, this is obviously a rather subjective judgment.

We have, then, essentially two forms of prejudice, and they are ordinarily found in combination. It is possible, of course, that one can be *ethically* prejudiced without being *empirically* prejudiced. One may dislike a group for reasons that are empirically valid, though it is difficult to fulfill the necessary conditions. It is difficult to sustain a categorical dislike for a group on empirical grounds because, as we have stressed repeatedly, it is virtually impossible to specify an "objectionable" trait that is characteristic of all members of any group. Also, we should not expect highly articulate statements of prejudice which specify the frequency of a trait in a group; nor can we expect a highly rational expression of prejudice. Typically one hears remarks to the effect that "they" are "selfish," or "dirty," or "pushy." One infers that this characterization is intended to apply to all members of the group object. But, if one presses the point some qualification may be attached, especially if the other person is not intensely prejudiced. "There may be a few good ones" is a common response under these circumstances.

That most instances of prejudice are not purely ethical in character can be gleaned from analyzing the empirical justifications cited for a group preference. If a person claims that his unfavorable attitude towards a particular group is due to their "aggressiveness" or "lack of ambition," one can conclude that this is something of a pretext, because

(1) the trait is surely not universal among the group, and (2) if the person really objects to this trait *as such* then it would be much more "efficient" for him to say that he dislikes all persons who have that trait. If a person says that he dislikes Blacks because they are lazy, one wonders which comes first; does he have an unfavorable attitude toward *all* lazy people? If not, then one can logically infer that there is an irrational prejudice towards Blacks *as such* and the reason given is merely a rationalization. To take a slightly different example, if somebody states that he doesn't care for Indians because they smoke tobacco, the rationality of this view is suspect on the grounds we have already cited, namely, that it is doubtful if all Indians would smoke, and the prejudiced person may not have any antipathy for non-Indian smokers. If someone does not like smokers, he can say so without confusing the issue by bringing in Indians! If he simply does not like Indians, he can attempt to justify his (ethical) prejudice by contending that he doesn't like them because they smoke. If we bear in mind that prejudice is essentially an irrational attitude, due to its emotional ingredient, we can understand more fully why efforts to justify it on empirical grounds are likely to be unsuccessful.

At the risk of redundancy we want to reiterate that there are real differences between groups, but they are statistical differences and should be interpreted accordingly. For example, if one conducted a survey inquiring about musical tastes of American citizens of African descent and American citizens of Polish descent, there would surely be differences. The statistical results of such a survey, however, are not the same psychological stuff that goes into "Polish jokes" and Black stereotypes.

Ethical inconsistency is a familiar component in prejudice. Some groups are admired because they are "aggressive" or "ambitious" while other groups are denounced for the same alleged characteristics. A good rule of thumb test of prejudice, in fact, is whether the same ethical standards of judgment are applied to all groups. Is the same insult coming from a Black more offensive than from a "white"? Is a crime committed by a Catholic less reprehensible than the same one committed by a Protestant? Is wealth or poverty more objectionable in one ethnic group than another? We can frequently conduct an objective analysis of ethical consistency. Prejudice inclines us to employ a "double ethical standard" in judging groups and their members. Rigorous logic can detect the process; if the same behavior or trait is praised in one group and condemned in another, we can logically conclude the existence of an emotionally rigid attitude.

Beyond the question of ethical consistency, the ethical brand of prejudice must be analyzed in its own terms, ethically. This does not necessarily mean, however, that only a "purely" ethical evaluation is possible. One can relate the ethical issues involved in judging groups to larger ethical principles. In American society, for example, there seems to be a general ethical axiom which holds that it is illegitimate to blame an individual (or group) for a condition or situation which he (or they) has not produced and cannot control. It is considered unethical, for instance, to reproach a person for a physical disability which he has inherited. By the same ethical principle one presumably should not disparage a group for living in slums if this is due to discrimination in employment and housing. There is likely to be controversy, however, over the question of whether these people dwell in slums because they must or because they lack the ability and ambition to secure better housing. Much the same issue is involved in the crime rate among Blacks in the U.S.[10] (The crime rate serves as a basis for some empirical prejudice, of course. There is doubtless both positive and negative prejudice which reflects underestimation and exaggeration of the actual rate. Let us assume here that impressions about the rate are essentially correct, for the sake of analysis.) If crime is produced by inadequate housing, unemployment, and slum conditions in general, can one fairly censure Blacks for a higher crime rate than non-Blacks, assuming that there are differences in such conditions? How much of Black crime can be "ethically excused" on these grounds? This is the kind of question which invariably arises when one pursues the ethical dimension of prejudice. It reaffirms what we have said about empirical and ethical forms of prejudice being closely intertwined. In the final analysis prejudice is reduced to the ethical question of whether or not it is fair to dislike a particular group and its members. Before this kind of moral issue can be resolved in the debate, it is necessary to establish what the group "is really like"; much of the argument will probably dwell on this question. Hence there are continuing vigorous arguments about whether Americans are materialistic, Germans are cruel, alcoholics are immoral, football players are stupid, Russians are trustworthy, and so on.

Perhaps the most fundamental ethical issue concerning prejudice is group judgment itself. There are two basic moral questions: (1) Should one judge an individual on the basis of his group membership? (2) Should one judge a group on the basis of an individual member? In the first case one's answer is likely to depend upon whether the individual has any influence upon the character of his group. A member of a racial group has limited influence in determining what the group "is like." A member of a club, on the other hand, would be expected to have a much larger voice in shaping the collective behavior and policies of the organization. Moreover, there is the corollary ethical question of grouping itself. Is it proper to judge Caucasians as a group in the same manner as judging, say, a labor union or an insurance company? It would seem fairer to judge a member of a political party (which formulates policy cooperatively) by his membership than it is to judge a member of an American ethnic group by his former society, since one can join or leave the political party at will but does not have that same degree of choice with respect to his ethnic heritage. Similarly, whether it is fair to hold a group responsible for the conduct and traits of individual members might hinge upon the degree of control the group has over the member. In law, a corporation is responsible for many of the acts of its agents, and parents may be held to account for the actions of their children. Should one blame (or credit) Frenchmen as a group for the behavior of a particular citizen of France? These are not merely academic, ethical questions. We must come to grips with them every day when we read the newspaper, walk down the street or engage in commerce. It should be obvious that the answers we give to these kinds of questions will reflect our theories about human behavior, motivation, and social causation, as well as our moral values.

To reiterate, prejudice is a complex phenomenon. The isolation of ethical and empirical forms enhances our appreciation of its nature, but these in turn require painstaking analysis. "Hard" intelligence about groups is difficult to accumulate, and one cannot reasonably expect more than statistical profiles which are constantly changing on the order of mortality tables devised by actuaries. These data may not satisfy the emotional appetite of one who is seeking a black and white portrait of a group; therefore, it is advisable to suspend one's judgment and to stand ready to modify it if one wishes to avoid empirical prejudice. The ethical form, as we have demonstrated, is equally complex. If one is prone to examine his prejudices critically and is concerned about the ethical dimension, the analysis can become quite involved. It is no simple matter to avoid ethical inconsistency and both positive and negative prejudice.

Donald Campbell, a social psychologist, regards attitudes towards minority groups as having five "subtopics," namely: (1) *social distance,* the tendency to deny intimacy to minority group members and to demand segregation from them; (2) beliefs regarding the *blame* of a minority group for social problems; (3) beliefs regarding the *capability* or intelligence of a minority group; (4) beliefs regarding the *morality* of a minority group; and (5) *affection*, the feeling of like or dislike for a minority group.[11] To relate these components to the two forms of prejudice we have previously distinguished, social distance and affection would constitute ethical prejudice, whereas beliefs concerning blame, capability, and morality would represent the empirical form of prejudice.

In short then, we can identify prejudice in two senses. One form is an inaccurate impression of a group and its members, resulting from false knowledge about the group, and the other form is the evaluation one makes of a group; his like or dislike of it. If one is correct in his perception of the group—an unlikely event in view of the heterogeneous nature of any group—then there is no empirical prejudice. Ethical prejudice exists whenever a person expresses an evaluative opinion about a group. Typically, of course, prejudice entails both a mistaken image of the group and a preferential judgment about the group.

STEREOTYPES

Closely related to prejudice, logically and psychologically, is the concept of stereotypes.[12] They provide intellectual raw materials for prejudice, one might say. These "pictures in our heads," as Walter Lippmann describes them, play an important functional role in prejudgments. For our purposes, we may regard (group) stereotypes as rigid mental images which purport to represent an entire group. As such, they are preconceptions and they induce prejudgments: they offer a kind of false mental economy, one might say, in that they attempt to reduce an entire group to a single mold. They are rather like figures in political cartoons whose prominent features are exaggerated.

Stereotypes, like prejudice, may be either negative (unfavorable) or positive (favorable); they may flatter a group or stigmatize it. As in the case of prejudice we are more likely to be concerned with the negative variety, since it is usually more productive of intergroup tensions. As we should expect, the favorable stereotype is generally associated with the in-group, and the unfavorable stereotype generally is identified with the out-group. A preconceived laudatory image would lead to a positive prejudgment and a derogatory image would produce a negative prejudgment.

Positive stereotypes are well illustrated in American advertising. The women in many advertisements, such as the ones for new autos for example, are quite beautiful, well dressed, poised, carefree, and gracious; their male companions are handsome, debonair, and well groomed. They are hardly typical people!

Stereotypes are not necessarily completely false representations any more than propaganda is false. They are, like propaganda, rather one-sided; they do not give a balanced, objective picture. Stereotypes contain germs of truth, but the fallacy is in their overgeneralization. Groups are too heterogeneous to be represented accurately in a single composite image, especially an emotionally rigid image. Stereotypes oversimplify, hence they misrepresent.

Stereotypes seem to exist for every major group in the world, whether it be racial, religious, ethnic, occupational, or national. There is variation in the rigidity of these stereotypes and how widely known they are. Most of us have some more or less fixed images in our minds concerning the appearance, conduct, and traits of football players, teen-agers, Indians, truck drivers, and many other group types. Some people cling tenaciously to these mental pictures, while others retain them as tentative hypotheses to be adandoned or revised as knowledge about the group is enlarged through interpersonal contact and experience.

Rigid stereotypes make for strong prejudice. An inflexible preconception tends to insure a strong prejudgment: the more pliable the image the less intense prejudice is likely to be. The intensely prejudiced person has a fixed idea of what a group is like and he knows that "they are all alike." They are all cut from the same pattern in his mind's eye, so that his perception of them coincides with his preconceived image. He is thus prone to ignore unique characteristics of group members. Since the group is perfectly homogeneous to his style of thinking, he needs only one (categorical) attitude for the whole group.

It is very doubtful that many individuals conceive their own stereotypes. Rather, they seem to reside in the culture and are acquired in the course of socialization. This may be inferred from the fact that their acquisition does not require contact with the group concerned. People who have never seen a Turk or Greek may have a fairly definite notion as to what "they" are like. Stereotypes are easily acquired from literature and the mass media of communication as well as from conversation. Another important source is humorous stories in which the minority group member is portrayed in a derogatory manner—the butt of the joke.

The fabrication and perpetuation of stereotypes is facilitated by categorical symbols which enable a person to evoke a single image for a whole group. A verbal symbol, such as "Frog" (for Frenchmen),

"Eight ball" (for Blacks), or "Gringo" (for American), serves to arouse these mental pictures and expedites the process of learning stereotypes. With only a limited vocabulary of such terms one can classify almost everybody. After one learns the term to designate a group he can associate the traits which constitute the stereotype more readily; the word provides a kind of "intellectual basket" into which he can place the various characteristics which are ascribed to the group being stereotyped.

A classic example of the Black stereotype was offered in the motion pictures of the 1930s, namely "Step'nfetchit." Appearing in numerous films, he was lazy, shiftless, superstitious, ignorant, cowardly, and dull witted. He moved with an indolent gait and was a comic and pathetic character. Many white people evidently found him quite amusing, but the portrayal was bitterly resented by many middle-class Blacks. He is still to be seen occasionally in old films on television and was praised a few years ago by Congressman John Bell Williams of Mississippi in the *Congressional Record*, presumably because Mr. Williams admired his performances. Another familiar example of Black stereotyping was the radio (and later TV) program of "Amos 'n' Andy." A character named "Kingfish" came to be the central one in the program, and he was presented as a somewhat ineffective, comically pompous, rather harmless, would-be big-time-operator who was usually scheming to make money without working, with the honest but naive and not-so-bright Andy frequently becoming the "fall guy." A lawyer was another major character, and he was pathetically inept, being a chronic stutterer and grossly ignorant of the law. It is small wonder that many Americans, especially in the South, were so astonished at the success of Black lawyers in pleading cases in the courts, in view of the image many of these people had of Black attorneys. The lawyer in the "Amos 'n' Andy" program was the most famous Black attorney in the U.S. for most Americans until the last decade or so. It is understandable that some southerners even claimed that the 1954 Supreme Court decision on segregation in the schools was a "communist conspiracy." Many were doubtless convinced that no Black barrister could have won such a case. More recently, especially in television, there has been a marked improvement in treatment of minority groups. Today one occasionally sees Blacks on television programs who are not "playing a Black;" that is, they may be playing the role of a police officer, soldier, taxi driver, or even a judge, when "race" is not a theme. In recent years, in fact, minority groups have become more conscious of their "image" as projected by the mass media and have protested stereotypical presentations. The general public also seems to have become more sophisticated in this respect and is apparently more prone to regard grossly stereotypical presentations as poor art and bad entertainment. Even the "westerns" have toned down the differences between the "good guys" and the "bad guys" in recent times.

An analysis of the content of American magazine fiction several years ago by Berelson and Salter revealed a consistent pattern of stereotyping of minority and majority characters. "The representatives of minority and foreign groups were usually tailored to the stereotypic dimensions of their respective groups. Of all the stories including one or more minority or foreign characters, familiar and usually disparaging stereotypic descriptions were employed in fully three-fourths." The investigators reported that stereotypes were found "for virtually every minority and foreign group in the fictional population." Blacks, Irish, and Italians were the most frequent groups mentioned, but there were also Jews, Poles, Filipinos, French, Chinese, Scandinavians, and South Sea Islanders who were stereotypically portrayed. They cited as samples "The amusingly ignorant Negro," "the Italian gangster," "the sly and shrewd Jew," "the emotional Irish," and "the primitive and 'backward' Pole." The heroes were generally the majority group members, "the Americans," and were described as physically attractive, of high status, and having superordinate roles.[13]

Stereotypes not only facilitate prejudice by providing a preconceived image of a group, they also serve to justify prejudice and discrimination. Allport, defining a stereotype as "an exaggerated belief associated with a category," contends that "its function is to justify (rationalize) our conduct in relation to that category."[14] Stereotypes are the excuses prejudiced people cite for their attitudes and discrimination; they constitute the "empirical" form of prejudice according to the analysis made earlier in this chapter. They are the equivalent of what John Dollard described as "defensive beliefs" in his study of *Class and Caste in a Southern Town*. "The function of defensive beliefs is to make the actions of white-caste members towards Negroes seem expedient and in line with current ideals; . . . they are, first, a method of justifying and perpetuating the gains of the white caste already described, and second, a technique for explaining the various types of aggression directed against Negroes."[15] The following passage from Dollard offers a specific illustration of this phenomenon.

Another line of belief about Negroes is that they are immoral, liars, and thieves, which is the equivalent of saying that they do not

follow our mores on one point and therefore cannot claim their
benefits at any other, i.e., such as voting. We must remember the
crime of rape in this connection and the defensive belief that
lynchings are mainly done as a result of sexual attacks on white
women. There is some truth in all these assertions; the poor are
more likely to be thieves and the threatened can turn out to be
liars. The fact of the matter would seem to be, however, that, if
the Negroes do not follow our mores it is not because they do not
wish to, but rather because they are not allowed, encouraged, or
compelled to follow them as the rest of us are.[16]

One of the most revealing studies on stereotypes was sponsored by
UNESCO a few years after the end of World War II. The survey was
international in scope, including Australia, Britain, France, Germany,
Italy, Holland, Norway, and the United States. Respondents were
asked to indicate which of the traits listed (backward, brave, conceited,
cruel, domineering, generous, hard-working, intelligent, peace-loving,
practical, progressive, and self-controlled) best described various
peoples. Some sample discriptions are offered below.[17] (The traits are
listed in order of frequency, with ties in brackets.)

Descriptions of Russians by:

Australians	British	French	Germans
1. Domineering	1. Hardworking	1. Backward	1. Cruel
2. Hardworking	2. Domineering	2. Hardworking	2. Backward
3. Cruel	3. Cruel	3. Domineering	{3. Hardworking
4. Backward	4. Backward	4. Brave	{3. Domineering
5. Brave	5. Brave	5. Cruel	5. Brave
6. Progressive	{6. Practical	6. Progressive	6. Practical
	{6. Progressive		

Descriptions of Americans by:

Australians	British	French	Germans
1. Progressive	1. Progressive	1. Practical	1. Progressive
2. Practical	{2. Conceited	2. Progressive	2. Generous
3. Intelligent	{2. Generous	3. Domineering	3. Practical
4. Conceited	4. Peace-loving	{4. Hardworking	4. Intelligent
5. Peace-loving	{5. Intelligent	{4. Intelligent	5. Peace-loving
6. Generous	{5. Practical	{6. Generous	6. Hardworking
		{6. Self-controlled	

Descriptions of British by:

Germans	Dutch	Americans
1. Intelligent	1. Self-controlled	1. Intelligent
2. Self-controlled	2. Peace-loving	{2. Hardworking
3. Conceited	{3. Practical	{2. Brave
4. Domineering	{3. Conceited	4. Peace-loving
5. Practical	5. Hardworking	5. Conceited
6. Progressive	6. Intelligent	6. Self-controlled

In the early 1930s Daniel Katz and K. W. Braly conducted a survey of Princeton students to determine their stereotypes,[18] and in 1950 this study was duplicated at Princeton by G. M. Gilbert. The students were given a checklist of traits, and the lists in table 5 indicate the frequency (percent) each trait was checked for the various groups.[19] The differences are shown in the third column.

Stereotypes are self-reinforcing as a result of their influence on perception. They produce a selectivity in our perception which makes us prone to ignore traits of group members which do not fit the pattern etched in our minds and which makes us inclined to pay attention to those characteristics which are in accord with our predispositions. Perception is conditioned by what one expects to see, and stereotypes represent visual expectations. Our perception tends to confirm our prejudices. We know from studies focusing on the relationship between prejudice, stereotypes, and perception that prejudice induces a distortion effect. A prejudiced subject reported that in the scene on a card he had examined a few minutes earlier a Black held a gun in his hand, whereas actually the Black was portrayed as a holdup victim.[20] Another study along this same line reported that white police officers who exhibited some prejudice towards Blacks were more likely to overestimate the Black crime rate in their area.[21] In other words, we are inclined to look for the best in groups toward whom we have a positive prejudice and the worst in those toward whom we are negatively prejudiced.

Implicit in stereotypes seems to be the idea that a group is responsible for its own image or reputation. Hence the admirable image of the in-group is intrinsically related to its virtues, while the adverse reputation of the out-group is also well deserved. Groups represented by a negative stereotype are expected to reform themselves so that they present a profile of traits that will make them socially attractive.

TABLE 5

TRAIT				TRAIT			
	PER CENT CHECKING TRAIT				PER CENT CHECKING TRAIT		
	1932	1950	diff.		1932	1950	diff.
AMERICANS				GERMANS			
Industrious	48	30	−18	Scientifically-minded	78	62	−16
Intelligent	47	32	−15	Industrious	65	50	−15
Materialistic	33	37	+4	Stolid	44	10	−34
Ambitious	33	21	−12	Intelligent	32	32	0
Progressive	27	5	−22	Methodical	31	20	−11
Pleasure-loving	26	27	+1	Extremely nationalistic	24	50	+26
Alert	23	7	−16	Progressive	16	3	−13
Efficient	21	9	−12	Aggressive	—	27	+—
Aggressive	20	8	−12	Arrogant	—	23	+—
Individualistic	—	26	+—				
ENGLISH				JAPANESE			
Sportsmanlike	53	21	−32	Intelligent	45	11	−34
Intelligent	46	29	−17	Industrious	43	12	−31
Conventional	34	25	−9	Progressive	24	2	−22
Tradition-loving	31	42	+11	Shrewd	22	13	−9
Conservative	30	22	−8	Sly	20	21	+1
Reserved	29	39	+10	Imitative	17	24	+7
Sophisticated	27	37	+10	Extremely nationalistic	—	18	+—
Courteous	21	17	−4	Treacherous	13	17	+4
Honest	20	11	−9				
NEGROES				CHINESE			
Superstitious	84	41	−43	Superstitious	34	18	−16
Lazy	75	31	−44	Sly	29	4	−25
Happy-go-lucky	38	17	−21	Conservative	29	14	−15
Ignorant	38	24	−14	Tradition-loving	26	26	0
Musical	26	33	+7	Loyal to family ties	22	35	+13
Ostentatious	26	11	−15	Quiet	13	19	+6
Very religious	24	17	−7	Reserved	17	18	+1
Stupid	22	10	−12	Industrious	18	18	0
Pleasure-loving	—	19	+—				

Trait	Per Cent Checking Trait			Trait	Per Cent Checking Trait		
	1932	1950	diff.		1932	1950	diff.
Jews				Irish			
Shrewd	79	47	−32	Pugnacious	45	24	−21
Mercenary	49	28	−21	Quick-tempered	39	35	−4
Industrious	48	29	−19	Witty	38	16	−22
Grasping	34	17	−17	Honest	32	11	−21
Intelligent	29	37	+8	Very religious	29	30	+1
Ambitious	21	28	+7	Industrious	21	8	−13
Sly	20	14	−6	Extremely			
Loyal to family				nationalistic	21	20	−1
ties	15	19	+4				
Italians				Turks			
Artistic	53	28	−25	Cruel	47	12	−35
Impulsive	44	19	−25	Very religious	26	6	−20
Passionate	37	25	−12	Treacherous	21	3	−18
Quick-tempered	35	15	−20	Sensual	20	4	−16
Musical	32	22	−10	Ignorant	15	7	−8
Imaginative	30	20	−10	Physically dirty	15	7	−8
Very religious	21	33	+12	Sly	12	7	−5
Talkative	21	23	+2				
Pleasure-loving	—	28	+—				

Source: G. M. Gilbert, "Stereotype Persistence and Change Among College Students," *Journal of Abnormal and Social Psychology* 46 (1951): 24. Used by permission.

If capitalists are "greedy" then they are supposed to become more humanitarian in their sentiments in order to shed the stereotype. If Blacks are "lazy" then it is presumed that if they become ambitious and industrious a more positive stereotype will result. (What happens if Blacks become capitalists? We should bear in mind that stereotypes, like prejudices to which they are so closely related, are not highly rational phenomena. Consequently, if people want to hate Blacks they can be hated as conveniently for being capitalists as for being lazy.)

It also is implicitly assumed that a particular group member has some measure of responsibility for the conduct and characteristics of "his" group. When we stereotype a group we seem to expect that there should be some kind of internal discipline in that group. The group should police itself, and "they" should pull themselves up by their bootstraps. Hence one hears talk about "racial pride" which seems to suggest that Blacks should display greater unity and self-improvement. At the same time other groups are criticized for being too "aggressive" and "clannish."

We have noted that stereotypes may contain a grain of truth. It is true that empirically false beliefs can be perpetuated for generations, especially when they have a strong emotional appeal or when they justify some advantage or privilege, but if there is some element of truth in a stereotype it should favor its propagation. In the case of attribution of laziness to Blacks, for example, credence is lent to the belief when one considers the conditions of slavery. There was hardly any point for a slave to be industrious; on the contrary, a clever and ingenious slave would innovate techniques for "soldiering" on the job. Indeed, it does not always "pay" for a Black to be ambitious and aggressive today; his success may bring him more problems than poverty, especially in the deep South. If the school drop-out rate among Black youth is an index of a low level of aspiration, then this could be cited as evidence to support the stereotype. How much of this should be written off as discouragement about prospects for equal employment opportunities is a related question, of course. Then, too, one might ask how many generations does the influence of slavery extend through to depress aspiration?

Stereotypes, we have indicated, tend to be emotionally rigid, like prejudice. This is the principal differentiating factor between the process of stereotyping and the social classification done in the social sciences. Bogardus has made such a distinction, referring to stereotyping as rigid and "sociotyping" as fluid.[22] The latter process is a scientific one, which means that the model of a group or social category is flexible, and probabilistic, and it is revised as new data become available. When sociologists compare criminals and noncriminals it is on a statistical basis, the object being to ascertain the distinguishing characteristics, if any, of criminals. A statistical profile of "the criminal" is developed, but this is something rather different from the popular stereotype of "the criminal."[23]

TOLERANCE-PREJUDICE MEASUREMENT

A rigorous definition of prejudice and tolerance is of limited utility unless it can be applied to the problem of attitude measurement. It is rather academic merely to formulate definitions of tolerance-prejudice without reference to techniques of determining how prejudiced or tolerant people are. Moreover, coming to grips with the problems of measurement should also enhance one's insight into the nature of tolerance-prejudice, since successful measurement necessarily entails an intimate acquaintance with the object under consideration. The definition we have already advanced should facilitate the task of understanding the process of assessing prejudice quantitatively. We have emphasized that prejudice (and tolerance) is a matter of degree and can be either positive or negative in direction. We also have postulated a zero point of prejudice, or maximum tolerance, which is the dividing line between negative and positive prejudice. Similarly, we can apply the continuum concept to the problem of measurement, as we did in demonstrating our definition diagrammatically. In other words, we have already established a conceptual foundation for discussing the measurement of intergroup attitudes.

The measurement of tolerance-prejudice is a special challenge because of the controversial nature of the subject. One cannot simply inquire of people whether or not they are prejudiced and to what degree and expect to obtain valid results. Most of us are not prone to confess our prejudices, even if we are aware of them, and strongly prejudiced persons are not usually possessed of great self-insight.

We should bear in mind that in seeking to measure tolerance-prejudice we are dealing with an *attitude* that one of the chief reasons for our interest in attitudes is that, within limits, they are indicative of overt behavior. Prejudice, for example, is an indicator of discrimination, though it is an imperfect one. Prejudice, like other attitudes, is important in itself, however, quite apart from its relationship to discrimination. We are concerned not only about how we are treated by other people but what they think of us is significant to us also.

Traditionally prejudice has been measured in much the same manner as other attitudes, but the concept of tolerance has not received much attention as far as measurement is concerned. *The emphasis has been on negative prejudice.* By and large the procedure has been to present a series of statements about a particular group, usually derogatory propositions, to which the subject has been asked to respond, favorably or unfavorably. For example, a respondent might be presented with the following statement: "Japanese are ruthless and callous." He would be asked to agree or disagree with this item. It is inferred that agreement with the statement indicates some prejudice against Japanese. It is rather ambiguous, of course, whether or not disagreement reflects a positive prejudice towards Japanese. In other words, scales composed of these kinds of items do not make it possible to ascertain a zero point of prejudice easily.

Intergroup attitude scales can be constructed by various techniques, but the most popular ones seem to be those developed by Rensis Likert, L. L. Thurstone, and Guttman. The following brief scale, for example, was constructed by the Likert method.

Instructions: Read each of the following statements carefully and respond to it by drawing a circle around one of the options at the left of the statement; SA (Strongly Agree); A (Agree); U (Undecided); D (Disagree); SD (Strongly Disagree). Give *your* sincere opinion.

SA   A   U   D   SD   I don't think I would want a Black as a close friend.

SA   A   U   D   SD   Marriage of Blacks and whites should be prohibited by law.

SA   A   U   D   SD   I wouldn't want a youngster of mine taught by a Black teacher.

SA   A   U   D   SD   The Black race is inferior to the white race.

SA   A   U   D   SD   Blacks should not be permitted to swim in the same swimming pools as whites.

SA   A   U   D   SD   Most Blacks would become overbearing and disagreeable if not kept in their place.

These items cover various kinds of social relations as well as beliefs about Blacks. Some students of intergroup attitudes would distinguish between willingness to engage in various forms of social relations and beliefs about the group in question in measuring prejudice. This distinction would correspond roughly to the one we have made between ethical and empirical prejudice. It is possible, as we have pointed out, for a person to have some affection (or hatred) for a group even though he has some mistaken notions about the group. As a general index of prejudice, however, scales containing both kinds of items are highly useful.

The Bogardus Social Distance Scale was designed especially to appraise attitudes towards groups. The concept of social distance seems to embody the feelings associated with prejudice. Social distance might be said to refer to how much social intimacy one is willing to grant to others, or conversely, how much social aloofness one demands in relations with other people. The range of social intercourse stipulated in these scales usually starts with "marriage" and ends with "exclusion from my country." The subject is typically expected to react categorically to the groups specified in the scale. The net result is a rank ordering of groups by the respondent, from the group toward which he expresses the least social distance to the one with which he wishes the least social contact. Bogardus instructed his subjects to check the groups whose members (as a class) they would willingly admit to the following classifications:

1. To close kinship by marriage
2. To my club as personal chums
3. To my street as neighbors
4. To employment in my occupation
5. To citizenship in my country
6. As visitors only in my country
7. Would exclude from my country

These items rather obviously constitute a scale, but one can construct a social distance scale by adapting other scaling methods: for example, one can use the Thurstone method of submitting items to judges. The reliability and "coefficient of reproducibility" of these scales are quite high, which simply means that rarely will a subject agree to have, say, a Mexican as a neighbor but deny citizenship to members of that group. Respondents seem to grasp intuitively that they are expressing their attitudes on a scale and are prone to "cooperate" with it. Scores can be compared over a span of time to determine whether various groups are rising or falling in social favor.

A modified form of social distance scale has been developed by Westie which features a zero point. Known as a Summated Differences Scale, it has been applied to the measurement of the attitudes of Blacks toward whites as well as the attitudes of whites toward

Blacks without any alteration.[24] This device also attempts to overcome the objection of many scales which tend to force the respondent
into a categorical judgment. This instrument asks the respondent if he
would be willing to have such individuals as "a Black lawyer" or "a
white bookkeeper" to "live in my neighborhood" or "as a member of a
veterans' organization" and other scaled social distance questions.
Response options (Strongly Agree, Agree, Undecided, Disagree,
Strongly Disagree) are provided to gauge the intensity of the attitude. The specification of occupation in the items serve to control
the socioeconomic variable. The underlying logic of this instrument is
the experimental logic of the laboratory: with all other variables held
as nearly constant as possible, the impact of one variable on another
is studied. In this case, one variable is the group membership specified in the items (e.g., Black or white) and the other variable is the
response (agreement or disagreement) of the subject with the social
distance statements. If a person agrees with the statement that he
would be willing to have a Black bookkeeper as a neighbor or as a
fellow club member and disagrees with the same statement later in the
scale about a white bookkeeper, then one can logically conclude that
there is a group preference on his part.

The scale yields a summated differences score which is the total net
difference in responses to all the items for the two groups specified.
(It would be possible to assess attitudes toward more than two
groups at the same time by increasing the number of items.) For each
item referring to Blacks there would have to be an identical item for
whites elsewhere in the scale, probably on another page of the scale
so that the subject would not be conscious of the comparative judgment he is making. Thus if a respondent checks "strongly agree" to
an item about a Black lawyer but checks "strongly disagree" to a
subsequent item of a similar nature about a white lawyer, the difference would be scored as 5, and the summated score would simply be
the aggregate of difference for all the items. The score could be anti-
Black/pro-white or anti-white/pro-Black, or a zero summation which
would indicate a lack of group preference. It measures negative and
positive prejudice and can render a zero score if the subject does not
make any group distinctions. Attitudes toward the occupations as
such do not have any effect on the tolerance-prejudice score of course.

The principal advantages of this device are (1) its zero point, which
permits differentiation between positive and negative prejudice; (2)
its ability to measure the prejudices of and toward two (or even

more) groups without alteration; (3) its control of the socioeconomic variable; and (4) its concealment of its purpose to compare responses toward hypothetical individuals whose only visible difference is in group membership. The major objection to this kind of scale is that it is somewhat cumbersome to prepare and requires more time to administer than most other scales. The scoring also is more time consuming, especially if several difference occupations are used in the items and if several areas of social distance are covered, such as residence, personal contact, and political participation. The theory and logic behind this scale are sound, and it would seem to be one of the most objective and effective instruments available today, despite its awkwardness in preparation and application. It is hardly the final word in tolerance-prejudice measurement, but it seems to be a step in the right methodological direction.

Another possible approach to the quantitative assessment of prejudice would be to infer its presence or absence from overt acts. This is complicated by the difficulty of obtaining controlled conditions, and by the fact that acts sometimes mask attitudes as well as reveal them. It is seldom feasible to establish laboratory conditions to observe overt behavior such as group discrimination, though some resourceful researchers have accomplished this. [25] Although we ordinarily assume that attitudes actuate much of our outward behavior, it is well to recognize that occasionally we act overtly in a manner to disguise our inner attitudes. Under social conditions where there are overwhelming pressures to manifest prejudice towards some group, those who are tolerant may not wish to betray their true feelings by their observable actions. Similarly, where there are strong negative sanctions against prejudice it may be advisable to appear outwardly to be tolerant. Nevertheless it is sometimes useful to check *expressed attitudes* against *overt behavior*, and vice versa. This can be done by formulating hypothetical situations and asking subjects to indicate how they would respond. For example:

> You are invited by a friend to go on a blind date. When you meet your date you discover that he (she) is a Black (Caucasian for Black subjects). How would you react to this situation? Check your response below.

> _____1. Walk out in indignation.

> _____2. Excuse myself politely and leave.

_____3. Explain that I am not personally prejudiced against Blacks (Caucasians), but I am opposed to such forms of social contact as dating.

_____4. Be courteous and cordial, but suggest that it would be embarrassing to everybody concerned to go out together in public.

_____5. Be gracious and friendly, but decline any invitation for another date with the person.

_____6. Be gracious and friendly, and judge later whether or not to accept another date with the person.

_____7. Other reaction (specify) _____

_____.

There is the possibility that the subject will not select the same option on the scale item as the behavioral options he would elect in a real situation, but experience would indicate that a high correlation could be expected.

Frank R. Westie and Melvin L. DeFleur undertook to determine the relationship between prejudice and overt acts by comparing prejudiced and unprejudiced groups, matched with respect to social class, sex, age, residential history, religion, marital status, and previous contact with Blacks, in an imaginative experiment.[26] After showing these two categories of (white) subjects photographs of two persons of opposite sex (one Black and one white person) seated together, the respondents were asked whether they would give their written consent to pose for similar photographs for various purposes. They were asked to sign a "standard photograph release agreement" with options which would authorize uses of the photographs to be taken for laboratory experiments only (the most restricted use option), or for more lenient uses. Permission to use photographs for a national publicity campaign to promote racial integration was the most liberal use option. Thus it was possible to compare attitudes (toward Blacks in this case) with overt behavior through the signing of a form which would permit the subject to be photographed with a person of a different race and would authorize use of the photograph according to the degree of restriction or leniency elected by the subject. It was found that eighteen of the prejudiced subjects were below the mean "level of agreement" with only five above the average. Within the unprejudiced category, fourteen were above the mean and nine were below it. These results would seem to demonstrate a considerable degree of consistency between prejudice and overt acts, though there were a number of subjects who showed considerable inconsistency between their expressed attitudes and their actions.

The inference of prejudice from direct observation of "real" behavior has the merit of eliminating the problems connected with "paper and pencil" type scales, and the disadvantage of the subjectivity associated with ascribing motives to actions. One could surmise with some confidence that a participant in a Ku Klux Klan rally would have some prejudice against Blacks, but this is a somewhat cumbersome and inexact method of measuring prejudice, especially if one wishes to subject the attitudes of a number of persons to statistical analysis. The ideal conditions for measurement would provide a situation which was genuine to the participants but contrived by the investigator so that the relevant variables could be controlled. This would be approximated in the case of a minority group member, accompanied unobtrusively by a researcher, entering some public accommodation where prejudice and discrimination might be expected. Some research along this line has been conducted, and it has shown, for example, that discrimination is less likely to occur in face-to-face situations than in more impersonal communications, such as in letters inquiring about reservations.[27] It also has been demonstrated that an expressed attitude can indicate what the person would ideally prefer to do, rather than what he would actually do in a face-to-face situation. In one study letters requesting reservations in public accommodations from a minority group member were ignored or denied on spurious grounds, but the people were accepted as guests when they arrived in person.[28]

Muzafer Sherif, in his experiment in the boy's camp, actually created prejudice by encouraging the development of in-group/out-group distinctions along controlled lines and demonstrated that these conditions could be produced (and also be eliminiated subsequently) under experimental controls.[29] The boys were not aware that they were participating in any kind of scientific experiment, so that their behavior was presumably "natural." There are obviously practical limitations upon this research approach. In Sherif's study, for instance, the research staff had to intervene to prevent violence between the two groups. There are ethical and legal considerations to be taken into account; one can hardly provoke some kind of intergroup disturbance for purposes of scientific study.

Since emotion is an important factor in prejudice, an attempt to gauge this reaction to a group member of some symbolic representation (such as language or photographs) of a group would seem to be logical. An effort has indeed been made along this line by means of a galvanic skin response device. This apparatus measures the physiological concomitants of emotional reactions; the same principle is employed in lie detectors. A study by S. B. Cooper and another by Westie have demonstrated that the degree of emotion aroused by a group is a fairly good index to the degree of prejudice toward the group.[30] Cooper reported that the galvanic skin responses of his subjects, chosen for their highly favorable or unfavorable attitudes toward various ethnic groups, were much stronger for statements (either complimentary or derogatory) about groups toward which they had strong positive or negative prejudices than for statements about groups toward which they had rather neutral attitudes (as measured previously by other means). Westie also found that those with strong prejudices had more pronounced reactions to scenes (photographs) in which persons of different races appeared in various forms of social contact, such as dancing together.[31]

We should not delude ourselves into thinking that it is feasible to construct some kind of apparatus comparable to the polygraph (lie detector) which will enable us to detect prejudice and measure its intensity in a rigorously objective and systematic fashion. Such a device could be useful, however, for checking on the validity of other instruments such as scales, and for testing the sincerity of responses. The limitations of this technique can be realized when one considers that a person may sincerely believe that he is unprejudiced and his emotional-physiological responses tend to confirm it, but he may nevertheless be prejudiced because he has "successfully" deceived himself. Prejudice is evidently not a completely conscious phenomenon. It is coy, elusive, and complex, and it is a vexing challenge to the science of attitude measurement.

Much of the measurement of intergroup attitudes has been concerned solely with prejudice toward a single group. It is difficult to assess prejudice confidently toward a given group without some kind of comparison with attitudes toward other groups. Some people are rather friendly toward all groups, but more favorably disposed to some than others, and some people are rather misanthropic but do not hate all groups with equal intensity. In the measurement of prejudice it is the *differential* preference that is important. It is only by some kind of comparative approach that we can talk meaningfully of positive and negative prejudice toward a group. The Bogardus Social Distance Scale enables us to ascertain the amount of social distance the subject expresses toward various groups, but it does not indicate where negative prejudice ends and positive prejudice begins for these groups. What we would like to know is the degree of positive or negative prejudice of subjects toward a number of groups. With this kind of data we could plot a profile of a person's prejudices, such as the hypothetical example in figure 1.

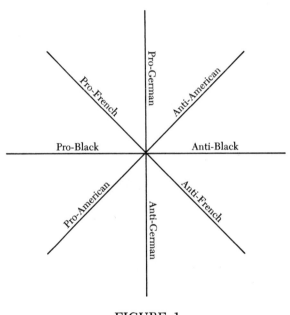

FIGURE 1

In this hypothetical case, our diagram indicates that the subject exhibits negative prejudice against Germans and Americans and positive prejudice toward Blacks and Frenchmen, with varying degrees of intensity. Actually, our present techniques of tolerance-prejudice measurement probably would not allow us to prepare such a precise graphic profile. Ordinary social distance scales would not yield data that would permit plotting scores along a scale with a zero point differentiating positive and negative prejudice. Westie's Summated Differences Scale would be more suitable for this purpose, but it seems to require the juxtaposition of groups for measurement; that is, one would presumably have to compare responses to items about a French Doctor to a German Doctor and so on in order to determine anti-French or pro-French prejudice. The zero point on this scale represents a zero net difference in the responses to all of the paired social distance items about the two groups involved. With more than two groups one cannot establish such a zero point unless one compares the scores of only two of the groups toward which prejudice is being measured. Thus one can say that there is a negative prejudice against the French only in relation to, say, a positive prejudice toward Germans or Americans. When more than two groups are involved we can only describe the rank order of group preferences and we cannot logically specify a zero point of prejudice or social distance. One could compare each group with all the other groups in turn, but this would only inform us as to positive or negative prejudice of the respondent toward the two groups in *relation to each other*.

The foregoing discussion should instruct us that prejudice is a relative concept and consequently we can measure it only in relative terms. We can establish an operational zero point of prejudice in comparing attitudes toward a pair of groups, but a fixed zero point from which we can judge positive and negative toward a single group is unavailable. We do not have a scale for accurately ranking several groups above and below a point of no prejudice, so that we can say that a person is positively prejudiced toward these groups and negatively prejudiced toward those groups, at least with any high degree of confidence. It behooves us, therefore, to view prejudice in the context of the groups being compared. A person may be positively prejudiced toward Mexicans in comparison to Indians but may express a negative prejudice toward Mexicans in relation to Canadians. (To be sure, he can avoid group prejudice by refusing to make judgments of individuals on a group basis, but this is easier said than done in a world where one is confronted with many highly visible group boundaries.) We can only refer to positive and negative prejudice toward particular groups in rather subjective terms, except for the direct comparison of attitudes toward paired groups. It is also somewhat arbitrary to pair groups. Should one gauge attitudes toward Blacks in relation to whites or some other "opposite" group? It is advisable too to take into account that positive and negative prejudice are usually associated with in-group and out-group distinctions, and that there are various levels of this kind of identification, so that American includes Jews. Christian includes Blacks, Southerners include Blacks and whites. The complexity, subtlety, and relativity of prejudice should not cause us to despair about the prospects of accurate measurement of tolerance and prejudice. More sophisticated and refined instruments will almost certainly be forthcoming and should be stimulated by advances in the conceptualization of prejudice.[32] We should not overlook the potential assistance of electronic devices in the construction and refinement of scales. Greater interest is being shown in the problem, and this will eventually pay dividends. Meanwhile, we must be satisfied with imperfect techniques and temper the generalizations and conclusions which they yield about prejudice accordingly.

Notes

1. For example, Mack found that more than 50 percent of Air Force squadrons studied were ranked first in prestige by their own members; R. W. Mack, "The Prestige System of an Air Base: Squadron Ranking and Morale," *American Sociological Review* (June 1954): 281-87. Caplow and McGee reported that 51 percent of 122 university departments were rated by their own department chairman as among the top five in the country. Theodore Caplow and R. J. McGee, *The Academic Marketplace* (New York: Basic Books, 1962), table 5-5. Also see Robin Williams, *Stranger Next Door* (Englewood Cliffs, N.J.: Prentice-Hall, 1964), pp. 17-29 on ethnocentrism.

   The concepts of racism and sexism are discussed in other chapters in this book, but the obvious relationship to our concept of prejudice should be noted in passing. Racism can be usefully regarded as a kind of ideology and broader in scope than a particular group prejudice. The flavor of racism is richly conveyed in the "Kerner Report," Report of the National Advisory Commission on Civil Disorders, 1968, and in Pierre L. Van Den Berghe, *Race and Racism* (New York: Wiley, 1967).

2. See William R. Catton, Jr., and Sung Chick Hong, "The Relation of Apparent Minority Ethnocentrism to Majority Antipathy," *American Sociological Review* 27 (April 1962): 178-90.

3. See Hans Kohn, *The Age of Nationalism* (New York: Harper and Bros., 1962), and *Nationalism* (Princeton, N.J.: D. Van Nostrand, 1955); Boyd C. Shafer, *Nationalism* (New York: Harcourt, Brace and Co., 1955); and Louis L. Snyder, *The Meaning of Nationalism* (New Brunswick, N.J.: Rutgers University Press, 1954).

4. The meaning of the concept of prejudice is also discussed in William Vickery, "A Redefinition of Prejudice for Purposes of Social Science Research," *Human Relations* I (1948): 419-28; H. S. Dyer, "The Usability of the Concept of Prejudice," *Psychometrika* 10 (1945): 219-24; Gordon W. Allport, *The Nature of Prejudice* (Cambridge, Mass.: Addison-Wesley, 1954), pp. 7 ff; and Peter I. Rose, *They and We* (New York: Random House, 1964), chapter 4.

5. Allport, *Nature of Prejudice*, p. 9.

6. Substantially the same definition is discussed by one of the present authors. See James G. Martin, "Intergroup Tolerance-Prejudice," *Journal of Human*

Relations 10, nos. 2 and 3 (1962): 197-204, and *The Tolerant Personality* Detroit, Mich.: Wayne State University Press, 1964), chapter 1.

7. See Oliver C. Cox, *Caste, Class, and Race* (New York: Doubleday, 1948), and "Race Prejudice and Intolerance—a Distinction," *Social Forces* 24 (December 1945): 216-19.

8. Pierre L. Van Den Berghe, "The Dynamics of Racial Prejudice," *Social Forces* 37, no. 2 (December 1958): 138-41.

9. Cf. Martin, "Intergroup Tolerance-Prejudice."

10. See John Fischer, "The Easy Chair," *Harper's*, July 1962.

11. Donald Campbell, "The Generality of a Social Attitude" (Ph.D. diss., University of California, 1947).

12. For further discussion of the concept of stereotype see Maurice Richter, "The Conceptual Mechanism of Stereotyping," *American Sociological Review* 21 (October 1956): 568-71; Forrest LaViolette and K. H. Silvert, "A Theory of Stereotypes," *Social Forces* 29 (March 1951): 257-62; and Allport, *Nature of Prejudice*, chapter 12.

13. Bernard Berelson and Patricia J. Salter, "Majority and Minority Americans: An Analysis of Magazine Fiction," *Public Opinion Quarterly* 10 (1946): 168-90.

14. Allport, *Nature of Prejudice*, p. 191.

15. John Dollard, *Class and Caste in a Southern Town*, 3rd ed. (New York: Doubleday Anchor, 1957), p. 364.

16. Ibid., p. 375.

17. William Buchanan and Hadley Cantril, *How Nations See Each Other* (Urbana: University of Illinois Press, 1953), pp. 51-52.

18. Daniel Katz and K. W. Braly, "Racial Stereotypes of 100 College Students," *Journal of Abnormal and Social Psychology* 28 (1933): 280-90.

19. For a study of Indian university student stereotypes of Chinese see Sri Chandra, "Stereotypes of University Students Toward Different Ethnic Groups," *Journal of Social Psychology* 71 (1967): 87-94. For a study of stereotypical perception of "live persons" (Indians and Canadians) see Anees A. Sheikh, "Stereotypes in Interpersonal Perception and Intercorrelation Between Some Attitude Measures," *Journal of Social Psychology* 76 (1968): 175-79.

20. Unpublished research at Northern Illinois University by James G. Martin. See Gordon W. Allport and Leo Postman, *The Psychology of Rumor* (New York: Henry Holt, 1947), chapter 4, for a similar study.

21. William M. Kephart, "Negro Visibility," *American Sociological Review* 19 (August 1954): 462-67.

22. Emory Bogardus, "Stereotype versus Sociotypes," *Sociology and Social Research* 34 (1950): 286-91.

23. For examples of its application see E. L. Hartley, *Problems in Prejudice* (New York: W. W. Norton, 1949); Katz and Braly, "Racial Stereotypes of 100 College Students"; and Bogardus, "Racial Distance Changes in the U.S. During the Past Thirty Years," *Sociology and Social Research* 43 (1959): 286-90.

24. See Frank R. Westie, "Negro-White Status Differentials and Social Distance," *American Sociological Review* 17 (October 1952): 550-58, and Westie and David H. Howard, "Social Status Differentials and the Race Attitudes of Negroes," *American Sociological Review* 19 (October 1954): 584-91.

25. For examples see Muzafer Sherif and Carolyn Sherif, *Groups in Harmony and Tension* (New York: Harper and Bros., 1953); Frank R. Westie and Melvin L. DeFleur, "Autonomic Responses and Their Relationship to Race Attitudes," *Journal of Abnormal and Social Psychology* 58 (May 1959): 340-47; and Melvin L. Kohn and Robin M. Williams, "Situational Patterning in Intergroup Relations," *American Sociological Review* 21 (April 1956): 164-74. Also, a variety of studies of intergroup attitudes employing various methods may be

found in Herbert H. Hyman, "Social Psychology and Race Relations," in *Race and the Social Sciences,* ed. Irwin Katz and Patricia Gurin (New York: Basic Books, 1969).

26. Melvin L. DeFleur and Frank R. Westie, "Verbal Attitudes and Overt Acts: An Experiment on the Salience of Attitudes," *American Sociological Review* 23 (December 1958): 667-73. For other interesting variations on this same theme see S. W. Cook, "Studies of Attitude and Attitude Measurement," mimeographed (National Science Foundation, October 1966); S. W. Cook and J. J. Woodmanse, "Dimension of Verbal Racial Attitudes: Their Identification and Measurement," *Journal of Personality and Social Psychology* 7 (1967): 240-50; and L. S. Linn, "Verbal Attitudes and Overt Behavior," *Social Forces* 43 (1965): 353-64.

27. Bernard Kutner, Carol Wilkins, and Penny Yarrow, "Verbal Attitudes and Overt Behavior Involving Racial Prejudice," *Journal of Abnormal and Social Psychology* 47 (1952): 649-52.

28. R. T. LaPierre, "Attitudes versus Actions," *Social Forces* 13 (1934): 230-37.

29. Sherif and Sherif, *Groups in Harmony and Tension.*

30. J. B. Cooper, "Emotion in Prejudice," *Science* 130 (1959): 314-18; G. W. Lott and A. J. Lott, "Galvanic Skin Responses and Prejudice," *Journal of Personality and Social Psychology* 5 (1967): 253-59; and Westie and DeFleur, "Autonomic Responses and Their Relationship to Race Attitudes."

31. Melvin L. DeFleur and Frank R. Westie, "The Integration of Interracial Situations: An Experiment in Social Perception," *Social Forces* 38 (October 1959): 17-23.

32. To cite two imaginative examples: Bause D. Cheson, George Stricker, and Charles F. Fry employed subscales of the Minnesota Multiphasic Personality Inventory (MMPI) to explore the relationship between "repression-sensitization" and various measures of prejudice, *Journal of Social Psychology* 80 (1970): 197-200, and Claire Selltiz and Stuart W. Cook analyzed the connection between attitudes toward Blacks and the rating of the plausibility of statements about segregation and integration, "Racial Attitude as a Determinant of Judgments of Plausibility," *Journal of Social Psychology* 70 (1966): 139-47.

Theories of Tolerance-Prejudice

7

As stated in chapter 1, a principal function of theory is to explain empirical data. Theory formulation, however, does not necessarily have to *follow* the accumulation of facts; it may precede collection of empirical data because another function of theory is to guide the search for relevant facts. Typically the formulation of a theory, or theories, does occur after *some* facts are known, when there is a manifest need for some kind of integrated explanation to account for these facts in a meaningful way and to direct the search for additional pertinent data.[1]

In the area of intergroup attitudes we find a number of conceptual frameworks referred to as theories (many of them only partly developed). With the exception of a few notable contributions to the area, most of the explanatory schemes do not conform to prerequisites for a theory. However, there are general approaches salient to tolerance-prejudice and, for the sake of clarity, we will refer to these approaches as theories. Many of these theories purport to give explanations of the same set of facts, but sometimes seem to be in conflict.[2] Upon closer examination, however, these theories are not so much conflicting as complementary. They are not mutually exclusive explanations; it would be more nearly correct to say that they represent differing degrees of emphasis upon essentially the same factors. It is really a question of how much relative emphasis a particular theoretical approach places upon a given factor. For example, the role of personality factors in prejudice may be advanced as the foremost influence in the acquisition of prejudice, or it may be relegated to a secondary consideration.

The lack of a comprehensive, unified theory acceptable to all schools of thought is due in part to the fact that there is no single discipline which has sole responsibility for the study of intergroup attitudes. The area is shared by sociology, anthropology, and even history and economics to some extent, as well as the obvious fields of psychology (and psychiatry) and social psychology. Consequently, several different philosophical perspectives are brought to focus on the problem, and the resulting theories reflect these different viewpoints. It also should be noted that some theories do not clearly delineate between prejudice and discrimination, that is, between the attitude and overt behavior. In many cases it seems to be tacitly assumed that discrimination stems from prejudice almost automatically, and that an explanation of one should also serve to account for the other. This is not an unreasonable assumption, but there are some instances in which the distinction needs to be invoked, as we shall see later.

Some of the theories which purport to explain the facts of prejudice and tolerance have been formulated expressly for the explanation of these attitudes, whereas others represent an application of a more general theory to this specific scientific problem. There are applications of Freudian theory and Marxist theory to intergroup attitudes, for example. The numerous theories offered also vary in scope, some purporting to explain all forms of prejudice while others restrict themselves to attitudes toward a single group.[3]

There are different levels of explanation of any event or phenomenon, and prejudice is no exception. Allport has demonstrated this graphically in the diagram of figure 2. The funnel device is a useful one for depicting "causation" in the behavioral sciences since "multiple causation" is generally assumed to be the rule. The wide mouth of the funnel symbolizes the more general influences producing prejudice, and as it narrows the more specific and immediate precipitants are presented. (One might disagree, of course, as to what the proper sequence of factors should be, as well as to their relative weights in the process.) The several segments of the funnel should be roughly equated with different theoretical emphases or approaches, although these various theoretical viewpoints are not always labeled in the same way.

The exposition of the various theories of prejudice presented later in this chapter will amplify this diagram, although the designation of the different theoretical approaches will differ slightly. We should frankly acknowledge that the "names" of these explanations are subject to a certain amount of variation, though this does not mean that the theories themselves are unstable.

In judging the utility of these theories it is necessary to realize that each theory is obligated to explain not only why some people are prejudiced, but also why others are not. This is why we prefer to

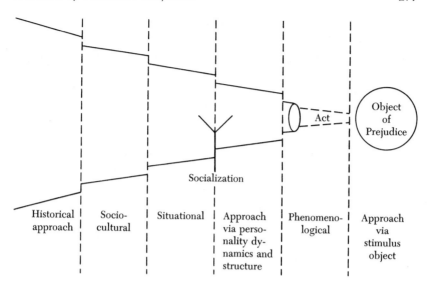

Theoretical and methodological approaches to the study of the causes of prejudice. From Gordon W. Allport, *The Nature of Prejudice*, 1954, Addison-Wesley, Reading, Mass. Used by permission of the publisher.

FIGURE 2

call them theories of "tolerance-prejudice." Likewise, both negative and positive and minority and majority prejudice should be explained. It is legitimate, as we have already implied, for a theory to restrict itself in scope, but if it claims to account for prejudice it cannot logically avoid accounting for the absence of it, too. On the other hand, if one undertakes to explain anti-Semitism, we should not demand that his theory inform us fully about some other form of prejudice.

In all fairness to the theorists in this area, it must be said that prejudice is a complex phenomenon, entailing affectivity, cognition, perception, motivation, and many other variables. We should not be disappointed if its etiology has not been explicated as fully as that of certain diseases, such as malaria or typhoid fever. However, we *should* expect that as knowledge of intergroup relations increases, integrated and explicit *theories* of the phenomenon will be developed.

In evaluating the extant theories of prejudice it behooves us to be at least critical of the content of such theories. This is especially necessary in view of the fact that some of the approaches are partly ideological as well as scientific. Also, there are the almost inevitable biases which stem from professional position; economists and psychiatrists will almost surely proffer somewhat different views on the reasons for prejudice, or the lack of it. With these reservations and insights in mind, let us proceed to examine the major theoretical offerings that are available to "explain" prejudice and tolerance. We will refer to these as "theoretical approaches," for reasons we have previously stated and implied.

THE SOCIOCULTURAL NORMS APPROACH

Since it is rather obvious that prejudice is a learned attitude, and since most attitudes are acquired from our society and culture, it is plausible to argue that prejudice in the individual is cultural in origin. It is quite unusual for a person to develop attitudes which are not to be found in his culture; few persons originate novel attitudes and are hailed as creative thinkers or denounced as heretics. Consequently, it does seem indeed unlikely that most prejudiced persons have innovated the idea; it seems more reasonable to believe that their prejudices have been instilled in them by society or its subgroups.[4]

The essence of this theoretical position is that most cases of prejudice can be adequately explained in terms of social contagion: the individual acquires prejudiced attitudes in substantially the same manner that he forms other attitudes, that is, by absorbing the norms of his sociocultural environment. The socialization process is designed to inculcate within the individual values, attitudes, and habits which society regards as legitimate and proper, and group prejudice is frequently included. Hence prejudice is acquired as "normally" as conventional religious, political, and economic attitudes. If intergroup prejudice does not exist in a society as a cultural tradition, the individual will rarely develop it.

Like other theories, the normative position, as it is sometimes called, offers a particular *level* of explanation. In its case, it does not especially concern itself with describing how a norm of prejudice becomes established in a culture. In other words, it answers only part of the "why?" of prejudice. A more comprehensive answer would include a description of the process whereby the social norm of prejudice evolved. This is the historical approach which Allport presents in his diagram. Depending upon what level of understanding one is seeking, one could claim that the normative explanation is incomplete and insufficient in that it does not fully inform us about how the cultural tradition of prejudice toward a particular group or groups became established in the first place. One may consider this to be an especially important question if he wishes to determine the roots of prejudice in order to eliminate it as a social tradition.

It is incumbent upon a theory of prejudice to account for individual differences with regard to the phenomenon. More specifically, even in areas where it is almost socially imperative to exhibit prejudice, there are invariably a few persons who do not. The explanation offered by this theoretical approach is that there is differential exposure to cultural norms, so that variation in the possession and intensity of the attitude is to be expected. Furthermore, there are subcultural systems with differing norms in complex cultures, so that there will be different patterns of prejudice and individual variation. More comprehensively, differences in prejudice among individuals in the same sociocultural environment can be attributed to a differential susceptibility to prejudice due to personality needs (which are also at least partially learned) and traits. There is an interaction of culture and personality, and presumably some persons are more prone to become prejudiced than others, even with the same degree of exposure to the social norms defining it as proper and desirable. It is supposed that some individuals will succumb to the appeal of prejudice quite readily because it will fulfill important psychic needs for them, while others will be quite resistant to it because it does not perform this kind of personality function for them. This sort of explanation obviously partakes of another theoretical approach, one which emphasizes the psychodynamics of prejudice, which we shall discuss presently. Thus, the sociocultural approach must resort to some supplementary concept to account adequately for individual differences in intergroup attitudes. Otherwise it is haunted by the basic and significant question of why some persons are substantially unprejudiced while others are intensely intolerant.

One of the major ways in which prejudice is acquired from the sociocultural environment is the learning of stereotypes.[5] The culture provides these as it provides other definitions, explanations, and meanings. It is a source of categorical images of other groups which gives the person a definite impression of the group even though he has never come into contact with it. Every culture seems to contain a supply of these ready-made group portraits. They are contained in folklore, literature, and the visual arts; in modern society they are propagated and reinforced by numerous mass media of communication. Stereotypes, as we have previously observed, contribute to prejudice by facilitating group prejudgment; they provide a preconceived image which is the psychological wherewithal for the attitude. One can hardly avoid exposure to stereotypes, any more than one can escape other elements in his cultural heritage. For instance, they are acquired in the course of learning a native language, and one has little choice but to accept them as valid, at least tentatively, unless his own experience contradicts them. Even if such experiences seem not to square with one's own perception of the group in question his perception may be subsequently modified to correspond with the cultural definition. As a result it is not easy, social-psychologically, for a person to reject elements of one's culture—even if such elements are prejudices.

Culture also produces prejudice in the individual by conditioning his definition and perception of groups. It presents a classification system which enables him to identify people by group membership. It designates social categories such as race, class, and ethnicity. Prejudice becomes a *possibility* when a number of people are identified and labeled as a social unity, and it becomes a *probability* when a stereotype is developed to portray them. Under these conditions prejudice is likely to be the rule rather than the exception. Culture points to people, tells us what they are like and why, and indicates what our attitude should be toward them. To ignore or to violate these injunctions is to swim against the current of one's culture.

Although the culture is the general reservoir of intergroup attitudes, social class and family perform a mediating function in the transmission, as the following passage from Lillian Smith's *Killers of the Dream* reveals.

> I knew by the time I was twelve that a member of my family would always shake hands with old Negro friends, would speak gently and graciously to members of the Negro race unless they forgot their place, in which event icy peremptory tones would draw lines beyond which only the desperate would dare take one step. I knew that to use the word "nigger" was unpardonable and no well-bred southerner was quite so crude as to do so; nor would a well-bred southerner call a Negro "mister" or invite him into the living room or eat with him or sit by him in public places.[6]

One can become prejudiced from cultural conditioning in favor of or against groups without ever having any personal contact with the people themselves. Contact with the social norms which require or encourage prejudice is ordinarily sufficient. One does not need to know people to prejudge them. Hartley demonstrated this by including the names of three ficticious groups, the "Daniereans," "Pireneans," and "Wallonians" in a list of actual groups, and discovering that the subjects who exhibited prejudice towards the real groups also prejudged the ficticious ones.[7] He reported a positive correlation of 0.80 between social distance scores for the real groups and the imaginery ones.

The social practice of group segregation (whether due to law or informal social convention) also contributes to the formation of prejudiced attitudes. Segregation heightens the visibility of a group; it facilitates classification of people into a group and perception of them as a unit. By reducing intergroup contact it fosters the formation of social stereotypes. It creates the impression of group differences and tends to magnify them. It is particularly conducive to prejudice when it is involuntary. Social barriers make it difficult to avoid prejudice even when the individual is opposed to it as a matter of principle. He is almost forced into prejudice because of the difficulty of surmounting the social barriers erected by segregation. It is difficult to make friendships, to entertain, to marry, and to engage in many other forms of social intercourse when segregation exists. Often, it is quite awkward for whites and Blacks who are "friends" to enjoy a meaningful relationship, given past and current cutural practices of racial segregation. This tradition also severely limits communication between the separated groups, and consequently tends to promote misunderstandings and tensions. Conflict, which will almost certainly stimulate and reinforce prejudices, is more likely to occur when groups confront each other across boundaries. Prejudice is the handmaiden of segregation; it is almost impossible to eliminate the attitude when groups are required by custom (historical or contemporary) or law to live apart from each other.

Segregation almost invariably means a superordinate-subordinate relationship between the groups involved. This is implicit in the following passage from a prize-winning novel about life among Blacks in the South. The character referred to was a member of the board of trustees of a college for Blacks.

> Wilbur Daniels was fond of saying that no one was a greater friend of the Negro than he was; that is, he would add, providing that the nigger knew his place. The place was clearly defined in his mind, and it resembled nothing so much as an endless assembly line of Negroes he had seen in the movies. He yearned for bosomy mammies with handkerchiefed heads, kindly old family retainers

with gray hair and gnarled black hands bearing trays of frosted
juleps, and erect young chauffers and strong-backed boys who
would gladly lay down their lives for Old Massa Daniels.[8]

Under conditions of segregation these kinds of relationships and attitudes are encouraged. Prejudice is easy to acquire in a segregated
society.

Social structure weighs heavily in the production of prejudice, since
it defines the position and relationships of groups within society. A
group's position within the social structure can be shown to have an
apparently decisive effect on attitudes towards that group by the rest
of society. Historically, the status of "middleman trader" can be cited
as having been linked to prejudice; there are such instances as Christian Armenians, Jews, Indians, Chinese, and other groups in various
countries who have been objects of unfavorable attitudes. This social
role entails a certain visibility, and it may not be a popular one because
of the profit that is made in commerce. Such groups are frequently of
minority size, and if they are also religiously different it is not difficult
to understand prejudicial attitudes towards them. To be sure, this is
not invariably the case; Sheldon Stryker has pointed out the Parsis in
India as an exception to this pattern of prejudice and has suggested
that ". . . a complex of structural and associated value variables—
characteristic of the minority peoples themselves and the host societies
—underlie the appearance of such systematic prejudice and discrimination."[9] Prominent among these may well be political factors, such as the
emphasis upon national unity. The ardent nationalism in Nazi Germany
and the demand for political conformity would be a case in point.

Prejudice seems to be encouraged by a cultural emphasis upon
competition for social status. This makes prejudice an "advantage" in
the contest, in that it can be used to gain status by claiming that
another group is socially inferior to one's own. Often, prejudice is
appealing because it elevates one's social standing. Myths such as racial
superiority thrive under these conditions since they serve to rationalize
a favored social position. As long as competition is on an interpersonal
basis, group prejudice would not appear to be a tool used to differentially stratify persons. In a society with diverse groups, however, it is
difficult to restrict competition to the personal level; there is the
temptation to invoke group distinctions to enhance one's social position.

It is axiomatic that all cultures eulogize themselves. Ethnocentrism is
apparently a universal phenomenon; it exalts the native over the
foreign. In fact, culture itself might be referred to as a "bias." It induces

prejudice not only against foreign cultures and people, but it also defines the status of groups within society. It identifies groups which are low in merit and those which are suitable targets for scapegoating.

Some who espouse the cultural norms theory of prejudice set forth an expanded version of it which includes reasons why the folkways of prejudice originated. This origin is generally explained in functional terms: prejudice is seen as performing certain functions which account for its conception and continuation. The political, economic, and social advantages of prejudice are cited—advantages which have been useful as a device for justifying political power, as in the case of Nazi Germany; as an instrument for economic domination, as in South Africa; as a device of majorities in many societies for gaining social power and general social subordination.[10] When historical or contemporary circumstances combine to produce a situation in which prejudice is conceived and incorporated into the culture, individual contagion of the attitude may persist even after the initial function of prejudice for the society or subgroup has faded. There are social and personal functions which prejudice can perform of course. Socially, prejudice can justify the institution of slavery or some other form of exploitation, and personally it can serve to gratify the ego strivings of an insecure individual. This cultural norms theory then can be expanded or contracted to offer explanations of prejudice of varying scope. By extending it to take into consideration the social roots of prejudice it becomes a broader explanation of the phenomenon.

In sum, according to this theoretical orientation culture is the principal source of prejudice in individuals. However, the theory does not necessarily account for the origins of the sociocultural norms which define prejudice as a legitimate and desirable attitude. Within itself, it does not fully explain individual differences in prejudice; although, in conjunction with the theoretical approach which emphasizes personality factors it becomes a stronger explanatory scheme. Its basic theme is that prejudice is acquired by social contagion; the more saturated the sociocultural environment is with prejudice the more likely a given person will develop the attitude. Prejudice becomes a process of social learning, the internalization of social norms by socialization. It holds that elaborate and complex psychological explanations which dwell on unconscious forces and defense mechanisms are not necessary to explain most cases of prejudice, because prejudice is often a "normal" attitude in the sense of being normative in the sociocultural environment of the person. Prejudice is as easy to explain as any other social attitude which a person learns by "social osmosis" from his culture.

This is the main thrust of the theory, and it is difficult to refute or accept in its entirety. Most other theoretical approaches, as we shall presently observe, grant it some degree of validity.

THE ECONOMIC APPROACH

Economic determinism has many adherents and as a monistic theory it is advanced to explain many social phenomena. Prejudice is no exception. Economic explanations of prejudice assume essentially two forms, namely those which emphasize the role of competition in generating intergroup prejudices and those which regard prejudice as a means and rationalization of economic exploitation. These two emphases are merely two variations on the same theoretical theme and should not be regarded as two distinct theories. The economic competition version is well represented by the writings of Oliver C. Cox, though he also dwells on the idea of exploitation.[11] The exploitation conception is to be found in its "purest" form in Marxist doctrine, though there are non-Marxists who also embrace this thesis.[12] This theoretical orientation is likely to impress and appeal to those who view life in an economic frame of reference; those who believe that bread, profits, or jobs are what "make the world go round," and this includes both communists and capitalists.

The main thrust of the economic competition theory is that different groups view each other as competing for scarce economic rewards and therefore come to employ prejudice (and discrimination) as a means of defense and offense in economic warfare. One group seeks to dominate another by economic weapons; there is economic conflict along ethnic, racial, religious, and other group lines. Black and white workers, for example, supposedly perceive each other not as common members of the working class, but as enemies in the struggle for limited employment opportunities. Each group strives to gain the upper hand and to establish monopolistic rights to the most remunerative jobs. If this can be accomplished, the subordinate group will have to be content with the employment "leftovers"; the low-paying, low-status, menial jobs. They will be "the last hired and the first fired." If there is a labor surplus the dominant group will be protected from unemployment, and even if there is a labor shortage the subordinate group will still get only the less attractive positions. It is a "bread and butter" matter, and prejudice is an effective rationalization for any advantage that can be gained. The competition is encouraged by any group differences which heighten the visibility of the groups. It also is stimulated by an economic system which stresses competition as an economic process.

Cox has expressed the thesis quite succinctly:

> Race prejudice in the United States is the socio-attitudinal matrix supporting a calculated and determined effort of a white ruling class to keep some people or peoples of color and their resources exploitable. In a quite liberal sense the white ruling class is the Negro's burden; the saying that the white man will do anything for the Negro except get off his back puts the same idea graphically. It is the economic content of race prejudice which makes it a powerful and fearfully subduing force. The "peonization" of Negroes in the South is an extreme form of exploitation and oppression, but this is not caused by race prejudice. The race prejudice is involved with the economic interest. . . . Thus race prejudice may be thought of as having its genesis in the propagandistic and legal contrivances of the white ruling class for securing support of its interest. It is an attitude of distance and estrangement mingled with repugnance, which seeks to conceptualize as brutes the human objects of exploitation. . . .

> Race prejudice, then, constitutes an attitudinal justification necessary for an easy exploitation of some race. To put it still another way, race prejudice is the social-attitudinal concomitant of the racial-exploitative practice of a ruling class in a capitalistic society.[13]

This theory certainly has a ring of plausibility when applied to the treatments of Blacks in American society, especially after the end of slavery. It is quite obvious that slavery was a form of economic exploitation of one group by another, but it was only after emancipation that Blacks and whites became direct competitors in the job market. It is true that there was some indirect competition previous to that time, and that the wages of white workers were affected by the existence of slavery. It is often alleged that employers have encouraged competition between the races in the South in order to keep wages low. One of the effective arguments used by employers in dissuading workers from unionizing has been that it would mean having to accept Blacks as "brothers." Another tactic was to hire Blacks as strikebreakers, which made everybody keenly conscious of the racial competition and stimulated prejudice. Charges that labor unions, integration, or FEPC are "communist inspired" have served a similar purpose. In the North, the industrial unions have achieved some degree of success in promoting labor unity and discouraging race identification. In the craft unions, however, it has been a different story, with various unions exercising effective exclusion policies against Blacks. With wages obviously dependent upon labor supply and seasonal unemployment a problem (especially in the building trades), restricting union membership along racial lines has been regarded as an advantage to the racially "in" group.

Other evidence to support the theory can be found in the treatment of American Indians, Japanese, Jews, and other minorities in American society. Prejudice against Indians, conveniently supported by the "savage" stereotype, has been useful in depriving them of land—a great deal of land, in fact. The prejudice seemed to diminish somewhat after those Indians who survived the U.S. Cavalry were restricted to reservations, and the Indian population declined. As one might expect, the reservations were not on the best quality land, but even these were often infringed upon as efforts were made (usually successfully) to deprive Indians of their mineral rights. Today there is hardly any of the kind of prejudice implicit in the saying that "the only good Indian is a dead one," and one even encounters a sentimental, romantic attitude toward them. Perhaps this is because they no longer have any land which can be expropriated and are not perceived as any kind of economic threat.

The Japanese prospered as farmers on the west coast prior to World War II despite some prejudice and discrimination against them.[14] The advent of the war offered an opportunity to their competitors to gain an advantage; 110,000 Japanese, some 70,000 of whom were American citizens, were taken from their farms and homes and sent to "relocation camps" for the duration of the war. In some cases they wound up working on farms for their former competitors. Although there was some restitution after the war, the losses suffered by the Japanese in economic terms were enormous. To be sure, the economic motive was not the only factor operating to produce the internment, but there had been political agitation against them for many years in California by nativist organizations which seemed to be prompted in part by economic considerations. In fact, one can argue with some persuasiveness that the economic factor loomed large in the whole process, directly and indirectly.

Proponents of the economic competition theory can marshall impressive evidence to account for anti-Semitism, both historically and currently. In the U.S., for example, it seems significant that anti-Semitism is often stronger among the middle- and upper-class people in contrast to the pattern of anti-Black prejudice. This could be attributed to the role of business and professional competition. One can hardly deny that there has been systematic exclusion of Jews in many businesses, industries, and professions. This has resulted in the concentration of Jews in certain economic activities that are marginal and frequently high in financial risk, such as small scale retail clothing stores, the salvage and scrap business, the garment industry, and the like. The familiar stereotype to the contrary notwithstanding, the percentage of Jews in finance and heavy industry is disportionately small. Gentiles often display the kind of fear and hostility toward Jewish business competitors that the "native sons" of California displayed toward competing Japanese farmers in the 1930s and 1940s (when the prejudice was at its peak). One of the most frequent defensive arguments advanced for discrimination against Jews in business is that once the group secures a foothold they will proceed to gain control. The ethic implicit in this argument is that group loyalty takes precedence over rational business practices. It also seems to imply that there should be "business segregation," that is, a Christian business world and a Jewish one. Theoretically, in a capitalist system competition should be free, but intergroup prejudice induces attempts to gain monopolistic advantages. The same principle applies to employment, promotions, launching new businesses, but in modern society it is employment and promotion that are of crucial importance. Ownership is "free" in the sense that anybody can presumably buy ownership in the form of shares of stock without discrimination on an exchange, but ownership and control are not necessarily coterminus. Furthermore, consumers may be influenced by group prejudices in their patronage of businesses rather than by rational economic criteria.

The evidence which supports the economic competition explanation of prejudice is indeed impressive and can hardly be completely refuted, but it is an incomplete explanation and it tends to ignore other variables. A major shortcoming is its failure to indicate why there is a competitive relationship between some groups but not others. The people in a line at the employment office could be classified in many (group) ways. Blacks and whites are relatively visible to each other, but so are men and women. We tend to view some people as our economic competitors, but not others, and some competition we resent while some we regard as permissible and even desirable. Furthermore, some people are not prejudiced who would have good reason to be according to this theory. Then there are situations in which prejudice exists but where economic competition does not seem to be present; a possible example of this would be anti-Semitism in the Soviet Union. The theory takes little note of individual psychological differences in the etiology of prejudice nor does it adequately account for differential intensity.

The "exploitation" version of this theoretical approach stresses the profit motive in prejudice; it regards prejudice as an excuse or rationalization for exploiting a group for financial purposes. It is a "mask" for economic (and political and social) privileges; it justifies slavery, low wages, and job discrimination. Racism has been a favorite and effective device for colonialists, and expressed as "the white man's burden" it has even been made to sound noble and magnanimous. The native is supposed to be the beneficiary of paternalism by the colonialist. By stigmatizing a group as "savages" or as "racially inferior," it seems less reprehensible to live off their labor and to appropriate their resources. The exploited are stereotyped as lazy, irresponsible, lacking in thrift, incapable of self-government, and so on by the colonialists.

Behind prejudice, according to this view, is some kind of economic gain; a higher profit, cheaper labor, a larger share of the market, a higher standard of living. In terms of Marxist doctrine, the exploitation is fundamentally a matter of *class* conflict, and race and ethnic prejudice is only the apparent and not the real consideration. The capitalists merely foster this kind of prejudice in order to prevent working class solidarity and to conceal the real basis of the conflict. Worker dissatisfaction can be expressed in the form of hostility or prejudice toward another racial or ethnic group, thus preventing it from being directed toward employers. The capitalist is supposed to be the villain in the whole process with the workers merely innocent victims of a conspiracy.

Economic determinists, Marxian and otherwise, consider political organization and power distribution to be inextricably related to economic structure. Economic domination automatically means political control; so if a group is economically exploited it also will be politically subordinated. There are some theorists who disagree with this viewpoint and argue that, especially in a democratic society, economic relief can be obtained by political means. In cases such as South Africa and Rhodesia, it is rather obvious that there is both economic exploitation and political subjugation. Perhaps the dominant groups in these instances choose to employ political means to sustain economic advantages. To the Marxist, the working class has no real political power because the capitalists control the means of production and the instruments for controlling public opinion. (In evaluating this contention one must recognize that it is a compound of scientific theory and political ideology.) Given political power, economic advantage is usually a concomitant, but the critical question is the relative influence of the two factors in the etiology of prejudice.

The most conspicuous fault of this exploitation thesis is that it tends to be a monistic explanation, disregarding other factors. Its most ardent subscribers are frequently economic determinists who see behavior and society shaped by materialistic forces; hence they are prone to regard intergroup attitudes as a simple function of economic processes. That prejudice or tolerance could be due solely to "bread and butter" factors seems improbable, though in a particular case it might be the dominant influence. Another objection to the theory is that economic gain does not always come from prejudice; in some instances it is patently a liability.[15] Once again, however, we must remind ourselves that prejudice is an irrational attitude, and if people subjectively *feel* that they are better off because of the social distance they insist on maintaining toward various groups, then this is what really counts. A more telling criticism is that this theory simply does not explain adequately many types of prejudice and tolerance. Why is there relatively little prejudice against white sharecroppers in the South? Can the attitudes of Moslems and Hindus toward each other be attributed to economic elements? One must acknowledge that a group which is economically superior to another is likely to show a certain amount of disdain or even contempt, but this does not always mean that it is a prejudice induced by an exploitative advantage. Unfortunately for scientific objectivity, this theory is often applied in tautological fashion, so that whenever prejudice and economic differences are found together it is assumed that prejudice is the dependent variable. It is true that we find prejudice in capitalist, communist, and socialist societies, and during all phases of the business cycle. Consequently, this proposition has considerable validity in explaining the origin and continuation of many forms of prejudice; however, we cannot accept it as the final theoretical word. The influence of economic forces in shaping intergroup attitudes must be ascertained by a dispassionate, nonideological analysis; any affection for a particular economic arrangement or any fear of recrimination for placing the blame on the existing economic system should not condition our conclusions.

THE SITUATIONAL APPROACH

It is debatable whether the situational approach is a theoretical position clearly distinct from the one which emphasizes culural norms. It also pays heed to the influence of social norms, but in a more dynamic way according to its adherents. In any event, it strikes us as sufficiently different in emphasis to warrant separate consideration. The central theme of this approach is that prejudice is not an attitude which is consistently displayed in all social situations; rather, there is considerable variation ranging from scarcely any manifestation to violently overt discrimination. It is misleading to refer to a person as being prejudiced to some particular degree in the sense of a fixed level because he is likely to show considerable prejudice in one situation but relatively little in another.

> Not only do prejudiced attitudes differ widely from one individual to another, but they tend to differ from one situation to another for any given individual. For an attitude is not a thing—it is a process; it is an interaction. It is an interaction involving not only the person and the object, but all the other factors that are present in any situation.[16]

A "prejudiced" individual might not give any evidence of his attitude in interacting with members of another group in a supermarket but could reveal intense hostility towards the same group at a lodge meeting. In the same vein, a person welcomes a member of another group as an employee but would balk at living in the same neighborhood. Moreover, the social distance pattern is often illogical in that it does not follow consistently any rule of intimacy; that is, there may be no objection to having a member of an out-group care for one's children, but there can be vigorous opposition to riding in the same taxi with "them." How the person responds in a given situation is partly determined by cultural influences, partly by how he "structures" the situation, and partly by the collective dynamics which are operating, that is, how the situation is collectively defined by the group or collectivity involved. The attitudes of the individual are of some consequence in defining the situation, but it is difficult to predict accurately how a person will react in a variety of social situations from a score on a "static" attitude scale for measuring prejudice. Each behavioral situation is unique and contains its own dynamic elements; the individual's actions are strongly conditioned by collective forces peculiar to the situation.

Much of our social participation nowadays is as role-playing members of collectivities which provide standardized definitions of situations and rationalizations for various behaviors. Many of these collectivities are of the "deliberately organized" variety and serve as important reference groups for individuals. They often have policies and norms which members are under obligation to follow, so that the attitude of the individual is of rather minor consequence.

> Thus it is more frequently the policy, strategy, and tactics of deliberately organized interest groups, rather than the folkways, rather than the individual dimensions of personal prejudices or racial amity, which control behavior in specific situations.[17]

This is especially so in modern mass society in which the individual has a variety of allegiances and identifications with subgroups rather than a sense of membership in an integrated community or tribe. Intergroup attitudes are not so much a matter of individual predilection as they are a function of definition and structuring of situations by the various collectivities with which we identify and in which we participate. These include organized groups with special interests and informal associations based on common tacit objectives. Since any individual can be expected to have a variety of such memberships and identifications, his behavior towards a racial or ethnic group will vary considerably. This can explain some behavior which appears to be otherwise contradictory, especially if it had been assumed that each person has a given amount of prejudice which is independent of situational factors. The same person who votes for a Black for a union office may vote against admission of a Black to a fraternal organization. It is patently arbitrary to refer to him as prejudiced or unprejudiced in any general sense. As Earl Raab and Seymour M. Lipset put it:

> In short, an individual does not typically have "an attitude" towards Negroes; he has many different attitudes depending on the circumstances.[18]

Melvin L. Kohn and Robin Williams share this viewpoint and claim empirical support for it:

> There is now abundant research evidence of situational variability in intergroup behavior: an ever-accumulating body of research demonstrates that allegedly unprejudiced persons act in a thoroughly egalitarian manner in situations where that is the socially prescribed mode of behavior, and that allegedly unprejudiced persons discriminate in situations where they feel it socially appropriate to do so.[19]

This theoretical position is popular among those who are students of collective behavior in sociology and social psychology. Prominent among these is Herbert Blumer, whose views are suggested in the following passage from a paper on race relations theory.

> Any careful scrutiny of the relations between racial groups compels a recognition of the following points: (1) such relations are the product of a complex number of factors; (2) they are markedly dependent on the peculiar character of happenings and of situations; and (3) they are subject to much change, occasionally approaching pronounced transformation.[20]

Blumer had developed a similar theme in an earlier paper in which he observed that:

> The fact that race prejudice is not a constant accompaniment of race relations, and that it is variable in its nature, indicates that it is a product of certain kinds of situations and experiences.[21]

The advocates of this thesis are quite critical of the concept of prejudice as it has been traditionally applied in intergroup relations. Similarly, they pay relatively little heed to personality factors. Rather, they stress prejudiced *behavior* instead of attitudes, and they point out that there is frequently considerable disparity between a covert attitude and the overt expression of it. According to Raab and Lipset:

> Perhaps the most effective and workable approach to understanding the phenomenon of prejudice is through an investigation of the kinds of *social situations* which give rise to and sustain prejudiced behavior and attitudes. This is a sharply different approach from that which would investigate what kinds of *people* are prone to prejudice.[22]

Prejudice is learned, according to this viewpoint, by involvement in social situations in which there are prejudicial behavior patterns. This prejudiced behavior is situationally learned; the person perceives and participates in the community patterns, such as segregated schools or housing, and various forms of discrimination. He learns when prejudicial behavior is obligatory and when group distinctions should not be made.

The situational approach bears the imprint of "field theory" in psychology; prejudicial behavior is seen as occurring within a particular psychological field, that is, a situation or context. The behavior of the person will depend upon the structuring of the field and the relative weights of the forces that are operating within it. In order to change this behavior and atitude, it is necessary to redefine the social situation for the individual and to change his perception of it so that he will respond in a different manner.

The situational theoretical viewpoint cannot be divorced from an approach to the alteration of prejudicial behavior. In fact, one usually finds that its proponents cite evidence of the elimination of prejudicial behavior as evidence for the validity of the theory. They argue that it is not necessary to change "attitudes" in order to modify behavior, because there is an imperfect correlation between attitudes and actions, and attitudes often "follow" behavior rather than "precede" it.

The desegregation of restaurants in Washington, D.C., was not due to a campaign to persuade the residents to abandon their group prejudices; rather it was accomplished effectively "in one fell swoop" by the court decision which declared such discrimination illegal. The situation was suddenly and completely restructured so that Blacks were no longer to be refused service in the city's restaurants. Behavior was changed overnight but presumably there was no corresponding wholesale change in attitudes: the situation was merely redefined so that everybody—restaurant owners, waiters, customers—was obligated to behave differently in the restaurant situation. If this form of segregation were simply due to the mores, it is hardly likely that the behavior could have been reversed so suddenly.

The remedy for prejudiced behavior, then, for those who embrace this theory, is social action which will redefine or restructure behavioral situations in such a way that it will no longer be considered appropriate to discriminate. (These theorists tend to use the phrase "prejudiced behavior" to refer to what others normally label "discrimination," because they do not make a sharp distinction between prejudice as an attitude and overt behavior which is discriminatory. This is consistent in terms of their theoretical posture.) The process should not be piecemeal, equivocal, or gradual; if a community wishes to desegregate its educational facilities it should announce its decision in an authoritative manner, indicating that this is now the law and official public policy, that it will take effect on a particular date, and that the new policy will be firmly enforced. It is assumed that this will have the effect of defining the educational situation as one in which one is not supposed to act in a prejudiced manner. This strategy, it should be noted, presumably does not call for an attempt to eliminate prejudiced behavior in all areas of social contact at the same time. Rather, it seems to favor a situation by situation approach, but it is certainly not identified with a "gradualism" viewpoint. This does not mean that there is not prior planning for the transition by those concerned with promulgating the policies and enforcing them, but the psychology of the *fait accompli* is a strong element in the strategy.

There is also present an overtone of social action in this position. Its subscribers are fond of pointing to examples where its application has effected a sudden and dramatic change in behavior patterns. Such an example would be President Truman's executive order ending segregation in the military. A tradition of segregation was suddenly halted by an order which redefined behavior in the military situations; segregation was no longer the acceptable pattern. There was no grandiose indoctrination program to eliminate prejudice attitudes, and outside the military situation many members of the armed forces followed other behavior patterns in which prejudice was expected, but racial distinctions were no longer standard operating procedure within the military context.

An underlying assumption of this approach is that most persons will follow a pattern of behavior in a situation that is prescribed for them by some kind of authority or authoritative suggestion. There may be a few rebels or nonconformists, but the vast majority will go along with what appears to be the officially sanctioned behavior for a situation. It is not necessary to convert each individual to a new attitudinal position in order to change the behavior of the whole group or community; this would be very inefficient. By altering the structure of the situation, the collective behavior can be changed, and after this has been accomplished attitudes can be expected to adjust to the new behavior patterns. Once the scales of behavior have been tipped in a new direction by a new social policy declaration, it is supposed that the majority will conform to the new norm.

Even the most enthusiastic proponents of this social action strategy admit that there are limits to its application. Public opinion operates as a brake on radical changes in public policy by legislators, executive orders, and even court decisions. There is a point at which resistance to a new definition of situational behavior will prevent its implementation. The advocates of this action strategy argue that it is usually advisable to attempt to change one situation at a time, so that the new policy will not be resisted so vigorously. The general public is not likely to challenge all legal authority to resist change in one area of intergroup relations. It is considered important not to have to retreat from an announced change or to equivocate, since this encourages opposition.

In the long run, of course, there must be some larger collectivity which supports the new policy, whether it is world public opinion, the national government, or the state government. Also, there must be a certain amount of bold and dynamic leadership for such programs to succeed.

It might be disputed whether the situational approach is really a theory of prejudice, since it seems to concentrate more on what other students of intergroup relations would call discrimination. This criticism is mitigated somewhat by the fact that the most important reason for studying attitudes is to be able to predict overt actions. It is weak on accounting for the origins of prejudice and indicating why certain groups are prime targets. Furthermore, it does not explain fully individual differences in intensity of intergroup attitudes. It does suggest that membership or identification with various interest groups affects reactions to other groups, but the questions of why and how these different groups are formed and why and how individuals come to affiliate or identify with them is a more involved question. One must grant that the theory is instructive for purposes of changing patterns of prejudiced behavior by social action, though it is by no means a magic formula for that, as current violations of the "law of the land" would attest. Its validity and utility seem to be greater when it is applied to mass society, wherein behavior is greatly affected by reference group attachments and situational factors, a condition which is increasingly characteristic of human existence.

THE PSYCHODYNAMIC APPROACH

Prejudice and tolerance also can be explained in terms of factors that operate primarily within the individual. This theory does not necessarily overlook culture as the basic seedbed of prejudice, but it emphasizes psychic processes in the individual in accounting for the acquisition of prejudice.[23] There is some lack of accord as to the designation of this theoretical emphasis; one can find reference to the "scapegoat theory" and to the "frustration-aggression theory," and even to a "prejudice and personality theory." For convenience of analysis we shall adhere to the designation of "psychodynamic approach" although it is patently arbitrary. The various shades of emphasis which center around this approach will be described and illustrated.

Perhaps the most common formulation of this theory is the one which views prejudice as something of a mechanism for ego defense. According to this version the attitude is due to the effort of an individual to compensate for some psychic insecurity or anxiety on his own part. The prejudiced person thrives on his prejudice because it is a means of relieving and covering his own frustrations and shortcomings. Hence he employs minority groups as an outlet (scapegoat) for his pent-up hostilities. Instead of blaming himself for his failures and dissatisfactions he is prone to *project* the blame on a convenient scapegoat group. Projection is an unconscious ego defense mechanism; therefore, a person cannot be expected to be aware of the process. The researchers who authored *The Authoritarian Personality* (and who embraced a psychodynamic theory which has a strong Freudian flavor) referred to "extropunitiveness" as a trait common among their prejudiced subjects. This means essentially the same thing: people are inclined to assign blame for their frustrations and problems to others rather than themselves. The more tolerant subjects in the study were more frequently "intropunitive"; that is, they tended to find fault with themselves under similar conditions.

This theoretical orientation embodies the concept of "frustration-aggression" which was developed at the Yale Institute of Human Relations and which John Dollard applied in a classic study of Black-white relations in the South.[24] It regards prejudice as essentially a form of aggression, which is an almost automatic response to frustration. It does not always follow, however, that the real source of the frustration will be the object of the person's aggressions. The aggressive behavior, which can assume many forms, can be expanded on a substitute object. In Freudian terms, *displacement* occurs; that is, the person unconsciously vents his hostility against some other object. Experimental studies have supported this theory: subjects in a boys' camp exhibited greater prejudice on a scale when they were prevented from attending movies.[25]

In a hypothetical case of prejudice, Mr. Smith, a businessman whose business has failed (*frustration*), expresses hostility (*aggression*) towards Greeks (*scapegoat*) because he blames them (*displacement*) for his predicament. He attributes his failure to unethical practices on the part of Greek competitors (*projection*), although he is guilty of such behavior himself and is unconsciously ascribing this to Greeks. To be sure, there are real cases in which an individual is persecuted by a group and he can legitimately hold them responsible, but we are referring to those instances where the prejudiced person seeks to avoid blame by accusing a scapegoat group for his troubles.

Historically, there are numerous familiar examples of the process this theory describes. Religious groups have often been the subjects of such attentions, partly because of their visibility. The early Christians were often blamed by the Romans for various social problems, and they were sometimes forced into the arena with hungry lions as punishment. Catholics and Protestants have served as scapegoats for each other in many historical instances. One could safely say that there is hardly any major social group which has not been used as a scapegoat at some time or other. In some cases, however, there has been a persistence of abuse directed against one particular group which almost defies rational explanation, as in the case of the Jews. They have, seemingly, been an "ideal" scapegoat group throughout history. Since they have always been a rather small minority, attacking them has not been especially dangerous, and because Jews have not been a national minority in most instances, they have not been afforded the protection of a "home nation," as have many other ethnic groups in foreign societies.

The most obvious limitation of this psychodynamic approach is the matter of "choice" of the scapegoat or target of aggression. As Bohdan Zawadzski has reminded us, in a critique of the theory, not all objects of prejudice are necessarily victims of scapegoating in the traditional sense of the term. Some groups are better suited for scapegoats than others.[26] The prejudiced person cannot attack groups indiscriminately with impunity. It would be inadvisable for a Soviet citizen to blame the Communist party for shortages of consumer goods. In the United States, on the other hand, there is hardly any risk in blaming communists for any problem. One must be careful to choose a "safe" group, as McWilliams points out.[27] It is rather obvious that the identification of appropriate targets for venting our spleen is provided by the culture; it informs us, though often in subtle terms, what groups can be saddled with blame for our personal frustrations and social ills.

An interesting application of this theoretical approach to anti-Semitism highlights the problem of choice of a scapegoat. It has been suggested that prejudice against Jews is the result of displaced hostility towards capitalism. According to this view Jews are a symbolic substitute for capitalism. Resentments which could not be conveniently expressed against the economic system—because the person consciously approves of the system or because of the hazards of criticizing it—can be channeled instead against Jews, who can be stereotyped as capitalists. Hence, if one is contemptuous of Jews because he regards them as "profiteers," he has an outlet for any unconscious hostility he harbors toward capitalism without exposing himself to the negative sanctions which might be forthcoming for attacking the system directly. Thus his "choice" of a scapegoat group is made in part because of cultural influences and in part because of unconscious forces in his own psyche.

The psychodynamic theoretical approach to prejudice is a sophisticated and plausible one, and yet it is not a complete explanation, as we have already noted. It does not, in itself, explain why a person vents his pent-up aggressions against a particular group, nor does it tell us, in itself, why some groups are such attractive targets while others seem to be immune. Another possible weakness is the almost exclusive emphasis upon the prejudiced person, ignoring the group-object of prejudice. It tacitly assumes that the attitude is substantially independent of the group-object. The prejudiced person argues vigorously to the contrary of course; he claims that his hatred of a group is due entirely to the characteristics and behavior of "them." We should be skeptical of comments from this quarter, but scientific objectivity requires us to consider the possibility that there is some validity in the proposition that prejudice is due to the nature of the group-object. The theoretical orientation under consideration virtually excludes any such idea, and yet we can hardly deny that groups do differ, at least in relative frequency of characteristics. A complicating factor in the analysis is that some "offensive" (a subjective word, we must remember) traits may be due to past prejudice and discrimination. The response to this criticism by the adherents of the theory is that a scapegoat group is "a living inkblot" which, like the Rorschach projective test in clinical psychology, can be perceived and interpreted in accordance with the dynamics of the subject's personality. This poses the question of whether groups can escape prejudice by changing their behavior and characteristics. Could Jews reduce the prejudice against them by migrating to rural areas and by switching to a different occupational pattern? Would there be less prejudice against Blacks if they were more affluent? It seems plausible to conclude that this would occur, but when one examines the reasons given for dislike of groups by prejudice people, one is impressed with the contradictions and irrationality of them. It is not at all unusual for a person to dislike one group for its alleged economic success and another for its lack of ambition. It is well to bear in mind, in this connection, that prejudice is partly an irrational attitude, and that we cannot reasonably expect prejudiced people to be rational and consistent. This fact complicates the problems of theory formulation.

The psychodynamic theoretical approach to prejudice necessarily involves an emphasis upon personality factors in the etiology of the attitude. Most versions of the theory claim, in effect, that certain persons are predisposed to prejudice because of their personality structure and dynamics. Some persons are more prone to acquire prejudice because of certain personality characteristics which render them susceptible. The critical traits would be those which would cause the person to experience frustration and to attempt to cope with them by the expression of aggression against scapegoat groups. It is implicitly assumed that certain personality "types" exist for whom prejudice has a very strong appeal, and conversely, for whom it is distasteful. In some individuals prejudice seems to perform the function of bolstering the ego or giving a sense of social esteem, while in others being tolerant apparently gives personal satisfaction. People do vary considerably in their toleration of frustration as well as the amount which they actually encounter. There also is considerable variation among different personalities in the way they react; some display direct aggressive behavior, some tend to repress and inhibit, and others may engage in socially constructive behavior to consume the energies aroused by frustration. To understand the dynamics of prejudice, therefore, this theory counsels us to explore the personality in order to discover why some people thrive on prejudice and others find it repulsive.

The relationship between intergroup attitudes and personality is a significant one apart from the question of a functional connection. Consequently, we will devote an entire chapter to examining it (chapter 8). Suffice it to say at this point that the personality differences which exist between the prejudiced and the tolerant are of considerable interest to us and can be quite instructive about the nature of prejudice even if these differences are related only in a correlative way as distinct from a cause and effect connection. We shall analyze the personality differences between the strongly prejudiced and those substantially disinterested or tolerant in their attitudes at some considerable length in the next chapter, and in the process we will necessarily reconsider the psychodynamic theoretical approach to prejudice.

THE "WELL-DESERVED REPUTATION" APPROACH: THEORY OR RATIONALIZATION?

This is an utterly simple theoretical approach to prejudice; it asserts that if prejudice is expressed toward a group it is merely due to the reputation which the group has "earned." There is a perfect correlation, so to speak, between attitudes towards a group and the behavior of that group. If it is "well behaved" it will not be the object of prejudice, and any group which suffers prejudice must have done something to deserve it. In the same vein, the stereotype of a group is regarded as an accurate image of that group. Prejudice is not the fault of the prejudiced person, but rather of the group-object. Prejudice is viewed as some kind of infallible folk wisdom which does not make errors in judgment of groups. Consequently, groups which are the object of prejudice do not deserve any sympathy; their treatment is just. In order to understand prejudice it is necessary to study the group-object rather than prejudiced people.

To put it in terms of our distinction between ethical and empirical forms of prejudice, those who espouse this theory claim that prejudiced people are not guilty of empirical prejudice and that the ethical judgment is consistent with the ethical principles of society governing such judgments. The prejudice is an accurate judgment and it is also a fair one in terms of prevailing ethical standards. If people wish to avoid being the object of prejudice they should reform their groups and then others would automatically change their attitudes toward them.

This approach stands in sharp contradiction to psychodynamic theories which emphasize the role of frustration and scapegoating, and regard prejudice as an emotionally distorted and irrational attitude. The "well-deserved reputation" theory holds that "prejudice" is something of a misnomer for unfavorable attitudes toward groups, because these attitudes are reasonable and fair judgments. One approach assumes that the phenomenon is essentially due to errors in perception and cognition on the part of the individual, whereas the other assumes that it is an accurate assessment of the faults and misbehavior of the group. Bohdan Zawadzski has reminded us that both of these explanations cannot be completely correct.

> It seems obvious that, while both the "well-earned reputation" theory and the "scapegoat" theory are *monistic*, onesided, and therefore unsatisfactory, a theory that would give a complete answer to the problem of origin of prejudice must be a *dualistic*, *"convergence"* theory which would take into account both the internal factors within the individual (his drives and needs) and the objective characteristics of the stimulus and object of his reaction, i.e., the minority group. This statement does not imply that the two sets of factors producing prejudice should be assigned equal weight. It is most probable that if the "forces" producing

prejudice could be measured and reproduced in a parallelogram
of forces the "objective vector" would be smaller than the one
representing the subjective factors. Nevertheless, the objective factors do exist and should be investigated as well as the subjective
ones.[28]

As one might expect, this theoretical approach is strongly favored
by those who would be defined as prejudiced by other theories, though
not all of its advocates are necessarily strongly prejudiced. This invites
the suspicion that it is as much a rationalization of prejudice as it is an
explanation of it, especially since it absolves the "prejudiced" people
of any blame for their group antipathy. Consequently, social scientists
generally give little credence to the thesis, though they are not inclined
to reject categorically the idea that the characteristics of a group have
some influence on the attitudes that exist toward it, even though these
traits may be unevenly distributed and due to previous discrimination,
and some members of the group may be unimpeachable with respect
to "proper" characteristics.

One of the problems in the application of this theory is defining
what constitutes objectionable or obnoxious traits in a group. In its
simplest form, the theory deals with the matter in a tautological
fashion, that is, it recognizes the contentions of "prejudiced" people
as correct on the subject; whatever they claim to be "objectionable"
must indeed be so. This really only begs the question, of course, because it is a self-verifying proposition. It is apparent that there is
vigorous disagreement as to what traits and actions are obnoxious,
and that there is considerable inconsistency in applying these judgments. In the final analysis, what traits are obnoxious is rather subjective and a matter of value judgment. Subtle semantic distinctions may
mislead us; the in-group is "proud" and the out-group is "arrogant,"
our religious group is "pious and devout" while "they" are "superstitious and fanatic." Still, there are real differences between groups,
as well as fancied ones, and there are surely honest and sincere differences in values, tastes, and ethics which result in different judgments.
One group may prize a stoic, benign, composed behavioral posture,
and another may genuinely place a premium on expressiveness, flam-
boyancy, and extravagant gestures. The theory under discussion seems
to imply, however, that there are certain differences which are uni-
versally and intrinsically despicable. This may be so at an abstract
level; we can all agree that something called "rudeness" is irritating and

improper conduct, but there is lack of accord on the meaning of rudeness and what groups are guilty of rudeness. It also tacitly assumes that groups are rather homogeneous in traits.

The most glaring defect of this explanation of prejudice is that it fails to account for negative cases, or tolerance; why don't some people despise unpopular minorities? Even the most oppressed group is admired by some people; there is no group which everybody dislikes, not even Gypsies, who have suffered considerable mistreatment as a perennial out-group, or gangsters, who are sometimes regarded with a kind of romantic admiration. The well-deserved reputation approach does not tell us why some people are hostile toward a group while others are rather friendly toward it. To do this one would have to redefine and elaborate the theory, pointing to the role of differential contact, experience, and exposure to a group and its reputation. It is not a sophisticated theory, and as it is popularly applied does not pay much attention to the subtleties of prejudice and tolerance. The trend in intergroup attitudes theory in recent times has been away from an emphasis upon the study of the group object, and scholars in the field are generally unfavorable to explanations which focus on the "faults" of minorities.

It would be unscientific and naive to ignore or reject this approach completely because it is a "popular" one and is the favorite of those people who are obviously strongly prejudiced by any other standard. This would be comparable to rejecting the scapegoat theory, as the favorite of the victims of prejudice, because it tends to absolve groups of responsibility for prejudice against them. In order to determine whether or not the accusations of the prejudiced about a group are valid, it is patently necessary to study the group in question as well as the prejudiced themselves. We cannot afford to ignore either variable, although experience has taught us that there is considerable distortion in the perception of these groups by prejudiced people. The matter becomes quite complicated when one takes into account the influence of stereotyping on groups and the possibility of the operation of the "self-fulfilling prophecy" phenomenon. We must make allowance for the possibility of a group assuming, perhaps unconsciously, some of the traits which are constantly attributed to it by means of the stereotype. Can people be influenced in their behavior by accusations and allegations? Do some people merely capitulate and conclude that if they are going to be blamed for certain reproachful actions and traits anyway, they might as well enjoy them?

This theory is not easy to test. Its proponents and critics cannot agree on what would constitute adequate evidence. Also, there are sharp differences of opinion as to why a trait or rate of behavior prevails within a group. For example, there are differences among racial and ethnic groups in crime rates, but there are many possible explanations. The differences could be due to some other variable, such as economic status rather than race or ethnicity per se, or they could be partly the result of discrimination in law enforcement, job discrimination, residence in slum areas, or prejudice. The argument rages over whether the higher crime rate is largely the fault of the group or is the result of circumstances which the group has little power to control. Consequently, it seems unlikely that this theoretical approach will be validated or refuted to the satisfaction of both its advocates and critics.

OTHER THEORIES

Still other theories have been formulated to explain particular forms of prejudice. As a case in point, there is a theory of anti-Semitism, advanced by Maurice Samuel, which explains this prejudice as a symbolic rejection of Christ.[29] The Christian who is anti-Semitic supposedly vents hostility toward Jews because they symbolically represent Christ, whose teachings cannot be accepted and followed because these require compassion, love, tolerance, self-denial, and so on. They cannot bring themselves to reject or attack these noble standards or Christ consciously, but by the unconscious process of displacement, they can hate Jews who can be conveniently substituted (unconsciously, presumably) for Christ since he was a Jew. Samuel refers to this as "Christophobia," a logical term since it is an irrational process. These anti-Semites usually profess, at the conscious level, subscription to Christian principles and beliefs, but unconsciously they cannot abide them and so they scapegoat Jews who remind them of Christ and Christianity. Hence their ambivalence toward Christ and Christianity is accommodated. It is an interesting theory, but difficult to confirm conclusively.

A somewhat more complicated theory of anti-Semitism was developed previously by Freud, from which Samuel's theory is apparently derived.[30] Freud suggested that anti-Semitism had its roots in the crucifixion of Christ as a symbolic act intended to expiate guilt that ensued from the previous killing of Moses. Moses was identified with a stern and repressive God, and after he was assassinated feelings of guilt arose. The crucifixion of Christ, according to St. Paul (as interpreted by Freud), defined this as an effort to expiate this guilt, since Christ was the son of "God the father." That is, Christ gave his life as punishment, but the Jews who followed Christ, and later St. Paul (the Christians, in other words), would not forgive the killing of Moses or accept the sacrifice of Christ as an act of redemption for the death of Moses. Hence those Jews who became Christians persisted in their hostility toward those Jews who did not. To appreciate the full significance of this theory one must have considerable understanding of the concepts of myth, unconscious guilt, symbolism, and many other Freudian ideas as well as insight into the origins of Christianity and its relationship to Judaism.

The various theories that have been advanced to explain particular forms of prejudice can generally be subsumed under the general theoretical categories we have already described, although there are some explanations which incorporate elements from more than one of these categories. These general theories can be applied to many different forms of group prejudice, usually with little adaptation necessary.

Attempts have been made to develop an "integrated" or "synthesized" theory of prejudice, but the results, as one would expect, have not proved satisfactory to all theoretical tastes; there is too much disagreement as to what the proper proportion of the various theoretical ingredients should be. Additionally, as pointed out earlier, at best the offerings have been conceptual frameworks with little predictive, explanatory, or controlling power. Ideally, we would eventually be able to develop unified, well-integrated, and parsimonious theories of intergroup relations which could be subjected to empirical test. Undoubtedly, then we will be able to specify the relative influence of the different theoretical approaches outlined in this chapter.

Notes

1. Cf. Robert K. Merton, "The Bearing of Empirical Research upon the Development of Sociological Theory," *American Sociological Review* 13 (October 1948): 505-15.
2. See Frank R. Westie, "Toward Closer Relations Between Theory and Research: A Procedure and an Example," *American Sociological Review* 22 (April 1957): 140-54, for a discussion of the relationship between theory and empirical evidence in the area of prejudice. Also Hubert Blalock, *Toward a Theory of Minority-Group Relations* (New York: Wiley, 1967), and John Rex, *Race Relations and Sociological Theory* (New York: Schocken Books, 1970).
3. See Westie, *Toward Closer Relations Between Theory and Research.*

4. For an excellent explication of this position, see James Vander Zanden, *American Minority Relations*, 3rd ed. (New York: The Ronald Press, 1972).

5. See the discussion of stereotypes in chapter 6.

6. Lillian Smith, *Killers of the Dream* (New York: W. W. Norton, 1949), p. 19.

7. Eugene L. Hartley, *Problems in Prejudice* (New York: Kings Crown Press, 1946).

8. Bucklin Moon, *Without Magnolias* (New York: Doubleday, 1949), p. 90.

9. Sheldon Stryker, "Social Structure and Prejudice," *Social Problems* 6 (Spring 1959): 352.

10. See Vander Zanden, *American Minority Relations*, chapter 7.

11. See Oliver C. Cox, *Caste, Class and Race* (New York: Doubleday, 1948).

12. The Marxist viewpoint is well stated by Herbert Aptheker in his *The Negro People in America* (New York: International Publishers, 1946). Also, see Carey McWilliams, *A Mask for Privilege* (Boston: Little, Brown, 1948).

13. Cox, *Caste, Class and Race*, p. 475.

14. For a detailed account see Leonard Bloom and Ruth Riemer, *Removal and Return* (Berkeley: University of California Press, 1949), and E. V. Rostow, "Our Worst Wartime Mistake," *Harper's*, September 1947.

15. See Norval Glenn, "White Gain from Negro Subordination," *Social Problems* 14, no. 2 (Fall 1966): 159-78.

16. Earl Raab and Seymour M. Lipset, "The Prejudiced Society" in *Racial Conflict*, ed. Gary I. Marx (Boston: Little, Brown, 1971), p. 33.

17. Ibid.

18. Ibid.

19. Melvin L. Kohn and Robin Williams, "Situational Patterning in Intergroup Relations," *American Sociological Review* 21 (April 1956): 164.

20. Herbert Blumer, "Reflections on Theory in Race Relations" in *Conference on Race Relations in World Perspective*, ed. Andrew Lind (Honolulu: University of Hawaii Press, 1955), p. 9.

21. Herbert Blumer, "The Nature of Race Prejudice," in *Race*, ed. Edgar T. Thompson and Everett C. Hughes (Glencoe, Ill.: The Free Press, 1958), p. 485.

22. Raab and Lipset, "The Prejudiced Society."

23. The classic work in the area is T. W. Adorno et al., *The Authoritarian Personality* (New York: Harper and Bros., 1950).

24. John Dollard, *Caste and Class in a Southern Town* (London: Oxford University Press, 1937).

25. John Dollard, Neal Miller, and Leonard Doob, *Frustration and Aggression* (New Haven, Conn.: Yale University Press, 1939), p. 43.

26. Bohdan Zawadzski, "Limitations of the Scapegoat Theory of Prejudice," *Journal of Abnormal and Social Psychology* 43 (1948): 127-41.

27. McWilliams, *Mask for Privilege*.

28. Zawadzski, "Limitations of Scapegoat Theory," p. 25.

29. Maurice Samuel, *The Great Hatred* (New York: Alfred Knopf, 1940).

30. Sigmund Freud, *Moses and Monotheism* (London: Hogart Press, 1951).

Tolerance-Prejudice and Personality

8

Whether or not prejudice or tolerance is a *function* of personality factors is debatable, but it is difficult to deny the significance of personality differences between tolerant and prejudiced persons. One does not need to subscribe to a theory of intergroup relations which views attitudes as essentially the product of personality dynamics to agree that it is worthwhile to study the personal and social characteristics which differentiate tolerant and prejudiced people; furthermore, it is not necessary to assume that these differences in personality characteristics are directly due to being prejudiced or tolerant.

It should be instructive to examine how these two categories of people differ; this should aid us in judging the validity of the various theories discussed in the previous chapter. The data on personality differences have obvious relevance for the psychodynamic approach, but they can also be revealing for other theoretical viewpoints, at least indirectly. If we should discover that strongly prejudiced people have pronounced paranoid tendencies, for example, this fact would be quite significant in assessing the validity of the "well-deserved reputation" theoretical approach. It would suggest that the source of the prejudice might be the irrational suspicions and judgments of the prejudiced people.

Thus we shall address ourselves to the task of studying the personality differences that have been discovered by research and clinical analysis. In addition to examining the data, we will also consider the theoretical implications of these findings. In large measure, this will entail a consideration of the alleged personality function of tolerance and prejudice. It is perhaps unfortunate that most of the research and theorizing has focused on the prejudiced person to the extent that much of our knowledge of the tolerant personality is inferential.

PERSONALITY FUNCTIONS OF TOLERANCE AND PREJUDICE

One of the basic assumptions of researchers who have investigated the personality characteristics of prejudiced people is that prejudice is intimately and functionally related to certain personality traits; indeed, that there is a particular constellation or syndrome of traits which characterizes such persons. A corollary assumption is that the possession of certain personality traits renders the individual more or less susceptible to the formation of prejudice. It also seems to be tacitly assumed that the possession of prejudice itself will tend to favor the acquisition of certain other traits and attitudes, though ordinarily it is the other way around.

What functions does prejudice perform for the personality? In general, it is theorized that it fulfills certain psychic needs or satisfies various social psychological motives. There is some difference of opinion as to whether these needs are essentially innate or are partly or mostly social and acquired. Is there an inherent psychic need or drive for recognition or esteem or is this primarily acquired through socialization? Is it possible to disagree on this subsidiary issue and still subscribe to the view that prejudice is attractive to individuals because it serves certain functions in the personality? Stated in general terms, the most common conception of the role of prejudice in personality is that it is ego enhancing; that is, it enables the individual to regard himself as superior to other groups. It gives him something of a guaranteed status, in that his mere membership in his in-group insures his social superiority over the whole out-group. Prejudice, supposedly, is almost irresistible to persons whose egos *require* this kind of support; it might be said to relieve their status anxieties. To say that prejudice serves to allay anxieties about social status is to admit tacitly, of course, that the function is partly social.

Some people are especially prone to prejudice, some are strongly resistant to it, and others seem to require it as an ego support and adjunct to their personality. Theoretically, it would be possible to rank order persons according to their prejudice proneness, ranging from those to whom it would be anathema to those to whom it is an indispensible personality trait. The standard analogy is disease contagion; some persons are highly immune to poison ivy, whereas others contract it as a result of the slightest exposure. As in the case of disease, however, prejudice can hardly be acquired if it is not present in the environment; if it is not present in the cultural atmosphere, it is unlikely that the individual will become prejudiced, regardless of his psychic propensities.

One of the most important functions of prejudice in personality hypothesized is that it serves as an outlet for frustrations.[1] The source of the frustration need not be related to intergroup relations; it may be associated with the person's work, marriage, family relations, childhood experiences, political affairs, financial matters, sex. Prejudice provides a means for venting pent-up frustrations at fairly low "social costs"; that is, presumably one will not suffer any great social stigma for his prejudice. It should be noted that this depends upon how prejudice is evaluated in the person's culture; if it is regarded as extremely reprehensible, then it would be a "socially expensive" means for expressing frustration. The process by which frustration is converted into prejudice is not necessarily a conscious one. The process is known as "displacement," which is defined as an unconscious process. It is probable that the prejudiced person fails to associate his feelings of frustration with his dislike of various groups. Prejudiced people customarily "explain" their attitudes towards a group in terms of behavior and traits which they claim characterize the group. The frustration may be general and diffuse, as in the form of a general social-psychological insecurity. Group prejudice would relieve this frustration by providing the person with a sense of social importance. Hence the strong appeal of racism; it offers a social-psychological security of knowing that one is inherently superior to a whole group of people.

A culture that emphasizes strongly the competitive pursuit of scarce rewards and goals, tangible or intangible, would probably encourage the development of the kind of frustration which seems to be converted into prejudice. A study by A. A. Campbell is suggestive of how this process operates.[2] A sample of white, non-Jewish subjects in the United States was interviewed and the subjects were rated according to (1) their degree of anti-Semitism, (2) their satisfaction-dissatisfaction with their own personal economic situation, and (3) their satisfaction-dissatisfaction with the national political situation. (These latter two ratings were made independently of the rating on attitudes toward Jews.) Those persons classified as dissatisfied with their own economic situation expressed hostility toward Jews more frequently than those who were economically satisfied (10 percent of those economically satisfied expressed hostility but 38 percent of those economically dissatisfied expressed hostility), and those classified as dissatisfied with the contemporary political scene were disproportionately inclined to express dislike or hostility toward Jews. (The category of "economically dissatisfied" is, of course, a mix of cultural, social, and personal variables, including social class, which may have a bearing on such attitudes.)

The functions which prejudice may perform for a person are varied; some of them are "justifying pathological hostility, rationalizing culturally unacceptable wants and behavior in the service of culturally acceptable aspirations, managing repressed wants, enhancing feelings of self-regard, protecting the self against threats on self-esteem, helping a person to become wealthy, providing a 'reasonable' explanation of why one remains poor."[3]

Before going further, it is necessary to point out that some investigators have disagreed over the importance of psychodynamic factors in prejudice and tolerance. Van Den Berghe has stated that prejudice for some individuals probably *is* a function of deeply rooted psychological problems, however, for most persons it is a convenient rationalization for rewarding behavior. Succinctly, the more overt, blatant, and socially sanctioned racism is, the less variance in both racial prejudice and discrimination can be accounted for in psychodynamic terms.[4] Thus, for Van Den Berghe and others, the sociopathology of prejudice is of greater importance than the psychopathology of prejudice. This contention should be borne in mind as we proceed with an analysis of the relationship between prejudice and personality.

The role of prejudice and personality is illuminated by evidence which indicates that prejudiced people are more inclined to be extrapunitive, assigning the blame to somebody else—frequently a minority group, than tolerant persons. The latter are more disposed to be intropunitive, that is, they tend to blame themselves for their problems, frustrations, and failures.[5] For the person who has strong extrapunitive tendencies, group prejudice is a "natural" outlet; he can displace the blame for his shortcomings on a scapegoat group which his culture designates as a vulnerable target. By the same token, one can understand why tolerant people are more intropunitive in posture; they find fault with themselves instead of with a scapegoat group. They have different psychic modes for handling frustration.

The process of *projection* is closely related to the personality functions of prejudice. It enables the person to rid himself of guilt and feelings of moral inadequacy by transferring them (unconsciously) to others, especially scapegoat groups. If he harbors lustful motives he can attribute such motives to other people and thereby "relieve" himself of some of the guilt and anxiety which he would otherwise have. By means of projection the person can divest himself of repressed guilt feelings and also justify hostility towards a group. Allport cites the Nazis' accusation that the Jews were "sadistic." "Nothing could be more directly projective. Not only are the traditions of Jewish culture singularly devoid of sadism, but the circumstances of life under extreme persecution would prevent any sadistic behavior even if a member of the Jewish group had this impulse. On the other hand, the conspicuous pleasure many Nazis took in torturing Jews showed that sadism was, in fact, an approved SS policy."[6] A similar example of projection is furnished by the following statement from an address by a leading Nazi party official in Germany in 1937 at a time when the Nazis were already in the process of killing vast numbers of Jews: "Look at the path which the Jewish people have traversed for millenia: Everywhere murder; everywhere mass murder."[7]

The functions of tolerance in personality may be less obvious but evidently they are of some consequence. In many respects a friendly attitude toward other people is much more satisfying psychologically than hostility. Scapegoating, displacement, projection, and other "techniques" of handling one's psychological problems are actually dysfunctional for the person; they do not solve the basic problems of frustration, anxiety, and so on. There is considerable ego gratification to be had from tolerant intergroup attitudes, and there are social values from which one can derive support. Furthermore, when tolerance is an unconventional attitude in a community or society, it can fulfill some of the personality functions associated with nonconforming and rebellious behavior. In fact, since Van Den Berghe alludes to the fact that in a racist society, most racists are not sick, they are simply conforming to social norms, is it possible to say that in a racist society some tolerants *may be* sick or at least personally disorganized? There are doubtlessly some people who are tolerant because it is a deviant viewpoint in their community. Tolerance, however, can be associated with a sense of moral righteousness which serves to embellish the person's self-image.

PERSONALITY CHARACTERISTICS OF PREJUDICED AND TOLERANT PEOPLE

Do prejudiced and tolerant people have distinctive personality characteristics, and if so, what are they? Bearing in mind that distinctiveness is a matter of degree, one may assert that people who are strongly prejudiced in their intergroup attitudes tend to be characterized by certain personality traits, habits, and attitudes which make them relatively distinguishable from people who are tolerant. These characteristics are not necessarily highly visible, even to the behavioral scientist or clinician, but the pattern reveals itself with various kinds of tests, scales, and interviews. There is a considerable body of evidence, which we shall presently examine, which indicates that there are fairly definite *syndromes* of personality characteristics associated with strong intergroup prejudice. However, we shall also examine evidence which is antithetical to this viewpoint.

The idea that personality characteristics are associated with strong intergroup prejudice is understandable in terms of what we have already said about the personality functions of prejudice and tolerance; these constellations of charactertistics are evidentally functionally interrelated and not merely chance combinations. The concept of syndrome implies that there is a configuration of personality characteristics which are interconnected and which make it possible to classify the person into a category with others with similar patterns.

In general it seems that a distinctive constellation of characteristics is more likely to be found among those who are very strongly prejudiced. The pattern is not so likely to be found among those whose prejudice is moderate or "conventional" or among those near a zero point of prejudice. Also, as in the case of all personality "typing" we should expect some variation in the traits.

The study of the prejudiced personality was stimulated by Erich Fromm's *Escape from Freedom* in which he suggested some general character traits and attitudes associated with what has come to be referred to as "authoritarian personality."[8] A. H. Maslow, evidently inspired by Fromm, subsequently developed a general profile of "The Authoritarian Character Structure."[9] He described the authoritarian viewing the world "as threatening and like a jungle," believing "that people can be ranked on the basis of quality," having a "drive for power," being "inclined to identify kindness as weakness," tending to be compulsive and to value "routine, order, fixity, and discipline," subscribing to the notion that "one is not responsible for one's fate," and being likely "to perceive moral issues as dichotomized absolutes." This interest in analyzing the prejudiced personality and in describing it was produced in no small measure by the rise of the Nazi ideology in Germany and the vicious persecution of various minorities by the Hitler regime. (Although the terms "authoritarianism" and "prejudice" are often used interchangeably, and although high correlations have been found between these two kinds of scales, they should not be regarded as synonymous, for reasons which will be discussed later in this chapter.)

The most ambitious study of prejudice and personality, and the one which provides us with much of the data on the subject, is the one undertaken at the University of California by a team of researchers after World War II and which yielded the volume *The Authoritarian Personality.*[10] The study was given impetus by the rise of fascist ideology and the events in World War II, and it in turn has given rise to a considerable body of research on the same theme. This study brought various psychoanalytical concepts and procedures to bear on the problem of prejudice and personality, although a good deal of criticism has been directed toward the study due to methodological problems. Nevertheless, research on the prejudiced personality enables us to identify certain personal characteristics which are common among persons of strong intergroup prejudice.[11] One of the most significant findings of this research has been that there is a high correlation among various kinds of prejudice; persons who are strongly prejudiced against a particular group also are likely to have unfavorable attitudes toward various other groups as well. There seems to be a basic ethnocentrism in these persons which is manifested in various specific group prejudices. We know, for example, that prejudice against racial and ethnic groups is associated with strong nationalistic sentiments. Eugene L. Hartley reported, for example, the following correlations between various prejudices of college students (including prejudices toward fictitious groups such as the "nonesuch" groups listed below): Blacks and Jews, 0.68; Blacks and Catholics, 0.53; Catholics and Jews, 0.52; nonesuch and Jews, 0.63; nonesuch and communists, 0.68; nonesuch and labor union members, 0.58.[12] This kind of evidence suggests a general hostility toward a variety of out-groups. This is a pervasive theme in "hate literature." Militant prejudice is seldom directed toward a single group, rather it is almost invariably correlated with prejudice against several other groups. This was the pattern found by the authors of *The Authoritarian Personality*, as the correlation matrix of table 6 indicates. These correlations among various forms of prejudice (the patriotism scale presumably measuring nationalistic bias) are impressively high, although the correlations of the subscales with total ethnocentrism is to be expected because it contains items from the subscales. The minorities subscale makes reference to a variety of groups, including Japanese, Okies, Zootsuiters, Filipinos, and others. Regarding the subscale intercorrelations, the researchers observe that: "The subscale intercorrelations, which range from 0.74 to 0.83, are of considerable

TABLE 6
INTERCORRELATIONS OF SUBSCALES OF
ETHNOCENTRISM SCALE AND SUBSCALES AND E SCALE

Subscales	Negroes	Minorities	Patriotism	Ethnocentrism (Total Scale)
Anti-Semitism	.74	.76	.69	.80
Negroes		.74	.76	.90
Other minorities			.83	.91
Patriotism				.92

SOURCE: T. W. Adorno et al., *The Authoritarian Personality* (New York: Harper & Row, 1950), p. 228. Used by permission of the publisher.

significance. The fact that they involve items dealing with so great a variety of groups and ideas suggests again that ethnocentrism is a general frame of mind, that an individual's stand with regard to one group such as Blacks tends to be similar in direction and degree to his stand with regard to most issues of group relations."[13]

A similar pattern of prejudices is reported by Campbell and McCandless from a study of nonminority students at a California college. Their findings are summarized in the correlation matrix of table 7.

TABLE 7

	Negro	Japanese	Jewish	Mexican
Japanese	.72			
Jewish	.73	.74		
Mexican	.75	.70	.66	
English	.32	.43	.47	.42

SOURCE: D. T. Campbell and Boyd R. McCandless, "Ethnocentrism, Xenophobia, and Personality," *Human Relations* 4, no. 2 (1951): p. 191. Used by permission of the journal.

The prejudiced personality, in sum, has a generalized hostility toward out-groups, although the prejudice may be more intense against some groups than others. This psychological posture seems to be functionally related to other personality characteristics, one of which is the person's social philosophy.

Philosophical-Psychological Posture

In comparing persons strongly prejudiced towards various groups with those who are substantially tolerant in their intergroup attitudes we find that there is ordinarily a fundamental and pervasive difference in social philosophy and social values. This is reflected, for example, in the literature of what might be called "hate groups" and "brotherhood groups"; we can refer to hate literature and tolerance literature, for example. Consider, for instance, the following two passages, the first from a publication of the Seaboard White Citizens' Councils by John Kasper entitled "Segregation or Death," and the other from a letter by a Black professor at Tuskegee Institute in reply to an anonymous letter from a member of a White Citizens' Council.[14]

PURGE CRIMINAL JUDGES

As to the Federal judiciary, we have continuous treason from that branch of government since Roosevelt came into power. The 9 swine on the U.S. Supreme Court, the present Attorney-General Brownell, Federal Judge Robert Taylor at Knoxville, Federal Judge Hoffman in Virginia, Federal Judge Rives of Montgomery, Alabama (race-mixing on busses infamy), and more than 75% of the present judiciary should be tried for treason to the American people, for treason to the Constitution of the United States, and for attempted genocide, as this same court once decreed in Nuremberg. Once convicted they should be "publicly hanged until dead, dead, dead," and drawn and quartered in some prominent public place (in front of the White House) to remind the public of the fate of judicial tyrants, all in the best Anglo-Saxon tradition. History shows that when despots set themselves up and flaunt the people by loving what they hate, or hating what they love, their natures become twisted and they come to a bad end, violent end, because they are acting contrary to nature.

Dear Sir:

I thank you for the very informative letter you sent me. . . . I am sorry that you have decided not to speak to Negroes whom you know "because of what their race is trying to pull," . . . Hatred is both expensive and dangerous. It takes time and effort to hate. And when one is hating, he cannot be loving. When he is acting on hatred, he cannot be engaged in noble efforts. Persons who hate

are unhappy persons. Many of them are afraid, and fear is dangerous. . . . Love is more satisfying and honorable than hatred.

. . . I hope that if you have read this letter you will accept it in
the spirit in which it is written. It is not my desire to offend. I do
not threaten you. I am sorry that you hate me. I do not hate you.
. . . Those who really know me say that I am gentle, kind, and
generous. I invite you and your associates to meet with my associates and me in friendly fellowship. You might discover that
we are good Americans.

Very truly yours,

The first example is rather extreme, even considering the source, but
it illustrates the hostile theme which permeates this kind of literature.
It is generally beligerent and punitive in tone and usually contains a
"conspiracy" theme. It seems to reflect a philosophy of revenge, retribu-
tion, and "Social Darwinism." The second passage obviously takes a
different tack on the problem of intergroup relations and reflects more
of a humanitarian social philosophy. Apart from these two examples,
one finds a pronounced contrast in the implicit and explicit social
values in the literature published and circulated by segregationist,
racist, and fascist groups on the one hand, and organizations devoted
to the promotion of tolerance and brotherhood on the other. A comparison of the literature distributed by the Christian Nationalist Crusade
and the National Conference of Christian and Jews seems to confirm
this difference in social philosophy; the former organization has a
much more belligerent posture and is rather hostile towards certain
groups, while the latter dwells strongly on the theme of tolerance,
understanding, and brotherhood. In extreme cases the contrast is between a militant, vicious hostility and maudlin, indulgent compassion
for minorities.

More direct evidence on differences in social philosophy is available
from a study made in Indianapolis in which tolerant and prejudiced
subjects were compared in their responses to the following "Threat-
Competition Orientation Scale."[15] It was validated by the Likert technique and designed to measure, as its name implies, a person's attitudes
on the general character of human relations and human nature, especially whether he conceived them to be essentially a matter of "struggle" or not. It was assumed that the tolerant subjects (toward Blacks
in this case) would be inclined to reject a competitive, conflict kind of
orientation while those strongly prejudiced would be likely to endorse
such propositions.

THREAT-COMPETITION ORIENTATION SCALE

SA A U D SD*   When you come right down to it, it's every man for himself in this world.

SA A U D SD   If a person doesn't look out for himself nobody else will.

SA A U D SD   A person has to be very careful these days to avoid being gyped or cheated by other people.

SA A U D SD   Human nature being what it is, there will always be war and conflict.

SA A U D SD   Most of the people on public relief are just too lazy to work.

SA A U D SD   You can talk about humanity and all that, but in reality life is a matter of the survival of the fittest.

SA A U D SD   A little charity is all right, but most people will just ask for more if you give them something.

SA A U D SD   Life is primarily a matter of struggle for survival.

* SA—strongly agree; A—agree; U—undecided; D—disagree; SD—strongly disagree.

The results were as anticipated; the prejudiced subjects had a significantly higher mean score on the scale, meaning that they were inclined to agree with a "threat-competition" orientation. They seem to view the world as an arena of conflict with human relations being dominated by self-interest and tough competition. This "jungle" *Weltanschauung* has been noted by other researchers and writers also; Fromm and Maslow have attributed this characteristic to the authoritarian and strongly prejudiced person, and the evidence from *The Authoritarian Personality* supports this conclusion. "Projection of one's inner impulses, particularly of aggression, onto others, will naturally lead to a conception of a dangerous and hostile world and consequently to a general suspiciousness of others. Thus it was found that typical high-scoring subjects tend to manifest *distrust and* suspicion of others. Theirs is a conception of people as threatening in the sense of an oversimplified survival-of-the-fittest idea."[16]

Various studies have found a close relationship between hostility and anxiety and group prejudice. Anthony Davids reported a positive correlation between manifest anxiety and authoritarianism (F) scale scores, and Saul Siegel found that those high on the F scale showed more hostility as measured by a scale constructed from Minnesota Multiphasic Personality Inventory items.[17] In a study of former Soviet Ukrainian citizens, designed to test the hypothesis that the prejudiced personality syndrome is not restricted to American society, Allen Kassof concluded that: "The prejudiced person, by comparison with the tolerant person, tends to be extrapunitive. That is, he tends to project rather than accept blame, and to perceive his environment as threatening and unfriendly."[18] Another researcher, studying anti-Semitic students by means of MMPI items, found that the strongly prejudiced were characterized by

> . . . a prevading sense of pessimism and lack of hope and confidence in the future; feelings of synicism, distrust, doubt, suspicion; a diffuse misanthrophy and querulousness; a hostile and bitter outlook which verged on destructiveness; and an underlying perplexity related to a feeling that something dreadful is about to happen.
>
> The overall picture which emerges from these item clusters is one of a harrassed, tormented, resentful, peevish, querulous, constricted, disillusioned, embittered, distrustful, rancorous, apprehensive, and somewhat bewildered person. The syndrome is almost paranoid in intensity, but is not equatable to paranoid because it lacks the excessive circumstantiality and self-deluding aspects of the latter. Nevertheless, it is clear that a set of characteristics such as those listed must be quasi- or near-pathological in its distorting and incapacitating implications for personality.[19]

In a similar vein, Margaret Hayes demonstrated that the prejudiced tend to blame others for their frustrations and problems whereas the tolerant subjects more often blame themselves or are "impunitive."[20] Also, Gardner Lindzey has reported that a comparison of those high and low in prejudice revealed that the prejudiced were characterized by more frustration placement, more outwardly directed hostility, more overt disturbance, and less frustration tolerance.[21] Still another study reveals essentially the same pattern. White boys whose prejudice increased during a stay at a biracial camp, as compared to those whose tolerance increased, showed the following characteristics: they had more aggressive and dominance needs; they had more hostility toward their parents; they felt their home environments to be hostile and threatening; they desired to defy authority, but feared the punishment that would result; and they were more dissatisfied with the camp and their fellow-campers.[22]

Mental Rigidity-Flexibility

There is a body of research evidence which indicates that persons with strong group prejudices are characterized by a greater degree of general mental rigidity than persons who are rather tolerant. There are logical and psychological reasons to expect such a relationship; inasmuch as prejudice is an emotionally rigid attitude, it should follow that those who are rigid in their modes of perception and style of cognition would be prone to prejudice. Sharp in-group and out-group distinctions are closely connected with prejudice and would also seem to be examples of mental inflexibility. Similarly, stereotypes, which are so intimately associated with prejudice, should appeal to persons with a penchant for hard and fast distinctions. The idea of race is probably another case in point, since it entails rather strict categories, such as black and white.

The psychologist Maslow postulated that authoritarian personalities (who are by definition strongly ethnocentric) tend to think in terms of dichotomized absolutes and to value order, fixity, and discipline. Another psychologist, Else Frenkel-Brunswik, developed a scale to measure "intolerance of ambiguity" and found a positive association between that variable and authoritarianism.[23] A similar scale was administered to subjects in Indianapolis, and those who were strongly prejudiced against Blacks also scored significantly higher on "intolerance of ambiguity."[24] Other psychological experimenters have found that prejudiced persons exhibit tenacity in judgments and perception in such situations as estimating the movement of a point of light and redrawing geometric figures. In somewhat the same vein Milton Rokeach discovered that ethnocentric subjects displayed greater mental rigidity in such exercises as arithmetic tests and puzzles.[25] Rokeach also has developed scales to measure two forms of mental rigidity, opinionation and dogmatism, and he has reported positive correlations between these factors and ethnocentrism and authoritarianism.

Research by Bernard Kutner involving children as subjects indicated that differences in mental rigidity between tolerant and prejudiced persons exist during childhood.[26] After testing mental functions (concept formation, deduction, and mental flexibility) characteristic of prejudiced and unprejudiced subjects, Kutner summarized the differences in the following comparison:

Prejudiced Child	*Unprejudiced Child*
1. rigidity	1. flexibility
2. overgeneralization	2. realistic generalization
3. categorizing and dichotomizing	3. individualizing
4. concretization	4. abstraction
5. simplification	5. retention of complexity
6. furcation	6. retention of totality
7. dogmatism (omniscience)	7. lack of dogmatism
8. intolerance of ambiguity	8. tolerance of ambiguity

He concluded that there are two major characteristics of the mental functioning of the prejudiced child, *mental rigidity* and *intolerance of ambiguity,* and he attributes these to the same kinds of influences as did Frenkel-Brunswik in her research on family relationships, socialization experiences in the family, and discipline patterns and their effects upon the ego. Evidently the presence of this psychic factor predisposes one toward tolerance or prejudice.

Superstition and Mysticism

On the assumption that prejudice itself entails erroneous judgments about groups induced by emotional influences, it would be logical to hypothesize that prejudiced people would score significantly higher on a scale measuring general superstition and mysticism. This hypothesis has been empirically verified; a significant difference was found between tolerant and prejudiced subjects in the Indianapolis study on the following "Superstition-Pseudoscience Scale."[27]

SUPERSTITION-PSEUDOSCIENCE SCALE

SA A U D SD   Every person has a time to die, which is fixed when he first comes into this world, and there is nothing a person can do to change it.

SA A U D SD   You can tell a lot about a person's character by the lines of his face.

SA A U D SD   It is instinctive for mothers to love their children.

SA A U D SD   With very few exceptions, criminals come from poor physical stock.

SA A U D SD   Some fortune-tellers can actually predict a person's future by studying the lines of his hands.

SA A U D SD   It will probably be shown one of these days that astrology can explain a lot of things.

SA A U D SD   If a person wants to raise a good garden crop he ought to pay attention to the signs of the moon when he plants.

SA A U D SD   It is more than a remarkable coincidence that Japan had an earthquake on Pearl Harbor Day, December 7, 1944.

As expected, educational level was negatively correlated with scores on this scale, but even when educational level was held constant the prejudiced respondents showed themselves to be more superstitious. This finding supports the results of the California study of *The Authoritarian Personality,* which identified superstition as a component variable in authoritarianism. Thus this factor appears to represent a basic personality factor differentiating tolerant and prejudiced people.

Among the strongly prejudiced there seems to be an affinity for mystical and bizarre explanations of phenomena; a definite "cognitive style" or intellectual appetite seems to be operating. Prejudice itself dwells upon myths, rigid emotional beliefs, and fantastic allegations about the out-group. This is convincingly demonstrated by hate literature which, in addition to derogatory material about out-groups, frequently contains unorthodox medical advice and dire warnings about such matters as fluoridation of water, polio innoculations, and "poison food." One such publication containing anti-Semitic and anti-Black materials also offers pamphlets and books for sale on such subjects as the Hoxey cancer treatment, "zone therapy," astrology, and the adverse effects of polio innoculation.[28] Another issue, offering the statement that "It is now quite obvious to every informed Southerner that the plan worked out by the Communist-Jewish conspiracy to mongrelize the

Southern White Man and hold him in economic bondage is well under way," also ran an advertisement entitled "Restore Your Health Without Treatment" which claimed that:

> Treatments, remedies, cannot change the Natural Law. You must want to live in harmony with this Law to regain your health. The Law (cause and effect) will resolve every disease that has not progressed too far. Regeneration improves the organism. This is TRUTH and LAW.[29]

Racist dogma is permeated with mystical ideas, race itself being a prime example. The idea of "blood" as the agent of heredity and race is the case in point. A fatalistic viewpoint, in the sense of supernaturalistic determinism, also seems to prevail among racists; thus segregation is regarded as divinely ordained and beyond human alteration.

The penchant of strongly prejudiced persons for superstitious-mystical explanations of reality has been attributed by *The Authoritarian Personality* researchers to a weak ego (in the Freudian sense of the term). Unable to cope with the complexities of reality and feeling insecure, the prejudiced personality is predisposed to accept irrational explanations of his confused world. Furthermore, if events are determined by capricious and incomprehensible forces then the individual is at their mercy; thus he is not morally responsible if a minority group is persecuted, for example.

Authoritarianism

Numerous studies have revealed a correlation between group prejudice and authoritarianism scale scores. Other research has suggested that this association may be somewhat spurious and that it can be partly attributed to the tendency of some unsophisticated subjects, especially those of low education, to agree with strongly expressed statements almost regardless of content and direction; this is known as "response set." It also has been demonstrated that there are regional variations in the U.S. in the association between prejudice and authoritariansim, such as a lower correlation in the South, although those who exceed the regional norm of prejudice are evidently more authoritarian than those who are more tolerant than the prevailing norm.

The authoritarianism scale was intended to provide an indirect measure of group prejudice and an implicit explanation of the psychological nature of the attitude. It was assumed that those persons who were inclined towards authoritarianism also would have a keen appetite for group prejudice; their psychological "style" would render them quite susceptible to the appeal of prejudice. The survey and clinical evidence marshalled by Adorno and his associates persuasively supported this contention and the many subsequent studies which were inspired by the California research tend to corroborate the conclusion. In general, however, it seems prudent to regard authoritarianism as a relative index of prejudice rather than an absolute measure of it since persons from different regions or cultures may be strongly prejudiced but may differ considerably in F scale scores. For a given social area with established norms for prejudice it seems likely that the more prejudiced will be more authoritarian. Essentially the same conclusion has been drawn by Thomas E. Pettigrew on the basis of a study of the prejudice and authoritarianism attitudes of white students in South Africa: "In areas with historically embedded traditions of racial intolerance, externalizing factors underlying prejudice remain important but sociocultural factors are unusually crucial and account for the heightened racial hostility."[30] It also should be noted that the term "authoritarian" has been applied to rigid ideologists of the political left whose objects of group prejudice are different.

Leo Srole has demonstrated that authoritarianism may be related to prejudice through another variable, *anomie* (a feeling of alienation, a condition of "normlessness"[31]), and later research indicated that the three variables of prejudice, anomie, and authoritarianism are all intercorrelated in a positive way but negatively correlated with educational level.

Child-Rearing Attitudes

People who differ significantly in their intergroup attitudes also are quite divergent in their views on child-rearing practices. This is hardly surprising when one considers that attitudes about child-rearing reflect one's basic social values. In brief, strongly prejudiced persons are inclined to favor rather stern discipline and to stress obedience, whereas those who are substantially unprejudiced seem to prefer a more lenient and permissive approach with an emphasis upon abstract ethical principles rather than physical punishment. Items such as the following have proven to be highly discriminating in studies of tolerant and prejudiced subjects:

"Obedience is the most important thing a child should learn."

"Spare the rod and spoil the child."

A high percentage of prejudiced respondents agree with these statements.

It seems very likely that parents who have authoritarian child-rearing attitudes also are prone to inculcate prejudice in their offspring. Moreover, this kind of social-psychological family atmosphere probably contributes to prejudiced attitudes in itself by rendering children more susceptible to cultural norms supporting prejudice. In the language of ego psychology the child fails to develop an adequate ego because of the repressive parental controls and therefore prejudice provides him with a sense of identity and ego support.

Associated with these kinds of child-rearing attitudes is a philosophy of human relations which emphasizes repression, punitiveness, hierarchical relationships, and power and force. The psychological connection with prejudice is manifest.

Status Anxiety

A ubiquitous characteristic of prejudiced personalities seems to be their anxious concern about their social status and the threats they perceive to it. One finds an uneasy feeling among these people that their social advancement and their current social station are insecure because there are other groups conspiring against them. They are inclined to be rather keenly status conscious and to emphasize the competitive nature of social mobility. Prejudice is a form of social snobbery and a way to rationalize a social advantage based upon discrimination.

The persistence of prejudice can be understood in terms of its function in relation to status anxiety. As Bruno Bettelheim and Morris Janowitz express it, "If prejudice can bolster a weak sense of identity, the loss of this psychological supportive mechanism may threaten a weak identity."[32] Efforts at racial integration threaten not only the social status and economic security of a prejudiced group but actually the inner sense of identity of its members. Steps towards integration mean criticism of their prejudices—a criticism that increases guilt feelings they may be unable to admit even to themselves. As a result they may feel psychologically trapped, because now both criticism and guilt threaten their sense of identity.[33] In their study of Chicago veterans of World War II, Bettelheim and Janowitz reported that "personal insecurity, subjective feelings of deprivation, anxiety, and hostility were found to be positively and meaningfully linked to prejudice."[34]

Prejudiced persons evidently feel that their social and psychological well-being is threatened by out-groups. They are inclined to view society and the world as a struggle for social-psychological security in which one must be on guard against the threats of other groups in order to preserve and enhance his own social status and identity. This tendency to perceive such threats is suggested by the results from the previously mentioned study by Campbell where he discovered that white non-Jewish Americans in a national sample who were rated as dissatisfied with their personal economic situation expressed more unfavorable attitudes toward Jews than those who were economically satisfied.[35] A similar result emerged from a study by James Martin in which tolerant subjects expressed a greater degree of economic security even though they had a lower average income than prejudiced respondents and, interestingly, even though they had a higher average amount of education and higher occupational level.[36] One surmises that tolerant personalities are not so prone to feel personally and socially threatened by out-group members, or indeed, to *perceive* social situations in group terms.

TOLERANT AND PREJUDICED PERSONALITY PROFILES

Research on prejudice and personality has led to formulations of general profiles of tolerant and prejudiced personalities. Some years ago Hartley studied differences between tolerant and prejudiced college students by means of a "personality assignment" in which each subject was asked to make a kind of self-analysis with the help of an outline which contained general questions about skills, anxieties, personal relations, and so on. From the findings Hartley developed general personality portraits, described as follows.

The relatively tolerant personality seemed likely to exhibit some combination of the following characteristics: a strong desire for personal autonomy, associated with a lack of need for dominance; a strong need for friendliness, along with a personal seclusiveness; a tendency to placate others along with lack of general conformity to the mores. He appeared to be fairly serious, to be interested in current events, to have ideas about bettering society, to be a member of a political group and to have need for personal achievement in the vocational area. He showed himself to be an accepting personality, disliking violence, able to be more or less alike and adopting a nurturant rather than a dominant attitude toward those younger than he. He manifested conscious conflicts concerning loyalties and duties and was very seriously concerned about moral questions. His interests centered about what are commonly called the social studies, and about reading and journalism. Although personally seclusive, he showed great need to be socially useful.

The relatively intolerant personality was found to combine in varying degrees the following characteristics: unwillingness to accept responsibility, acceptance of conventional mores, rejection of serious groups, rejection of political interests, desire for groups formed for purely social purposes and absorption with pleasure activities, a conscious conflict between work and play, emotionality rather than rationality, extreme egocentrism, and interest in physical activity, the body, health. He was likely to dislike agitators, radicals, pessimists. He was relatively uncreative, apparently unable to deal with anxieties except by fleeing from them. Often his physical activity had in it a compulsive component.

Robin Williams, who conducted extensive research at Cornell under grants from the Rockefeller Foundation (the Cornell Studies in Intergroup Relations), found

> that persons who express social distance toward ethnic, radical, or religious outgroups tend rather consistently toward a meaningful pattern of personality characteristics—of, if one prefers, a consistent pattern of beliefs and values. The greatest likelihood of prejudice attaches to those persons who (1) believe in *strict and unquestioning obedience* of children to parent; (2) advocate *severe punishment* of sex criminals; (3) acquiesce in statements of *moralistic condemnation* concerning youths, old people, or people who do not live upright lives; (4) manifest a *generalized distrust* of other people; (5) report feeling *uncomfortable about meeting strangers*; (6) indicate feelings of *personal frustration* and lack of secure group belongingness. Although quantitative measures of the relative importance of these several items are not feasible with the data at hand, the statistical relationships among the various attitudes and beliefs are such that they suggest that a primary dimension of the most highly prejudiced personalities is *moralistic punitiveness* toward other people, especially toward impulsive or deviant behavior.[38]

A set of profiles was prepared on the basis of the Indianapolis study, designed to ascertain the distinguishing characteristics of tolerant persons. A random sample of adult subjects was drawn from the community and screened to determine those most prejudiced and those who were near a zero point of prejudice on a scale measuring attitudes towards Blacks and whites. The following profiles were based upon interviews with forty-one tolerant subjects and fifty-nine prejudiced ones in which they responded to a variety of attitude scales and background questions.[39]

The Strongly Prejudiced Personality

The strongly prejudiced person tends to be ethnocentric; he makes sharp distinctions between his in-groups and out-groups; he might be called a "social reductionist" in that his reference groups reflect an *exclusive* rather than *inclusive* emphasis; he would not be likely to identify himself with "humanity," but rather would prefer more exclusive levels of identification; he thrives on selective membership with himself on the "inside." Such an orientation seems to provide a sustaining and compensating mechanism to satisfy psychological and social insecurity. Although he may be obscure himself, he borrows prestige from his "race," nation, and the like.

The strongly prejudiced person is inclined to be suspicious, distrustful, and extrapunitive. He tends to attribute ulterior motives to Blacks and other out-group members. The "Black problem" is due to Blacks; if their lot is not to their liking, it is because they are at fault. He avoids contact with minority groups and predicts adverse consequences from intergroup interaction. He urges segregation as a social-political policy because he "knows" that Blacks and whites cannot live peacefully as close neighbors.

He views the world as an arena of conflict, involving power struggles and competition among individuals and groups. Other people are not to be trusted (except, perhaps, for a few in-group members) because everyone is seeking to maximize his advantage at the expense of others. He prides himself on his "realism" and tends to regard "idealistic" people as foolish and even dangerous; he favors the "practical" over the "theoretical."

Cognitively, the strongly prejudiced person seeks certainty through the use of dichotomized absolutes. He would very likely subscribe to the proposition that "East is East and West is West." Relativistic thinking does not satisfy his intellectual appetite; he prefers dogmatism to doubt. Accordingly he views Blacks and whites as being essentially and markedly different; a person is either good or evil, and a statement is either true or false.

The strongly prejudiced person favors obedience and submission to authority. This trait is congruent with his zeal for definiteness and his basic distrust of the impulses and motives of other people. He prefers order, discipline, and conformity in the social environment. He is likely to be conservative in his social attitudes and interests and is often a vigorous supporter, at the conscious verbal level, of conventional morality. He is moralistic, but rather unsentimental and even anti-sentimental. Such a person evidently represses considerably and engages in projection, particularly in connection with conventional moral norms and their violation. Although there is not as yet conclusive clinical evidence, one might venture the speculative opinion that hostile and sexual impulses, especially those directed at authority figures such as parents, give rise to excessive projection, with minorities as frequent "targets." Associated with these processes are a general lack of self-insight and understanding of unconscious motivation. The prejudiced person is likely to be emotionally immature in the sense of a lack of self-understanding. Although he may appear to be emotionally stable on the surface, it is probable that there are deep-seated conflicts and anxieties in some instances.

The strongly prejudiced person also appears to be low on imagination, creativeness, humanitarianism, and compassion. He is inclined to be fatalistic and is pessimistic about the scientific study of human behavior. Superstition has a considerable appeal to this type of personality; the magical, the mystical, and the mysterious are attractive to him as explanations of events. It may be conjectured that he is prone to regard "psychological causation" as external to him; "he" is not responsible for his own fate or (and this is quite significant) for the fate of others; "they" determine what happens. He sometimes ascribes causation to impersonal, mysterious, and uncontrollable forces. Compared to the tolerant type, he tends to be more emotional and less rational, and he could be characterized as more moralistic than ethical. The strongly prejudiced "ideal type" is typically nonintellectual and frequently anti-intellectual; he is very often dogmatic in expression and angers easily when he meets with disagreement. He is likely to interpret intellectual disagreement as a personal affront.

In religion, modally speaking, he suscribes to the more fundamentalist, dogmatic, irrational, and authoritarian doctrines and beliefs. He is less likely to concur with ideals and values relating to brotherhood, basic humanity, "social welfare," or mutual aid. He is usually opposed to "modernism" in religion.

The Tolerant Personality

The very tolerant person tends to be generally tolerant of all groups, though it does not necessarily follow that he is always "well adjusted" in his inter*personal* relations. His trust of other people is a conspicuous trait. The tolerant person is inclined to look for the best in people; he gives them "the benefit of the doubt." He tends to judge individuals *as individuals* and to reject the practice of group stereotyping. He expects other people to be friendly, fair, and cooperative; and he is likely to suspend his judgment of others beyond the first impression.

The tolerant person apparently feels reasonably secure, or at least he does not seem prone to exaggerate actual threats from other people. He may be neurotic but he is rarely paranoid, for example. He is inclined to be rational, humanistic, liberal in social attitudes, and intropunitive. The tolerant person also is characterized by a high degree of empathic ability and is much more likely to be high on sympathy and compassion than the strongly prejudiced person. He is "sensitive" as distinct from being "tough"; he is opposed to cruelty, violence, and harsh discipline where the strongly prejudiced person would be likely to condone it. Whereas the prejudiced male is often ultramasculine to the point of having almost no compassion, the tolerant male is rarely "swaggering and arrogant" in his maleness.

Cognitively, the "ideal type" tolerant is able to perceive variation realistically; he therefore does not have a strong need for stereotyping and dogmatism. He recognizes that each individual is unique (though not *radically* different from any other person), and that good and evil, shortness and tallness, darkness and lightness, stupidity and intelligence are all relative concepts. Compared to the strongly prejudiced, he has no obsessive fear of being mistaken or wrong and is more willing to admit his own shortcomings and weaknesses. The tolerant personality is not a highly rigid one. (The tolerant subjects in the Indianapolis sample seemed, in conversation, to display more wit and humor, for example. The strongly prejudiced were more often grim and serious.)

Typically interested in, and optimistic about, the improvement of human society, the tolerant person is likely to stress cooperation over competition in achieving human progress. He is often idealistic and utopian, at least in his own judgment. His interests are often in intellectual matters. He values creative activities and is not prone to stress the "practical" over the "theoretical." Furthermore, the tolerant type is much less of a "social reductionist;" "humanity" would be an important reference group for him, while "exclusiveness" in membership has little appeal.

The unprejudiced person is rather "kindhearted," if not "softhearted"; he is typically in sympathy with the underdog and does not have the threat-competition orientation so manifest in highly intolerant people. The religious values and beliefs of *most* tolerants reflect an emphasis upon brotherhood, humanitarianism, charity, rationalism, and tolerance of personal deviation. (As we have previously noted, the changing character of religion, and especially its increasing concern for human relations, may mean that in the future even the more conservative adherents of religion will have more "liberal" intergroup attitudes.) Similarly, they are likely to be altruistic, somewhat sensitive, and appreciative of the aesthetic.

He is more concerned with *serving* than *leading*, is likely to be relatively autonomous, does not have a strong need for dominance, is rarely ever obsessively conformist, and dislikes both subordination and superordination of any appreciable degree. He tends to view his social interaction and social relationships as possibilities for expression, mutual assistance, affective response, rather than as opportunities for exploitation and manipulation.

Tolerant subjects seem to display somewhat more self-insight than the strongly prejudiced and deal with their emotional problems in different, perhaps more mature, and realistic ways.

Based upon the experience of informal conversations with subjects who qualified as "tolerant" after their tolerance-prejudice scale scores were tabulated, it can only be said that they seem rather more variable as a lot than the strongly prejudiced and do not fall into as neat a pattern as do the strongly intolerant. The intolerant type is evidently more "homogeneous," whereas the tolerants in the Indianapolis sample seemed to present a wider range of personality variation. Consequently, one must not expect a distinct pattern of characteristics which will fit all tolerant persons; to do so would be an instance of stereotyping. Some tolerant subjects in the Indianapolis sample were friendly and talkative while others were aloof and laconic. Some were evidently quite effective in interpersonal relations while others were evidently rather inept. There did not seem to be any particular temperamental quality that was characteristic of all the tolerant respondents.

Although the Indianapolis study did not reveal *great* differences in the reported childhood disciplinary environment, it seems reasonable to surmise that the tolerant type is *more likely* to have experienced a childhood family environment characterized by an absence of harsh discipline and authoritarian parental control. The pronounced differences in child-rearing attitudes exhibited by the tolerant and prejudiced subjects lend credence to this generalization. In any event, tolerant persons emphasize a relaxed, lenient, and affectionate approach to child-rearing. (Many of the prejudiced subjects would doubtless refer to this policy as "permissive" or even "indulgent.")

The tolerant person does not seem to suffer from the acute status anxiety that one observes so commonly among the strongly prejudiced. He apparently does not have an obsessive need to feel superior to other people. He is willing to take his chances for success on an "equal opportunity" basis; he is prepared to grant recognition where it is deserved regardless of group membership.

Although it is difficult to pinpoint one characteristic that distinguishes the tolerant person more than any other, one will not be far wrong by pointing to his "sympathy for the underdog." The attitude of "fair play," the refusal to hate people who could be hated with impunity, may be the basic psychological ingredient in tolerance. It is of interest to note, however, that there is some evidence to support the contention that tolerant personalities, when placed in an environment where prejudice and bigotry are norms, move toward such attitudes.

SOCIAL CHARACTERISTICS

In addition to these personal characteristics there are other differentiating factors of a more social nature. A social profile of tolerant and prejudiced persons is subject to a certain amount of variation depending upon the group-object of the attitude, but the following generalizations can be made about the relationship between various social categories and tolerance-prejudice.

Age

The available evidence indicates that younger people are generally more tolerant than older ones. Very young people may not have had time to learn prejudice, and if prejudice is diminishing generally in American society, one would expect the younger generation to have less of it. Furthermore, in our society there is a measure of emphasis upon group harmony and tolerance in the schools. This influence is compounded by the increase in the number of years of formal education. Idealism is frequently stronger among youth; age is likely to bring a more "practical" and ethnocentric attitude.

Social Class

Lower social class seems to be generally associated with more intergroup prejudice, though anti-Semitism is a possible exception to this pattern. The reasons for this variation, as Westie has pointed out, may be any of several, ranging from personal insecurity to economic competition.

Social Mobility

A variety of studies have demonstrated a close association between social mobility and prejudice. Perhaps the most intensive analysis of this relationship was the one by Bettelheim and Janowitz.[40] Viewing ethnic hostility as "a symptom of the individual's effort to maintain his psychic economy" they hypothesized that downward social mobility and extreme upward mobility would contribute to prejudice. The data confirmed this relationship and several subsequent studies also have empirically verified the hypothesis.

Income and Education

Since these two factors are closely related to class membership, the generalization about social class also would be applicable here. Numerous studies have shown that higher levels of education are negatively associated with prejudice. Education appears to influence a person's outlook and sufficiently inform him to the extent that misconceptions are eradicated.

Religion

As previously mentioned, there seem to be only slight differences between Protestants and Catholics, on the average. Jews are generally more tolerant toward other groups. Within Protestantism, the rule seems to be that the more liberal the theology the less the prejudice toward minorities.

Other Social Categories

Region, residence, political affiliation, occupation, ethnic background, and organization membership also may be related to tolerance-prejudice, but complete and reliable evidence is still lacking. There are regional variations in prejudice, at least in intensity. The political variation is most obvious at the extremes, though there are some important reservations to be noted on the "left." Political liberalism seems to be positively associated currently with tolerance up to a point, and that point is often where class prejudice becomes manifest (not that there is not a different form of class prejudice on the "right"). Suffice it to say that the extreme "left" is not without certain forms of group prejudice: political, religious, class, and so forth.

A summary of studies on authoritarianism and related social variables by Stewart and Hoult reveals that the authoritarian syndrome is "particularly evident" among (1) the less educated, (2) the aged, (3) the rural, (4) members of disadvantaged minorities, (5) people of lower socioeconomic status, and (6) those who have been reared in an authoritarian family environment.[41]

Notes

1. John Dollard, L. W. Miller, and N. E. Mowrer, *Frustration and Aggression* (New Haven, Conn: Yale University Press, 1939). See Gordon Allport, *The Nature of Prejudice* (Cambridge, Mass.: Addison-Wesley, 1954), chapter 21.
2. A. A. Campbell, "Factors Associated with Attitudes Toward Jews," in *Readings in Social Psychology*, ed. T. M. Newcomb and E. L. Hartley (New York: Holt, Rinehart and Winston, 1947).
3. James G. Martin, "Tolerant and Prejudiced Personality Syndromes," *The Journal of Intergroup Relations* 2, no. 2 (Spring 1961): 171.
4. Pierre Van Den Berghe, *Race and Racism* (New York: Wiley, 1967), p. 21.
5. Richard L. Simpson found both Blacks and Jews who tended to be intrapunitive were relatively unprejudiced. See Simpson, "Negro-Jewish Prejudice: Authoritarianism and Some Social Variables as Correlates," *Social Problems* 7, no. 2 (Fall 1959): 138-46.
6. Gordon Allport, *The Nature of Prejudice* (Cambridge, Mass.: Addison-Wesley, 1954), p. 365.
7. Mimeographed material, source unknown.
8. Erich Fromm, *Escape from Freedom* (New York: Holt, Rinehart and Winston, 1941).
9. A. H. Maslow, "The Authoritarian Character Structure," *Journal of Social Psychology* 18 (1943): 401-11.

10. T. W. Adorno et al., *The Authoritarian Personality* (New York: Harper and Row, 1950).
11. Martin, "Tolerant and Prejudiced Personality Syndromes," pp. 171-75. Also see James G. Martin and Frank Westie, "The Tolerant Personality," *American Sociological Review* 24 (August 1959): 521-28, and Martin, *The Tolerant Personality* (Detroit: Wayne State University Press, 1964).
12. Eugene L. Hartley, *Problems and Prejudice* (New York: King's Crown Press, 1946).
13. Adorno, *Authoritarian Personality*.
14. Mimeographed material received by one of the authors from an anonymous source.
15. Martin, "Tolerant and Prejudiced Personality Syndromes."
16. Adorno, *Authoritarian Personality*.
17. See Anthony Davids, "Personality, Intelligence and Intolerance of Ambiguity," *Journal of Abnormal and Social Psychology* 51 (1955): 415-20, and Saul Siegel, "The Relationship of Hostility to Authoritarianism," *Journal of Abnormal and Social Psychology* 52 (1956): 368-72.
18. Allen Kassof, "The Prejudicial Personality: A Cross Cultural Test," *Social Problems* 6 (1958): 59-67.
19. H. G. Gough, "Studies of Social Intolerance: A Personality Scale for Anti-Semitism," *Journal of Social Psychology* 33 (1951): 247-55.
20. Margaret Hayes, "Personality and Culture Factors in Intergroup Attitudes II," *Journal of Educational Research* 43 (1949): 197-204.
21. Gardner Lindzey, "Differences Between the High and Low in Prejudice and Their Implications for a Theory of Prejudice," *Journal of Personality* 19 (1950): 16-40.
22. See Muzafer Sherif et al. *Intergroup Conflict and Cooperation: The Robbers Cave Experiment* (Norman: University of Oklahoma Book Exchange, 1961).
23. Else Frenkel-Brunswik, "Intolerance of Ambiguity as an Emotional and Perceptual Variable," *Journal of Personality* 18 (1949): 108-43.
24. Martin, "Tolerant and Prejudiced Personality Syndromes."
25. Milton Rokeach, "Generalized Mental Rigidity as a Factor in Ethnocentrism," *Journal of Abnormal and Social Psychology* 43 (1948): 259-78.
26. Bernard Kutner, "Patterns of Mental Functioning Associated with Prejudice in Children," *Psychological Monographs* 72, no. 7 (1958).
27. Martin, "Tolerant and Prejudiced Personality Syndromes."
28. According to a story in the Clinton, Tennessee, *Courier-News*, 16 May 1957.
29. See Martin, "Tolerant and Prejudiced Personality Syndromes."
30. Thomas E. Pettigrew, "Personality and Socio-cultural Factors in Intergroup Attitudes, A Cross-National Comparison," *Journal of Conflict Resolution* 2 (1958): 29-42.
31. Leo Srole, "Social Integration and Certain Corollaries," *American Sociological Review* 21 (1956): 709-16.
32. Bruno Bettleheim and Morris Janowitz, *Dynamics of Prejudice: A Psychological and Sociological Study of Veterans* (New York: Harper and Bros., 1950).
33. Ibid.
34. Ibid.
35. Campbell, "Factors Associated with Attitudes Toward Jews."
36. Martin, "Tolerant and Prejudiced Personality Syndromes."
37. Hartley, *Problems in Prejudice*.
38. Robin Williams, *Strangers Next Door* (Englewood Cliffs, N.J.: Prentice-Hall, 1964), pp. 109-10.
39. Martin, "Tolerant and Prejudiced Personality Syndromes."
40. Bettelheim and Janowitz, *Dynamics of Prejudice*.
41. Don Stewart and Thomas Hoult, "A Social Psychological Theory of the Authoritarian Personality," *American Journal of Sociology* 65 (1959): 274-79.

The Concept of
Discrimination

9

INTRODUCTION

This chapter will be concerned primarily with the *concept* of discrimination rather than existing patterns or areas of discrimination, as they will be the thrust of chapter 10. What we hope to achieve in this chapter is a rigorous analysis and exposition of the process of discrimination, hence our discussion will be essentially theoretical and actual cases will be cited primarily to illustrate principles. Educationally, we believe that understanding the concept of discrimination objectively is more valuable than a comprehensive and detailed description of contemporary forms and objects of discrimination. There is considerable historical variation in group discrimination and for that reason it is of critical importance that the student of intergroup relations be able to recognize discrimination when he encounters it in the future, as well as recognizing and understanding its manifestation in today's society.

Most discrimination is institutionalized and consequently not highly visible. Sanctioned by the culture and therefore regarded as natural and proper, it is a challenge to one's perception to recognize it. For example, discrimination against women has been an integral part of America's ethos for a long period of time. Yet *perceived* discrimination against women seems to be a relatively new phenomenon illuminated by the women's liberation movement. This movement has disputed the legitimacy of a pattern of treatment and statutes previously considered to be fair and reasonable and simultaneously has altered perceptions of how women are treated in American society.

CONCEPTUAL ANALYSIS

Group prejudice, we have observed, is an attitude; group discrimination entails some kind of overt action. Since discrimination refers to differential treatment, which in this case is based upon *group membership,* individual differential treatment does not concern us unless it is based upon group classification. This is a point that is often misunderstood in arguments about discrimination. Apologists for group discrimination are fond of citing the universality of discrimination in human behavior in the choice of food, clothing, friends, and so on. It is implied that this process is a part of human behavior and that it requires no moral defense. The participants in such arguments usually fail to distinguish between discrimination based upon individual criteria and that based upon such categorical factors such as race or ethnicity. This distinction is crucial for our purposes, and though it is sometimes difficult to make clear, such a distinction is easier to render than the distinction between individual and group prejudice, because prejudice does not necessarily manifest itself overtly whereas discrimination results in "tangible" behavioral evidence. It is easier to detect discriminatory hiring practices, for example, than the prejudicial attitudes which may motivate them.

Aaron Antonovsky has developed a sociological theory which stipulates the conditions and motives which produce discrimination. According to Antonovsky, discrimination may be defined "as the effective injurious treatment of persons on grounds rationally irrelevant to the situation. Individuals are denied desired and expected rewards or opportunities for reasons related not to their capacities, merits, or behavior, but solely because of membership in an identifiable out-group."[1] He contends that:

> Certain conditions are necessary before discrimination will emerge and persist: (1) There must be scarcity of rewards and opportunities, both material and psychic. The greater the scarcity, the greater the pressure for recourse to discrimination. (2) But scarcity is—beyond the sheer subsistence level—a culturally defined concept. There would be no such pressure unless both insiders and outsiders agreed upon the desirability of the scarce values. (3) In order for discrimination to operate, there must be an unequal distribution of power, which enables the insiders to impose their monopoly and perpetuate it. Thus scarcity, shared goals, and unequal power are the necessary conditions for discrimination. Under

such conditions, discrimination will become a reality given sufficient motive.[2]

There are several personal and social motives in Antonovsky's judgment.

First, there is the possibility of direct economic, social or political
benefit through exploitation. The Southern landowner who, as a
member of the Board of Elections, prevents Negroes from voting
and thus from exercising political power, may thereby achieve
gain through rigged laws and judicial practices.

Second, there is the gain that derives from monopolistic control
over desired values; for example, the union that restricts membership and thus gains economic advantage for its members.

Third, there is discrimination that is motivated by fear or loss,
or negative profit. This rests upon the discriminator's presumption
that he will be punished for failing to discriminate. The employer,
the union official, the real estate broker, the admissions committee
of a club or medical school, the employment agency, may or may
not be prejudiced; but they discriminate because they assume that
their economic or status interests will suffer if they do otherwise,
since they believe themselves to be dependent upon a prejudiced
work force, membership, body of alumni, clientele, or colleagues.

A fourth type of gain is that which, by pandering to prejudice,
diverts hostility which might otherwise be directed against the
discriminator. The employer who establishes himself as a "right
guy" by discriminating in hiring or upgrading, by exploiting the
prejudices of the labor force, may thereby divert attention from
other grievances.

In all these cases, the discriminator benefits from the persistence
of discriminatory policies. It should be noted, however, that once
discrimination becomes institutionalized, it may be perpetuated
even though its agent no longer receives any significant gain.

To these types of discrimination should be added the prejudice-
motivated type. Here there is psychic gain for the discriminator
independent of financial profit or avoidance of loss. The employer
who does not hire a Negro, even though he may be the most
competent candidate for the job, simply because he hates Negroes,
may take a material loss, but his action provides him with a
psychic satisfaction.[3]

In sum, according to this theory,

> For discrimination to exist, one or another of these motives (which are not mutually exclusive) must be present under the conditions of scarcity, shared goals, and unequal power. . . . Motivation without power is insufficient to effect discrimination.[4]

The distinction between discrimination motivated by prejudice (which is an irrational attitude as we have previously argued) and discrimination for rational reasons is worthy of further pursuit at this point because of its importance to the whole discussion of discrimination. It is our contention that most discrimination is a consequence of prejudice. Some discrimination is surely for rational reasons, such as gaining some kind of economic advantage; however, the social-psychological processes that are involved are such that it is quite likely that the person who practices discrimination for rational reasons at the outset will eventually come to rationalize (in the Freudian and unconscious sense of the word) his actions; he will, in effect, become prejudiced as a result of practicing discrimination. We submit that the typical process is to become prejudiced and then to discriminate, and that this accounts for most discrimination, but some people who discriminate (without prejudice) for rational reasons later become prejudiced for psychological reasons to excuse their behavior. In this connection we should remind ourselves of the general principle that detection of human motivation is a speculative matter, because one can only crudely simulate the psychological processes of another person. Furthermore, the process is complicated by the operation of unconscious motivation so that we cannot always be sure of our analysis of our own motives. That is why it is easier to detect discrimination than it is to ascertain the specific motivational circumstances. Our knowledge of the measurement of prejudice and its relation to discrimination does convince us, however, that in general it is the prejudicial attitude which leads to the discriminatory act.

Robert Hamblin, seeking to identify the antecedents of racial discrimination, hypothesized nine variables related to the tendency to discriminate.

> (1) The tendency to discriminate against members of a minority varies directly with authoritarianism, or the degree to which the individual's personality is characterized by fascist tendencies, that is, rigidity, projection, and punitiveness.

> (2) The tendency to discriminate against members of a minority varies directly with anomia, or the degree to which the individual perceives his milieu as being unpredictable or normless.

(3) The tendency to discriminate against members of a minority inversely with the amount of vertical mobility, or the degree to which the individual has experienced an increase (as opposed to a decrease) in occupational status.

(4) The tendency to discriminate against members of a minority varies directly with perceived nonconformity, or the degree to which the members of the minority group are perceived by members of the majority as violating the norms of the majority.

(5) The tendency to discriminate against members of a minority varies inversely with equal-status contact, or the degree to which the majority member has interacted with minority members who are his equals in occupational status.

(6) The tendency to discriminate against members of a minority varies directly with competition, or the degree to which the individual has experienced frustration in past competition with members of the minority group.

(7) The tendency to discriminate against members of a minority varies directly with the amount of fear of equal-status competition with members of the minority group.

(8) The tendency to discriminate against members of a minority varies directly with the strength of family pressures to discriminate against members of that minority.

(9) The tendency to discriminate against members of a minority varies directly with the strength of friends' pressures to discriminate against members of that minority.[5]

He reported the correlations given in table 8.

An economist, Gary S. Becker, has developed a comprehensive theory of discrimination from the standpoint of the marketplace that "supplements the psychologists' and sociologists' analysis of causes with an analysis of economic consequences."[6]

> The theory can be applied to "discrimination" and "nepotism" in all their diverse forms, whether the discrimination be against Negroes, Jews, women, or persons with "unpleasant" personalities or whether the nepotism be in favor of blood relatives, countrymen, or classmates, since they have in common the use of non-monetary considerations in deciding whether to hire, work with, or buy from an individual or group.
>
> This theory is applicable not only to discrimination and nepotism in the market place but also to non-market discrimination and

TABLE 8
PEARSONIAN CORRELATIONS BETWEEN THE
DISCRIMINATION INDEX AND NINE POSSIBLE
ANTECEDENT VARIABLES

Possible Antecedent Variables	r
Authoritarianism	.22
Anomia	.37
Vertical Mobility	.06
Perceived Nonconformity of Negroes	.29
Negative-Sympathetic Stereotypes	.28
Equal-Status Contact	−.17
Frustration from Past Competition	.41
Fear of Equal-Status Competition	.62
Family Pressures to Discriminate	.75
Friends' Pressures to Discriminate	.68

SOURCE: R. L. Hamblin, "The Dynamics of Racial Discrimination," *Social Problems* 20, no. 2 (Fall 1962): 109. Used by permission of the journal and the author.

nepotism and, indeed, more generally to other kinds of non-pecuniary motivation as well.[7]

Becker has formulated a "discrimination coefficient" based upon a "taste for discrimination" which not only represents a "non-pecuniary element in certain kinds of transactions," but also "is positive or negative, depending upon whether the non-pecuniary element is considered 'good' or 'bad.' "[8] (Thus nepotism is obviously a case of *positive discrimination*, which is discussed subsequently in this chapter.) "When an employer discriminates against employees, he acts as if he incurs non-pecuniary, psychic costs of production by employing them. . . ."[9] Application of Becker's kind of analysis yields the conclusions that: (1) Discrimination against Blacks seems to be positively correlated with their relative number. (2) Discrimination is greater against older and better-educated non-whites. (3) "Tastes in discrimination" (in 1940) in the South appear to have been, on the average, about twice those in the North. (4) Although some changes have occurred in both North and South, there has been little relative difference in the degree of discrimination against Blacks during the last few decades.[10]

Becker's analysis informs us that discrimination entails some form of payment for the "taste," or what sociologists would call the "social distance." This price is paid for the privilege of associating with some people, or for the privilege of being able to avoid contact with others. Thus the Black worker may receive a lower wage than a white worker for the same kind of work; he is being exploited in the sense that he must work for less when the employer acts as if it were psychically painful to have a Black working for him, and hence is not willing to pay as much. On the other hand, the employer may act as if it is worth a premium to have his white brother-in-law as an employee. Such taste for discrimination, according to Becker, includes both prejudice (preference) and ignorance (lack of knowledge of the efficiency of a Black, for example).

The role of discrimination in the whole economic process is complicated by unequal amounts of capital, work skills, and other relevant variables among different groups, which make analysis difficult. Becker's kind of theoretical approach to discrimination illustrates the utility of an objective, quantitative analysis of the process, although it is not always simple to apply.

Conceptually group prejudice and group discrimination have much in common. In many instances the latter apparently is produced by the former. In some instances it also is likely that the practice of discrimination leads to the development of prejudice to justify behavior. Both prejudice and discrimination may be either positive or negative, and both may be based upon ethical or empirical/logical factors. Both are categorical responses founded upon rather rigid images of groups, often entailing in-group and out-group distinctions. Although they are usually found in conjunction with each other, this is not invariably the case, for there are evidently genuine cases of prejudice without discrimination and of discrimination without prejudice. Some prejudiced people are restrained by various social controls from committing acts of discrimination while some nonprejudiced people are required or encouraged to discriminate by other social pressures.

The Detection of Discrimination

The detection of discrimination is essentially an exercise in experimental logic. If all other factors are held constant, and only group membership and treatment of the individual are variables, one can logically infer the impact of group membership upon the treatment of an individual. If the fact of group membership, *ceterus paribus*, affects response to the person, one can conclude that there has been group discrimination. Unfortunately, it is sometimes difficult to control all the variables except group membership and differential treatment. One is often at a loss to know whether discrimination is on a personal or a group basis.

In investigating group discrimination in employment, for example, the procedure would be to match applications which differed only on critical group membership. Any differential hiring practices could then be attributed to group discrimination. Again, this is not always a simple matter because the personnel selection process may entail a personal interview which introduces a subjective "personality evaluation." However, if there is a consistent pattern of rejection of members of a particular group on the basis of "personality" one is hard pressed to account for this rejection in terms of "chance." Discrimination requires some ingenuity when the application process is an impersonal one; the application form must be identified by race, or whatever the group object of discrimination is, by some means such as coding. When group discrimination is illegal or contrary to "official" policy some kind of secret coding must be devised. Discrimination is least likely to occur under conditions in which completed application forms which do not identify group membership are ranked in order of employment preference. If there is a personal interview in the employment process and the applicant's group membership is "visible" it is easier for the employer to discriminate if he is so predisposed.

The process of group discrimination can be studied empirically by means of the experimental logic we have discussed. One study, done in New York City, was designed to ascertain whether restaurants in that city discriminated against Black patrons. For this study discrimination was specifically defined in terms of various kinds of treatment, such as refusal to serve, delayed service, and overcharges. Teams of Black and white diners entered a number of restaurants of varying price range, dined, and then reported their experiences. The diners were matched in age, sex, socioeconomic level, and dress and were instructed to behave similarly. In short, all of the major variables except race were held constant so that the impact of race upon treatment by these restaurants could be ascertained. It was found that 42 percent of the restaurants in the sample tested gave the Black diners clearly inferior treatment.[11] Similar studies on discrimination in housing employ the same experimental logic, the only difference being substantive, that is, refusal to rent or sell because of group membership.

In its popular usage the term discrimination seems to connote unfair treatment; some kind of differential treatment which violates accepted codes of ethics governing human relations. Though discrimination is considered to be morally reprehensible, there is often sharp disagreement as to whether it exists in particular instances because of the subjectivity of its definition. Equal treatment is evidently regarded as the antithesis of discrimination in most cases, but "equal" tends to be defined in terms of traditional moral values rather than in the technical sense. Thus certain kinds of "unequal" treatment of women may not be considered as discrimination according to the popular usage of the term.[12]

POSITIVE AND NEGATIVE DISCRIMINATION

Membership in a given group can be an asset or a liability to a person as far as discrimination is concerned. It may enable him to obtain employment which would otherwise be unavailable to him or it may prevent him from getting a job. The fact that we are ordinarily more conscious of negative discrimination is probably due to our psychological vanity; we would rather not acknowledge preferential treatment. The advantages that accrue to us simply because of ascribed group membership are very easy to ignore while negative discrimination is more likely to be denounced as unfair. Rare is the person who modestly attributes his success to favoritism; less rare is the person who attributes his misfortunes to negative group discrimination.

Positive and negative discrimination parallel in-group and out-group distinctions, there being a propensity to give preferential treatment to members of one's in-group in contrast to out-group members. This favoritism ranges from the most subtle distinctions in responses in social intercourse to dramatic differences between comrade and enemy in war. Our reaction to others is sometimes significantly altered upon discovery of various group memberships, including not only the more visible categories such as "race," but also social class, family, political party affiliation, religion, occupation, club, school, community, and many other groupings. Learning that a stranger is a Mason, a physician, or a communist may profoundly affect the treatment we accord him. This is not entirely irrational, of course, because many "achieved" group memberships are informative about individual characteristics, at least on a probabilistic basis. Typically, however, discriminations seem to follow the lines of group boundaries, with those on the inside receiving advantageous treatment while those on the outside suffer disadvantageous treatment.

An important distinction to be taken into account in analyzing and evaluating positive and negative group discrimination is whether the group membership involved is *ascribed* or *achieved*. (Ascribed membership is automatically conferred by society, such as being classified as male or female; achieved status is the result of some action on the part of the person, such as being married or being a policeman.) In the former case it may be virtually impossible to escape negative discrimination by changing group membership; a person cannot change his race or sex to accommodate prevailing prejudices. Actually the dichotomy is by no means absolute, for religious affiliation or political party membership are not altogether voluntary. Social inheritance can be almost as rigid as biological inheritance. Family membership is ascribed for children, but achieved for parents. The practical problem for the individual, then, becomes "being" in the right groups to avoid negative discrimination. For many people the problem is not merely one of expediency but also of principle, since one may have strong ethical objections to changing group memberships, even when feasible, to gain some kind of social advantage. Changing one's name may eliminate some negative discrimination based on ethnicity, but it also raises serious ethical issues suggested by the phrase "ethnic treason" if one attempts to conceal his ethnic background.

Any given person will have a number of group memberships in a complex society, so that he will suffer or benefit from group discrimination depending upon which group or combinations of groups are relevant in a particular situation. His treatment will depend upon how he is perceived and classified and how the situation is defined by others. If an individual is perceived as a Black job applicant in an employment situation where racial discrimination is normative, he will be treated accordingly. One may be at a loss at times to know not only whether he is being treated in a particular way *because* of a group membership, but *which* of his group memberships is involved.

The most intense form of discrimination is that which is based upon a single group membership to the exclusion of all others. This means, for example, that because one is a Black, a Protestant, or an Indian, he is automatically treated differently regardless of whatever other group memberships or individual characteristics he may have. This is the most frustrating kind of negative discrimination one can encounter, and it is the most difficult to overcome. Unless the person can change his group membership he must endure unfavorable treatment. When such discrimination is positive it is a kind of "sociological windfall," especially if it is an ascribed membership which is involved. This kind of social advantage is likely to be highly rationalized and vigorously and emotionally defended if challenged. Such an advantage is not necessarily highly visible, however, because it may be firmly institutionalized, as in the case of a rigid caste system.

The logical antithesis of group discrimination is individualism, or an emphasis upon individual characteristics rather than group memberships in the evaluation and treatment of persons. Though societies differ with respect to this practice, there is no society in which group memberships of all kinds are ignored. In almost every society virtually all group memberships are ignored as a matter of principle in the dispensation of formal justice, even though group prejudice frequently affects the actual administration of the law. But such basic social institutions as the family and kinship tend to reduce individualism and encourage forms of group judgment and treatment. Societies vary also in terms of what kinds of group memberships are considered crucial in reaction formation; family connection was very important in ancient China, caste was of paramount significance in traditional India, while race (white or African) is of tremendous consequence in contemporary South Africa. One might even venture to classify societies as to whether or not they emphasize "groupism" or "individualism," and although dichotomous classification is patently impossible, ranking along a continuum would seem to be reasonable.

EMPIRICAL AND ETHICAL DIMENSIONS OF DISCRIMINATION

As in the case of prejudice, analysis of discrimination reveals two basic dimensions or forms, one representing the ethical issue, and the other the question of the empirical validity of the process. In other words, there are two fundamental questions to be asked about discrimination: (1) Is it ethically justifiable (that is, fair, moral)? and (2) Can it be justified in empirical terms (that is, is it logical and rational)? Discussions and arguments about discrimination inevitably revolve about these two issues. On an ethical level, the question is whether or not discrimination can be morally justified and what moral grounds exist for differential group treatment. On an analytical plane, the question centers on whether discrimination makes any logical sense, that is, whether it is rational in terms of given objectives.

As a moral issue discrimination is subject to the same kind of analysis as any other moral question. One can invoke many general ethical principles to sustain one's position; one can cite various moral authorities on the question; and one can argue that there are moral absolutes which govern such matters. In the final analysis, the question remains one of moral judgment, beyond the realm of scientific determination. Discrimination does seem to raise fundamental moral issues. This is not surprising when one considers that what is really at issue is how other people are to be treated. Should one respond differently to members of different groups? Should a person be treated in terms of his group membership? Should one offer a ride to a hitchhiker and is one morally justified in denying employment to a former convict?

In coming to grips with this question, it is necessary to take into account the time factor. One might postulate a kind of "sociological accounting system" which would attempt to assess the balance between positive and negative discrimination over some period of time. Similarly, one could conceive of a "moral accounting system" which would seek to redress grievances by balancing them with some form of positive discrimination; terms such as idemnification and reparations could be employed in this kind of analysis. *The issue, of course, is whether a group is entitled to some kind of sociological compensation for previous discrimination.* In contemporary American society, some institutions, in particular government agencies and subdivisions, have undertaken "affirmative action" programs in an effort to increase the number of minority group employees. The argument for such an approach is that previous discrimination has resulted in a very low percentage of minority group employees; consequently, it is necessary to make a special positive effort to recruit them and to facilitate their adjustment and success on the job.

The concepts of affirmative action and compensatory employment programs pose exquisite rational and moral questions about discrimination. Again the time span is a fundamental variable in assessing the rationality of these programs; for example, if there has been discrimination against one group over a period of time in, say, employment, then presumably this has created a pool of unemployed persons, everything else being equal, who are more talented, so that positive action in seeking out employees from this group is rational in the sense that it corrects the previous errors. Similarly, to switch from a discriminatory selection policy to an equal opportunity policy can be regarded as irrational in the sense that there is no opportunity for the victimized group to achieve equality because of previous disadvantages —to catch up, in other words. It is rather like a football game in which one team has thirteen players and the other nine during the first half of the game, and then at the beginning of the second half the rules are changed so that the two teams have an equal number of players; this is irrational in that the smaller team is likely to be behind in the score by half time and will suffer a handicap at the beginning of the second half. The exquisite moral issue, of course, is what time period to select; for example, should a labor union which now admits Black apprentices but did not ten years ago be compelled to forego or attenuate the apprenticeship process for some Black craftsmen while still requiring new white apprentices to serve the full apprenticeship? This is a very controversial moral question in American society. We frequently find Blacks on one side of the issue and various other ethnic groups holding contrary opinions. Some ethnic group members point to previous discrimination which they suffered when they first arrived in the United States but which they claim they were able to overcome by dint of effort, while American Blacks point angrily to the wholesale prohibition on membership in many craft unions for Blacks for many generations. The debate is robust and bitter.

The rationality of discrimination reduces itself to the question of whether the kind of group discrimination practiced is logically consistent with the objectives of the selective process. It is as logically sound to select students for music scholarships on the basis of a musical aptitude test as it is to hire secretaries on the basis of typing skill. Discrimination is rational to the extent that it is empirically valid, or efficient in terms of the established aims of selection. It is patently irrational and inefficient, according to this principle, to select students for medical school on the basis of religious affiliation, since there is evidently no demonstrable correlation between medical aptitude and theological perspective. Group discrimination based upon such categories as race, religion, ethnicity and the like is not likely to be logical or efficient for the selection of persons for such roles as occupations. These criteria are highly efficient only for selecting persons on the basis of race, religion, or ethnicity. To employ such groupings for other purposes simply indicates that the discrimination is irrational and suggests that it is motivated by a rigid emotional attitude, unless it is in connection with some kind of "affirmative action program" as previously discussed.

It is to be expected that efforts will be made to conceal the real basis of discrimination in many instances, and that there may even be self-deception. One is likely to encounter rationalizations of racial discrimination which hold that there is such a high correlation between racial group membership and certain skills, aptitudes, or traits that it is rational and logical to discriminate on the basis of these kinds of groupings. This argument seems very difficult to sustain because there are not high correlations. Consequently, it is really inefficient to discriminate on such bases *unless* there is an intent to treat these groups categorically in the first place. It would make much more sense to discriminate directly on the basis of a particularly desirable trait or combination of traits. Yet while many persons or organizations are not willing to admit irrational behavior, irrational discrimination is not uncommon, and in many instances it is patently the result of the intervention of an emotional factor, namely prejudice, which assumes that "they are all alike," and therefore they should all be treated alike.

In the case of organizations which select and admit members on the basis of certain criteria, one would expect logical consistency. Yet criteria for membership, in the final analysis, would be an ethical issue to be disputed on an ethical plane, being defended or attacked according to various ethical principles. If an organization is rational in its actions and sincere about its membership requirements, it should admit all persons who are technically qualified. Thus if it wishes to exclude certain racial or ethnic groups it should state this preference. Then it can proceed rationally to select members. However, to reject a group categorically from membership is irrational if rejection is justified in terms of alleged characteristics of their ethnic group, since no group is perfectly homogeneous. Evidently college social fraternities and sororities are often either guilty of infidelity to their admission criteria or hold their real criteria secret. At Portland State College, where six national sorority chapters were suspended for refusing to pledge Blacks, a spokesman claimed that two Black girls who were rejected for membership were "eminently qualified" and were "the kind of pledges all sororities are looking for."[13] To reject such pledges in advance because of group membership is tantamount to admitting an irrational prejudice against the group as a whole. Organizations which practice such categorical group discrimination seldom admit to this attitude publicly even though it may be tacitly understood widely. Ethically, it is exceedingly difficult in terms of any code or system to justify wholesale exclusion.[14]

Some forms of group (both achieved and ascribed group membership) discrimination are sanctioned by certain cultures, which is to say they are deemed to be morally legitimate. In American society it is considered right to discriminate in favor of war veterans (achieved group membership) in many areas of government employment and to give preference to physicians over visitors in parking space adjacent to hospitals. In some societies women (ascribed group membership) are not allowed to eat until after all males have been served, and some societies grant special privileges to holy men, children, soldiers, royalty, poets. Because the practice is taken for granted, there are many forms of discrimination which are not obvious or visible. In fact, such actions are not usually considered to be discrimination in the popular sense because there is no dispute about the ethical justification of them. There is no protest when blind persons are granted an extra tax exemption, or when students with high grades are granted scholarships. The popular view of discrimination identifies only instances in which differential treatment violates some cultural moral norm, as, for example, in the case of blind persons being assessed higher taxes, or high ranking students being rejected for scholarships in favor of students with mediocre grades. Of course, the sociological fact of the matter is that discrimination in the technical sense in which we have defined it occurs whenever there is any kind of differential treatment of individuals based on group membership, regardless of whether society considers such treatment morally right or wrong, or whether there is any consensus about it in the society. Discrimination may be considered a social problem when there are conflicting value judgments about it. When some social norms define discrimination as proper and desirable while others condemn it, the social problem exists in the sense of a controversial issue.

In sum, any kind of group discrimination can be defended or attacked on ethical grounds and analyzed in rational terms. Whether or not discrimination based upon some kind of social category or classification is fair or unjust must be argued as an ethical issue, the resolution depending upon the prevailing social values which pertain to how people should be treated. Given certain ethical premises for discrimination, such as the value judgment that persons over forty years of age should not be conscripted into the armed forces, there remains the empirical question of whether or not this judgment constitutes rational discrimination from the standpoint of selection of the most effective fighting men. These two basic questions are to be found in all instances of group discrimination, and this mode of analysis should enhance one's understanding of the nature of discrimination.

The concept of discrimination is comparable to the concept of race in that both terms are much easier to define than to apply. It is no great task to develop a reasonably rigorous definition of group discrimination, but it is a great challenge to apply that definition with precision. There is substantial agreement on the meaning of discrimination, but there are sharp differences concerning where and to what degree it exists in practice.[15]

There are many patterns, forms, and objects of discrimination; indeed, it seems unlikely that there is any group which does not suffer or benefit from some negative or positive discrimination.[16] The history and literature of mankind are replete with both dramatic and subtle examples. The following chapter attempts to provide some examples of the social effects of prejudice and discrimination with particular reference to contemporary American society.

Notes

1. Aaron Antonovsky, "The Social Meaning of Discrimination," *Phylon* 31, no. 1 (Spring 1960): 81. Used by permission of *Phylon*.
2. Ibid., p. 82. Used by permission.
3. Ibid., p. 85. Used by permission.
4. Ibid. Used by permission.
5. Robert L. Hamblin, "The Dynamics of Racial Discrimination," *Social Problems* 20, no. 2 (Fall 1962): 103.
6. Gary S. Becker, *The Economics of Discrimination* (Chicago: University of Chicago Press, 1957), p. 3.
7. Ibid.
8. Ibid., p. 7.
9. Ibid., p. 122.
10. Ibid.
11. Claire Selltiz, "The Use of Survey Methods in a Citizen's Campaign Against Discrimination," *Human Organization* 14 (1970): 19-25.
12. This is illustrated by the patterns in discrimination against women faculty in colleges and universities. For example, one study of women faculty in graduate departments of sociology reached this conclusion: "What emerges from our study is evidence of a systematic pattern of excluding women from the two organizational rewards that most influence an individual's prestige. Women are excluded from high-ranking departments and they are excluded from high-ranking positions in almost all departments. The data convincingly demonstrate that these exclusions are not justified by personal qualifications: In every personal characteristic related to merit scholarly performance, women sociologists are equal to men." Michele Patterson, "Alice in Wonderland: A Study of Women Faculty in Graduate Departments of Sociology," *The American Sociologist* 6, no. 3 (August 1971): 232.
   At the level of personal experience, the social psychology of discrimination against women in the academic world is conveyed by the following passage:
   "Recently my husband and I accepted a joint appointment at a university, he in the sociology department, I in the medical school. It is important for the rest of my story to note that not only are women rarely found among the faculty, but social science departments at medical schools are equally rare. Many lay persons as well as professionals have never thought of medicine as having anything to do with social science.
   One of my early extracurricular academic obligations at the medical school was to respond to an invitation to a small faculty reception. When I came to

the door of the room where the reception was held, a gentleman walked hastily toward me and positioned himself in such a way as to block my entrance. 'May I help you?' he asked politely, but uninvitingly. I asked him whether this was the reception of the premedical committee, 'Yes,' he said still blocking my way. A questioning look in his eyes seemed to ask for an explanation of my presence, and I said: 'I have been invited to this reception. I am Rose Coser.' 'Will Dr. Coser be coming?' 'I *am* Dr. Coser.' 'Oh,' he said, somewhat startled, and, stepping aside, asked if he could take my coat and directed me to the bar." Rose Coser, "Of Nepotism and Marginality," (letter to the editor) *The American Sociologist* 6, no. 3 (August 1971): 259-60.

13. Urbana, Illinois, *The Daily Illini*, 28 October 1963.

14. See James G. Martin, "Group Discrimination in Organizational Membership Selection," *Phylon* 20, no. 2 (1959): 186-92, and Ahrea Mchung Lee, *Fraternities without Brotherhood* (Boston: Beacon Press, 1955).

15. Discrimination is also legal concept which has been defined by legislation and court decisions. A landmark court decision was *Brown v. Board of Education* in 1954, which was followed in later years by a number of other decisions relating to segregation laws discriminating against Blacks. In 1971, a Superior Court judge in the State of Washington ordered the University of Washington to admit to law school a white student who contended he was discriminated against when thirty black students with poorer qualifications were accepted for admission. In his opinion, the judge stated "It seems to me that the law school here wishing to achieve a greater minority representation in accomplishing this, gave preference to the members of some races. . . ." He found that the plaintiff had not "been accorded the equal protection of the law guaranteed by the fourteenth amendment. . . . In my opinion, the only safe rule is to treat all races alike, and I feel that this is what is required under the equal protection clause. . . ." It is noteworthy that the plaintiff also claimed he was further discriminated against because some of those admitted to the law school were non-residents, but the judge declared "there is no constitutional restriction upon admitting non-resident students." *Higher Education and National Affairs* 20, no. 36 (October 1971): 3.

16. For a summary of a comprehensive study of discrimination in American society see Walter Mendelson, *Discrimination* (Englewood Cliffs, N.J.: Prentice-Hall, 1962).

Social Consequences
of Prejudice
and Discrimination

10

INTRODUCTION

As previously observed, prejudice tends to result in discrimination. Together, the two variables produce a variety of social and personal consequences. In this chapter we will attempt to examine the principal ramifications of prejudice and discrimination.

One of the more *visible* products of prejudice and discrimination is the *segregation* of groups by various means such as place of residence, school attendance, and membership in social groups. A more *dramatic* product of prejudice and discrimination, however, is intergroup conflict in its various forms, such as lynchings, interrace warfare, and race riots. To be sure, all forms of prejudice and discrimination do not produce overt intergroup conflict, yet it is doubtful that long-term subjugation of a group of people will be accepted passively by these subordinated persons.

With respect to the effects of prejudice and discrimination, one can observe both societal and personal consequences. For instance, the economic system of a society is affected by group discrimination, because it influences the allocation of human resources and the distribution of wealth. At the personal level one encounters a variety of *psychological reactions* to prejudice and discrimination; this behavior can be viewed as a question of the "psychic strategy" to be used by an individual to cope with frustration.

While a major portion of this chapter will be devoted to the aforementioned effects, we also feel that it is important to examine the effects of prejudice and discrimination upon the *person who is prejudiced* and who engages in discrimination, because such effects have profound implications for the personality and behavior of such a person. Succinctly then, the principal consequences of prejudice and discrimination to be explored in this chapter will be segregation, conflict, economic effects, power and status, and the psychological reactions of the oppressed and the oppressor. No single comprehensive theory is adequate to account for the myriad of effects of and responses to prejudice and discrimination. Thus we have not attempted to wed our analysis to any monistic theory. Some forms of reaction to prejudice and discrimination may be understood by reference to collective behavior theory, such as that of Blumer or Smelser, while Merton's response paradigm of conformity, innovation, ritualism, retreatism, and rebellion could explain some other patterns of reaction.[1] At the level of personal response to prejudice and discrimination one must eventually resort to clinical explanations. Our task in this chapter is basically expository rather than theoretical explanation although we have made some references to theories where it seemed helpful to the analysis.

SEGREGATION

Segregation refers to the social separation of groups by various means, principally by some form of physical separation such as residence. Although group segregation may be either voluntary or involuntary, we are primarily concerned with the involuntary variety, that which is motivated by prejudice and has a negative discriminatory effect. Such segregation is essentially a form of rejection and implies an attitude of social distance on the part of the dominant group. The group which is involuntarily segregated is viewed as socially inferior or undesirable, and segregation is a process used to prevent certain kinds of perceived repugnant interaction. A case in point would be the apartheid system in the Republic of South Africa which prohibits various forms of social contact between Afrikaners and the native African population. Hence there are a variety of restrictions on where Africans may reside, and in general they are excluded from living permanently in South African cities. An insight into the nature of apartheid is provided by the following passage from Pierre Van Den Berghe's book on the subject.

> The basic constant in the South African story is the concern of the white man for his survival and security and his determination to maintain his racial identity and his dominance. Over the centuries he has achieved a position of privilege and power which

few of his kind are willing to forego. While there are differences and conflicts within the white group, whites of all classes benefit by membership in the white hierarchy. White workers, particularly the incompetent and semi-skilled, are protected by their race. Aside from the economic advantages, there are imponderables, such as the sentiment of superiority and the prestige and power to rule. To whites generally, security is inconceivable in a system of equality; and dominance is seen as essential if the white man is to be protected against biological, social, cultural and political innundation.[2]

Segregation itself is a form of discrimination and it is likely to be associated with other forms of discrimination. A striking example of this is offered in the case of the town of Shaw, Mississippi, where the population (1971) has been approximately 2,500 with about 1,500 Blacks and 1,000 whites. Nearly 98 percent of all houses on unpaved streets in Shaw were occupied by Blacks and 97 percent of the houses not served by sanitary sewers were in Black neighborhoods. All modern street lighting fixtures were in white neighborhoods which also had effective storm sewers and drainage ditches; Black neighborhoods had only a few haphazard and unmaintained ditches. A lawsuit was filed by the NAACP and Educational Fund, Inc., and the United States Court of Appeals ruled that the town of Shaw had to provide services on a racially equal basis.

The above example is particularly striking in that one of the most visible and repressive measures a majority can employ to subjugate a minority group is to confine them to a physical area in terms of residence and other activities. Other examples include American Indian groups that have been confined to reservations; Jews, Gypsies, communists, and various other groups that were sent to concentration camps during the Nazi regime in Germany and in the United States; and Americans of Japanese ancestry who were sent to relocation camps during World War II.[3]

Usually less subtle forms of involuntary segregation are more commonplace. The expressions of prejudice which often result in segregation are manifold: the contemptuous stare, calculated rudeness, condescending courtesy, studied avoidance, harrassment by epithet, all convey emphatically the idea that a group is not welcome and should "keep to itself." Involuntary segregation might be called pernicious incivility or a form of social snobbery. Whatever the nuances of method, the message is clear—the dominant group rejects the minority group and insists that members keep to themselves in various areas of social interaction. The implication is strong that there will be some kind of contamination if the sociologically inferior or undesirable group is not kept at proper social distance. This is the spirit of prejudice and discrimination, and it is the social-psychological force behind involuntary segregation.

Residential Segregation

Despite civil rights legislation at the national, state, and local levels, residential segregation in American society based on race is a persistent sociological fact of life. The current trend in American cities is an increase in proportion of the Black population as whites move to the suburbs as table 9 shows. For example the 1970 census revealed that fourteen cities joined Washington, D.C., and Bessemer, Alabama, in having predominantly Black populations during the 1960s.[4] (Charleston, South Carolina, changed from a Black majority in 1960 to a white majority in 1970.) Although some of these cities are in effect "Black suburbs," in the central areas of most major American cities the Black-to-white ratio is increasing steadily. Furthermore, research indicates that the residential segregation patterns of central cities are reappearing in the suburbs.

The term ghetto is frequently applied to segregated residential areas although it is not a precise sociological term. In Europe in the Middle Ages the term was applied to restricted areas in which Jews were required to live, but nowadays it is more suggestive of the Black areas of American cities with the connotation of poverty and a physically deteriorated area. There is one school of thought which holds that the ghetto is like a colony and can be understood by that analogy as the following passage suggests:

The Ghetto As Colony

The key relationships which must be demonstrated before the colonial analogy can be accepted are the existence between two distinct and clearly separate groups of a superior-inferior status relationship encompassing both (1) economic control and exploitation, and (2) political dependence and subjugation.[5]

The author concludes that "an historical comparison of the forms which colonialism has taken, and a description of the place of Blacks

TABLE 9
AMERICAN CITIES WITH BLACK POPULATIONS IN
EXCESS OF 50 PERCENT

Percentage Black	
71.1	Washington, D.C.
54.2	Newark, New Jersey
51.3	Atlanta, Georgia
52.2	Bessemer, Alabama
71.1	Compton, California
69.1	East St. Louis, Illinois
52.8	Gary, Indiana
53.1	East Orange, New Jersey
82.3	Willowbrook, California
80.6	Westmont, California
58.6	East Cleveland, Ohio
56.0	Florence-Graham, California
55.3	Highland Park, Michigan
55.2	Petersburg, Virginia
52.0	Greenville, Mississippi
50.5	Prichard, Alabama

SOURCE: Constructed from U.S., Bureau of the Census, *Current Population Reports*, Series P-60, no. 80 (Washington, D.C.: Government Printing Office, 1971).

in the American economy, make clear that internal colonialism is an apt description of the exploitation of Blacks in our society."[6]

Similar arguments have been advanced by Kenneth Clark and by Robert Blauner among others.[7] Blauner maintains that the Black ghettos represent a colonized status because of involuntary segregation, because they persisted over several generations in contrast to the immigrant ghettos, and because the European ethnic ghettos soon acquired ownership of their areas including commercial as well as residential property. The colonial model holds that Black ghettos have been dominated by external economic and political forces so that they are an "internal colony." Nathan Glazer is of the opinion that today's Black youth do not subscribe to the traditional ethnic ghetto vision in American society in which assimilation and social mobility enabled a person to achieve economic social and political success.[8] He believes that some other option such as a form of pluralism, separatism, or even a separate nation may become the prevalent choice.

Social Affiliation Segregation

An historical example of social affiliation segregation in American society would be the seating restrictions imposed upon bus passengers in the South before they were prohibited by civil rights legislation in the 1960s, especially the Civil Rights Acts of 1957 and 1964. Social custom and state laws in many southern states required that Black passengers sit in the rear of the bus. (The Interstate Commerce Commission banned segregation on busses, in waiting rooms, and on coaches in interstate commerce in November, 1955.) This practice was dramatically challenged by a Black female passenger, Mrs. Rosa Parks, in Montgomery, Alabama, in 1955. Mrs. Parks, a department store seamstress, was arrested for refusing to move to the back of the bus as required of Blacks by a city ordinance. She was taken to police court later in the day, and with 2000 people in attendance, charged with violating the corresponding state law and was fined $10.00.[9] This led to a highly publicized bus boycott in December, 1955, by Blacks under the leadership of Dr. Martin Luther King, Jr., and launched, in turn, a civil rights movement to eliminate other forces of segregation and discrimination.

There are many who would argue that support for racial segregation in all areas of American life is based upon the desire of persons to maintain social autonomy. It is common to hear persons say that "I don't mind working with them, but I don't want to live next door to them." Implicit in this statement is the contention that a neighbor is much more intimate than a colleague or fellow worker, in the sense that the former has social access to one. No doubt there are many who would counter that it is the economic factor (resale, property value) that looms large in their minds. This rationale, however, is suspect since there is very little evidence which would support the position that Blacks ruin property values though there is evidence that when Blacks move in whites move out rapidly—often selling cheaply to avoid interracial contact—thus the decline in property values.

To be sure, the question of which type of segregation is being attempted in a given situation is admittedly difficult to answer. What is apparent, however, is that different types of segregation often are used by majority groups simultaneously to disenfranchise minority groups politically and to exploit them economically.

Stereotype Reinforcement and Marginality

One of the adverse effects of involuntary segregation of minority groups is that, because they are out of the "sociological mainstream," they suffer a constriction of opportunities. Their opportunity structures are more limited as is their knowledge of how to succeed by established social rules. This is borne out in a study on school integration and achievement which demonstrated that Blacks graduating from integrated high schools had a greater likelihood of breaking out of "traditional jobs." Apparently attending an integrated school provided more information about the job-finding process which seems to be based largely upon informal means of communication.[10] Another study of Blacks and whites in the consumer financial system reported that "compared with white families with similar incomes, Black families use fewer savings and insurance services but more kinds of credit, have a smaller total amount of financial resources and tend to use the less advantageous type of financial services."[11] This is attributed to lack of knowledge about the consumer financial system. Thus, there is a cyclical effect of prejudice and discrimination with respect to the eradication of stereotype and the marginal status of a minority group. If prejudice and discrimination are directed toward a group to the extent that their life chances are adversely affected, then there is an increase in the likelihood that members of this group will suffer a constriction of opportunities. Basically this means that the marginal status of the group will be increased, adding substantial credence to stereotyped knowledge others might have about the minority group.

CONFLICT

Group prejudice and group discrimination engender and precipitate intergroup conflict. People who are objects of prejudice and discrimination tend to resent it and to develop hostility against those who practice it against them. Conflict is also stimulated by the ill will and condescension which underlie prejudice and discrimination; aggressive behavior is prompted by the same kinds of emotions and situations which produce prejudicial and discriminatory behavior.[12] Conflict may be viewed as an effort to redress the grievances of a victimized group and an effort to maintain the subjugation by a group practicing prejudice and discrimination. In its most extreme form conflict aims to commit genocide to eliminate the other group entirely. It is important to point out, however, that not all forms of intergroup conflict have these overtones. Let us consider several forms of conflict which will include relatively mild *and* violent conflict.

Obvious examples of relatively mild conflict should come to mind when one recalls the days, and to be more precise, years immediately following the arrest of Mrs. Rosa Parks in 1955 in Montgomery, Alabama: bus boycotts, lunch counter sit-ins, and the like in the South in the late 1950s and early 1960s. In all of these examples, one group had internalized and practiced an ideology of nonviolence which was opposed to victimization and subjugation of the other group. Elimination of the out-group was not the intent of the activities sanctioned and carried out by organizations such as the NAACP, SCLC, CORE, and others. Conflict was in evidence, however, since basic values, norms, ideals, and so forth were being nonviolently challenged. However, it is rather difficult for two groups to be in severe conflict when one group refuses to enter the combat arena.

As a general rule the repression of a minority group encourages violent reactions but this is dependent upon the cultural and political context. For example the systematic effort on the part of the Nazis in Germany to eliminate the Jewish population met with relatively little violent reaction, partly because the ultimate aim of the Nazis was often not apparent to the victims until it was too late. There was a violent uprising in a Jewish ghetto in Warsaw during the Nazi occupation but it ended in tragedy for most of the participants.[13] Some individuals are more inclined to react violently to prejudice and discrimination than others; for example, a study of the participants in a 1964 riot in the Bedford-Stuyvesant ghetto in New York City found that "although violence-oriented Blacks were found in all segments of the community, the young, recent newcomers to the area and males were more likely than the old, long-term residents and females to be violence-oriented."[14] Also, Blacks in the lowest income groups are more likely to be violence-oriented than those in the highest income group. One might interpret the finding that Blacks in the lowest income group are more likely to be violence-oriented as being due to the fact that they are the most oppressed by the social system. Thus, cultural, political, and structural as well as social-psychological factors must be taken into account if any adequate explanation of different types of protest is to be given.

The increase in violent protest among American Blacks in the 1960s seemed to reflect a growing bitterness about what the Kerner Report called "white racism." The inclination to violence seemed to be associated with a sense of alienation and powerlessness; a study of participants in the Watts riots in 1965 found that "isolated Blacks and Blacks with intense feelings of powerlessness and dissatisfaction were more prone to violent action than those who were less alienated."[15]

A crucial but subjective question about the role of violent protest is whether it subsequently increases or decreases prejudice and discrimination for the minority group. Like many other questions in the field of intergroup relations it is one which is saturated by emotion. It seems unlikely that minority individuals engaging in acts of violent protest during riots or other forms of disturbances do so as a result of deliberate plans, and that they have calculated the impact of such actions on the majority group. However, one may find that majority group members are unable to separate their attitudes toward violent protest behavior from their attitudes *and* behavior toward the minority group. This is understandable when one takes into account the fact that reactions to violent protest are generally emotional and complex; for example, reactions of fear and anger and perplexity can be expected, but on the other hand, rigorous objectivity indicates that there are other reactions which may benefit the minority group. Thus a spontaneous violent disturbance may call dramatic attention to the frustrations and grievances of a disadvantaged group and stimulate some efforts to reduce discrimination and improve conditions as well as to prevent a recurrence of violence. This process is suggested in an old American political proverb, "The squeaking wheel gets the grease."

One student of protest in American society, Jerome Skolnick, finds mass protest "an essentially political phenomenon engaged in by normal people" and he claims that violence "when it occurs is usually not planned, but arises out of interaction between protesters and responding authorities; that violence has frequently accompanied the efforts of deprived groups to achieve status in American society."[16]

The impact of violent protest on the attitudes and behavior of the majority group depends upon their perception of the motivation of the violent action. A study of the Watts riot by Edward Jeffries, Ralph Turner, and Vincent Morris yielded such a conclusion:

> Finally, it is important to consider what contribution our study
> has made to a better understanding of how those interested in

improving the conditions of blacks and other disadvantaged groups may most effectively pursue their attempts to attract and mobilize the good will of what is usually an apathetic and often hostile majority. If the assumption that support of needed social reforms is closely linked to perceiving a collective disturbance as social protest is correct, then an understanding of the reasons for such a definition can be of considerable value. Our findings indicate that the previous recognition of existing injustices is of central importance. For example, even among those whose basic attitudes towards blacks are relatively antagonistic, almost half (48%) see the Watts riot as a protest if they believe discrimination exists in some degree, as compared to only 36% of respondents seeing the disturbance as a protest among those who are favorable in this basic attitudes toward blacks but believe there is very little or no discrimination. Thus credibility due to awareness of injustice is more important than a basically favorable attitude toward the protesting group in its effect upon a protest definition. Consequently, devising ways to intensify public awareness of the extent of prejudice and discrimination continues to be a promising strategy toward reducing racial inequality in the United States.[17]

The dilemma, which seems to be an unconscious one, for the majority group is to react to violent protest in a way which does not encourage and reinforce these methods of protest. One can argue reasonably that the appropriate time to make reforms and take measures to improve the lot of American Blacks would be during a "cool summer"; that is, to implement programs to correct the inequalities from which American Blacks suffer during a tranquil period, so that there is a reward for tranquil methods of protest, rather than after violent disturbances. However, such a strategy is rarely used by a majority group vis-à-vis a minority group even though it is obviously a more rational approach if one's objective is to discourage minority group members from violent methods of protest. This is not unusual due to the fact that groups enjoying a power advantage ordinarily *do not* initiate reduction in their power unless there are other advantages which can be ascertained. For example, a minority group may, as we have pointed out, use many techniques in an effort to create conditions which make it advantageous for a majority group to release its power. Violent methods of protest represent one of these methods and reinforcement appears to be a by-product.

During more tranquil times, a majority group most certainly could reduce its power, however, it does appear that some form of protest by the minority group is necessary in order to bring its plight to the attention of the majority group.[18] The precise nature of the protest is undoubtedly open to question and acceptance and endorsement to a very great extent, depending upon one's position in the social structure.[19] As we suggest in chapter 11, such techniques as moral suasion may alienate fewer members of the majority group than a technique of violent protest, however, at least in the past, they have achieved success much more slowly. Thus, for a growing number of Blacks in the United States, violent protest appears to be a superior technique of achieving intergroup equality, while many whites in the United States, in spite of the perceptual variable discussed, must long for the days when moral suasion was the chief mode used by Blacks. Let us turn to some more specific instances of violent conflict in the United States.

Race Riots

The most bitter fruit of prejudice and discrimination, American style, has been what is commonly referred to as the "race riot." The phrase race riot connotes violent conflict between racial groups and in twentieth-century American society this means Blacks and whites. Most of the violent protest on the part of Blacks during the sixties and early seventies has not involved any *significant* fighting between Blacks and whites, in fact in some cases a few whites have joined with Blacks in looting behavior during disturbances. The classical American race riot is illustrated by the 1917 riot in East St. Louis, Illinois, the Chicago riot of 1919, and the one in Detroit in 1943.[20]

The East St. Louis riot occurred during the month of July and was triggered by the assault on Blacks by white gangs. Blacks retaliated by attacking an automobile which they thought contained some of their previous tormentors but which turned out to be a police squad car. Two white detectives were killed. A large-scale battle between Blacks and whites followed the next day, resulting in numerous injuries and the deaths of nine whites and thirty-nine Blacks.

In Chicago during the summer of 1919, friction developed between Blacks and whites concerning bathing beach boundaries. Rumors spread rapidly that a white man had been responsible for the drowning of a Black youth and that a white policeman had refused to arrest the guilty man. The active rioting lasted for a week and was concentrated in the stockyards area and the "black belt" area, especially along the street car routes. Individual Black passengers on street cars were often attacked by white gangs. The police were unable to control the rioting and the state militia was called in to restore order; the Black community seemed to welcome the militia because they were more effective in protecting Blacks from the roving bands of whites.[21] Many of the deaths (fifteen whites and twenty-three Blacks reported) occurred when a Black or white found himself in an area where the other racial group had numerical superiority.

In Detroit during the summer of 1943 a riot was precipitated by fights between whites and Blacks at an amusement park and by a false rumor that a Black woman and her baby had been killed there. The Detroit riot involved a considerable amount of property destruction, especially white-owned businesses in Black neighborhoods, which marked a significant change in the previous patterns and was in that respect more like the disturbances by Blacks in America during the summers of the 1960s.[22]

The eruption of violence seems to be generally attributable to an accumulation of frustrations and grievances which finally become intolerable. In the language of the report of the National Advisory Commission on Civil Disorders (the Kerner Commission): "Our investigation in the 1967 riot cities establishes that virtually every major episode of violence was foreshadowed by an accumulation of unresolved grievances by whites spreading dissatisfaction among Negroes with the unwillingness or inability of local governments to respond."[23] The commission offered the following generalizations about the patterns of disorder in twenty-three American cities:

> The final incident before the outbreak of disorder, and the initial violence itself, generally took place in the evening or at night at a place in which it was normal for many people to be on the streets.
>
> Violence usually occurred almost immediately following the occurrence of the final precipitating incident, and then escalated rapidly. With but few exceptions, violence subsided during the day, and flared rapidly again at night. The night-day cycles continued through the early period of the major disorders.
>
> Disorder generally began with rock and bottle throwing and window breaking. Once store windows were broken, looting usually followed.
>
> Disorder did not erupt as a result of a single "triggering" or "precipitating" incident. Instead, it was generated out of an increasingly disturbed social atmosphere, in which typically a series of tension-heightening incidents over a perior of weeks or months became

linked in the minds of many in the Negro community with a reservoir of underlying grievances. At some point in the mounting tension, a further incident—in itself often routine or trivial—became the breaking point and the tension spilled over into violence.

"Prior" incidents, which increased tensions and ultimately led to violence, were police actions in almost half the cases; police actions were "final" incidents before the outbreak of violence in 12 of the 24 surveyed disorders.

No particular control tactic was successful in every situation. The varied effectiveness of control techniques emphasizes the need for advance training, planning, adequate intelligence systems, and knowledge of the ghetto community.

Negotiations between Negroes—including young militants as well as older Negro leaders—and white officials concerning "terms of peace" occurred during virtually all the disorders surveyed. In many cases, these negotiations involved discussion of underlying grievances as well as the handling of the disorder by control authorities.

The typical rioter was a teenager or young adult, a lifelong resident of the city in which he rioted, a high school dropout; he was, nevertheless, somewhat better educated than his nonrioting Negro neighbor, and was usually underemployed or employed in a menial job. He was proud of his race, extremely hostile to both whites and middle-class Negroes and, although informed about politics, highly distrustful of the political system.

A Detroit survey revealed that approximately 11 percent of the total residents of two riot areas admitted participation in the rioting, 20 to 25 percent identified themselves as "bystanders," over 16 percent identified themselves as "counter-rioters" who urged rioters to "cool it," and the remaining 48 to 53 percent said they were at home or elsewhere and did not participate. In a survey of Negro males between the ages of 15 and 35 residing in the disturbance area in Newark, about 45 percent identified themselves as rioters and about 55 percent as "noninvolved."

Most rioters were young Negro males. Nearly 53 percent of arrestees were between 15 and 24 years of age; nearly 81 percent between 15 and 35.

In Detroit and Newark about 74 percent of the rioters were brought up in the North. In contrast, of the noninvolved, 36 percent in Detroit and 52 percent in Newark were brought up in the North.

What the rioters appeared to be seeking was fuller participation in the social order and the material benefits enjoyed by the majority of American citizens. Rather than rejecting the American system, they were anxious to obtain a place for themselves in it.

Numerous Negro counter-rioters walked the streets urging rioters to "cool it." The typical counter-rioter was better educated and had higher income than either the rioter or the noninvolved.

The proportion of Negroes in local government was substantially smaller than the Negro proportion of population. Only three of the 20 cities studied had more than one Negro legislator; none had ever had a Negro mayor or city manager. In only four cities did Negroes hold other important policy-making positions or serve as heads of municipal departments.

Although almost all cities had some sort of formal grievance mechanism for handling citizen complaints, this typically was regarded by Negroes as ineffective and was generally ignored.

Although specific grievances varied from city to city, at least 12 deeply held grievances can be identified and ranked into three levels of relative intensity:

First Level of Intensity

1. Police practices
2. Unemployment and underemployment
3. Inadequate housing

Second Level of Intensity

4. Inadequate education
5. Poor recreation facilities and programs
6. Ineffectiveness of the political structure and grievance mechanisms

Third Level of Intensity

7. Disrespectful white attitudes
8. Discriminatory administration of justice
9. Inadequacy of federal programs
10. Inadequacy of municipal services
11. Discriminatory consumer and credit practices
12. Inadequate welfare programs[24]

The most general conclusion was that "white racism is essentially responsible for the explosive mixture which has been accumulating in our cities since the end of World War II."[25] The principal ingredients of this mixture were: pervasive discrimination and segregation in employment, education and housing, which have resulted in the continuing exclusion of great numbers of Blacks from the benefits of economic progress; Black immigration and white exodus, which have produced the massive and growing concentrations of impoverished Blacks in our major cities, creating a growing crisis of deteriorating facilities and services and unmet human needs; the Black ghettos where segregation and poverty converge on the young to destroy opportunity and enforce failure; crime, drug addiction, dependency on welfare, and bitterness and resentment against society in general and white society in particular are the result.

The critical question which must be asked about the Kerner report is the extent to which the collective disturbances were motivated by the participants' desire to rectify racial injustices or whether they were reactions to specific incidents such as provocative police actions.

A reasonable answer would seem to be that a general sense of relative deprivation and frustration is a necessary condition for these events and when combined with a provocative incident, such as police action which is perceived as discriminatory and motivated by prejudice, the social dynamite is ignited. We are inclined to concur with Joseph S. Himes' conclusion in his theoretical explanation of the racial conflict in the 1950s and 1960s: "The times produced that conjuncture of motivations, power resources, social organizations, and tactical devices that triggered conflict as the expected outcome of change and by the same token virtually eliminated any other possible outcome."[26]

ECONOMIC EFFECTS

John Dollard, in a classic work, included economic prestige and power advantages among other gains experienced by whites as a direct function of Black subordination.[27] The "economic gain" concept has been explored empirically, and recently by Sidney Wilhelm, Edwin Powell, Norval Glenn and Philips Cutright, among others. Wilhelm and Powell contend the economic "need" for Blacks has attenuated to the point that if Blacks were to disappear, they would hardly be missed. Since, in all likelihood, this does not appear to be forthcoming, it can be claimed that a major question remains unanswered. That question is related to the profits majority groups extract from prejudice and discrimination.

The question of the economic consequences of discrimination is a rather complex one and answers depend in part upon the kind of economic theory and analysis one applies. For example, Gary Becker has argued that discrimination by whites against Blacks involves costs which whites are willing to pay in order to avoid association with

Blacks.[28] Lester C. Thurow, on the other hand, has advanced the theory that whites in American society realize gains of some fifteen million dollars per year because of certain monopolistic economic powers they possess.[29] The crucial answer one requires to resolve this paradox is whether the total productivity of a society would be increased or not if discrimination were eliminated. One's economic intuition may suggest that since discrimination obviously prevents the most efficient use of human resources, then the total productivity of a society is limited accordingly. On the other hand, it is plausible that a dominant group should profit from the economic subjugation of a minority. Thus it is conceivable that if discrimination against Blacks were eliminated the total productivity could be increased by an amount which would increase Black income equal to whites if one accepts Thurow's theory—or that whites would not be charged the *cost* of their discrimination. The latter alternative, of course, tends to beg the question because according to Becker's theory whites are willing to pay this price to avoid contact with Blacks.

Thus, if discrimination were eliminated then whites would not be *able* to pay to avoid contact with Blacks.

Prejudice and discrimination seem to impose a kind of sociological tax on minority groups, a tax which is paid to the dominant group. This is why one must give some credence to the proposition that economic motivation lies behind prejudice and discrimination. It should be noted that this does not argue against the thesis that prejudice and discrimination are economically inefficient for society, it only asserts that within the economic structure of a society prejudice and discrimination result in the transfer of the allocation of goods and services on the basis of noneconomic criteria.

One does not have to be an economic determinist to acknowledge the role of pecuniary motivation in prejudice and discrimination. The most visible and dramatic illustration would be slavery based on race. The plantation system in the American South enabled whites in general to enjoy a higher standard of living and allowed a few whites to indulge in the luxury of personal slave servants and lead a life based primarily on leisure. (Something of this life style in the plantation system with its economic stratification can be garnered from Margaret Mitchell's famous novel *Gone with the Wind.*) More recent examples of the role that economic motivation assumes in prejudice can be seen in the median income and family unemployment rates by race, the total money income for minority and majority families, and the proportion of Blacks and whites in various occupational categories.

While there has been a good deal of speculation concerning the relationship between economics, prejudice, and discrimination, certain objective indicators of prejudice and discrimination can be gleaned from an examination of demographic data. For example, if one looks at the statistics concerning total money income for Blacks in 1960 and 1970 and other minorities from 1947 and through 1970, it is possible to arrive at the conclusion that economic discrimination is gradually attenuating. Data in table 10 show that in 1947 the median income of Blacks was $1,614.00, whereas in 1970 the amount was $6,516.00.

TABLE 10

DIFFERENCE IN MEDIAN INCOME BETWEEN WHITES
AND BLACKS (AND OTHER RACES) FROM 1947 TO 1970
(IN DOLLARS)

YEAR	WHITES	BLACKS AND OTHER RACES	DIFFERENCE
1947	3157	1614	1543
1948	3310	1768	1542
1949	3232	1650	1582
1950	3445	1869	1576
1951	3859	2032	1827
1952	4114	2338	1776
1953	4392	2461	1931
1954	4339	2410	1929
1955	4605	2549	2056
1956	4993	2628	2365
1957	5166	2764	2402
1958	5300	2711	2589
1959	5643	2917	2726
1960	5835	3233	2602
1961	5981	3191	2790
1962	6237	3330	2907
1963	6548	3465	3083
1964	6858	3839	3019
1965	7251	3994	3257
1966	7792	4674	3118
1967	8274	5141	3133
1968	8937	5590	3347
1969	9794	6191	3603
1970	10236	6516	3720

SOURCE: U.S., Bureau of the Census, *Current Population Reports*, Series P-60, no. 80 (Washington, D.C.: Government Printing Office, 1971).

In this table we have presented data for Blacks and whites. If these data are analyzed *comparatively*, it is easy to see that while the median income of Blacks *has* risen in the last twenty-three years, except for seven intervening years (1948, 1950, 1952, 1954, 1960, 1964, and 1966), there has been an *increase* in the gap between Black and white median income. Thus, in 1947, the difference between Black and white median incomes was $1,543.00, while in 1970 the difference was $3,720.0. While it may be difficult to attribute the rise in median income differences to prejudice and discrimination, it does appear to be the case that if economic inferiority of Blacks were alleged to be correlated with prejudice and discrimination in 1947 (and earlier), then there is little evidence to support an attenuation of this relationship. In fact, one may wonder if the increase in Black-white income differences is not accompanied by an increase in the social-psychological variables—prejudice and discrimination.

Another set of data is equally as interesting though not as dramatic. These data are related to the total money income of Black and white families in the United States in 1960 and 1970, as shown in table 11.

TABLE 11
FAMILIES BY TOTAL MONEY
INCOME IN 1960 AND 1970 BY RACE

Total Money Income	Whites		Blacks and Other Races	
	1960	1970	1960	1970
Under $3,000	19.1	7.5	46.5	20.1
$3,000 to $4,999	19.9	9.5	24.4	17.0
$5,000 to $6,999	24.5	11.3	15.4	16.4
$7,000 to $9,999	21.3	20.1	8.7	18.2
$10,000 to $14,999	11.2	27.9	4.3	17.3
$15,000 and over	4.1	23.7	0.6	10.9
percent	100.0	100.0	100.0	100.0

SOURCE: U.S., Bureau of the Census, *Current Population Reports*, Series P-60, no. 80 (Washington, D.C.: Government Printing Office, 1971).

If the proportion of Blacks and whites with total income are compared, the greatest gain for Blacks is made on income levels below $10,000. For instance, in 1960, 46.5 percent of Blacks' total income was $3,000.00 or below as compared with 19.1 percent for whites. In 1970, the percentages were 20.1 for Blacks and 7.5 for whites. Thus, the proportion differential decreased. However, there was an increase in the differential at the $3–4,999.00 level. On the third level ($5–6,999.00), differences between proportions decreased while at the $7–9,999.00 level, there was a substantial gain for Blacks. It should be remembered, however, that the median income for whites in 1970 was $10,236.00. The implication of this, of course, may be enhanced if one compares the difference in proportions of Blacks and whites with total income $10,000 and above for 1960 and 1970. Combining the two economic levels, one can note that in 1960 the difference in proportions for the economic levels was 10.4 percent, while in 1970 this difference was 23.4 percent.

Another oft-used measure of discrimination is the proportion of minority group members in the various occupations in a society. Occupational status is highly correlated with social status in general in American society; it is also closely associated with education and income. In table 12 Norval Glenn compares the actual proportion of employed nonwhite workers and various occupation groups over a span of three decades with the percentage that would be expected if there were proportionate representation of nonwhites in each occupational category.

Glenn and Charles Bonjean have interpreted this table in the following manner:

The white-nonwhite occupational gap is summarized by the index of dissimilarity at the bottom of the table. The index is the percentage of nonwhites (or of whites) who would have to change occupational categories to make the white and nonwhite distributions identical. The index declined by 7.6 points from 1940 to 1950, by 2.4 points from 1950 to 1960, and by 6.6 points from 1960 to 1968. If the index declines at the 1960–1968 rate until 1970, the total decrease for the decade will be 8.3—an unprecedented ten-year rise in the relative occupational standing of nonwhites in the United States.

The data in table 12 reveal that representation of blacks in United States business is still meager. The ratio of real to "expected" or proportional representation of nonwhites is only .28 for managers, officials, and proprietors and .30 for sales workers. In fact, the picture is even bleaker than it seems from superficial examination of these data. A substantial proportion of the nonwhites in these categories are undoubtedly Orientals rather than

TABLE 12

RATIO OF ACTUAL TO EXPECTED° PROPORTION OF
EMPLOYED NONWHITE WORKERS IN EACH OCCUPATION
GROUP, 1940, 1950, 1960 AND 1968

Occupational Group	1940*	1950*	1960*	1968*
Professional, technical, and				
kindred workers	.36	.40	.49	.59
Farmers and farm managers	1.31	1.22	.78	.52
Managers, officials, and				
proprietors, except farm	.17	.22	.23	.28
Clerical and kindred workers	†	.29	.46	.67
Sales workers	†	.18	.23	.30
Craftsmen, foremen, and				
kindred workers	.27	.38	.49	.60
Operative and kindred workers	.57	.94	1.08	1.27
Private household workers	4.66	5.92	5.46	4.22
Service workers, except				
private household	1.53	2.00	2.02	1.81
Farm laborers and foremen	2.57	2.28	2.46	2.08
Laborers, except farm and mine	2.06	2.56	2.59	2.00
Index of dissimilarity‡	47.8	40.9	38.5	31.9

° The "expected" proportion is the proportion of all employed workers in the
   occupational group.
† In the 1940 census reports, clerical and sales workers are not separated. The
   ratio for clerical, sales, and kindred workers for 1940 is .12.
‡ This index is the percentage of nonwhites (or of whites) who would have to
   change occupational categories to make the white and nonwhite distributions
   identical.
* The ratios and indexes for 1940, 1950, and 1960 are computed from decennial
   census data gathered in April of those years. The 1968 figures are computed from
   data from a sample survey conducted in June. See United States, Department of
   Labor, Bureau of Labor Statistics, Employment and Earnings and Monthly
   Report on the Labor Force (July 1968).
SOURCE: Norval Glenn, "Changes in the Social and Economic Conditions of
   Black Americans during the 1960's," in Norval Glenn and Charles
   Bonjean, *Black in the United States* (New York: Chandler, 1968), p. 45.
   Used by permission of the publisher.

blacks, and unless the situation has changed dramatically since
1968 (which is unlikely), the nonwhites are highly concentrated in
low-paying managerial positions, ownership of marginal small business, and low-paying retail sales jobs. The representation of blacks
as executives, as prosperous entrepreneurs, and in sales jobs in

which high commissions are possible almost certainly is still miniscule.[30]

The measurement of the economic gains of discrimination is not a simple process and different studies report different degrees of benefits. There is one rather stark, simple, and dramatic measure in American society, however, namely, unemployment. Since 1954, for example, the unemployment rate for Blacks has been approximately twice that of whites. In simple human terms this means that it is obviously easier for whites to obtain and retain jobs than Blacks. Unemployment has been particularly acute for teenage Blacks; for example in the year 1967 the national average unemployment rate was 3.8 percent but it was 3.4 percent for whites, 7.4 percent for Blacks, and 26.5 percent for teenage Blacks—and this was the lowest unemployment rate for the decade.[31]

POWER AND STATUS

One of the principal consequences and indeed, the implicit aim, of prejudice and discrimination is to reduce or control the amount of power a minority group has. As a matter of sociological fact one way to define a minority group is to say that it is a group which lacks sufficient power to achieve equal status in a society. A case in point is to be found in a study by the Chicago Urban League of the decision-making process in the Chicago community as influenced by Blacks. An attempt was made to assess the extent of Black participation in policy-making decisions, the kinds of policy-making positions occupied by Blacks, the relationship between Blacks in policy-making positions and the Black community, and how an increase in the percentage of Black policy makers would affect socioeconomic conditions for Blacks in general. It was found in 1965 that, out of the top 10,997 policy-making positions in major institutions in the Chicago area included in the study, Blacks occupied only 285, which is 2.6 percent although the city of Chicago was 28 percent black. It also was found that the number of posts held by Blacks tended to be inversely related to the power invested in these positions—the more powerful the post, the fewer the Black policy makers. Thus, there should be little doubt that there are certain "power" gains to be derived by whites from prejudice and discrimination.

Status Deprivation

Status in a society is socially determined. That is, members of the social structure assign rights and privileges to position. If the majority opinion in any society relegates a category of persons to an inferior position with respect to social rank while simultaneously elevating another group of persons to a lofty position on the status hierarchy, it can be assumed that the latter group enjoys a prestige advantage. Not only does the group member who belongs to one of the status categories enjoy a particular status rank because of group membership but his esteem (evaluation of role performance) in many social interaction areas, such as education and occupation, is greatly influenced by group membership. As pointed out by Dollard, this means that the majority group member, regardless of his objective personal worth, remains superior to all members of one group simply by virtue of his membership in another. Obviously, the implications are similar for minority group members whose status remains constant in at least one area of their lives regardless of successful role performance in other areas of social life. Numerous instances of "successful minority group members" suffering the consequences of prejudice and discrimination attest to this. To paraphrase the American Black entertainer, Sammy Davis, Jr., the successful Black in America is just as enslaved as his brother and sister in Watts, California.

The general character of the psychological problem of minority group status is illustrated by the following passage by Eli Ginzberg concerning the development of attitudes toward work in Black children:

> How can the Negro child develop positive attitudes toward work when he early comes to recognize that almost all of the desirable jobs in the community are closed to him? To the extent that a high proportion of Negro men are more or less dissatisfied with the lack of opportunity at work, to that extent will their children tend to grow up with a negative orientation towards the world of work—to view it largely as an unpleasant necessity bereft of any positive quality. The problem is compounded by the fact that in a high proportion of Negro families the man is not the responsible head. In part, this is a legacy of slavery; in part it reflects the heightened instability of family life as more and more men and women seek to escape the confines of segregation through relocating themselves in more favorable areas. In brief, a high proportion of Negro youth grows up without any understanding of, or belief in, their capacity to shape their lives through work.[32]

PSYCHOLOGICAL REACTIONS TO PREJUDICE
AND DISCRIMINATION

Gary T. Marx has studied "the reaction of Black Americans to their oppression and quest for justice," "the hostility of Black Americans toward Whites and the extent to which protest is linked to this hostility."[33] He found the most privileged and least socially isolated Blacks the most militant and the main reason for this was "because they have the necessary psychological outlook to support and encourage militancy: morale, sophistication and pride in self." He also notes that when this outlook is found among the less privileged and more isolated, militancy also accompanys it, and similarly, when those who are privileged do not have such a view they are not militant.

Other investigators have discussed the inimical effects of prejudice and discrimination for the self-image of minority group members. Elliot Liebow in *Tally's Corner: A Study of Negro Street Corner Men* illuminates the fact that the psychological effects of prejudice and discrimination are demeaning for minority group members. He states that the Black male in American society is likely to experience painful problems of self-image.[34] Liebow further contends that

> . . . one of the major points of articulation between the inside world and the larger society surrounding it is in the area of employment. The way in which the man makes a living and the kind of living he makes have important consequences for how the man sees himself and is seen by others; and these, in turn, importantly shape his relationships with family members, lovers, friends and neighbors.[35]

Burdened with problems of inadequate education and a lack of success models to inspire him, a menial job is a likely fate, if not joblessness. This in turn compounds his marital problems with the result that "sometimes he strikes out at her or the children with his fists, perhaps to lay hollow claim to being man of the house in the one way left open to him, or perhaps simply to inflict pain on this woman who bears witness to his failure as a husband and father and therefore as a man."[36] Increasingly he turns to the streetcorner where a shadow system of values constructed out of public fictions serves to accommodate just such men as he, permitting them to be men once again provided they do not look too closely at one another's credentials."[37] Bitterness and disillusionment are commonplace reactions to prejudice and discrimination but the degree depends upon the personality and the experiences of the individual. One can observe the process of embitterment in the case of Robert F. Williams who was president of the NAACP Chapter in Monroe, North Carolina.[38] When a County Court acquitted two white men of brutal assaults on two Black women but sentenced a mentally retarded Black to imprisonment as a result of an argument with a white woman, Williams made an angry public statement that "We cannot take these people who do this injustice to the Court, and it becomes necessary to punish them ourselves. If it is necessary to stop lynching with lynching then we must be willing to resort to that method." After his dismissal as NAACP Chapter president by the national organization, kidnapping accusations, and apparent harrassment by the police, he fled to Cuba and founded an exile organization known as the Revolutionary Action Movement. He has since returned to the U.S. though his legal difficulties have not been solved.

Repression and Denial

This type of minority group reaction is a defense mechanism used to expel the disturbing and painful effects of prejudice and discrimination from conscious perception. Minority group members in the United States have often used repression to escape the stark realities of prejudice and discrimination. E. Franklin Frazier, in his classic monograph *Black Bourgeoisie*, contended that the Black middle class lived in a world of make-believe and unreality. Characteristically, this class of Blacks sought recognition only from whites, avoided direct competition with whites, and generally emphasized social life and consumption. Thus, the Black middle class that Frazier spoke of tended to repress the effects of prejudice and discrimination by psychologically rejecting their assigned inferior positions and living an idealistic type of life. The extreme form of psychological repression and denial for minority groups has been "passing." To be sure, only a small minority of Blacks could accomplish this feat—that is, the shedding of one's blackness and the adoption of a white role. The obvious restriction on large numbers of Blacks assuming a "white" identity was physical characteristics. In recent years, however, passing seems to have been on the decline though objectively this is very difficult to validate.

Sidney Kronus, in a recent study of the Black middle class, has suggested that the predictions of St. Clair Drake and Horace Cayton rapidly are becoming fulfilled.[39] That is, that the Black middle class is fast emerging as a group best described in terms of racial advancement, stable family, achievement-oriented, and skeptical regarding the intentions of most white people. Based on these contentions, the use of repression and denial by Blacks appears to be on the decline as reactions to prejudice and discrimination.

Guilt Feelings

Closely associated with repression and denial is the tendency of successful minority group members to feel guilty because they are not making sufficient contributions to the minority group cause. While minority group members can and often do experience guilt feelings apart from repression and denial, the ultimate recognition by the minority group member that he is perceived by his own group as a "scab" reinforces his own feelings of self-doubt. Thus prejudice and discrimination operate in such an inimical fashion that even when minority group members achieve some measure of success, it may be nullified by reference group feelings. As a result, many successful Blacks have begun to return to the fold and even those who were already active in the Black movement feel pressured to the extent that elements of guilt can be seen in their observations.

Compensation

A psychological reaction which may be closely related to repression and denial is compensation. Minority group members have often used compensation as a type of protective mechanism whereby the individual engages in alternative activities in order to protect himself from the inimical effects of prejudice and discrimination. Frequently, persons predisposed to the utilization of compensation overindulge in the activity. For instance, the middle-class Black of whom Frazier has spoken may be responding to prejudice and discrimination as he engages in conspicuous consumption activities. As previously suggested, repression and denial involve subordinating prejudice and discrimination to the realm of the unconscious. Compensation, on the other hand, implies recognition of prejudice and discrimination; however, once they have been recognized, the individual shields himself behind other activities and patterns of prejudice and discrimination are weakened. While we have suggested that repression and denial may be declining as reactions among Blacks, compensation is still used by a large num-

ber of Blacks—the economically and socially disadvantaged Black who
seeks solace in deviant behavior as well as the Black economic and
social striver who enmeshes himself in economic and social functions.

Counter-Prejudice

From a majority group's perspective this may be one of the most be-
wildering reactions to prejudice and discrimination. For the more
ethnocentric member of the majority group, it is indeed puzzling to
discover that members of a minority group have negative attitudes
toward them because they devalue many characteristics of the majority
group, and, minority group members, if given an opportunity, would
elect not to engage in social interaction with majority members. On the
other hand, less ethnocentric majority group members find it difficult to
understand how minority group members who bemoan prejudice and
discrimination can use these devices on others, and thus practice what
they preach against!

The phenomenon of counter-prejudice is seldom a novel development in intergroup relations characterized by subjugation, oppression,
and, in general, conflict. While an historical analysis of intergroup relations may reveal few overt indicators of counter-prejudice and discrimination, there is reason to believe that they are emergent properties
which accompany majority group prejudice and discrimination. Tilman
Cothran pointed out that Blacks in the United States held unfavorable
predispositions toward whites long before the current emphasis on
Black nationalism.[40]

As a reaction to prejudice and discrimination, it is difficult to assess
the value of counter-prejudice, since any assessment must be made
from the standpoint of the oppressed and the oppressor, and the goals
to which each ascribe. One thing which appears to be fairly certain,
however, is the fact that if equality and harmonious relations are to
exist between majority and minority groups in any society, prejudice
and discrimination and counter-prejudice and counter-discrimination
must be eradicated.

Cynicism

Cynicism, as a majority group member's reaction to prejudice and
discrimination, takes the form of an obsessional doubting of majority

group members' motivations for any behavior directed toward the minority group. To be sure, dubiousness regarding some behavior is not unwarranted. However, obsessional elements enter in when all behavior by majority group members, regardless of analyzed intent, is placed in a particular category. To express this idea differently, cynicism suggests that because a person is a member of the majority group, all behaviors he emits are directed toward the maintenance of his superior position. Obviously such a position assumes that individuals are static; they do not change nor can they be changed. In those instances where a minority group has experienced a long history of subjugation with few meaningful changes in imbalanced intergroup interaction patterns, it is easy to see how such an attitude might emerge. Whether the attitude correctly assesses intergroup relations is, of course, another matter.

It is perhaps the subtle forms of prejudice and discrimination which lead more directly to the emergence of cynicism. This is due to the fact that subtle prejudice and discrimination implies deception, and deception is a violation of social trust and unspecified obligations. It involves actual rejection of the minority group member after pretending to accept him. The effect of such rejection is to attenuate the individual's tendency to trust. There is nothing mysterious about this, since the gradual attenuation of trust is a result of socialization. The minority group member is punished in social interactions with majority group members and simply devises ways to avoid punishment. A most effective way to avoid punishment is to withhold trust, and while this may not be the first reaction to prejudice and discrimination, the minority group members may gradually come to feel that it is the most effective; at least, this appears to be the trend among a growing number of Blacks in the United States.

Impact on the Prejudiced and Discriminator

Perhaps one of the most neglected areas in intergroup relations in recent years has been the impact of prejudice and discrimination on the perpetrators of the phenomena. Let us direct our attention to this problem.

The inimical effects of majority group prejudice and discrimination are felt by members of the *majority* group as well as minority group members toward whom the phenomena are directed. Undoubtedly, the effects of prejudice and discrimination on the majority group are numerous. Moreover the effects probably are latent as well as manifest. However, this section will be devoted to an examination of three manifest deleterious effects of prejudice and discrimination which are defined as moral schizophrenia, rationalization, and unconscious guilt feelings.

Moral Schizophrenia

Social psychologists have stated that once prejudice and discrimination against an outgroup are routinized in the social structure, accompanying cognitions and feelings concerning the out-group acquire normative qualities. That is, members of the in-group are expected to conform to existing norms, and this may include holding certain attitudes about the out-group in addition to displaying certain behaviors toward out-group members. In many societies, prejudice and discrimination are not the only characteristics of the normative order. Contrarily, part of the society's prescriptions may be directed toward equalitarianism, liberty, and justice for all.

The majority group individual in the United States who internalizes society's norms often internalizes a conflicting set of prescriptions. On the one hand, he may be taught to assume a superior role in interaction with minority group members while simultaneously being taught "All men are created equal." This type of socialization can render the individual a moral schizophrenic in the sense that he exhibits behavior and feels in diametrically opposed ways. It is not uncommon to find persons who, for example, feel that Blacks have a right to live wherever they can afford to just like members of the majority group (62 percent of white respondents in a study by Campbell and Schuman felt this way) and yet not favor laws to prevent discrimination against Blacks in buying or renting homes and apartments (only 40 percent of the sample favored such laws). In fact, 40 percent of the sample also felt that a limit should be placed on the number of Blacks that could move into a white residential area.[41]

The behavioral pattern described is but one form of inconsistency characteristic of many members of majority groups in societies with conflicting norms concerning equalitarianism. Succinctly, the moral schizophrenic in intergroup relations is a personality laden with seriously ambivalent, mutually contradictory views of life regarding in-group—out-group relationships. In social-psychological terms, it is a personality characterized by severe cognitive dissonance.[42] Finally, it is important to point out that as long as prejudice and discrimination and ideologies of equalitarianism and justice prevail in a society, moral confusion is likely to exist.

The Need for Rationalization

A final effect of prejudice and discrimination on majority group personalities to be discussed here is the phenomenon of a need for rationalization. Lillian Smith implies this need as she gave what George Simpson and Milton Yinger have called "an insightful account of the costs of white men and women of the race-sex situation in the South United States."[43] Because of the juxtaposed ideas of Christianity and slavery, whites found it psychologically comfortable to deny slaves a soul. Such reasoning was fraught with many ambiguities in view of the often close relationships established between Blacks and whites, such as Black women caring for white children in a servant role.

The need for rationalization as a consequence of imbalanced intergroup relations can be psychologically debilitating in that the rationale is likely to be under constant attack by new or different cognitions. Furthermore, a need for rationalization often means that there is some uncertainty about the legitimacy of some behaviors, cognitions, or feelings. We have already discussed the emergence of moral schizophrenia from conflicting cognitions, however, we suggest that the likelihood of such a personality developing is enhanced when the availability of a feasible rationale is not commensurate with the need for rationalization. The discrepancy between the supply and demand of rationales does not always lead to severe personality disorganization. Indeed there is evidence that individuals can stand a certain amount of inconsistency though the precise nature of this phenomenon has not been revealed. One reason why this may be true is due to a tendency to reject new information which is contrary to existing opinions. For instance, in spite of numerous empirical and humanistic studies which reveal that the Black man's lot in America is largely due to the forces of prejudice and discrimination, Campbell and Schuman found that only 19 percent of the whites in their sample felt that discrimination was the main reason why Blacks had worse jobs, education, and housing than whites; another 19 percent felt that it was due to Blacks themselves and discrimination; and a majority of 56 percent contended that it was mainly due to Blacks themselves (6 percent did not know).[44] While these persons reject biological determinism ideas concerning the status of Blacks, it is obvious that a new rationale has probably developed which can provide justification for maintaining power imbalances in intergroup relations.

Guilt Feelings

According to psychoanalytic theory, the ego represses ideas, wishes, actual external events, memories and so forth if the recognition of these leads to a disruptive increase in energy-produced tension in the personality system. Presumably, one alternative for ideational components is that the energy generated by them may be channeled toward different objects or activities in the form of behavioral symptoms. We will not attempt to refute nor support the psychoanalytic interpretation of the processes of repression in this book. Of interest to us are the behavioral symptoms prejudiced and discriminatory persons appear to exhibit. We submit as sociologically obvious that there are powerful value conflicts in American society about such questions as race and that it is virtually impossible for any individual to escape the psychological consequence; we see guilt as an almost inevitable personal result of these clashing social values.

Members of majority groups often display behaviors which are apparently motivated by feelings of guilt. This guilt may stem from direct personal subordination of minority group members to indirect (majority group members) subordination of the minority group. The severity of this guilt complex probably depends upon the extent to which the individual internalizes the principles of fair play, justice, and equality for all. The nature of the guilt obviously takes many forms and may range from a professor prostituting his profession by giving unearned grades to minority group students to accepting and condoning abuses. Whether guilt feelings must be experienced before harmonious relations between groups can be achieved is an empirical question, and we do not offer an hypothesis concerning the relationship between guilt feelings and intergroup harmony.

SUMMARY AND IMPLICATIONS

Prejudice, as we have frequently observed, tends to produce discrimination, and discrimination, in turn, encourages majority group responses such as segregation, subjugation, and general subordination of minority groups. Segregation as a response heightens the visibility of a group, thus facilitating prejudice and discrimination. Moreover, segregation is likely to reinforce existing group differences by stimulating the evolution of a distinctive subculture. A group that suffers discrimination and is segregated often develops counter-prejudices as well as other defensive behaviors which intensify the process. Such behavior may then be cited by majority members as a confession of sociological guilt and viewed as verification of the allegations of the majority group against the minority, thus justifying their prejudicial attitude. For example, one hears majority group members claiming that they are perplexed by the "rude" behavior of minority group persons. Instead of attributing the behavior to the psychological effects of prejudice, they cite it as justification for differential attitudes. They are unable to comprehend or to acknowledge that prejudice encourages responses of bitterness, cynicism, and belligerence. Majority group members, however, not only experience gains but also suffer certain consequences of the prejudice and discrimination they perpetuate. The consequences include moral schizophrenia, guilt feelings, a need for rationalization, and, as Simpson and Yinger point out, a "loss of purpose and solidarity that are the strength of a people."

Notes

1. See Robert K. Merton, *Social Theory and Social Structure* (New York: The Free Press, 1957), chapter IV, "Social Structure and Anomie."
2. Pierre L. Van Den Berghe, *Race and Racism* (New York: Wiley, 1967), p. 110.
3. See Dorothy S. Thomas and Richard S. Nishimoto, *The Spoilage* (Berkeley: University of California Press, 1969).
4. U.S., Bureau of the Census, *Current Population Reports,* Series P-60, no. 80 (Washington, D.C.: Government Printing Office, 1971).
5. William Tahli, "Race Relations Models and Social Changes," *Social Problems* 18, no. 4 (Spring 1971): 443.
6. Ibid.
7. See Kenneth Clark, *Dark Ghetto: Dilemma of Social Power* (New York: Harper and Row, 1965), and Robert Blauner, "Internal Colonialism and Ghetto Revolt," *Social Problems* 18, no. 4 (Spring 1971): 431-44.
8. Nathan Glazer, "Blacks and Ethnic Groups: The Difference and the Political Difference It Makes," *Social Problems* 18, no. 4 (Spring 1971): 461.
9. See Clyde W. Franklin, Jr. "A Comparison of Two Social Movements in Two Southern Cities: Montgomery, Alabama and Albany, Georgia" (master's thesis, Atlanta University, 1962).
10. U.S., Commission on Civil Rights, *Racial Isolation in Public Schools* (Washington, D.C.: Government Printing Office, 1967).
11. See Joseph S. Himes, "The Functions of Racial Conflict," in *Race, Class and Power,* ed. Raymond Mack, 2d ed. (New York: The American Book Company, 1968), pp. 401-13.
12. For a lengthy discussion of sources of conflicts see Vernon J. Dixon, "Two Approaches to Black-White Relations" in Vernon J. Dixon and Badi Foster, *Beyond Black or White* (Boston: Little, Brown, 1971), pp. 42-48.

13. This pattern tends to hold for most minority uprisings unless aid is received from external sources.
14. The National Advisory Commission on Civil Disorders Supplemental Studies, 1968, pp. 221-48.
15. See H. Edward Ransford, "Isolation, Powerlessness and Violence: A Study of Attitudes and Participation in the Watts Riots," in Allen D. Grimshaw, *Racial Violence in the United States* (Chicago: Aldine, 1969). Also David O. Sears and T. M. Tomlinson, "Riot Ideology in Los Angeles: A Study of Negro Attitudes," *Social Science Quarterly* 49 (1968): 485-505.
16. Jerome Skolnick, *The Politics of Protest* (New York: Ballantine Books, 1969), pp. xix-xx.
17. Edward Jeffries, Ralph Turner, and Vincent Morris, "The Public Perception of the Watts Riot as Social Protest," *American Sociological Review* 36 (June 1971): 450.
18. James Vander Zanden's note on the function and dysfunctions of ethnic and racial conflict is pertinent for this discussion. For the entire discussion, see *American Minority Relations* (New York: The Ronald Press, 1963), pp. 185-87.
19. Hubert Blalock, *Toward a Theory of Minority-Group Relations* (New York: Wiley, 1967), pp. 214-18.
20. See Grimshaw, *Racial Violence in United States,* and William M. Tuttle, Jr., *Race Riot* (New York: Atheneum, 1970).
21. For a detailed account of the Chicago riot in 1919, see Tuttle, *Race Riot,* pp. 32-66.
22. Ibid.
23. Commission on Civil Disorders Supplemental Studies.
24. Ibid.
25. Ibid.
26. Joseph S. Himes, "A Theory of Racial Conflict," *Social Forces* 50 (September 1971): 53-60.
27. With the advent of the Black power movement in the United States, and the youth culture and increasing liberality of young whites, among other factors, the sexual gain Dollard spoke of in *Caste and Class in a Southern Town* appears to be less significant at the present time. Indeed, it can be contended that the stereotyped impression of the Black male as a super sex object has actually reversed the sexual gain principle. Though there is a dearth of empirical evidence to support such a contention, one is almost moved to state that Black males presently enjoy a sexual gain. The Black female, as a consequence of historical condition, appears to be less likely to sexually align herself with the white male while the Black male and white female have increasingly become familiar alliances—at least on college campuses. Only speculation exists concerning the incidence of actual mating between interracial couples, however, if as one study reports, approximately 44 percent of the females engage in sexual liasons, a good deal of interracial mating probably takes place. Furthermore, if a certain number of these couples are Black-male—white-female, then a reversal of the sexual gain might be in evidence—at least among a certain segment of the population.
28. Gary S. Becker, *The Economics of Discrimination* (Chicago: University of Chicago Press, 1957).
29. Lester C. Thurow, *Poverty and Discrimination* (Washington, D.C.: The Brookings Institution, 1969).
30. Norval Glenn, "Changes in the Social and Economic Conditions of Black Americans during the 1960's," in Norval Glenn and Charles Bonjean, *Blacks in the United States* (New York: Chandler, 1968), pp. 45-46.
31. Eli Ginzberg, "The Economist Who Changed His Mind," in Glenn and Bonjean, *Blacks in the U.S.,* pp. 534-37, admits that he attempted to convince

the Advisory Commission on Civil Disorders with statistics from his and Alfred S. Eichner's study, *The Troublesome Presence: American Democracy* (New York: Free Press of Glencoe, 1964). However, in this article he suggests that the most important thing for white Americans to do is to exorcise racism thereby granting Black humanity and citizenship.

32. Ginzberg and Eichner, *The Troublesome Presence.*
33. Gary T. Marx, *Protest and Prejudice: A Study of Beliefs in the Black Community* (New York: Harper and Row, 1967).
34. Elliot Liebow, *Tally's Corner: A Study of Negro Street Corner Men* (Boston: Little, Brown, 1967).
35. Ibid.
36. Ibid.
37. Ibid.
38. Robert F. Williams, *Negroes With Guns* (New York: Marzani and Munsell, 1962).
39. Sidney Kronus, *The Black Middle Class* (Columbus, Ohio: Charles E. Merrill, 1971).
40. Tilman C. Cothran, "Negro Conceptions of White Folk," *American Journal of Sociology* 16 (1951): 458-67.
41. A. Campbell and H. Schuman, "Black Views of Racial Issues," in Marcel Goldschmid, *Black Americans and White Racism* (New York: Holt, Rinehart and Winston, 1970), pp. 346-65.
42. For an elaboration of the concept cognitive dissonance, see Leon Festinger, *A Theory of Cognitive Dissonance* (Stanford: Stanford University Press, 1957).
43. George E. Simpson and J. Milton Yinger, *Racial and Cultural Minorities* (New York: Harper and Brothers, 1958), p. 268.
44. Campbell and Schuman, "Black Views of Racial Issues."

Moral Suasion, Education, and Direct Action

11

MORAL SUASION

Voluntary associations, movements, and institutions designed to eradicate intergroup injustice and hostility often have used techniques which are basically unidimensional. The techniques have been either affective, cognitive, or behavioral; however, rarely have they been three-dimensional. In other words, while moral suasion, education, and direct action are employed to effect change between majority and minority groups, such means more often than not are used in a singular fashion rather than in combination. The efficacy of this type of usage will be explored later in this chapter. First, however, we will examine the roles of moral suasion, education, and direct action in the amelioration of intergroup hostility.

It is often contended that, in the final analysis, all social problems are moral issues. Such a statement does not greatly enhance our understanding of the nature of problems such as prejudice and discrimination however, because it is virtually a truism and begs the question of how to solve these problems. Moral suasion occurs when attempts are made to change feelings, behavior, and cognitions, such as discrimination and prejudice, by appealing to moral principles. These efforts may assume the form of pleas to conform to existing moral codes which are currently being violated, or they may be directed at persuading people to adopt new standards which would alter their conduct. Moral suasion may mean that some persons attempt to persuade others to observe certain religious norms which proscribe prejudice and discrimination or that arguments are advanced to sustain and defend norms which endorse and justify prejudice and discrimination. The question is basically one of how to modify human motivation and behavior, and there are the usual corollary problems of how to influence opinions and habits and what techniques of persuasion and suggestion are the most effective. It is customary to regard moral suasion as only one side of the coin; propaganda which seeks to stimulate and reinforce intergroup animosity also constitutes moral suasion. We shall concede to convention in that we shall dwell primarily upon efforts to reduce intergroup hostilities, though the other moral viewpoint will not be entirely ignored.

The question of the effectiveness of moral suasion as a means of ameliorating intergroup tensions necessarily raises the larger question of how social changes occur. How does society change its norms and what social forces produce a higher rate of conformity to or deviation from existing norms? Can a society pull itself up by its moral bootstraps, or must there be some kind of factor "external" to the moral norms in order to produce any change? To what extent can "leadership" or "agitation" or "intellectual innovation" precipitate social change in the pattern of intergroup relations? In attempting to assess the role of moral suasion as a means for modifying behavior and social structure in intergroup relations, we must make certain tacit assumptions about these matters. In general we are prepared to say that moral suasion does seem to constitute a force of some magnitude in changing cognitions, feelings, and behavior, although it must not be assumed that social patterns can be suddenly and drastically reordered merely by exhortation.

One can point to such dramatic historical instances as the apparent impact of a force such as *Uncle Tom's Cabin* upon attitudes towards slavery.[1] Ideas are powerful social forces and their eloquent and timely expression enhances their effect. The question remains, however, whether or not an idea can register any profound impact until the social-historical conditions are ripe for it; to what extent can a noble idea create its own favorable sociological reception? There can be little doubt that *Uncle Tom's Cabin* was a factor in and of itself in generating enthusiasm and support for the abolitionist movement and promotion of a political atmosphere which culminated in the American Civil War. It dramatized the issue of slavery and focused attention upon the problem in a manner that encouraged vigorous campaigns to eliminate it. The critical question is whether or not the book would have had similar consequences if it had been written twenty years earlier. The position can be taken that the effect would have been minimal mainly due to the fact that the book's impact was primarily affective or emotional. In other words, while undoubtedly some cognitions were altered, it is suggested that the socio-historical conditions were of such a nature as to render *Uncle Tom's Cabin* primarily an affective force.

The 1954 U.S. Supreme Court decision on segregation in the public schools offers another instance of the operation of a moral force in modifying behavior and attitudes. Although it can be viewed in a narrow legal sense, this momentous decision was essentially a profound moral judgment about the character of human relations in a democratic society. This moral pronouncement is strongly implicit in one of the key passages of the decision: "To separate [Negro Children] from others of similar age and qualifications solely because of their race generates a feeling of inferiority as to their status in the community that may affect their hearts and minds in a way unlikely ever to be undone." To be sure, it is impossible, in practice, to determine what part of the impact of this decision has been due to the moral component as distinct from the legal component, but there is no gainsaying that it has exerted a moral force on the attitudes and behaviors of Americans.

Appeals to moral principles in attempts to modify intergroup relations do not occur in a sociological vacuum, of course. Typically, the approach is to attempt to convince people that certain of their attitudes and behaviors are incongruous with some of the basic moral doctrines of the society. Basically, it is an effort to change cognitions and behavior by changing feelings or affectivity. Opponents of racial segregation may argue that it is diametrically contrary to the Christian ethic and to democratic political principles, and therefore should be eliminated. The underlying assumption of this strategy is that almost everybody is strongly committed to these values and if the contradiction between this position and segregation can be brought forcefully and dramatically to their attention, they are likely to become more favorable to integration. The plan is to emphasize the ethical inconsistency and thereby create a state of "moral dissonance" with the expectation that this will lead almost automatically to a new moral balance or equilibrium.

This strategy principle seems to underlie much of the civil rights movement in the United States. The various protest demonstrations are designed to dramatize the moral contradictions implicit in racial discrimination. It is hardly coincidental that much of the leadership and sponsorship of the movement has come from religious organizations and churches, institutions responsible for instilling a sense of purpose in life and various other affective functions.

Moral leadership is exceedingly difficult to measure accurately. One can only speculate, for example, about the relative influence of Presidents Eisenhower, Kennedy, Johnson, and Nixon who have followed quite different policies in regard to presidential responsibilities in intergroup relations. Mr. Eisenhower chose to remain silent on such controversial issues as school segregation and was criticized by many who felt that he should have spoken out in condemnation of such violent incidents as those at Central High School in Little Rock, Arkansas. Mr. Kennedy was more vocal on racial issues and is seen in retrospect by many Blacks as the president who finally heeded the Black man's call. Mr. Johnson pursued an even bolder course; he uttered some rather strong statements of a moral/political character regarding Black voting rights and the right of peaceful protest and demonstration. We cannot be entirely certain that the latter approach was significantly more effective, but if the gains in Black civil rights during his tenure in office were any index it would appear to be.

Mr. Nixon's policy, on the other hand, has been perceived as one of "benign neglect," although his administration has been involved in the introduction of the idea of "quotas" or "goals" in minority employment. Whether this is an accurate description of his moral leadership in the intergroup relations arena, one cannot say. From all indications, however, minority groups' rhetoric would tend to substantiate this connotation.

In a similar vein, it would appear that the passage of the 1964 Civil Rights Act has had a considerable moral impact on race relations in the U.S. If this is true it may seem ironic in view of the fact that one of the most frequently expressed arguments against its passage was that "morality can't be legislated." The response to the bill, and to the great national debate which preceded its enactment, would seem to indicate that it did indeed exert a moral force of some magnitude; compliance with the law in the South was quite at odds with the dire predictions of militant resistance to it by those who opposed the bill. It seemed as though a new moral consensus had emerged from the debate and the passage of the law.

It also is possible for a dramatic incident to have a profound moral effect which results in new laws, such as the death of a white clergyman at the hands of segregationists in Alabama in 1965. This incident followed the use of force by state police in preventing a peaceful protest march by Blacks and whites demanding that Blacks be permitted to register to vote. The moral conscience of the nation was surely aroused by these events; President Johnson's address to a special session of Congress and to the nation a few days later are indicative of the moral tone of the reaction to this episode.

> There (Selma, Ala.), long-suffering men and women peacefully protested the denial of their rights as Americans. Many were brutally assaulted. One good man—a man of God—was killed.
>
> The real hero of this struggle is the American Negro. His actions and protests—his courage to risk safety and even life—have awaked the conscience of the nation. His demonstrations have been designed to call attention to injustice, to provoke change and stir reform. He has called upon us to make good the promise of America.
>
> For at the heart of the battle for equality is a belief in the democratic process. Equality depends not on the force of arms but the force of moral right—not on recourse to violence—but respect of law.[2]

The moral conscience of the nation had obviously been pricked by the concatenation of events in Alabama, and the president seemed to articulate these feelings; the Congress responded by approving legislation protecting voting rights.

One effective technique of moral suasion employed in the American civil rights movement has been nonviolent, passive resistance. Inspired by the success of Ghandi in the Indian independence movement, American civil rights protestors have sought to focus public moral attention on the issue of racial discrimination. They have often evoked sympathy from the general public when they have been subjected to violent suppression; in instances where they have been largely ignored and there has been little publicity given to their protest actions, it would appear that they have been less effective in arousing moral indignation in their favor. It is ironic that this nonviolent approach is evidently most successful when it is met with brutal suppression. There have been some situations in which demonstrators—pickets, sit-in—have not elicited support for their cause because of the creation of antagonisms.

In fact, it would appear that as protests have grown less peaceful and more violent, there has been a decrease in alteration of the affectivity of whites. A counterargument, and one which is quite penetrating, is that while affectivity has decreased, majority group behavior has been dramatically altered in some instances.

In the final sociological analysis the effectiveness of any form of moral suasion in intergroup relations will depend upon its congruity with the cardinal moral principles of the society. Unlike some form of direct action, as we will see, it is essentially a process of promoting moral consistency rather than effecting revolutionary changes in the whole moral system. Hence the efforts of Blacks to achieve full civil rights in the United States by highlighting the moral contradiction between the provisions of the Constitution and the practices in America is a case in point. It is not so much a matter of attempting to alter radically the moral foundations of society as it is an effort to produce a higher degree of moral integration.

The Impact of Religion

The role of religion in preventing and eliminating intergroup prejudice is paradoxical, in that religion is frequently both a unifying and divisive force in human affairs. Religious groups tend to be ethnocentric about their faith, but they also claim, in many cases, to be universal and to endorse the idea of human brotherhood accordingly. Also, the diversity of religious groups and beliefs frustrates generalizations about their influence on prejudice and discrimination. In American society, for example, we find that denominations such as the Unitarians have been active in promoting racial equality, while some of the more fundamentalistic sects have been ardent defenders of racial segregation.

That religious allegiance itself has close psychological kinship to predudice is illustrated in a UNESCO study by Gardner Murphy concerning Hindu and Muslim relations in India.[3] He concluded that to be a "good" Hindu or a "good" Muslim required believing the derogatory traits and behaviors ascribed by one's own group to the other. This is in line with the findings of Milton Rokeach, who concluded that "on the average those who identify themselves as belonging to a religious organization express more intolerance toward racial and ethnic groups (other than their own) than do non-believers. . . ."[4] Similarly, Clifford Kirkpatrick compared subjects on their scores on religiosity and humanitarian scales and discovered a slight negative correlation between the two variables. In general, it seems that persons without religious affiliation are less prejudiced than church members.[5]

Gordon Allport has suggested that there is an important distinction to be made about the *motivation* for religious participation which bears on the question of the relationship between religion and prejudice.

When religious group membership and activity stem from a desire to conform, rather than an earnest concern with the problems of mankind, it is more likely to be associated with various forms of group prejudice. If one attends church largely because it is *de rigueur* or confers a certain amount of respectability, he is more likely to be prejudiced than the person whose religious involvement is a product of an interest in human betterment.

Research on the relationship between religion and prejudice points to the conclusion that religious participation per se is not especially correlated with tolerance or prejudice. It is true that there are some differences in the degree of prejudice among various religious groups— Jews tend to be more tolerant of Blacks than Baptists are, for example —but a simple index such as frequency of church attendance is of relatively little predictive utility. Theological doctrine itself may have a direct bearing on race attitudes; for example, Mormon theology, as it is generally interpreted, does not allow Blacks to serve as clergy.

Religion also is capable of inspiring noble thoughts and deeds; all religions seem to encourage altruistic sentiments. We find embodied in religious doctrines moral principles which define ideal relationships with other people. In general, these moral principles counsel a magnanimous, charitable attitude toward others, even members of outgroups. To be sure, these moral admonitions to be kind and tolerant are often taken to apply primarily to one's own religious kind, but they do provide an ideal norm which surely has some influence on behavior. The extent of this influence is a matter of conjecture, as there are those who would contend that in the absence of this force intergroup relations would be much less harmonious, and others who assert that religion is a crucial independent variable which leads to intergroup disharmony.

In recent times in the United States there has been a noteworthy increase in interest and activity on the part of clergymen and lay leaders of religion in the problems of intergroup prejudice and discrimination. It is true that the vast majority of white clergymen have not exhibited any great concern about the plight of minorities or intergroup tensions but the number of those whose conscience has been aroused is increasing and there is a segment of the clergy which is actively participating in the civil rights movement. Among Blacks, ministers have been in the forefront of the leadership of the struggle for equal rights.

A basic question which remains unanswered is whether a change in affectivity, cognition, and behavior of majority group members in regard to a minority group can be effected successfully through the use of an affective technique such as moral suasion. While there is social-psychological research support for such a process, many groups advocating more militant forms of action express dubiousness. Part of the skepticism may be due to the fact that affective techniques tend to be slow in effect and many more activistic minority groups are unwilling to wait for the process to reach its completion. Hence many "Black militants" were critical of the moralistic approach of Martin Luther King, Jr., for this reason. The following rather vitriolic words of Nathan Hare also express this sentiment. (In fairness to Mr. Wilkins and NAACP it should be pointed out that they relied heavily upon legal action as well as moral appeals.)

> "Appalling" is the only word I know that begins to describe the sneaky way in which critics like Roy Wilkins accuse us of "separatism." Our cries for more black professors and black students have padded white colleges with more blacks in two years than decades of whimpering for "integration" ever did.
>
> We blacks at white colleges remain associated with racists physically, although we seek social and psychological independence from their oppression. The Amos 'n' Andy administrators at Negro colleges, by contrast, are physically separated but accommodated to their dependence on white racism as well as the establishment's remote control of their black destiny.[6]

EDUCATION

Formal Education and Prejudice

Almost everybody seems to favor an educational approach to the problem of prejudice; some favor it as the principal and only means whereas others argue that although it should be employed it should not be relied upon as the exclusive instrument for the task. As far as deliberate instruction is concerned, it seems doubtful that it is a very effective technique for changing attitudes significantly. This is evidently due to the fact that it is exceedingly difficult for a formal educational institution to modify attitudes that are normative in the community. Teachers themselves, for example, are very likely to share the social attitudes that prevail in the community, including the various forms of group prejudice present. Hence a teacher of white pupils in

Mississippi who attempts to promote tolerance of Blacks may jeopardize her job, and it is improbable that a teacher would be hired in the first place who had expressed opposition to racial segregation. Educational institutions are more likely to reflect *and* reinforce the social norms of the community than to lead in their revision.

Moreover, verbal abstractions in the classroom about equality and justice are not likely to be effective against the background of a social system in which segregation and discrimination are normative. Ashley Montagu has expressed this idea very forcefully in an essay on human relations education: "No matter what we teach in the schools concerning the equality of man, unless these teachings are provided with a social milieu in which they can be practiced, they will wilt and die in the breasts of those who are forced to adapt themselves to the world as they find it."[7]

The effect of formal education on prejudice is by no means uniform or simple. Attitude change depends upon the content of the education, the personal and social characteristics of the student, the social-psychological context of the learning, and whether cognitions can cause affective and behavioral change. A higher level of education is correlated with prevention and reduction in "autistic distortions" in the perception of out-groups, i.e., the more blatant stereotypes. The specific nature of the education influence depends upon the operation of a number of other variables, however. For example, Charles Stember found that the effects of education in reducing prejudice were greater among women than men (especially on prejudice against Blacks), greater among the nonreligious than the religious, greater among persons with a foreign-born parent than among those of native parentage, and greater in urban areas and in the South than elsewhere.[8]

The complexity of the relationship between education and prejudice can be appreciated by attempting to assess the relative weight of various concomitants of education such as income and social prestige. Inasmuch as increased amounts of education lead to higher income and higher social standing it is exceedingly difficult to determine to what extent any change in intergroup attitudes is a function of these variables rather than education per se.

Educational programs and methods designed to promote intergroup tolerance have been employed by many schools and teachers but their effectiveness evidently has not been great. Formal instruction seems to have less of an impact upon intergroup attitudes than the individual's primary group experiences. Thus the school is at an initial disadvantage in any effort to shape social attitudes. The family has already had an opportunity to exert an influence on the child's sentiments and habits before he is exposed to formal education. Moreover, because of the intimate affective relations between parents and children, the degree of parental influence is likely to be much greater than that of teachers. Obviously, there is some combination of affectivity and informal education which makes the parental influence variable exceedingly effective. Respect and affection for parents tends to increase their influence on their children's attitudes, and many cases of sharp divergence in social attitudes between parents and children seem to be due to lack of esteem for the parents. If one is extremely fond of his father, who happens to be strongly hostile towards a minority (or majority) group, we can expect some "transfer" of this attitude. Similarly, attitudes towards school and teachers may condition the effects of instruction concerned with intergroup relations.

Another circumstance which has weakened educational efforts to improve intergroup relations has been various forms of group segregation in the schools themselves. Whether as a result of deliberate social policy or because of residential segregation the public schools have, in effect, taught segregation and discrimination by precept. Consequently, much of the conceptual teachings about tolerance and brotherhood apparently have not registered deeply on the emotions of pupils. Although the ideals of democratic society may be accepted at a verbal level by the children, the visibility of segregation can make a deeper impression, especially in terms of overt behavior. The presence of a Black teaching in a "white" school is likely to influence pupil attitudes toward Blacks to a greater extent than instruction in scientific facts about race.

Although it is evident that formal education does not dramatically reduce group prejudice in the short run, it is equally obvious that persons with the lowest number of years of formal education also tend to be the most prejudiced. This relationship has been confirmed in a number of studies; to cite one example, Melvin Tumin found in a study of attitudes of whites toward Blacks and desegregation in North Carolina that "the higher the education, the more favorable the attitude toward the Negro."[9] Thus one may be inclined to conclude that in the long run, formal education is favorable to more tolerant intergroup attitudes. The exact nature of this influence is more difficult to specify; it seems partly due to the greater economic security which a higher educational level ordinarily brings, as well as the general "liberalizing" effect of education. Similarly, the higher social status which is associated with more education also presumably contributes to less prejudice. Hence the greater tolerance which is correlated with educational level may be due as much to the "side effects" of education as a consequence of the substance of it.

There is some evidence supporting the view that "higher" education has a greater impact on intergroup attitudes than other levels. Stember suggests that "reduction of prejudice against Blacks is principally a function of college training; earlier schooling generally produces little favorable change."[10] He concluded that "only a high level of education seems to have any appreciable impact on the more deeply rooted prejudices."[11]

Various studies have attempted to assess the amount of change in intergroup attitudes as a result of educational experiences. The design and methodology of these studies have varied; some have employed control groups but others have not; the subjects have usually been high school or college students; different techniques of measuring attitudes have been used; attitudes toward various groups have been measured with Blacks being the most frequent; and the educational variable has consisted of such experiences and activities as a course in race relations, viewing films dealing with intergroup relations, and tours and visits to neighborhoods. The results of these "before and after" studies have been reviewed by Robin Williams and by Arnold Rose; the general pattern of the findings is that there was usually some slight attitude change in a more favorable direction due to these educational experiences. However, in almost as many instances no change was reported. Hence it is not reasonable to anticipate any dramatic consequences of such educational programs. On the other hand, it does seem probable that attitudes can be significantly modified if there is a concerted and sustained educational program employing multiple techniques and activities.

Educational Organizations

There are several important organizations in the United States which devote themselves to combatting prejudice and discrimination and promoting harmonious intergroup relations by educational means. Prominent among these are the National Conference of Christians and Jews, the Anti-Defamation League of B'nai B'rith, the American Jewish Committee, and the American Friends Service Committee (Quakers). These groups have published and distributed considerable amounts of literature to schools, educators, and others interested in improving human relations. In addition they have supported research projects, sponsored workshops in intergroup relations, and promoted human relations education in the schools.

The ADL, for example, has programs "directed in particular to combatting discrimination against minorities, to fighting the threat of all forms of totalitarianism, and to promoting intercultural understanding and cooperation among all the religious faiths of America." The organization also offers "consultant services to fraternal, civic, church, educational, labor, and other organizations working on behalf of better intergroup relations." Its catalog of publications lists pamphlets and reprints on such topics as anti-Semitism, civil rights, desegregation, education, human relations, intergroup relations, immigration, prejudice and discrimination, programmatic aids for human relations, research studies, totalitarianism, and understanding your Jewish neighbor.

The National Conference of Christians and Jews has been active in providing educational materials on intergroup relations to schools and teachers and it also has sponsored workshops in human relations for teachers and civil leaders. NCCJ is probably best known to the general public for its sponsorship of national "Brotherhood Week."

The American Jewish Committee has devoted itself to these goals:

> To foster mutual respect among the many religious, ethnic and racial groups within America.
>
> To increase self-respect and self-understanding among American Jews.
>
> To protect freedom of speech, press and religion and strengthen such institutions as the public school which help keep democracy strong.
>
> To ensure equal opportunities for all Americans in education, employment, housing and every facet of life, so that each man may advance on his own merits, not be penalized for his religion, color or ancestry.
>
> To help Jews in other lands to live in security and dignity as equals among their countrymen; to affirm their Jewish faith and to strengthen their communal and religious institutions.
>
> To promote the principle of human rights throughout the world.[12]

AJC also provides pamphlets on such topics as civil liberties, discrimination, immigration laws, understanding Jews and Judiaism, and improving intergroup relations. The organization has sponsored research on prejudice, including the five-volume "Studies in Prejudice," of which *The Authoritarian Personality* is the best known.

The program of the American Friends Service Committee "attempts to relieve human suffering wherever it is found and ease tensions between individuals, groups and nations. It operates on the belief that there is that of God in every man and that love, expressed through creative action, can overcome hatred, prejudice and fear." Although the organization does not devote itself exclusively to the area of improving intergroup relations by educational programs it does publish some literature on the subject and, through its Community Relations Program, has been involved in such projects as promoting equal housing opportunities.

Effectiveness of Programs and Practices

Although it is a complex task to judge the success of various strategies to reduce intergroup tensions because so many variables are involved, there are some general guidelines which have been formulated. Dean and Rosen, as a result of field research, suggest the following criteria for evaluating "good intergroup relations practices."

1. Is genuine two-way communication taking place between the majority and minority groups, especially between the leaders?

2. Is the minority participating effectively in the formulation of policy and program in organizations that have different ethnic groups as members or staff?

3. Are the staffs of mixed organizations trained and experienced in intergroup relations?

4. Have those activities been desegregated that can reasonably be expected to be carried on jointly by different groups?

5. Are integrated activities being used to broaden the individual's understanding of other groups and to reinforce a personal creed devoted to democratic intergroup practices?

6. Are intergroup action organizations working for realistic objectives?

7. Is intergroup action working effectively organized, and has it involved key influential leaders in community life?

8. Are effective strategies being used by action organizations in negotiating for intergroup change?

9. Are practitioners in intergroup relations continuing to grow professionally in their understanding of intergroup relations?[13]

DIRECT ACTION

The distinctions between social action, and moral suasion and education are somewhat blurred, but the phrase "direct action" connotes overt behavior designed to produce improvement in one group's social position vis-à-vis another group or other groups. Although direct action may assume many forms, its most dramatic expression in recent years has been public protest demonstrations, ranging from various versions of the sit-in to destruction of property *and* persons. Theoretically, direct action would range from exhortation to violent revolution, and the 1960s and early 1970s have produced direct action along this range.

The general purpose of direct action programs and measures is to effect a change in the relative status of groups. Direct action is supposed to accomplish this end by (1) dramatizing the issue, such as inequality, (2) influencing public opinion favorably for the group, (3) bringing pressure to bear on public officials and the power elite of the community or society, and (4) demonstrating the determination and power of the group. The success of these tactics will depend upon the kind of publicity received, the attitudes of the society toward this form of protest, and the merits of the case of the group as judged by the prevailing social norms. In contemporary society mass media coverage of the events is an important consideration in determining their impact. While some direct action appeals to the collective conscience of the larger community; other action does not make this concession. Instead, "by any means necessary" becomes an ideological motto and does not take into account the collective conscience of the society.

Public demonstrations by civil rights groups in the late 1950s and early 1960s in the United States represented a new strategy to eliminate discrimination. They were almost exclusively nonviolent, and there was a strong adherence to the Ghandi theory of passive resistance. The apparent assumption was that violence would harm the cause, and furthermore was not in keeping with the Christian doctrine of brotherly love. Although this approach compares in some respects with the efforts of industrial workers to gain union recognition in the 1930s by means of sit-down strikes, and although some of the criticisms of the movements are comparable, the civil rights protests during that era did not produce as much violent conflict.

However, in the late 1960s the civil rights movement began to take on a new look—one which was much less passive and more oriented to behavioral alteration, at least rhetorically.

One's judgment of the success or failure of these various endeavors is likely to be colored by one's sympathy or antipathy for the objectives of them. A disinterested opinion might hold that the organizers and participants have tended to be pragmatic themselves about the utility of the specific mode of direct action. It is dubious that the public demonstrations would have been continued as long as they were had they not produced some tangible and manifests results. Quite apart from the question of the ethics and legitimacy of this technique of protest, the evidence seems to indicate that demonstrable effects were achieved in the early 1960s in such areas as public accommodations and employment. At least there were significant changes in the patterns of public race relations in the U.S.A. which were preceded by mass protest actions. There were definite modifications in the system of segregation in the South, even though it is more speculative to say that there were discernible changes in attitudes.

A question often asked by many majority group members within the U.S., especially those who were active in or sympathetic to, the early civil rights movements, is "why did the movement become violent?" Among many possible reasons are the following two: an increase in the perceived ineffectiveness of nonviolent protest and "rising expectations." Because the two factors operated in concert, it is difficult to discuss the relative weight of each variable. In other words, it is possible that an increase in expected outcomes produced perceived ineffectiveness of peaceful protest and, likewise, an increase in perceived ineffectiveness of peaceful protest may have led to an increase in Blacks' expectation regarding equality in American society.

As previously discussed, the civil rights movement in America in the early 1960s was primarily a morally suasive effort. Thus, while there were perhaps many intangible changes resulting from nonviolent protest, tangible change was deemed negligible by many Blacks. Moreover, these few instances of change may have mobilized Blacks in the sense that suddenly they realized that they, too, were Americans and should enjoy America's privileges as well as perform its duties . . . and America *did* have some privileges which it *could* extend to *them.*

The shift from a nonviolent protest pattern in the middle 1960s to widespread incidents of violent protests also can be interpreted as indicating that the former strategy had reached the limits of its success. The Civil Rights Act of 1964 *did* prohibit most of the forms of discrimination against which the NAACP, SNCC, CORE, SCLC, and other organizations had been crusading, but many Black Americans evidently felt quite frustrated about the actual results as far as their daily lives were concerned. It is plausible to infer that some people felt they had been deceived; court decisions and legislation had not brought the tangible improvement in the quality of their lives that they had come to expect. This sense of frustration may be what led to the violence in American cities in the middle 1960s, such as Watts (Los Angeles), Rochester, New York, and Newark, New Jersey.

The form and timing of social action can be understood against the background of certain social changes in American society, especially a general stimulation of aspiration for (1) material advancement and for (2) political freedom engendered by the "Cold War" competition, both by the impact of the mass media of communication on these attitudes. Modern advertising, for example, does not really discriminate effectively in terms of its audience; underprivileged minorities are exposed to the allure of "the good life" as portrayed explicitly and implicitly in ads—the ranch house in the suburbs, new automobiles, and the other objects associated with upper middle-class living. This is said to create a certain restlessness among those who cannot attain these valued appurtenances and perhaps a measure of resentment against the barriers. Similarly, the ideological propaganda necessary to prosecute the Cold War has been consumed by minorities suffering from discrimination. The message about freedom, human rights, the dignity of man, and equal opportunity has evidently not been lost upon minority groups in the U.S.A., although the reference has been to people "behind the iron curtain." Consequently the aspirations of these minorities have been raised and converted into demands. The mass media have served to disseminate these messages on a broad scale; approximately 90 percent of American households have television sets.

The above factors nothwithstanding, it would be remiss if we did not mention another source of direct action—the active leader or spokesman. To be sure, Black leaders in the United States such as Malcolm X, Stokely Carmichael, H. Rap Brown, Angela Davis, and others have contributed to the direct action approach. However, their impact has been much more in the realm of cognitive awareness than *actual* leadership. It seems to us that their principal roles have been as communicators and educators, although some may disagree on this point.

To recaptitulate, this chapter has been devoted to an analysis of three independent variables (moral suasion, education, and direct action), and *one* dependent variable (reduction of intergroup hostility). We have discussed several indicators for each of the independent variables and the dependent variable. To this extent, the foregoing observations have been conventional. There have been, however, instances where "type" of change has been mentioned. Thus, it is entirely possible that an adequate discussion of the "change" variable should include a delineation of types of change in intergroup relations.

Technically speaking we have identified these forces of change factors as affective, cognitive, and behavioral. We believe that change in intergroup relations, itself, may be labeled in a similar manner: affective, cognitive, and behavioral. If this assumption can be accepted, and if we assume that change in either affectivity, cognition, or behavior can lead to change in the remaining two, then it is possible psychologically to examine the relative effects of the three independent variables discussed here. Because each technique of change tends to be used in isolation, the effect on intergroup relations is relatively weak. This is due to the fact that if, for instance, moral suasion is used, majority group affectivity change occurs; if education is the chief weapon, majority group cognitions are modified; and if direct action is employed, majority group behavior may be altered. We assume that eventually affectivity, cognition, and behavior will be congruent for majority group members, however, we do not specify when such congruency will occur. Thus, the effectiveness of one technique of change relative to another depends on the intent of those interested in change. One might say that if a minority group wants tolerance, it uses affective methods; if it wants recognition and awareness, it uses cognitive techniques; and if it wants behavioral change, it uses direct action.

It is well to remind ourselves here that these techniques can be used to increase prejudice and discrimination as well as to decrease it, just as knowledge of principles of accounting can be used to keep honest business records or for embezzlement. The history of American race relations is replete with examples of the use of violence and coercion to encourage and reinforce patterns of prejudice and discrimination.

In the American south, the Ku Klux Klan was successful in maintaining "white superiority" by means of terror, threats, and violence against Blacks and many whites who advocated racial equality. In more recent times bombings and murders have served to warn Blacks and their supporters in the South that promotion of integration was fraught with grave consequences. Economic retaliation against Blacks for voting registration and school integration activities by white employers and creditors has been reported in various southern states during this same period. White college students from the north who traveled to the South during the summers in the 1950s to assist and encourage Black voter registration encountered considerable hostility and harrassment from local citizens and local law enforcement officials, including murder in Mississippi. In 1955, George W. Lee, a Black clergyman who had been president of the local NAACP branch, the first Black in the county to register to vote, and who had been urging other Blacks to register despite threats, was killed in Belzoni, Mississippi. The NAACP Field Secretary for Mississippi, Medgar W. Evers, was shot and killed from ambush in 1963 in Jackson, Mississippi. A Unitarian minister from Boston, James J. Reeb, was beaten to death in 1965 by four white men in Selma, Alabama, where he had gone to participate in a voter registration campaign. Mrs. Viola Liuzzo of Detroit, Michigan, was shot and killed in 1965 from another auto as she was driving between Selma and Montgomery, Alabama, where she had gone to participate in a civil rights protest march.

It is obvious that violent direct action has a long history in American race relations and it can be used in both directions. It is not without irony that the Black Panthers, who are generally perceived by white Americans as being disposed towards violence, have had perhaps a score of their members killed (the exact number is subject to some dispute) by police. The violent explosions in American cities during the summers of the middle sixties, especially 1965 and 1966, to which we have frequently referred, represents a *new* chapter in the use of violence in American race relations. In the late 1960s and early 1970s the incidence of violence subsided and whether this is a lull or a new era is a question which challenges sociological prophecy.

In sum, we learn to be prejudiced and to discriminate by the same processes we have been discussing in connection with changing attitudes and behavior. Unfortunately for harmonious intergroup relations, a slight case of prejudice, unlike certain kinds of physical diseases, does not create subsequent immunity.

Notes

1. Harriet Beecher Stowe, *Uncle Tom's Cabin* (New York: Harper and Row, 1958). This Harper Classic was first published in 1852 by John P. Jewett and Company, Boston.
2. See Lynne Ianniello, ed., *Milestones Along the March* (New York: Praeger, 1965).
3. Gardner Murphy, *In the Minds of Men: The Study of Human Behavior and Social Tension in India* (New York: Basic Books, 1953).
4. Milton Rokeach, "Generalized Mental Rigidity as a Factor in Ethnocentrism," *Journal of Abnormal and Social Psychology* 43 (1948): 259-78.
5. Clifford Kirkpatrick, *Religion and Humanitarianism: A Study of Institutional Implications* (Washington, D.C.: Psychological Association, 1950).
6. Nathan Hare, "The Case for Separatism: Black Perspective," in *Black Viewpoints*, ed. Arthur C. Littleton and Mary W. Burger (New York: New American Library, 1969), p. 202.
7. Ashley Montagu, *Education and Human Relations* (New York: Grove Press, 1958).
8. See Charles Stember, *Education and Attitude Change* (New York: Institute of Human Relations Press, 1961).
9. Melvin Tumin, *Desegregation: Resistance and Readiness* (Princeton, N.J.: Princeton University Press, 1958).
10. Stember, *Education and Attitude Change*.
11. Ibid.
12. The American Jewish Committee, *This is Our Home*, vols. 1-12 (New York: 1957).
13. John P. Dean and Alex Rosen, *A Manual of Intergroup Relations* (Chicago: University of Chicago Press, 1955).

"The Politics of confrontation era has ended and is being replaced by a quiet revolution."

Warren Widener, Mayor
Berkeley, California

The Columbus (Ohio) *Dispatch*, 21 February 1973.

Prognosis and Prescriptions

Intergroup relations is the most dramatic problem on the world stage today. Actors include, among others, Blacks, whites, Indians, and Chicanos in the United States; Blacks and whites in South Africa; Mukhti Bahini (EPLA) and Pakistanis in East Pakistan; Protestants and Catholics in Ireland; Egyptians and Israelis in the Middle East; South and North Vietnamese in Indo-China; Chinese and Malayans in Malaya; Jews and Communists in Russia; and even men and women in various countries. These examples do not include all of the intergroup relations problem areas, yet, implicit in all of the relationships alluded to above are elements of prejudice and discrimination which create intergroup disharmony. There are, however, distinctions which can be made between the relationships. These distinctions stem from the diverse problem characteristics of the relationships. Power imbalances characterize the American, South African, Pakistani, Irish, Russian, and sex examples, though there are variations in degree. The Middle Eastern, Far Eastern, and Malayan examples are less clear with respect to power but prejudice and discrimination remain conspicuous features of social interaction between the matched groups. This chapter examines strategies which might be used to achieve balanced relationships between groups and offers a rather sweeping perspective on intergroup relations through the use of historical illustrations and by attempting to peer over the sociological horizon to envision future forms of intergroup relations. The retrospective or historical view would, ideally, enable us to exercise our sociological imagination about future kinds of intergroup relations. What have been the principal kinds of intergroup conflict in the past and what do they tell us about future forms of intergroup interaction?

An important inherent assumption of this discussion is that the existence of groups is a fundamental and irrefutable fact of human history, and that there is little prospect that group organization will be eliminated so that human existence would be simply a matter of individual relationships. The realistic question therefore is, what can we learn from the record of intergroup interaction that will enable us to predict and control it in ways we may desire in the future? Another fundamental and explicit assumption is that there has always been and there will continue to be change in the composition and boundaries of groups and the criteria for their establishment and identification. It is an intriguing sociological question to ask what new kinds of groups will emerge in the years, decades, and even centuries ahead, and how existing groups will fade, merge or even disappear. The history of human affairs is replete with examples of groups which have risen in meteoric fashion, illuminated the social horizon for a while and then faded from view.

ASSUMPTIONS UNDERLYING MINORITY GROUP STRATEGIES

The emergence and disappearance of groups is very much related to the types of relationships superordinate groups form with subordinate groups. In order to explain these relationships it is necessary to understand the assumptions under which minority groups operate.

George Simpson and Milton Yinger have stated, and rightly so, that due to the complex nature of hostility between majority and minority groups only multiple strategies can be effective in reducing prejudice and discrimination and thereby achieving positive intergroup relations.[1] They state further that strategies aimed at changing intergroup relations should be directed toward the alteration of individual attitudes and group influences which support and encourage discrimination. For instance, it may be desirable to attempt to change individuals' predispositions toward others, yet we cannot deny that persons who ordinarily display tolerant behavior may, in certain group situations, exhibit extremely prejudicial behavior. Thus, any attack on minority group subordination must be both individual and group oriented. Furthermore such opposition should be directed toward the eradication of prejudice *and* discrimination. Figure 3 illustrates the strategy being advanced. We submit that while the relatively simple chart presented in figure 3 illustrates a full-scale assault on minority group subordination, failure to include either cell in the attack lessens the likelihood that intergroup power imbalance can be decreased. The rationale for this statement is presented below.

	Prejudice	Discrimination
Individual		
Group		

FIGURE 3

It should be apparent by this time that prejudice is related to the cognitions and feelings of individuals and groups. Discrimination, on the other hand, is a behavioral phenomenon of individuals and/or groups. As previously pointed out, prejudice is not always translated into discrimination for numerous reasons, and there is evidence that every discriminator cannot be labeled prejudiced.

Because of the complexity of human behavior, it is often difficult to determine the meaning of acts of discrimination. If the meaning of action cannot be determined precisely, the difficulty of planning strategy to eliminate such action should be obvious. For instance, if a local supermarket manager refuses to hire Blacks only because he fears alienating his white clientele and not because he is prejudiced (admittedly, this may be difficult to assess), strategies aimed *only* at altering the manager's attitudes toward Blacks are obviously misguided. In the first place, the manager is discriminating in the absence of individual prejudice. Second, group prejudice is causing the manager to engage in selective hiring practices. Thus, attempts to alter the situation must be directed toward the eradication of *collective* prejudice.

An important assumption which emerges from the foregoing section is that the generic problem in eliminating group prejudice and discrimination is, of course, that group loyalty is encouraged and rewarded. Pride in group membership is fostered and group membership is instrumental as a means of achieving individual success. There is, in other words, a powerful social ethic about group loyalty; failure to pay allegiance to a group is punished and the highest honors are accorded a person who exemplifies the values of the group and makes sacrifices for its advancement and glory. The remedy for this situation is rather obvious, namely the cultivation of values which promote individual autonomy and stigmatize group identification and dependence. The crucial question is whether there is something about the social psychology of human beings which favors group involvement over individual autonomy. Is some kind of group support vital for the psychological well-being of man? Would human beings suffer a painful sensation of alienation without some sense of group belonging?

In attempting to answer this question about man's basic propensities to organize groups or to cherish his individuality we should recognize that there are practical advantages for individuals organizing into groups; these incentives mean that the existence of groups is virtually assured for human beings. It is obvious that banding together for protection and to achieve the advantages of division of labor are powerful motives for the organization of groups.

Because the sources of specific instances of minority subordination are often obscure, a "total" assault on the problem seems the better strategy to employ. This total effort must combine strategies aimed at reducing both individual and group prejudice as well as individual and group discrimination. In order to illustrate the reasoning behind this statement we will examine some of the basic strategies used by minority groups in an effort to achieve equalitarianism: the protest, the law, the riot, and the alteration of individual behavior.

BASIC PROTEST STRATEGIES

The Protest Movement as a Strategy

Protest movements, which may range from passive resistance to violent retributive activities, have been used by Blacks in Alabama, Catholics in Belfast, Biafrans in Biafra, and Bengla Desh in East Pakistan, among others. Specific activities have included sit-ins, sit-downs, boycotts, and outright warfare and have produced varying degrees of success (and failure). The key question which must be answered, however, is "what is success?" If by success one has reference to open lunch counters, token hiring policies, continued and heightened antagonism, then many of these movements have been successful. We are inclined to feel somewhat differently about success and contend that harmonious intergroup relations implies more than this—that it is indicative of a type of union between groups. Vernon Dixon and Badi Foster express the nature of this union for Blacks and whites in the following manner:

> If Black and White Americans adopt the diunital conceptual approach to race relations, racial harmony can follow. According to the diunital concept of ordering experiences, I resolve my identity crisis in this way: I simultaneously embody a Black ethnic identity and a White American or national identity; I am both these different identities without inherent antagonism; I am at once Black and not Black. This is my Blackness.
>
> Each opposite fully confirms the existence of the other. They cannot deny, replace, or destroy each other. They are both present, i.e., "co-present." Unlike the dialectical approach in which the inherent antagonism of coexisting thesis and antithesis causes a synthesis or new opposite, in the diunital approach, no destruction of opposites occurs; no synthesis of opposites takes place. The union of opposites is perpetual. Further awareness, analysis, and comprehension of the opposite enlarges not only the definition of that opposite itself, but also concurrently informs and expands the definition of the other. The opposites, therefore, change continuously.[2]

A union of the type discussed above is very difficult to achieve, and the variables of group loyalty and disloyalty contribute immensely to the difficulty. Group disloyalty is punished, sometimes severely so. For example, treason is one of the most serious of offenses and almost all nation-states have laws which provide for capital punishment even though this sanction may be prohibited for any other kind of crime. Similarly, nation-states reserve their highest awards for citizens who have been extraordinarily effective in action against the enemy, which is to say, killing out-group members. The reinforcements and sanctions are less powerful and less dramatic for other forms of group ethnocentrism, but the persistent sociological fact of the matter is that groups insist upon a certain amount of ethnocentrism even though they may call it something else, such as loyalty. Perhaps it would be in the best interests of mankind to establish some kind of international agency which would reward acts of principled resistance to group pressures which urge acting in a prejudicial manner.

In the contemporary world the dominance of the nation-state and the prevalence of the concept of sovereignty means that there is little recourse for a minority group within such a system to redress its grievances. A subjugated group may appeal to public opinion beyond the borders of the sovereign state of which it is a part and this might result in certain political sanctions such as a trade embargo, but the concept of national sovereignty is so widely respected that there are no really effective legal measures which can be taken. There is no world court to which a minority group can turn to sue for some kind of sociological equity, nor is there any formal mediation service which can be automatically called in to settle such a dispute. The United Nations and the World Court have not been notably effective in this realm despite good and earnest intentions, primarily because of the strength of the principle of national sovereignty among member nations. It is ironic that there is one dramatic form of intervention which is employed from time to time ostensibly for the purpose of coming to the rescue of a persecuted minority within a state, namely, war. One of the justifications cited for the military action of the United States against Spain in 1898 was that Spain was mistreating Cubans. The Nazi regime in the 1930s in Germany claimed that German minorities in Poland and Czechoslovakia were being repressed and this was cited as justification for a military invasion.

When minority groups resort to military action in order to gain relief from discrimination, often their aim is to establish a separate independent sovereign state of their own. One variant of this theme is for a minority to attempt to gain independence or to secede from one national state to join another one, as in the case of Italian Tyrol from Austria, the Irish in Northern Ireland, and the Turks in Cyprus. Although each one of these cases is unique and complicated, the basic theme is essentially the same. After India gained independence from Britain following World War II, there was a subsequent division involving Pakistan and more recently uprisings involving Bengalis in East Pakistan who sought some degree of independence, resulting in a bloody conflict with the Bengalis coming off much the worse. To add paradox to irony and to illustrate the kind of sociological cycle we are discussing, tensions between Pakistan and India then increased because (according to Pakistan) the Bengalis were assisted and encouraged by India.

As suggested earlier, protest movements center on discrimination, attacking prejudice only indirectly. Strategies built *solely* on the extirpation of discrimination are unlikely to be completely successful because the root source remains unruffled. While we are not saying that such movements do not have results, we are saying that these movements alone do only part of the job. For instance, a minority group may be successful in altering one form of behavior, however, this does not mean that other forms of behavior will disappear. A university may be forced to open its doors to Black students, however, this does not mean that the students will not be the recipients of other forms of discrimination once they enter the educational institution. As a result, while gains are made, losses are also incurred.

The Riot as a Strategy

Although riots may result in some apparent gains, the principal and visible ones are likely to be temporary. Furthermore, in virtually every instance of a full-blown confrontation between a majority and a minority group, the minority group has experienced the most severe losses in terms of property, wealth, and lives.[3]
The most serious deficiency of this method though lies in the fact that it may yield few changes in discrimination or prejudice, depending upon the perception by the dominant group. It is not a "rational" process of communication and the "message" of the event depends upon a subjective interpretation. If a riot is simply individuals fighting individuals and the sole "purpose" is one of eradicating members of the out-group without effecting real change in the social structure, it is a dubious strategy. The controversial question is the "purpose" of the disturbance; if it fulfills the function of alerting the majority group to injustices and problems they were not aware of, it may have a positive result. Also, if it convinces the majority that basic reforms are essential to avoid even more serious disturbance then it can result in some relief from discrimination. We believe that it is unrealistic to regard riots as a form of conscious strategy because we find little evidence of deliberate planning. It is more plausible to view them as collective, irrational, spontaneous expressions of social frustrations, and in that sense we agree with Jerome Skolnick that they are "political" expressions.

The Law as a Strategy

A strategy revolving around law accomplishes at least one thing that some other strategies do not—it attacks group discrimination. It does not, however, attack prejudice directly. One should be mindful of the propositions that protests lead to legislation and legislation *may* lead to a breakdown in discrimination. Yet there is a distinct possibility that laws may not be interpreted to encompass certain forms of discrimination nor enforced even if the interpretation is broad. [Lois Moreland, for instance, argues that protection from racial discrimination by private individuals is not a legal right under present judicial doctrine; there is a perceived discrepancy between civil rights and social rights:

> Protection from racial discrimination by private individuals is not a legal right under present judicial doctrine. It is only when the government discriminates that protection from racial discrimination can be sought. Despite the so-called liberal civil rights decisions of the Supreme Court of the United States, the Court perpetuates the institutionalization of racism.[4]

She goes on to say that:

> There is no clear distinction between civil rights and social rights. Civil rights generally are thought to be those rights which can be protected by law. Social rights are thought to be those rights outside the control of law and are left to individual choice to recognize and enforce. Social rights also may be viewed as including those rights which the civil rights protest movement sought to implement. They are rights which include those traditionally considered to be within the scope of private choice, for example, employment by private persons, residence in private housing, attendance in churches, admittance to social clubs and organizations. Social rights in this book will refer to that category of rights designated as social in the *Civil Rights Cases*. It should be noted that these were rights in areas of public accommodations, which, though considered to be private action, by their very nature already were subject to governmental regulation in 1875—hotels, motels, theaters, restaurants, public carriers. Property is subject to health, licensing, and inspection requirements. It is not free of governmental regulatory control.[5]

Implicit in the foregoing statement is that laws only attack discrimination and indirectly prejudice at the group level. Yet there is no legal justification for persons to discriminate at the individual level. Laws are institutionalized norms and tend to epitomize the collective will of many people who are to be governed by them. The social-psychological fact remains, however, that persons in collectivities may *act* differently from their individual predilections. Thus, laws may indirectly reduce group prejudice; the enforcement of laws may deter group discrimination; and, yet, *individuals* may be essentially unmoved.

The crucial distinction between public and private, or civil and social rights as Moreland has put it, remains essentially unsettled in American jurisprudence. The issue is posed rather sharply in such cases as discrimination by "private" clubs who are licensed to sell liquor by the state. The most recent Supreme Court decision (1972) ruled in favor of an Elks Club.

Alteration of Minority Group Behavior as a Strategy

A minority group's strategy can revolve around changing its own behavior in such a way that it is acceptable to the majority group. This often means that the minority group becomes practically indistinguishable from the majority group in such overt behaviors as speech, dress, mannerisms, expression of ideas, values and so on. The strategy of altering behavior is best accomplished by a minority group when physical differences between majority and minority group members are minimal. In other words, it is easy for a minority group, upon altering its behavior, to enter the social mainstream if majority group members cannot easily distinguish them on a physical basis.

Physical distinction appears to be a salient factor in the success of minority group strategies based on the alteration of an individual's own behavior. Part of the effectiveness is due to the fact that discrimination is undermined when groups are physically indistinguishable. Thus, while one may be prejudiced toward all Polish people and actually feel that all of the stereotypes apply, a person of Polish descent, by concealing his ancestry, could actually become an immediate family member without experiencing the effects of prejudice and discrimination. If, however, the person revealed his heritage, he probably *would* experience prejudice and discrimination from the "offended" party.

A minority group that *is* sufficiently physically different *may* alter its behavior and achieve some small measure of success in terms of majority group acceptance. However, this is a difficult feat to accomplish and the rewards which accrue to minority group members are minimal. The minority group member, if physically distinct, may evoke prejudice so intense that it distorts majority group perception and obscures any minority group member behavioral change.

On the other hand, perception of a physically different minority group member by majority group members may evoke discriminatory behaviors which thwart intergroup contact and thus negate the discovery of the behavioral modification of the minority group member. Yet, intergroup contact can and does occur, and majority group members may perceive modifications in the minority group's behavior; nevertheless, we suggest that intergroup relations usually remain essentially unchanged.

\The strategy of behavioral alteration has several drawbacks which combine to render it nearly impotent. The first drawback has to do with the accompanying psychological implications of its usage. Implicit in the strategy of a minority group altering its behavior to meet a majority group's acceptance criteria is the admission that the minority group's behavior leaves something to be desired. This is axiomatic if a society has not incorporated the minority group's existence as a legitimate part of its societal ethos. Accordingly, a group which attempts to alter its behavior acknowledges dissatisfaction with itself. Consequently, the strategy of behavioral modification serves to illuminate and perpetuate the idea that a group of people is inadequate. We can only suggest that this is inimical to individual members' self-concept and feelings of self-worth. \

A second drawback of this strategy is that it only attenuates group discrimination when physical differences between majority and minority group members are apparent. Additionally, group discrimination is only decreased to a certain extent. The majority group members as a collectivity generally will respond positively to behavior which furthers its own ends or at least is practically identical to its own. This type of majority group response is forthcoming even when minority group behavior runs blatantly counter to the interests of the minority group. As a result, one should not be amazed when a minority group American, who denounces all minority group efforts to attain equality and dignity as communist-inspired, is welcomed into the societal fold. Such a person is likely to be received by the majority group with few instances of overt group discrimination. We contend, however, that individual discrimination, and individual and group prejudice remain unmodified. Black Americans such as Willie Mays, Sammy Davis, Jr., Eartha Kitt, and Lena Horne rarely faced personal discrimination because they were well known for popular entertainment and sports exploits, however, they often were confronted with discrimination and prejudice when they were simply perceived as "Negroes."[6]

\ A final drawback of minority group behavioral attenuation considered in this book is that any gain in acceptance is tenuous. The majority group can, at its will, return the minority group to its previous status because the minority group is not perceived as a contributor to the society. This means that it is not *a part of* the structure, it *partakes of* the structure due to the goodwill of the majority. Indeed, the minority group is allowed to participate partially in the society as a reward for changing its behavior (emulating the majority group).

An excellent example of the foregoing discussion is the mass migration, concentration, and detention of approximately 110,000 minority group members of Japanese ancestry in 1942. As suggested in an earlier chapter a large number of them (approximately 80,000) were born in America, educated in American schools, and had been indoctrinated in democratic principles. It has been said that most of these (known as Nisei) were bicultural, though their habits and attitudes conformed to the American pattern to a far greater extent than to the Japanese. During the period prior to their detention Japanese in America were subjected to various forms of discrimination, yet they were able to compete sharply in economic activities. From all accounts these were people who had substantially altered their behavior to conform to American expectations and who were rewarded prior to December 7, 1941, with a modicum of upward mobility opportunities. By 1946, however, as Dorothy Thomas and Richard Nishimoto state, young Japanese-Americans had witnessed the loss of their parents' hard-won foothold in American's economic structure and their own deprivation of rights which American indoctrination had led them to believe inviolable.[7]

It should be obvious, then, that while the Japanese had, prior to the Pearl Harbor attack, experienced an attenuation of group discrimination as a direct result of behavioral alteration, individual prejudice and discrimination as well as group prejudice remained. In addition a reduction in group discrimination had *not* meant that the Japanese had become a part of America's social structure. Instead, their position was, and still is, one which is best described as "the majority group giveth, the majority group taketh, blessed it be the name of the majority group" (we hasten to add that this statement characterizes the status of any physically distinguishable group in any society which depends primarily upon behavioral alteration to gain a majority group's acceptance).

An Alternate Strategy

To paraphrase the words of two perceptive young scholars, a society bent upon establishing harmonious relationships between majority and minority groups must adopt an approach which starts from a conceptual position that acknowledges the majority group and the minority group as authentic, valid, and valuable. Their conceptual world of majority and minority must not be destroyed through the process of assimilation in an effort at reconciliation. Rather, there must be a union of opposite or different cultures.[8] Basically, these are the words of Vernon Dixon and Badi Foster as they advance what is called a *diunital* approach to intergroup relations. This approach is synonymous with the eradication of individual and group prejudice and discrimination approach that we have implied would be functional for a social structure. While their approach, by their own admission, remains in the stage of an intellectual formulation, the strategy to be presently outlined moves closer to the pragmatic phase.

There should be little doubt at this stage of our discussion of intergroup relations that majority group-minority group interaction is basically a power game. Protest in various forms is a means used by a relatively powerless group to achieve some measure of equality in relationships. Such activity often evokes widespread community hostility, which results in intense public action being directed toward diminishing the protest activity. This can be accomplished through suppression of the protest activity or through the granting of concessions. Whether one or the other occurs seems to depend upon whether the powerful group perceives the protest as legitimate. If articulation of the protest departs significantly and intensely from established community values, the legitimacy of the protest may be diminished. Michael Lipksy writes:

> Protest activity which edges toward the line of evoking widespread community hostility may threaten community values and thus excite intense reference public action directed toward diminishing protest group influence through granting concessions. This is the dynamic upon which militant black leaders play when they threaten the holocaust in presenting their demands. But articulation of goals or tactics which significantly depart from established community values, even if strong organized opposition does not develop, may offend sensibilities in such a way as to diminish the saliency of issues.[9]

Given the above contention, it would appear that if a society's values are in direct opposition to minority group advancement, the situation would be unsolvable. In fact, in the United States this is the stand often taken by Black and white separatists and, increasingly, by frustrated and apathetic citizens. Aside from the fact that both the Black and white separatist operate on a zero-sum power principle, they also, each in his own way, give tacit approval to resignation because of the failure of a culture. Many white separatists would argue, contrarily, that the culture is maintained as long as they are successful in the separatist strategy. According to Dixon and Foster, however, "White Americans are molded in Blackness after over three centuries of interaction, conscious and unconscious, with Blacks." Thus, a white separatist is an individual who actually attempts to deny parts of his culture. Quite similarly, the Black separatist also attempts to deny parts of his culture. Unlike the white separatist, though, he tends to be somewhat open and adamant about his intentions. In other words, the Black separatist knows he is trying to discard aspects of his culture and does not try to obscure this fact. Still, because the attempt is acknowledged does not make it pragmatically sound. To the contrary, it may be postulated that Blacks need not attempt to repress all of their white heritage; instead, they may want to use its valuable aspects to develop more fully their blackness.

To say that minority group advances cannot be made in a society controlled by a majority group is not a logically sound argument. In fact, such a statement is analogous to saying that because there have never been racial or ethnic disturbances in an area with a high concentration of ethnic and racial minorities, the expectations for the future are that there will *never* be disturbances. There are numerous examples which would render this proposition empirically inadequate. Consequently, doubt emerges when assertions are made that if a majority group has perpetuated its own culture for many years, it is going to do so indefinitely.

It is interesting to note that minority groups often have based their strategies on the above fallacious arguments. One could say that minority group reluctance to employ certain strategies is a direct function of past success and failure rates. In social-psychological terms (operant theory), such a minority group reaction is logically sound in some respects. What may be questioned on logical grounds is whether or not thwarted attempts to achieve equality in the past automatically mean that societal division is the only solution to problems confronting majority and minority groups. While the future may prove this to be a very sound strategy, exception is taken here on logical and empirical grounds as illuminated by the fact that instances of full-scale massive assaults on intolerable intergroup relations are relatively rare. While it is possible to point to certain limited programs and activities designed to obtain equality in specific areas, one is confronted with an almost insurmountable task if he is asked to recall one movement designed to reduce individual and group prejudice and discrimination simultaneously. Yet when other diseases have threatened the existence of societies, such as polio, diptheria, rubella, and smallpox, we have seen massive movements constructed to break down resistance to acceptance of vaccines which would diminish the threat. This type of response to intergroup relations has never occurred in modern times and is only presently emerging in the United States. As a result, suggestions regarding the efficacy of reducing majority group prejudice and discrimination against minority groups other than through separation of groups remain empirical.

INDIVIDUAL PREJUDICE

The psychological dynamics of individual prejudice were treated in chapter 10. Because this type of prejudice is related to highly personalized response dispositions and response salience factors, reduction efforts also must be highly individualistic. The strategy of moral suasion is especially suited for the eradication of individual prejudice. While users of the strategy have had varying degrees of success at the group level, it is submitted that moral suasion can be an effective technique at the individual level. This is so because the success of the strategy is largely dependent upon perceived sincerity of the influence, relevance to the receiver, legitimacy of the issue, and captivity of the audience. Barring intergroup interaction complications, on a one-to-one basis, these criteria can be met.

Often times majority group members are resistant to new information about a minority group because it disturbs a customary way of thinking, feeling, and behaving toward members of that group. No doubt this can be a barrier to moral suasion. If, however, moral suasion is used simultaneously with socialization and resocialization strategies, successful reduction of individual prejudice is likely to be more pronounced. Obviously, if an individual's socialization period is characterized by a relative absence of instruction in prejudice, then in all likelihood the individual does not become prejudiced. This, however, is difficult to achieve in a society where prejudice is a part of the cultural ethos. Thus, all persons in such a society could probably benefit from resocialization programs and interpersonal resocialization attempts. The importance of the latter strategy in other influence efforts has been empirically substantiated by researchers such as Paul Lazarsfeld, Bernard Berelson, and Sanford Dornbusch, to mention a few. The "love, peace, and understanding" slogans must move from the rhetorical level to the everyday life level. How to achieve this is a problem of major importance in intergroup relations. What is evidently needed is some kind of psychological substitute or moral equivalent for prejudice.

INDIVIDUAL DISCRIMINATION

While individual discriminatory practices often are a direct function of group discriminatory practices, once the practice is begun by an individual, it may not respond to treatment even when group discrimination no longer exists. This suggests why an individual may publicly voice approval of open housing and yet deny a minority group member the opportunity to live next door to him. In a group situation, individuals may be constrained to display specific behaviors; outside of the group situation, he may revert to traditional ways of behaving. Regardless of the source or form of discrimination a person practices, the strategy most effective in decreasing individual discrimination is direct confrontation activities. Such activities are designed to make discrimination costly for the discriminator. These costs may range from extreme psychological insecurity to dire economic insecurity. This is attested to when one recalls the boycotts, sit-ins, and sit-downs, of the 1960s. Direct confrontation as a strategy used to alleviate individual discrimination entails realistic conflicts. In Lewis Coser's terms such conflicts "arise from frustration of specific demands within the relationship and from estimates of gains of the participants, and which are directed at the presumed frustrating object."[10] It should be remembered that even though discrimination is thwarted by direct confrontation, the source remains relatively intact and is perhaps best handled by other strategies. Cairo, Illinois, is an excellent example where numerous whites, individually and collectively, experienced the sharp costs of discrimination due to a successful economic boycott by Blacks because of discriminatory hiring policies in the business community. Yet the source of the original discriminatory practices has spun new forms of discrimination which Blacks in Cairo have had to resist. Of course this emphasizes the necessity for taking a multifaceted approach to balancing relationships between majority and minority groups.

COLLECTIVE PREJUDICE

As we have explained, group prejudice is a collective phenomenon, and eradication strategies successful with individual prejudice are not guaranteed to be successful with group prejudice. The personal techniques of persuasion, influence, and socialization cannot be used on an entire collectivity which is amorphous, loosely knit, and heterogeneous in daily activities and actually which should be referred to as an aggregate. Collective prejudice would appear to be best reduced through the use of such strategies as formal instruction, imparting of counterprejudice information, prompting noncompetitive contact, increasing dissemination of knowledge about minority group culture, and more constructive use of the mass media to promote harmonious intergroup relations.

The latter approach should permeate the other strategies listed above. This should be expected since some form of the mass media has to be used if the majority group is to be reached. Lipsky has reported that numerous writers contend that the success of protest activity seems to be, in part, a direct function of the amount of publicity received outside of the immediate area in which protest takes place. Lipsky goes on to point out that the effect protest has on majority and minority groups covered in the communication media will be related to the way in which media present their coverage. Media may present such coverage in a variety of ways ranging from support for a majority group in opposition to a minority, to support for a minority group opposed to a majority group. Since the success of most forms of mass media depend heavily upon majority group acceptance, the media tend to reflect the interests *and* values of the majority group. Thus, the media may conflict with the needs of the minority group. Floyd McKissick has argued that:

> . . . there are only two kinds of statements a black man can make and expect that the white press will report. . . . First . . . is an attack on another black man—The second is a statement that sounds radical, violent, extreme—the verbal equivalent of a riot—The Negro is being rewarded by the public media only if he turns on another Negro and uses his tongue as a switchblade, or only if he sounds outlandish, extremist or psychotic.[11]

The main point about the role of the mass media in the reduction of group prejudice is that the role can be one of support or refutation. As a result, minority group strategies aimed at reducing prejudice must include an emphasis on improving the use of the mass media in reducing prejudice—and this includes minority group usage as well as majority group usage.

The cry for Black studies was heard in the 1960s and became an issue around which many Blacks rallied. Though the general emphasis was in the direction of contributing to a reduction in minority group prejudice, specific demands by some minority group members that majority group members not be allowed to participate in the learning process negated the potential contribution in many instances. Majority group members also should have the opportunity to learn about the achievements and failures of minority group members. In this way the majority group member can achieve the dual existence necessary for a reduction in prejudice—he becomes a majority group member and a nonmajority group member.

Programs aimed at reducing intergroup prejudice must become a part of the basic institutions in a society. Such institutions, in turn, regardless of other goals, must become agencies which instruct majority and minority groups about majority and minority groups.

COLLECTIVE DISCRIMINATION

On the question of collective discrimination, similar, though even more uniform, strategies to the ones used in individual discrimination can be employed. Aside from protest types of activities already discussed, it is important to discuss two additional strategies which could attenuate discrimination: *law enforcement* and *coalition politics*.

It is reasonable to say that there is little need for additional laws to protect minority groups from majority group discrimination in the United States. In other societies the need may range from very great to very low. Because such laws exist, however, does not mean that a minority group will automatically experience a better position in a given social structure. *Enforcement* of laws, however, *can* contribute to the eradication of group discrimination. The 1954 Supreme Court outlawing school discrimination did not produce significant results for some twelve years but during two years of moderate enforcement, more desegregation of schools occurred than the entire twelve years before. We are not suggesting that this mode of eradication of discrimination is not without ill effects. Indeed, other forms of discrimination appeared but this was due to the lack of a "total" approach to the problem rather than the failure of *one* approach. The issue of coalition politics is discussed in a section below.

THE REALLOCATION OF POWER

The enforcement of norms and laws in a society cannot be accomplished without the participation of the majority group. Likewise, it is crucial to point out that reallocation of power in a society is in for

a severe test unless the majority group cooperates. Actually, reallocation of power often implies enforcing existing norms and laws. As
mentioned earlier, there are laws in the United States sufficient for
altering the position of minority groups, however, these laws have not
been enforced with enough regularity and vigor. The reason for enforcement irregularity is due to the perceived intimate relationship
between power and freedom. By and large, in the United States, we
tend to perceive that an increase in the power of one group is at the
expense of the freedom of the other group (it is plausible to think in
terms of a total pie in which a larger slice for one group means a
smaller slice for another).

Because intergroup relations have been couched in the power framework noted above, and when the question of power reallocation has
arisen, the corollary issue of a timetable has been debated also. In the
language of political slogans, one hears "now" and "never" and the expressions such as "you can't change human nature overnight." Then
there is more eloquent and noble rhetoric such as "with all deliberate
speed," the language which was used in the school desegregation
decision. It is not uncommon in these situations for majority group
members to acknowledge that there is some inequity in group relationships but to argue for a slower timetable for making changes in the
minority group demands. In some instances one encounters a naive
kind of faith or optimism about progress which implies that passage of
time itself will tend to improve intergroup relations. A more objective
viewpoint in our opinion is that time is essentially neutral. This theme
was eloquently expressed by Martin Luther King in a letter from the
Birmingham City Jail, written in reply to a letter from Alabama clergyman urging the observance of "the principles of law and order and
common sense."

> We know through painful experience that freedom is never volun-
> tarily given by the oppressor; it must be demanded by the op-
> pressed. Frankly I have never yet engaged in a direct action
> movement that was "well-timed," according to the timetable of
> those who have not suffered unduly from the disease of segregation.
> For years now I have heard the word "Wait!" It rings in the ear of
> every Negro with a piercing familiarity. This "wait" has almost al-
> ways meant "never." It has been a tranquilizing thalidomide,
> relieving the emotional stress for a moment, only to give birth to an
> ill-formed infant of frustration. We must come to see with the dis-
> tinguished jurist of yesterday that "justice too long delayed is

justice denied." We have waited for more than three hundred and forty years for our constitutional and God-given rights.[12]

One interesting phenomenon in many societies is that while the majority group has been a rather unified powerful actor, minority groups have been diverse dependents. Even within minority groups it has been difficult to attain unity. As a consequence, majority groups have been able to respond to individuals rather than groups. The effect of such an arrangement, of course, has been that the powerful group has always been able to overwhelm any one individual in an actor to actor relationship. In addition, if the majority group were in "need" of any service, it was always possible to find an individual minority group member who would perform the service.

COALITION FORMATION

Coalition formation implies that the minority group becomes united to the extent that when a member is confronted by the majority group, the entire minority group is being confronted. If other minority groups are involved, then the same principle applies. In addition, the success of coalition formation is dependent upon the coalition having the necessary resources to enter the policy-making process. Often there is a paucity of such resources among minority groups. As a result, coalitions frequently have to appeal to those with a surplus of resources and this means, according to Lipsky, that certain members of the majority group are activated. It is not unusual for some minority group member to resist this strategy for fear of expanding the coalition to a point where it does not constitute an effective alternative to the existing social order. Such a concern is a legitimate one since the expansion of any coalition beyond some unspecified number of core adherents is viewed by some authorities as evidence that the coalition's ideology is diluted. On the other hand, in order for a coalition, social movement, and the like to increase its strength numerically, and perhaps, resourcefully, it is necessary for the ideology to be sufficiently broad in scope so as to attract potential contributors. Thus there appears to be an inherent dilemma linked with the expansion of coalitions. Regardless of this dilemma, however, coalition politics appears to be an effective strategy which can be employed by minority groups to combat discrimination.

PROSPECTS FOR CHANGE IN
INTERGROUP RELATIONS

What are the prospects for substantial reduction or elimination of intergroup conflict? Is it possible to reduce group prejudice and discrimination to innocuous levels? These are not merely idle academic questions or current issues; these are fundamental questions about human relations and human nature. In grappling with these global questions, we need to bear in mind that group prejudice and conflict are much more visible and dramatic than harmonious intergroup relations. Indeed, the generalization is warranted that group conflict is exceptional rather than typical. Most of the time groups interact in a tolerant and peaceful manner, and from this same kind of broad perspective, we must conclude that most of the behavior of individuals does not involve a high degree of group membership consciousness, although we should note the important qualification that for those who are victims of rather strong prejudice and discrimination, group consciousness is a much more frequent psychological force in their lives.

Objective analysis and sober reflection lead us to the conclusion that it is naive and wishful thinking to suppose that group prejudice and group conflict can be eliminated from human affairs. Although social organization is never static, and although there is a constant ebb and flow of groups and group boundaries, it is a cardinal sociological fact that the human animal has a strong propensity to form groups of various kinds rather than to lead a solitary existence. Furthermore, human groups are inclined to stress loyalty to the group and protection of it for its members. Consequently, there is an inevitable conflict of interest.

It is virtually trite to say that there are no panaceas for intergroup relations' problems, and yet there are comprehensive solutions which have been offered. The Christian concept of the Kingdom of God on earth is one example, and the Marxist concept of a classless society similarly promises to eliminate group distinctions. The Marxist solution, of course, requires a revolutionary stage to overthrow a capitalist system; class conflict is a necessary prelude to the realization of the classless society. Christians have been guilty of burning other (heretics) Christians at the stake, presumably as a necessary means to achieving the goal of the Kingdom of God on earth. This century has witnessed one of the most ominous "solutions" to a "problem" in intergroup relations, namely, the so-called final solution to the so-called Jewish problem in Germany during the Nazi reign.

It should be candidly acknowledged that we lack effective social inventions in the field of group relations. Perhaps this is because we do not allocate enough of our mental energy, resources, and ingenuity to these problems, and because rewards for innovation and creativity in this area do not provide the incentives they do in the realm of material technology, where a patent on a better can opener or an automobile part may bring handsome monetary rewards.

Occasionally, however, some intriguing proposals are made; for example, in 1971 the president of the American Psychological Association, Kenneth B. Clark, a Black, suggested "development of a drug to be administered to successful politicians to prevent abuse of power in public office" and that "such a drug might be useful for all mankind to contain human cruelness and destructiveness and perhaps eliminate such social curses as racism and war."[13] Clark argued that politicians should be the first to receive such a drug because they hold "life and death power over mankind" in this nuclear age.

Another interesting possibility is in the area of child adoption, especially in contemporary American society where there is a "shortage" of children for adoption. Actually, there are many children available for adoption, but it is a matter of white couples seeking white children, who are currently scarce, while there is a plentiful supply of children of American Black descent or children of mixed European and African descent. It seems likely that the desire for children will overcome group prejudice, and this may create a "beneficent cycle" because such parents should be less prejudiced against the racial group of their children and these children in turn may be less inclined to have strong racial loyalties. To be sure this situation creates some moral dilemmas. One perception of this trend could be that it would deny Black children the opportunity to be reared in an environment where their cultural heritage would be transmitted to them; Black Nationalists in the United States have been extremely critical of both interracial adoption and birth control proposals from the government on the grounds that the former is perceived as cultural disenfranchisement and the latter as a form of genocide.

One of the great ironies of social change in the area of intergroup relations is that much of the change which occurs is virtually unnoticed, if not invisible, and is uncontroversial. A curious example is to be found in race and religious relations in American society. A quarter of a century ago in American society there was a passionate opposition on the part of almost all whites to Black-white marriages, and in recent years there has been strong resistance to the same idea by Black groups emphasizing Black racial identity and pride. This new attitude on the part of some Blacks appears to have had, along with other factors, the effect of moderating the attitudes of many whites so that Black-white marriages no longer arouse the indignation they once did among whites. Rather, there is a certain amount of indifference towards it. There is a strange psychology that seems to apply, in part, to these kinds of situations which says that if the out-group begins to oppose integration then even though some in-group members have previously argued that the out-group really didn't want the integration, opposition to integration on the part of these same in-group members decreases. The implicit psychological logic seems to be that if "they are now opposed to it then it's not necessary that 'we' oppose it." A certain apathy develops, resistance declines, and so when one of "us" marries one of "them" it arouses relatively little protest.

The process is seemingly tautological; integration occurs when prejudice subsides and prejudice subsides when the out-group's interest in integration declines, and so on. Thus there is a kind of "structural conduciveness" to change that develops with the increase in apathy, and this apathy is generated by the loss of interest on the part of the out-group to integrate with the in-group. The process is paradoxical but can be understood in psychological terms. There is a psychological concept known as *ressentiment* which offers some explanation of this process. It is a kind of sophisticated "sour grapes" theory about human motivation.

There are some reasons to be optimistic about the future of inter-group relations in American society. Although there have been episodes of racial violence in the United States during the decade of the sixties, they were fundamentally a violent protest against racism and were of a different qualitative character from the violence in other periods of American history when Blacks were lynched with impunity, and Blacks and whites engaged in open warfare. To a considerable extent, prejudice is now considered to be rather bad form in certain segments of American society, something that educated, sophisticated people are expected to disavow. There are various kinds of evidence for this trend, including surveys about political preferences; for example, the Gallup Poll in 1971 reported the responses shown in table 13 to the question "Suppose the presidential candidate of your choice next year picks a Black as his vice presidential running mate—would this make you more likely to vote for this ticket or less likely?"

It is obvious from this table that prejudice is less among younger people and those with more education. The trend toward less prejudice is clearly revealed in table 14 in the responses over a period of

TABLE 13

	No Difference	Less Likely	More Likely	No Opinion
National	57%	24%	13%	6%
Non-South	60	19	15	6
South	47	37	10	6
Deep South	37	36	20	7
Rest of South	51	37	7	6
Republican	59	26	10	5
Democrat	56	22	16	6
Independent	56	25	13	6
Under 30	60	15	20	5
30-49	58	23	14	5
50 and older	54	30	9	7
College	66	17	13	4
High School	56	24	14	6
Grade School	48	33	12	7
Protestant	54	27	13	6
Catholic	63	16	13	8

SOURCE: Gallup Poll, 1971.

years to the question, "There is always much discussion about the qualifications of presidential candidates—their education, age, race, religion and the like. If your party nominated a generally well-qualified man for President and he happened to be a Black, would you vote for him?" (The same general question also was asked pertaining to Roman Catholics and Jewish nominees.)

It is not the intent of the authors to convey the impression that all is well in America and that we are definitely solving intergroup problems. We do feel, on the other hand, that there is some progress being made due to increased minority and majority group efforts. Obviously, the extent of the progress is debatable. Perception of the extent of progress varies with group membership; if one is a minority group member, progress is painfully slow; and if one is a majority group member, progress may be too rapid.

An objective viewpoint of progress entails an examination of the goals toward which the society should move. If the goals involve harmonious intergroup relations, then progress apparently is slow. It

TABLE 14

	Negro Candidate		
	Yes	No	No Opinion
1971	70%	23%	7%
1969	67	23	10
1967	54	40	6
1965	59	34	7
1963	47	45	8
1958	38	53	9
	Catholic Candidate		
1969	88	8	4
1959	69	20	11
1958	68	25	7
1940	62	31	7
1937	64	28	8
	Jewish Candidate		
1969	86	8	6
1958	62	28	10
1937	46	46	8

SOURCE: Gallup Poll, 1971.

is felt, however, that concerted and concentrated assaults on group prejudice and discrimination by minority and majority groups can speed up America's movement toward harmonious intergroup relations.

In sum, specific intergroup relations can be handled within the prejudice and discrimination eradication framework adumbrated earlier in this chapter. However, as Hubert Blalock has suggested, in a field such as intergroup relations, explanations and interpretations may not be generalizeable from one intergroup interaction situation to another. A more reasonable objective of investigators in intergroup relations, therefore, would seem to be to look for statistical regularities consistent with models that allow for unexplained variations.[14] Consequently, harmonious intergroup relations in Ireland, the U.S.S.R., East Pakistan, South Africa, Vietnam, and elsewhere are dependent upon reducing certain types of prejudice and discrimination. We should acknowledge that specific strategies and techniques which might be used will vary from one social structure to another.

In view of these factors and because one must take into account the type and stage of intergroup interaction, predictions about the prospects of harmonious intergroup relations for any social structure must be made with caution and with adequate knowledge of that structure's basic institutions, values, and norms.

Notes

1. George E. Simpson and L. Milton Yinger, *Racial and Cultural Minorities* (New York: Harper and Brothers, 1953), p. 779.
2. Vernon J. Dixon, "Two Approaches to Black-White Relations," in *Beyond Black or White: An Alternate America* by Vernon Dixon and Badi Foster (Boston: Little, Brown, 1971), pp. 48-50. It should be pointed out that this position recently has been attacked by William Nelson in his review of Dixon and Foster's work. Nelson suggests that the authors are preaching social theology and concludes that in America the diunital approach is doomed to failure. While Nelson's review is a penetrating one, he only vaguely considers the interactive relationships between cognition, affectivity, behavior, and power equilibrium which are implicit in the diunital approach. See William E. Nelson, Jr., "Book Review Symposium: Beyond Black or White: An Alternate America," *The Journal of Afro-American Issues* 1, no. 1 (Summer 1972): 99-109.
3. See Robert C. Cipes, *The Crime War* (New York: New American Library, 1968), and Louis H. Masotti, *A Time to Burn?* (Chicago: Rand McNally, 1970).
4. Lois B. Moreland, *White Racism and the Law* (Columbus, Ohio: Charles E. Merrill, 1970), p. 1.
5. Ibid., pp. 1-2.
6. If one reads the biographies of these famous Americans, there are glaring instances of overt prejudice and discrimination. See for example Sammy Davis, Jr., *Yes I Can*, edited by Jane Boyar and Burt Boyar (New York: Farrar, Straus and Giroux, 1965).
7. Dorothy S. Thomas and Richard S. Nishimoto, *The Spoilage* (Berkeley: University of California Press, 1969), pp. 1-5, 161.
8. Dixon, "Two Approaches to Black-White Relations," p. 58.
9. Michael Lipsky, *Protest in Politics* (Chicago: Rand McNally, 1970), pp. 191-92.
10. Lewis A. Coser, *The Functions of Social Conflict* (Glencoe, Ill.: The Free Press, 1956), p. 49.
11. Floyd McKissick, New York *Times*, 21 April 1967, p. 22.
12. Martin L. King, Jr., "The Negro is Your Brother," in *Black Viewpoints*, ed. Arthur C. Littleton and Mary W. Burger (New York: The New American Library, 1969), p. 235.
13. Des Moines *Register*, 5 September 1971.
14. Hubert M. Blalock, *Towards a Theory of Minority Group Relations* (New York: Wiley, 1967).

Index

About the Authors

JAMES G. MARTIN is presently Vice-President and Provost of the University of Iowa. He received his B.A. and M.A. from Indiana State University and his Ph.D. from Indiana University. He has published another book, *The Tolerant Personality*, 1964.

CLYDE W. FRANKLIN is an associate professor of sociology at The Ohio State University. He received his B.A. from AM & N College, his M.A. from Atlanta University, and his Ph.D. from the University of Washington. He has published several articles in various journals.